All about Hinduism

All about Hinduism

From Vedas to Devas and Past to Present

Ashok Tyagi

SHIPRA

Rs. 1250; US$ 67.50

ISBN: 978-81-7541-796-0

First Published in India in 2015

All about Hinduism: From Vedas to Devas and Past to Present

Published by:
SHIPRA PUBLICATIONS
LG 18-19, Pankaj Central Market, I.P. Ext.
Patparganj, Delhi-110092
Tel: 91-11-2223 5152, 2223 6152
E-mail: info@shiprapublication.com
www.shiprapublication.com

Preface

Most of the educated, urban and modern-day Hindus proudly identify themselves as being liberal, tolerant and more secular than followers of some other belief systems. However, when it comes to deeper questions relating to the finer doctrines, theology, metaphysics of religion, mythology vs. reality, and the forms of God, one tends to get entangled in generalities rather than having specific answers. A question that may seem simple at first like the difference between Hinduism as a way of life and as a religion may baffle many of us as Hinduism like any other religion is a complex subject with many mysterious facets which is difficult for most to comprehend.

Although there is a rich literary stream replete with explanations claiming to present interpretation of esoteric concepts in apparently intelligible way, there is an obvious dearth of a genuine source of information about a macro-perspective on the subject. One can always find bits and pieces of information on the history and growth of Hinduism but to put together all the pieces of the puzzle not only requires the tedious task of dealing with varied languages, styles and aphorisms but also trusted translations and commentaries that offer an analysis that is not overly academic or abstruse for an ordinary man to understand.

Most Hindus today are aware of Hinduism's esteemed heritage where several *Rishis* and *Munis* achieved insurmountable accomplishments in all spheres of humanity and much ahead than a lot of other cultures, both surviving and dead. In spite of the challenges posed by the modern day life pressures, more and more adults are keen to get in touch with their spirituality or connect with their roots like never before. More and more people are aspiring to gain a deeper understanding of their religion out of sheer curiosity as well as with a desire to pass on such knowledge about their culture and "*Sanskar*" to their next generations. Studies suggest that youngsters today are more inclined towards acquiring theological knowledge in comparison to the previous generations – one reason may be their heightened exposure to information in comparison to previous generations who were preoccupied with either the freedom struggle or struggling to arrange their economic means of survival.

India's cultural evolution is full of steep ups and downs as well as twists and turns similar to most long journeys passing through unchartered territories. To make matters worse, a good part of it dates back to an epoch when all forms of knowledge and wisdom were passed onto generations merely by the spoken word. No wonder that a large part of our history is recorded in the form of thoughts and words. It is a different matter, however, that these very words and thoughts became revelations recorded as sacred scriptures that came to be known as Vedas and Upanishads that are highly regarded and appreciated by the entire world as one of the finest human creations relating to the inner psychic world of human beings.

We often see panelists on prime time national TV programmes representing different religions embroiled in debates trying to prove the superiority of their own religion over others. In such situations, one generally feels under-qualified to form an opinion or even sceptical about the truths. At that point it becomes clear that to have an understanding of the comparative positions between different religions, one should not only have a grasp of his/her own religion but also a certain degree of exposure to the basics of other religions as well. In a secular society like India that is truly a bouquet of diverse flowers, it becomes a necessity to gain an insight on the fundamentals of other religions lest real facts be overlooked.

I am able to relate myself with these scenarios completely. My own childhood was typical of children from middle-class families where we all get from our parents regular words of encouragement for doing good deeds to accumulate good *karmas*(deeds) and instilling fear of God for all wrong-doings. These teachings were coupled with occasional visits to temples to cement the belief in the existence of an omnipresent God. However, having lived a major part of my initial childhood with my grandfather, I was constantly nudged by him to read religious books (including Ramayana, Mahabharata, Puranas and story books such as Panchatantra). He would also cross-examine me about references from various books as riddles and answering those correctly meant earning brownie points. It was his ideas that drew me closer to our scriptures and other concepts that, much later, I was to understand as tenets of Hinduism (not sure if such tricks can be played anymore on youngsters from current generation). In his later years, my father also was to spend more of his spare time in reading of Hindu scriptures and I used to wonder why one should spend so much time with religious books and why should he need to read the same book so many times over. It didn't make so much sense at that time.

After school and college, professional education takes lot of energy and there is no time for exploring God and his designs as His endless hurdles of real life become more urgent to cross over. Later life grips with all its pulls and pressures. Marriage, career advancement, and children result in forced suppression of time for learning for everything religious. Desire still remains, sometimes even strong, but neither there is inclination to pursue nor vigour to go deep in developing understanding for religions in a serious way. Real world, in that respect, is certainly cruel and demanding.

For many of us who are exposed to working with people from other cultures and religious leanings, the desire for seeking deeper understanding about our own religion may also come from external corners. For example, in my first ten years of working outside India, I got into situations with people from very diverse cultural backgrounds who came out showing obvious curiosity for Indian culture in general and Hinduism in particular.

On my own part, sharing unique features from Indian culture was always fulfilling and at one such engagement, my guest preferred discussing about specific role of Brahmins in Indian religious evolution and cultural landscape. On being told that I myself am a Brahmin by birth, his questions became even more penetrating and embarrassing. Apparently he knew well in detail about our caste system, Vedas, Shastras and the likes. Honestly, I was found wanting on quite a few questions and felt very small that he knew about Indian heritage much more than I did. And this was not the first time that I felt so.

Surely, knowing about Hinduism is very complex. There are so many versions for each issue and everything always remain in a flux of uncertainty. Nobody seems to be eying for finality in any manner. It is like a miracle that we are all Hindus inspite of all the 'Diversities' that we have. Clearly, that so called 'Unity' evades the naked eye on every plain. After all, there are so many scriptures, so many Gods, so many branches and so many languages. Then we have a vast history of over five thousand years with so much of transformations happening all the time. One constantly hears that Hinduism is not a religion but a "way of life" or as Atal Bihari Vajpayee often said "Unity in Diversity" but one can better appreciate this entire philosophy after going over following ruling by Supreme Court of India in one of its landmark judgment and it said:

> *"Unlike other religions in the world, the Hindu religion does not claim any one Prophet, it does not worship any one God, it does not believe in any one philosophical concept, it does not follow any one act of religious rites or performances; in fact, it does not satisfy the traditional features of a religion or creed. It is a way of life and nothing more."*

I am sure every reader will appreciate this dilemma in very clear light by the end of the reading of this very book. Because more we know about Hinduism, more we tend to realize how little we knew about it. It is indeed beyond any single human to completely understand every single concept and aspect of Hinduism in one's lifetime.

Coming back to my own experience, soon after completing my fiftieth year, events culminated fast, one after another, and made it possible for me to opt for a life of Vanprashtha, albeit in modified form. Today, I will certainly call it some divine intervention that prompted me to give up the career as CEO of an established company, at the age of 51 and pursue learning about Hinduism and its surroundings as a full-time passion with a new found vigour. Over next couple of years, I could switch from one source to another sniffing about Vedas, Upanishads, and evolution of Hinduism and all other social surroundings influencing and getting influenced with its evolution. Soon came the realization that just going deep into Hinduism is not enough as nothing grows in isolation. Every development has a cause and effect, and sometimes an interlinked chain of events is inseparably intertwined with each other.

This guided me to look for historical perspectives on one side and study of parallel religions of Buddhism and Jainism as home grown faiths on the other side. Similarly, Islam has been communicating with Hinduism in India for over a thousand years and at times involving strong arguments and even violent confrontation. Even Christianity has been in direct communication with Hinduism for last three hundred years or so and, for most part, as a religion of the rulers of the land. A good reflection on these religions is, therefore, quite essential for understanding some twists and turns within Hinduism. Never before had I realized the extent of influence absorbed by Hinduism emerging out of some sweet and some sour interactions with these religions. This study also brought out the unique ability of Hinduism of its readiness and openness to absorb new concepts and traditions from other religions almost so regularly. Its open arm ability to absorb new concepts and traditions help it maintain its virility all through its journey. There is no parallel to this ability of Hinduism in any other religion the world over. Similarly, deeper understanding about other religions helps one establish stark similarities and differences which in turn force you to go to the logics and take a call on its being right or wrong.

Understanding of history (*Itihaas* in Sanskrit which means 'that what happened') answered some key questions like 'why' part of many developments. Study of only religious matters and theology never brings out the ever-lasting impact of some key actors and events. For example, without study of Mauryan dynasty and works of King Ashoka, one is unable to appreciate its shadow on the character of Ramayana and Mahabharata. Some one reading only scriptures may never believe that both the characters of Rama and Yudhishthira actually came to life after the demise of King Ashoka and that his real life character directly influenced both. And that the concept of *Rama-Rajya* was nothing but the Ashoka's period in closing centuries of BC. Good study of historical developments over the centuries help in correctly comprehending other questions like When? How? and by Whom? Most printed material on Hinduism does not provide any direct linkage between the progress on religious front and their correlation with specific historical developments. This book is an absolute exception to this as all major historical background has been properly touched to let the reader understand clearly.

Differentiation of our religion as a religion of temple worship vis-a-vis whole concept of Sanatan Dharma, is yet another unique take away of this book. Most Hindu practitioners of my age and background may not have understood the knitting of Vedas, Upanishads, Yoga, Indian Philosophies and Ayurveda together with unique doctrines to make the complete Sanatan Dharma. Unfortunately, many will relate Hindu religion with only temples and Idols or, at best, with some additional rituals and external symbols. But nothing can be far from the truth. Hinduism is much greater than mere forms of worship.

I have made sincere efforts to touch upon all aspects of Sanatan Dharma and have also included most obvious aspects of this great tradition. I am sure that, by end of this book, the respect of my readers for Hinduism would have risen to a higher level from the point they started. Their appreciation for other religions, similarly, would have improved significantly.

Both these points combined are the real litmus test for the success of this book.

Throughout this journey, whenever I came across something revealing, the constant thought flashing through my mind was how little did I knew about it? Also, whether other people in my age and our gen next knew about it? Many other questions followed including—Will they experience similar pride and pleasure about their heritage like I did? Is it not of similar importance to them? This book is the reply to all those questions. The desire to share experiences of that beautiful journey are the sole cause of my 'pains in penning' or, shall I say, 'purpose of punching' all the words on following pages.

Undoubtedly, there are numerous books already in the market about Hinduism and one may wonder what new can be written about it. But greatness and vastness of Hinduism has its own challenges. Most of the books available cater to specific aspects of it but to begin with, people like me and our next generation need to have an instrument for glancing over its full landscape from the very beginning till today. They also need to know the impact and counter impacts of competing religions. They certainly wish to know what road blocks it has faced and what the future has in store for it. But they don't have time to read all voluminous scriptures or translations thereof. As it is, only reading of scriptures can not lead one to proper conclusions as a great deal of comprehensive analytical criticism is required to reach the firm conclusions out of such readings. Expecting so much of time and energy in today's world is a pipe dream.

This book is specifically designed for all such Hindu practitioners who wish to know everything about it in a cursory manner. Later, they can pursue specific subjects of their orientation in greater details. This book is also a must read for all youngsters who must know about their shining past and lineage of great ancestors of this wonderful land called India. In a way it is the responsibility of my generation to pass on the mantle over to next generation similar to those Brahmins who have preserved Vedas just by memorising for over a thousands of years. But for them the Vedas would have been lost long ago. And if we fail to pass on the mantle to next generation, these traditions will get lost once again.

The power and pride of Hinduism can be compared with Hanuman from Ramayana who always had the power of crossing the ocean to reach Lanka in search of Sita but never knew himself and was to be told by others. Had others not told him about his powers, Sita might not have been located. Exposing our next generations to our proud past will only help them develop their strong awareness and certainly help them in locating their place in the new world of tomorrow where their position of 'Global Gurus' awaits them.

Interested people from outside the Hindu world are yet another potential beneficiary of this book as they may not have the benefit of finding all about Hinduism in a single place in the language that they can easily relate to. Most importantly, it is a book by a Hindu by birth but someone who has physically been away from its home land for a while and, in the process, developed an outsiders approach about Hinduism without ever loosing the insiders view. So this book is by an insider with outsider's perspective using global language and universal relevance.

In order to help the reader, efforts have been made to cover most topics in a chronological manner but Hinduism is like a banyaan tree where some branches go to the ground and soon convert into roots such that, after some time, it is difficult to identify and differentiate the branch from the root. In the process, some overlap is just inevitable. Similarly, many developments under a single topic have occurred over a long period but explained under a single chapter itself.

As it is, all religious developments never happen in a clean linear manner. The landscape of Hinduism all over the Indian Subcontinent was always a large geography where different things were happening at different parts almost continuously. There were exchanges based on religions, based on languages, based on written or verbal practices, based on sects, based on level of orthodox view points of practitioners, based on influence of rulers and their clouts and based on pulls and pressures from aggressors from within and out side the Indian territories. Such large variations have contributed as threads/strands of different colours in shading the entire spectrum of Hinduism. Under this situation it is not always possible to know which colour came first and which one later.

Let me also share a word of caution. Some sections may not be found interesting as they deal with very serious subjects like Philosophy or original Yoga practices. Difficulty in clear understanding of these sections for the first time reader is completely understandable. Such subjects always require multiple readings for absolute comprehension. But these are some critical aspects and are worth the pains and cannot be kept out. These are integral part of Hinduism and no serious attempt to discuss Hinduism is complete without these concepts. The suggestions from readers are welcomed, and for any errors and omissions, I take the responsibility.

Happy reading to all my readers!

Ashok Tyagi

Contents

Glossary

Adivasi: Aboriginal tribal people living off forest produce.
Advaita: Vedantik doctrine of non-dualism of atman and brahman.
Agama: Scriptures dealing with working of temples.
Aghnya: Forbidden to be killed, used for Cow during Vedic time.
Aghori: Person following extreme practices under worship.
Ahamkara: Involving atman and brahman.
Ahimsa: Lack of desire to harm loosely called non-violence.
Ajivika: One of the nastic school of Philosophy.
Akhara: Organization of ascetics having unique set of traditions.
Amrita: Nectar, a source of immortality of Devas.
Anartha: Finances earned with morally wrong means.
Antyesthi: Last rites performed after death of human.
Artha Shastra: Text book of political science.
Anulom vilom: A combination of breath control exercise.
Ayurveda: The Veda of long life.
Apsara: Beautiful supernatural female being.
Arya: A term used for a noble being; 'nobles'.
Aryans: English borrowing of the word 'Arya'.
Aryavarta: Area of north India as referred in Classical Sanskrit literature-from Himalaya to Vindhya and from Arabian Sea to Bay of Bengal-Land of Aryans.
Asana: Place offered to a guest to make him get comfortable and feel welcome.
Ashram: Stages of life and dwelling place of sages where they lived and run academies for training young pupils.
Ashtanga Yoga: The 8 fold Yoga by Patanjali Yoga Sutras.
Atman: True self of any individual; inner-self; soul.
Aum: Sacred incantation; mystical sound of Hindu origin; mantra par excellence.
Avatar: Deliberate descent of a deity to earth; incarnation.

Avidya: Lack of correct knowledge; antonym of 'Vidya'.
Bhakti: Devotion of a devotee in the worship of the divine.
Bhasm: Also called Vibhuti is residue ash after incineration.
Bhastrika: Yet another exercise under Pranayam.
Bhukti: Enjoyment of all worldly and carnal desires.
Brahma: Hindu God of creation; one of the Tri-murti Gods.
Brahman: Unchanging, highest, ultimate reality; sat-cit-anand.
Brahmin: Top class of 'Varna Vyavastha' having absolute dominance on all activities in learning and teaching.
Brahmvarta: State on confluence of Sarasvati and Drishadvati rivers where sages are said to have composed Rig-Veda.
Buddhi: Intellect.
Cankam: Early Tamil literary assembly.
Carvaka: One of the Nastik school of Indian Philosophies which believed in materialism; also called Lokayats.
Darshana: Sanskrit word to refer Indian Philosophy.
Dharana: Aspect of mind which is attracted to Brahman and makes wisdom possible; a divinely oriented intellect.
Dharma Sankat: Cross roads where following path of moral high ground is made difficult by unpleasant and unwanted alternatives
Dualism: School that differentiates between God and universe.
Doab: The area irrigated by Ganga and Yamuna, the cradle of Vedic culture.
Dvaita: School of Vedanta Philosophy by Madhavacharya.
Ekagrata: A stage in meditation – total concentration on object of choice.
Ekdandi: Wandering ascetics carrying a single stick.
Guna: "Quality", term for the three strands of matter under Sankhya school of philosophy.
Garbha Griha: The central space in a temple housing main deities.
Gopuram: The outer precincts of Hindu Temples in South India.
Grihaspati: The male head of the family in Vedic societies.
Grihaswamini: The wife of head of the family in Vedic societies.
Hath Yoga: Present day Yoga emphasizing difficult physical postures, exercises and techniques rather than philosophical content.
Havan Kunda: The place where offerings are made into consecrated fire under a Vedic ritual for pleasing Gods.
Isht Devta: The Deity of personal choice.
Zazia: Tax imposed on subjects who did not participate in military services of Muslim rulers.
Janeu: The three strand thread worn by all twice born Hindus.
Kalpa-taru: The mythological tree offering any object of choice.
Kamadhenu: The mythological cow offerings choice of food at all times.

Kapalbhanti: Yet another breathing exercise under Pranayam.

Khap panchayat: The caste congregations held to address social issues of their respective castes and sub castes infamous for taking orthodox lines on many social norms.

Khariboli: A western Hindi dialect popular in and around Delhi and West UP.

Kshatriya: The class under Varna Vyavastha for all military matters.

Kumkum: Colored powder made of turmeric and saffron used for markings in Hindu religion.

Kundalini: Spiritual energy capable of awakening with practice.

Linga: Sign of the male sexual organ of Lord Shiva; also used as abstract symbol of Lord Shiva.

Mahesh: A name of Lord Shankar.

Mandir: Space designed for bringing human and God together.

Mantra: Sacred sound, word or syllable having psychological and spiritual power.

Matha: Monastic religious establishment.

Maya and Bhrum: Illusions and secrets.

Maryadapurushotam: An ultimate human ideal, an address for Shri Rama.

Mimansa: A astika school of Indian Philosophy, literal meaning being 'investigation'; the philosophy of logic.

Moksha: Also known as Vimoksha, Mukti or Vimukti; ultimate libration or release from the cycle of death and rebirth.

Mukti: Same as Moksha.

Nastika: People who believe "it does not exists"; atheists.

Naga sadhu: Naked ascetics in Hindu traditions.

Nilakantha: Another name of Lord Shankara, man with blue color neck.

Nirakar: One without any form; reference to Paramatma, the Ultimate God at the helm of entire Universe.

Nirguna: Same as Nirakar.

Nirvikalp Samadhi: Stage of Samadhi where all mental activities are absorbed within Self vanishing distinction on knower and knowing.

Nishkama: Unique concept of Gita, Self-less or desire-less actions.

Niyam: Obligations to be adopted by a spiritual aspirant; must dos.

Nyaya Darshan: An Astika school of philosophy based on 'examination'.

Para Brahma: Same as Nirakar God.

Parmartha: Combination of Param and Artha; 'The Right Way'.

Prakrit: Several vernacular languages of Vedic society from which Sanskrit originated as a much superior language.

Pramana: Correct knowledge of any object based on full reasoning.

Prana: Life force or cosmic energy responsible for life in body.

Pranayam: Set of Breath exercises combining inhaling, retaining and discharging vital life energy (*Purak, rechak and kumbhak*).

Prasad: Edible food offered to deity and than distributed.

Pratima: Idol, a perceived object having God's manifestation.

Pratyahara: Withdrawal of senses, 5th stage of 8 stage Patanjali Yoga.

Pratyaksha: Clear and distinct direct evidence beyond any doubt.

Puja Vidhi: Way of worship which is proper and complete in all respect.

Punar Janm: Re-incarnation, an Hindu concept of constant cycle of death and re-birth called, '*Samsara*'.

Purana: Ancient Hindu texts eulogizing various deities through divine stories; compendium of myth, ritual and history.

Purva Paksha: Unique concept of ancient India where full understanding of opponent's point of view was necessitated before criticizing it.

Purusha: The Primeval Man from Vedas; used as 'spirit' or 'self' in Samkhya philosophy school.

Purushartha: That which is sought by man; human purpose or aim.

Pushpak Vimana: Originally referred to flying chariots used by Gods but Epics using the term to refer to flying object.

Rama Rajya: Ideal state ruled by a just king with happiness all around.

Raj: Short form of 'Rajyam' the kingdom used exclusively for British rule over India.

Raja yoga: Just another name of Classical or Asthanga Yoga by Panini.

Rajas: One of three *Gunas* rep. excitation/action/motion/energy.

Rudra: A Vedic God later promoted to be Shiva or Shankara.

Sadachar: Combo of '*Sat and Achar*'; Behavior suitable for pure soul.

Sadhna Kriya: A stellar all-around Kundalini Yoga workout.

Saguna: God represented by definite form.

Sakar: Same as Saguna, a God with definite form.

Sakshatkar: To be visibly present before eyes.

Samadhi: Superior stage of still mind, one-pointed consciousness.

Samsara: The Hindu doctrine of cycle of birth, life and death.

Sandhi: A system of rules based phonology in many Indian languages used for combining sounds and words.

Sankhya: Yet another Indian Astika School of Philosophy; number.

Sannyasa: The last and final life stage of Renouncer.

Samskara: Imprints left on the subconscious mind impacted by present or previous lives.

Saptasindhu: Seven rivers of north India mentioned in Rig-Veda.

Sarasvati: One of the main Rig-Vedic river, having Sutlej and Yamuna as major contributories, later got completely dried up.

Sati: The custom where a women was made to end her life upon untimely death of her husband; technically means a good women or a devoted wife.
Sattva: One of the three *Gunas* representing purity and knowledge.
Satyam vada: The doctrine of speaking truth and nothing but truth.
Shastra: Type of Sanskrit literature having detailed technical or specialized knowledge in a defined subject area.
Shloka: Largest used metered verses of classical Sanskrit poetry almost exclusively used in Mahabharata/Ramayana.
Shraddha: A unique combination of qualities like Faith, Trust, loyalty, Devotion, Dedication but without exact word in English.
Shramana: A religious movement parallel to Vedic system contributing to rise to Yoga, Jainism and Buddhism.
Shunya: Nothing, empty and vacuum; zero.
Siddhi: Supernatural/magical powers/abilities/practices obtained using spiritual practices of Meditation/Yoga.
Smriti: Type of Sanskrit literature compiled by contribution from multiple verbal and/or written sources.
Somras: Special beverage made for Gods having curative powers, made from some botanical source since extinct.
Sruti: Ancient Sanskrit literature including Vedas, Upanishads, Shastras, Sutras where no alteration was admissible.
Sudra: Lowest placed traditional social class – artisans and laborers.
Sva-dharma: One's own particular dharma in contrast to common dharma called 'sadharana dharma'.
Svetasvatara: One of the prominent Upanishad.
Swargaloka: One of the many planes as per Hindu cosmology.
Swastika: A very sacred and auspicious symbol of Hinduism like cross.
Swayamwara: Ancient competitive system of choosing a husband by a girl of marriageable age from among the invited guests.
Tamas: One of three *Gunas* representing ignorance and inertia.
Tantra: One sect of Hinduism and texts of that tradition.
Tilak: Mark worn on forehead to denote sectarian identity.
Trimurti: The trinity of Brahma, Vishnu and Mahesh.
Tripitaka: One of the religious text book of Buddhism.
Vaani: Speech.
Vairagya: Renunciation of worldly passions.
Vaisheshika: One of the major Upanishads.
Vaishya: The third of the four classes of ancient Indian society included entrepreneurs, merchants and farmers.
Vanprashtha: The third of four stages of life focused on meditation.
Varna: The system of social class division based on professions.

Vasana: Smell; the memory traces left by the previous lives.
Vatta, Pitta, Vayu Dosha: Three category of bodily humors that makes one's bodily constitution, the foundation under Ayurveda.
Vichchheda: Breaking up of words under well defined Grammar rules
Virah: An unique type of feeling of separation from lover.
Vishishtaadvaita: Qualified Advaita school, one of the Vedanta school.
Yagyopaveet: Sacred thread ceremony before initiation to schooling.
Yajna: The fire ritual under Vedic system.
Yama: The prohibitions advised under Yoga school of Philosophy.
Yuga: Era within four age cycle of *Satya, Treta, Dwapar* and *Kali.*

1
Hinduism: An Introduction

Long time back a large triangular plate of Indian Continent drifted from Madagascar, sailed across Indian Ocean and collided with south Asian Continent at Tibet Plateau with a bang so large that Himalayas came into existence. From Himalayas came Mount Kailās and from Mount Kailās came Lake Mansarover—a lake considered as personification of purity—which is the source for some major rivers of Indian Subcontinent. Rivers Sindhu, Sutlej, Brahmaputra and Ghaghara (a very important tributary of River Ganga) all have their common origin from this sacred single source. Not far from there, Gomukh at Gangotri glaciers gives rise to Bhagirathi, which joins with Alaknanda at Devprayag to form the 'Ganga' (The Ganges).

Rivers have great contributions for sustaining human life in many ways. They acquire greatness by merging with other rivers and letting their tributaries merge with them. Soon after joining, the identity of the merging and the merged obtains unity with no trace of separateness. Constant flow ensures purification of all pollutants that is discharged by its ignorant natives. Turbulent currents and its eco system works as filtrates to separate the dirt which gets sidelined on the banks so that purified water continues to flow down the path. The river keeps sustaining all villages and towns on its banks by providing them everything it can and unwillingly keep accepting all their liquid effluent, garbage and what not. Barring exceptional cases, a river continues to serve humanity till the time it gets merged into the ocean or it dries up on the way.

Depending upon the spread and purity of its source, its gradient and speed, its width and depth, its span and its length, the river is also used for generating electricity, navigation, fishery, tourism, feeding canals, industrial uses and such other uses that its native are capable of harnessing. Any major obstacle brought in its way is dealt with full power and when it comes across something bigger and unmovable, the river changes its course and keeps moving on its way. Calamities, both natural and unnatural, flood it at times, compels it to take catastrophic proportions causing great agony and destructions. But depending on its capacity, it tries hard to flow out the extra burdens and resorts to normal flow as soon as possible.

A religion also takes its course to serve the humanity similar to a river. Most certainly, it originates in purest possible form. It obtains its greatness by accepting ideologies from different streams. It is also considered as crucial and useful by its beneficiaries in as many ways it serves them. It is also bound to accept waste and garbage from its users on the way. Its own capability of purifying itself remains as crucial for its purity down the time lines of history. If it is unable to purify itself regularly, it will soon render itself unusable for its people and will get discarded similar to a river, which after losing its capacity to purify itself, ultimately turns into a sewage drain. Its own gradient and flow determines how much it can be harnessed for generating unseen power of its philosophical content. It is also destined to face roadblocks and its own bypassing capacity is as essential to keep it going on and on. Its greatness is also judged by the fact of how much population has been served by it, for how long and in how many measures. Religion also, at times, forced to handle calamities with devastating impacts. And finally, similar to vanishing of many rivers, religions also have perished on the way and became extinct. Some religions are comparable to river Sindhu, Brahmaputra and Ganga due to their size, miles covered and proportion of humanity served. Some other religions of the world are like great river *Sarasvati*, which was once a great river but got extinct long back.

But no other river touches the life of its people and commands respect from them as river Ganga. Considered as a life giver, it is associated with them from birth to death in innumerable ways. People worship it like their Goddess. It is considered most auspicious, pure, saviour, salvation provider and what not. People come to it for many reasons to get benefits from it in their everyday life. Some other gets drawn to visit its bank just to admire its beauty and grace. This mystic river demands adulation from its natives at every step of their life. She is a symbol of long standing culture and civilization and is called "Ganga Maiyya", the mother Ganga. Yes, there are several other rivers in this world which are longer or broader but none serves its natives and none gets adoration as much as "Ganga".

> *"Hinduism" to the Indian Subcontinent is one such religion out of many, as the "Ganga" is the river to the people of India out of many other rivers.*

Ganga is known to create Indo Gangetic Plains where it now flows by bringing sediments and filling the place. So also, Hinduism is known to serve all the human inhabitants of this great land called India right from the time that civilization took roots.

Describing Hinduism is not as easy as some other religions of our times. Because most others are like canals with specific place of origin, with well-defined banks, with predefined path, with a single guide book (Sole Scripture) while Hinduism is like a free river. It is called a conglomeration of many religious, philosophical and cultural ideas and practices originated and largely practiced on Indian Subcontinent over a long period of history, contributed by a large number of great human souls. Its doctrinal content has been debated and tested over millenniums.

In the absence of religion as understood today, ancient India was binding residents together based on culture, traditions, forms of worship and beliefs and inclusive acceptance of variations in all these. Hindus did not develop a strong sense about them or considered their system as a separate religion for a long time until there were other religions and there was a necessity to stand against them and until it was forced to compare/compete with others. Actually, before arrival of foreign origin aggressors and invaders, Indians never felt the need of defining religion. It was never 'we' versus 'they' because there were no 'they'. Local identities of people were initially based on locality and languages and later on castes and sects in a way that there was never a need to bring in religion as a defining or distinguishing factor. So, the very classification of Hinduism as a religion is a recent phenomenon.

For the sake of simple segregation, at this primary stage itself, we shall call that overarching social structure of ancient traditions and customs as "Sanatan Dharma" as any other segregation fails to capture the complete grandeur of the great religion called Hinduism.

And religion being much more a narrow term in its meaning, my reader is well advised to understand and appreciate the real meaning of "Dharma" as a word out of our great language, Sanskrit. Also, we should take note that the word "Hinduism" will refer to "Indian Dharma" which is much wider than "Hindu Religion". Suffice to note that Hindu Religion will get referred as "way of worship" alone where there are temples, gods, mythological stories, idols, pujas, etc. All these are part of Hinduism but only a small part and exclude the bulk which will be discussed soon. Infact, the subject matter of this book is the other part of Sanatan Dharma rather than the worship part.

Let us also understand that unlike most other religions, Hinduism doesn't have a single founder or institution to enforce any single set of the traditions. This situation works in its favour as much as against but this is a reality. There is no Pope or Prophet here. It is a rainbow kind of situation where there are many colours of its own and where mixing of colours bring in new shades depending on the angle of the person looking at that. Afterall, there are no tight boundaries that someone will not be a Hindu if he crosses that over or some one will become Hindu if he does certain things. This is probably the only case where all major ideas like existence of God or its absence, belief in God or lack of it, God being with a form or without, one God versus many Gods, ways to reach Him, violence or non-violence, vegetarianism versus meat eating etc. have been in debate for as long as it exists and where living without a finality is well accepted. The result of this ongoing debate has greatly helped these traditions in getting refined or reinvigorated to respond to the changes happening all around in the societies that it has been serving.

As a result, there are various versions of Hinduism and each of these continue to flourish, albeit, with varying levels of influence. In this series, one can easily identify Vedic Hinduism, Brahmanical Hinduism, Upanishadic Hinduism, Pauranic Hinduism, Sanatani Hinduism, Yogic Hinduism, Tantrik Hinduism, *Bhakti* laced Hinduism, Modern Hinduism and Universal Hinduism, etc. And this process continues even at present with many new versions expected to emerge over periods. That is why it is rightly called a plethora collection of attitudes and personal experiences; methods of worships and methods of reaching spiritual experiences; and finally an essence which is better defined by individual behaviours than imposed beliefs.

Hinduism appreciates variations among individual beings conditioned by their social, intellectual and spiritual needs and one of the best features which is worth valuable is that it allows every person to righteously choose a path that suits him/her best. Normal Hindu may not appreciate this aspect as they take this freedom as guaranteed. It is only in Hinduism that you may be worshiping one or more Gods and you still qualify to be a good Hindu provided your values are not causing harm to any person, being or thing; if you don't worship a God, you are still a good Hindu; and even if you don't believe in the very existence of God, you are still a good Hindu. Other than having faith in a set of universally inclusive righteous path of following Dharma, there is nothing else which can make you bigger or smaller Hindu.

This diversity also brings its own issues relating to classifications of scriptures of importance to Hinduism. It is blessed with a large corpus of some great literary creations. Even after bulk of scriptures lost to history, the material available today is larger than ever written for any stream of knowledge. With longest line of critical compositions over the centuries and millenniums, it is hard to expect all Hindu followers to clearly reply as to what are their main scriptures and what is the right sequence of their importance; it is clearly a case of problem of plenty. We don't know which one is superior because there are so many of them and all of them so unique and so great.

Unlike other religion of this world, Hinduism has its own complex bagful of beliefs, traditions, and advanced systems of ethics, meaningful rituals, philosophies and theology. One of the most important and basic beliefs is that there is only one absolute called "*Brahman*" and people are free to look at it in any of its diverse manifestations. Other basic beliefs that are commonly accepted by most Hindus, without much opposition, include acceptance of Vedas as supreme scriptures and key doctrines of Karma, Dharma, Reincarnation, *Varna Vyavastha* (Class based segregation), *Ashrams* (Stages of life), *Moksha*, and *Ahimsa*. Each of these shall be discussed in some details in due course.

Appreciative acceptance for accommodating the views of others, even when they are in opposition, is yet another distinguishing characteristic of Hinduism. It is absolutely unique feature and not found in any other faith. The logic behind such acceptance and appreciation is probably inherent in the very way in which human culture evolved and flourished in the Indian subcontinent. The whole system is based on complete inclusiveness; there is no provision of keeping any view outside. Many other contemporary religions are based on very strict basis of exclusion but Hinduism is probably the only exception in the world which is truly inclusive. Actually, any one who has the audacity of considering most opposing faith as intolerant, cannot be a true Hindu.

Indian subcontinent has been the pious land where Hinduism has grown from time immemorial. In due course, some people stepped out of this culture as Buddhists, Jains, Sufis (which is a mix of Hinduism with Islamic influence), and Sikhs, etc. and some came in. Some of the people who stepped out initially, returned back later. Hinduism allowed them to go at will and welcomed them back without any fear or favour. There are numerous examples of people experiencing with alternate beliefs at will while remaining part of main Hinduism stream. Recorded history of rise and fall of the number of followers of Buddhism and Jainism clearly points to this fact. Side by side, Indian subcontinent always created space for many other religious traditions to seek refuge here from oppressions in their own homelands. Many such groups from out of India landed in here, got accepted, soon became integral part of India, made their place in the cultural space and exchanged their traditions with already existing traditions. These include Zoroastrians, Baha'i's, Christians, Jews and many smaller groups. Later on, many Islamic aggressors came from central Asia, Afghanistan and got settled here in increasing numbers. The last example of this acceptance comes from Tibetans who came here from oppressions of Chinese rule in 1959. The Hinduism of today has absorbed many traditions and practices from most of them as well. Undoubtedly, any system which comes out of churning of so many fluids, over thousands of years, will hardly ever get solidify into a tight mould.

This background also comes handy to understand how today's Indians can handle multiple thoughts in their mind at the same time—the art of multi tasking resulting in dominance of Indian mind in IT revolution. Probably it is out of this DNA in our genes where we were always exposed to different sides of the argument and contrary arguments at the same point of time. Similarly, an average Indian is exposed to many languages at the same time. Young children learn multiple languages at schools in normal course without making much of it. Compare that with most countries where kids are exposed only to a single language and where the rulers with oppression force languages on people.

In Hinduism, multiple narratives covering different points of view coexist peacefully without anyone getting antagonized in any way. It promotes holding different views in the mind at the same time. Most other religions strongly reject everything out of their perceived line of religious doctrine but Hinduism has been very open and inclusive all along. Our scriptures are full of *Purva Paksha* (counter arguments or views from opponents) while debating subjects which is basically to accept different points of view on equal merits at all times. This is also the reason that there are many elements within Hinduism which a Muslim recognizes as Islamic, a Buddhist recognizes as Buddhist and a Christian recognizes as purely Christian thoughts.

Probably, this background also justifies as to why it is only in languages of Hinduism that the same word has many times more than one competing meaning attached to it or alternatively one single object has many words. I came across in Indonesian language that their word for 'Sun' is 'Matahari' where 'hari' actually means day and 'mata' means eye. Imagine that they don't have a separate word for something like Sun. Contrary to that, any Indian language will have words running in double digits for each of these three i.e. Sun, Day and Eye. This tendency is most true for Sanskrit which has largest influence on all languages, specially, in north of India.

Hinduism allows one to look at the ultimate Supreme as a God without face, name, form; the *Nirakar* or to look at the same Supreme as a God with particular form and name; the *Sakar*. Within *Sakar*, there is no advocacy of worshipping any deity in particular. Different people over different periods have worshiped thousands of gods with the belief that each and every God represents different aspects of the same Absolute *Brahman*. A follower is completely at his own liberty to choose his own *Isht Devta* without any demeaning to the others. The most fundamental deities are trinity of Brahma, Vishnu and Mahesh but one comes across thousands other deities along with their several Rupas.

As a basic concept of Hinduism, soul continues its journey from one life to another accumulating good and bad karmas created by it. Pains and pleasures are understood as the way of settling bad and good karmas. Ultimately when all karmic effects are exhausted by going through pains and pleasures endured by the body, over various lives, soul will achieve salvation and merge with the Absolute. This concept of reincarnation is yet another defining and distinguishing feature of Hinduism when compared to other popular religions of our times. With the onslaught of globalization where people are able to know about far off places, work with people from diverse backgrounds, scientific advancements are increasingly reducing the unknown, the concept of reincarnation is getting increasingly accepted as the logical approach for humanity.

"*Brahman*", the ultimate Supreme God, in Hinduism is considered as unchanging, infinite, immanent, reality which is divine cause of all matter, energy, time, space, being and everything beyond in this Universe. It is said to be eternal, without gender, omnipresent, omniscient and ultimately indescribable in human language. In short, it is Soul to the universe as we understand Soul to a human body.

Hinduism since the beginning has been a very receptive system in contrast to sharply exclusive systems of Christianity and Islam. In fact, putting Hinduism in comparison of these religions is not fit and proper comparison. Surely, a great deal of historical understanding has to be applied over the evolution process of Hinduism to understand that it is not a watertight religion in comparison of Christianity and Islam. That is why it is better called a "way of life" than a religion.

Because of its own strong merits, openness, flexibility, adaptability, etc., Hinduism has survived many aggressions from Greek, Persians, Pathans, Mangolians, French, Dutch and English people without any major impact on its core values. On the contrary, Hinduism has constantly borrowed from such influences and has enriched itself constantly. Hinduism, always context sensitive, responds to what is happening, at roughly the same moment, not only on the political, social and economic front but also within other religions in India or among people from other cultures entering India.

Now, let us look at the key components of this big jigsaw puzzle called 'Hinduism'. The sequencing of the topics taken for understanding has been attempted in terms of what comes first. But all the topics of interest, unfortunately, can't be graded cleanly as there is an unavoidable overlap; there are many periods in history where more than one development was taking place simultaneously. Similarly, there are sub-topics which have accrued over a longer time span and hence, can't justify the sequential priority. Another important effort made out here is to peep at defining historical developments happening and contributing to the evolution of Hinduism which is expected to help in appreciating the developments within and having far reaching consequences. It is neither possible nor plausible to look at Hinduism or any other religion without looking at historical developments in the society served by the said religion.

They say that every development is a product of its time. Hinduism is no exception to that rule as there are a number of turns and twists that it has witnessed at each turn of its journey. With the glimpse of historical perspective of a particular period, readers should find it simple and logical to appreciate what happened and why. However, focus is undoubtedly on evolution of Hinduism as a religious thought-process. But in order to avoid getting trapped with the history, historical developments are brought in only at particular intervals and only when there is impact on relevant context. Idea is not to explain history unless and until there is a direct impact of historical development on the evolution of Hinduism.

Effort is also made to highlight only such points which are not commonly understood and hence, many points generally known to most Hindu practitioners have been kept out of the discussion. Similarly, the length of discussions on most points is just to provide an overall view of our great "way of life". Each of the topics already has many books available all across. It is neither the subject matter nor possible to deal any topic with complete details. Idea is to expose the reader with basics of the topics and to arouse their interest in pursuing topics of their choice in further greater details.

The aim of this effort is to bring in glimpses of fabulous journey of Hinduism to the attention of its believers of twenty first century in the language which is contemporary and easier to connect with and to provide them exposure of basic aspects of this great heritage. Having sailed through the end of this book, if the reader is inspired to feel proud about Hinduism and the readers are prompted to pass on outlines of this great landscape to their next generation, the objective of this effort will get completely rewarded. So this book is meant for people who wish to know about Hinduism in general but don't know where to begin and neither have time and attention to cover everything in detail. But be ready, you would come across issues forcing you to rethink about what you already knew; some concepts that you may not have known so far; some concepts you wish you have known earlier; and surely, some concepts that you would love to pursue further in detail.

Before going any further, let us look at the time-lines of major developments beginning from ancient times to date. An accurate time-line certainly helps to provide cross connections of developments over longer periods. Good understanding of sequential developments also provides insight of the evolutionary process which helps in better comprehension of the subject matter. Unfortunately, historians from India and abroad have not been able to agree on many dates on most events and variations are sometimes very large. It is sad but true that historians are not known for impartial narrations. People have their own understanding and their own conclusions and their own galleries to play for. At times, they have altogether different level of understanding of the same development. This is particularly the case with historians from Western world of pre-independence era. Some of them are to be squarely blamed for not being fair to great traditions of Hinduism. They did not understood Hinduism in full detail and also had ulterior motive of proving that their own culture is richer and stronger than Indian culture. The saying that history is always written by rulers, applied to them clearly.

With reference to exact dates, maps and chaps, our past is as unclear as our future. One has to live with many unknown facts without certainty. This gets further accentuated when we deal with situations where there are no clear evidences and most conclusions are to be inferred based on words than objects. Most of the uncertainties on dates relates to ancient matters of composition of Vedas, Upanishads and some events mentioned in epics like Mahabharata and Ramayana. Beginning 3rd to 4th century CE, however, we certainly have more accurate account of recorded history. But even in the absence of exact information, it is better to work with approximation rather than not having any perspective of time lines. For the limited purpose on hand, even approximations will serve as good indicators for my readers.

Estimated Time Lines of Major Developments in Hinduism

Begins	Ends	Cultural, Social and Religious Development
50000 BC		Stone Age
30000 BC		Bhimbetka cave paintings got created at Raisen dist., of MP
10000 BC		Approximate period of start of agriculture on Indian subcontinent
7000 BC		Pastoral nomad societies start emerging in North West
4000 BC		Early settlements in Sindhu and Sarasvati basins
3000 BC	2500 BC	Harappa culture emerges and achieves its peak
2500 BC	2000 BC	Early Rig Veda compositions are made
	1900 BC	Sarasvati River dries up forcing spread of its populace to Punjab and other areas in South and North
1500 BC	1000 BC	Yajur, Sama and Atharva Vedas are composed
1200 BC	1000 BC	Vedic texts contain mention of *Doab* as centre of culture
1000 BC	900 BC	Early Cities of Kaushambhi and Kanshi are founded
1000 BC	800 BC	Composition of Brahamanas and Aranyakas takes place
800 BC	500 BC	Various Upanishads are composed in Forest Academies in North India
600 BC		City of Patliputra is founded
	468 BC	Mahavira, Founder of Jainism, leaves this world
483 BC	410 BC	Life and Works of Gautama Buddha
300 BC		Earliest surviving Tamil literature is said to have been composed
300 BC	100 BC	Dharma Sutras are composed
327 BC	325 BC	Alexander the Great invades North West and South Asia
324 BC	298 BC	Chandragupta founds Maurya Dynasty and rules
269 BC	233 BC	King Ashoka rules one of the biggest empires of its time
250 BC		Buddhist Council at Patliputra takes place
300 BC	200 CE	Period over which Mahabharata evolves and takes final shape
200 BC	200 CE	Another Great Epic, Ramayana is composed
200 BC	100 CE	Trade between Mediterranean and South India is established

Begins	Ends	Cultural, Social and Religious Development
185 BC	73 BC	Shunga Dynasty establishes and perished
180 BC	150 BC	Buddhist Stupas at Bharhut (near Satna) and Sanchi are built
166 BC	78 CE	Greeks, Scythians, Bactrians and Parthians entre India
100 BC	100 CE	Tamil poetic collection of Purunanuru are composed
78 BC	140 CE	Kanishka rules and promotes Buddhism
	100 CE	Indian Spice trade with Italy reaches to its height
	100 CE	Cankum are composed in South India
	100 CE	Expected period of completion of Manu *Smriti*, Dharma *Shastra*
150 CE		First Sanskrit based Inscriptions emerge in Gujarat
	200 CE	Expected time for writing of *Artha Shastra* by Kautilya
	300 CE	Expected time for composition of Kama Sutra by Vatsyayan
300 CE	400 CE	Kalidasa composes Sanskrit poems and plays
320 CE	550 CE	Gupta Dynasty rules from Patliputra, the Golden period of Hinduism
375 CE	880 CE	Pallavas founded and thrives
455 CE	467 CE	The Huns attack North India
460 CE	477 CE	The caves at Ajanta are completed
350 CE	750 CE	Early *Puranas* are composed and redacted
500 CE		Aryabhata describes orbits of the Planets
550 CE	575 CE	Cave Temple of Shiva at Elephanta is carved
606 CE	647 CE	King Harsha rules from Kannauj, UP
600 CE	700 CE	Islam is introduced in southern India by Arabian traders
711 CE	715 CE	Arabians invades North West of India
765 CE	773 CE	Ellora's Shiva Temple by Raja Krishna I is built
788 CE	820 CE	Adi Shankaracharya from Kerala establishes Hindu Order
871 CE	907 CE	Rise of Cholan Empire in South India
900 CE	1150 CE	Temple complex at Khajuraho is built by Chandellas
1001 CE		Mohammad of Ghazni (979-1030) raids North India
1162 CE	1227 CE	Chenghis Khan attacks India multiple times
1192 CE	1206 CE	Muhammad of Ghor establishes Capital in Delhi
1238 CE	1258 CE	Konark Temple is built by Narsimhadeva at Cuttuck
1210 CE	1526 CE	Delhi Sultanate establishes in Delhi and spread in east

Begins	Ends	Cultural, Social and Religious Development
750 CE	1500 CE	Later *Puranas* like Agni, Bhagvata, *Brahma*, Garuda are composed
1325 CE	1351 CE	Muhammad bin Tughlaq reigns from Delhi
1193 CE	1386 CE	Qutub Minar in Delhi is completed in many stages
1336 CE	1565 CE	Empire of Vijaya Nagar achieves its peak
1398 CE	1448 CE	Sant Kabir lives in Kanshi, works on Social reforms
1399 CE		Timur, ruler of Central Asia destroys Delhi
1469 CE	1539 CE	Guru Nanak Dev founds Sikkhism in Punjab
1486 CE	1533 CE	Chaitanya Mahaprabhu lives to spread *Bhakti* in Hinduism
1498 CE	1597 CE	Period of Mirabai's life in *Bhakti* of Girdhar Gopal (Krishna)
1532 CE	1623 CE	Tulsidas lives and works for Popularising Lord Rama
1526 CE		Babur establishes Mughal Empire in India
1530 CE	1707 CE	Humayun, Akbar, Jahangir, Shah Jahan and Aurangzeb rules
1600 CE		Queen Elizabeth I charters British East India Company
1757 CE		East India Company defeats Muslim Ruler in Bengal
1857 CE	1858 CE	Mutiny, leads to wave of English Rule
1863 CE	1902 CE	Life and works of Swamy Vivekanada
1869 CE	1948 CE	Mahatma Gandhi lives and leads India's freedom struggle
1896 CE	1977 CE	Life of Swamy Prabhupada, lives and establishes ISKCON
1918 CE	2008 CE	Maharishi Maheshyogi of Transcendental Meditation lives
1931 CE	1990 CE	Self Proclaimed Bhagwan Rajneesh, OSHO lives
1970 CE		Hindus start building Temples across Europe and America

Social Structure during Early Vedic Period

Let us now look at early Vedic period to understand how the society organized itself at that point in time. This will work like the sounding board for appreciating all later developments and will pave way for building our story line in proper sphere.

While one does not have direct information about the social life in early Vedic period from any recorded literature as such but early Vedas are strongest words available about human contemplation and a good study of the surroundings reveal a clear picture of life at that point in history. The contents of Rig Veda do provide references about various aspects of social life around that time and these references are strong enough to be used as bits and pieces to put together a detailed sketch of the social scenario of early period. The remarks mentioned below, therefore, are a result of compilation of hints from Rig Veda, the earliest composition among all the Vedas.

Early Vedic people were pastoral in nature and cattle rearing was their main occupation. Agriculture was taking roots and that lead to settlements of families near the fields used for agriculture. The society so formed was patriarchal where family was the basic foundation. Within a family, father was the head and was called by the name of Grihapati or Grihaswami. Wife and children were subject to the will of the Grihapati. He was supposed to be emblem of kindness, compassion and magnanimity. As head of the family, he was vested with all major decisions in the family. The most common form of relationship between man and women was monogamy but there are some instances of polygamy especially among elite class. Woman position was quite strong in early period. In spare time, they were engaging in songs, dance and merrymaking activities. Education was given due importance and sons were to be sent to best possible gurus who run their academies in separate location where pupils lived on residential basis.

Women were given high level of respect and freedom but were also extended protection and safety. The concept of Goddesses was certainly towards appreciation of woman's qualities as feminine embodiment of important aspects and powers. Women were held in high esteem and regularly participated in all sacrifices and rituals along with their husbands. The wife was the lady of the house and controlled servants, slaves and own children as well as unmarried siblings of her husband. The position of women in Vedic times is best understood by the often-quoted verse which translates to "where women are worshipped, there the Gods dwell". This kind of respect for women is unique to Vedic culture and does not have any parallel in human history.

Life of these people was ascribed to many objects of nature. People were mesmerized with natural forces like Sun, Moon, Earth, Wind, Fire, Rain, and Thunder and these forces were considered divine powers. These natural powers were personified into many

Gods and Goddesses and were worshipped for their blessings and favours for better life. Holding *yajnas* was the central feature for early Vedic people. Many people conducted *yajnas* at home while *Rajas* conducted *yajnas* on larger scale on special occasions, which got celebrated like festivals. They believed that Gods arrive to the pits of *yajnas* for accepting offerings made during the rituals. Hence, there was a direct contact expected with Gods during *yajnas*.

Houses were made of clay, bamboo and later they started using wood items. Roofs were thatched with long grass and leaves. Each family had their own house. Most of the people were able to do all jobs themselves as self-reliance was high. Houses had kitchen in a separate corner, which was considered very pure with fire kept burning on continuous basis for rituals and cooking.

Marriage was not mandatory and there are references where a girl reached to advance age living in her father's house without marriage. Person interested to marry someone's daughter was to send his friend or father as a messenger to ask her hand from the Grihapati. Marriage generally happened only after permission from girl's father. Interestingly, many customs prevailing in present day Hindu society can be traced to early Vedic time without any dilution over last five thousand years. These included groom going to brides house with his friends and relatives, preparing grand meal for all guests, marriage ritual by taking rounds around the sacred fire and offerings gifts for groom and his family members.

Abundance of sons was constantly the subject matter of pray as that was the way of expanding family lineage. Most auspicious blessing to a married woman was for having many sons. Not having son was considered being equal to poverty. Adoption from near family members was a poor substitute. Rather unfortunate but fact of life was that having daughters was considered as having misery. These were early seeds of a long journey of gender discrimination in our culture. We may be talking of five thousand years history but it sounds so contemporary. Alas, so many other customs and traditions got diluted over all these years but gender bias has remained alive all through the history of Hinduism. Plight of half of the population has remained conspicuously pathetic.

Morality was high, adultery and rape were considered serious offences. Illegitimate births were there but efforts were made to conceal such happenings. Cattle lifting were most common offence. Clothes were made of sheep's wool and deer skin. Ladies did popularly used necklets, bracelets, anklets and earrings made from various items including metals. Ladies are also depicted as oiling and making out their long hairs with lot of attention. Men braided their hair and wound the same as a shell. Incidentally, you must have seen many pictures of Lord Shiva in that very getup.

Cow milk was main nutrient among various kind of foods. It was used for drinking, cooking grains as well as offering to Gods. Next in line was *Ghee*, the purified butter which was used for adding to all types of cooking and for oblations to Gods. Numerous types of vegetables and fruits were consumed together with wheat and maize. Rice was not yet grown so much as other grains. Flesh was used mostly on ceremonial occasions. Bulls were chief offering at important *yajnas*. Cooking vessels were made of earth and base metals. Drinking water was always stored in earthen pots. There are repeated references of 'Som-ras' which is supposed to be some intoxicant juice of Soma plant which has since been extinct. Som-ras was offered to Gods and later distributed among all as '*Prasad*'.

Cattle breeding and agriculture were the main stay of livelihood for all. Cattle was pride possession and considered wealth. Cows were used for barter trading as well as initial currency. Prosperity of a person was measured in terms of how many cows he possessed. Hunting and gambling with pieces of dices together with chariot races and war dances were social recreational activities and some people got hooked on to these as vices. They have developed 'Sura' (some variety of country made liquor) using maize and many people are described as regular user of sura.

Gram (village) was lowest unit of society followed by Gana (tribes) and Rajya. Most settlements were near rivers and were to spread inside forests based on how much land was required for agriculture. Density of population was very thin. Most *Rajas* were hereditary but if Ganas were not happy, they could choose some other person as their Raja. Fights were regular. These were largely on foot with bow and arrow as main weapons. Later, chariots drawn by horses came on the scene.

People were initially self-reliant which means that there was no profession based segregation to begin with. But later portion of the Vedas do mention class-based categorization suggesting that later on different people branched out to undertake different professions. In between, came some initial activity of industry. The first industry was in wooden activities followed by chariot making, melting, forging metals and tanners. Women were known to engage regularly in sewing, plaiting mats from grass or making dresses and ornamental wears. Later developed traits also included rope maker, jeweller, elephant keeper and actor. Music instruments used were drums, flute and Veena. Vocal music was very popular and was resorted to on all auspicious occasions.

Composing of poetry was considered a great blessing of gods as only few people had mastery over playing with words. Such people were looked up as knowledgeable and to some extent as specially blessed people. They were later called "*arya*" in Sanskrit (Aryan in English). *Arya* literally means 'noble person' and was referred to designate people who believed in Vedic culture of performing rituals and *yajnas* and worshipped Vedic Gods. Coming from a common society, Aryans were certainly first among equals. It was out of this learned category of blessed people that composition of the Vedas got started.

2

The Vedas: A Great Human Heritage

The Vedas are considered the earliest literary record of not only India but the entire humanity and are certainly considered as most sacred books of Indian thoughts. They are the original scriptures of Indian teachings, and contain spiritual knowledge encompassing all aspects of human life. The Vedas are the fundamental part of Vedic literature. Philosophical maxims contained in Vedas have stood the test of time and the Vedas are considered the highest religious authority for all sections of Hindus in particular and for mankind in general.

"Veda" means wisdom, knowledge or vision, and it manifests the language of the gods in human speech. The laws of the Vedas regulate the social, legal, domestic and religious customs of the majority of inhabitants in entire Indian subcontinent to the present day. All the obligatory duties of the Hindus at birth, marriage, death, etc. owe their allegiance to the Vedic rituals. They draw forth the thought of successive generation of thinkers, and so contain within it the different strata of thought. All philosophies based out of Indian thoughts, similarly, owe their origin to the Vedas.

The Vedas are probably the earliest documents of the human mind and is indeed difficult to say when the earliest portions of the Vedas came into existence. The Vedas got composed when there were no scripts and writing was not yet invented. As such there is no proof of the exact period when these were composed. People have different timelines ranging from 1500 BC to 3000 BC where most expected period indicate to 1500BC or around as the period of beginning of compositions for these great literature for the entire mankind.

While the Vedas contain Hymns in praise of various Gods, the *Brahmanas* and Aranyakas contain prose text on sacrificial rites and ceremonies (those rituals and ceremonies had very special position in social cultural space of Vedic community) while the Upanishads are philosophical texts which clearly reveal very high level of abstract thinking by the Rishis of that time. All these four parts combined are called Vedic Literature. For right appreciation of Vedic scriptures, one must understand that nowhere on the earth has humanity developed so much at that point in history. Also whatever is available had been preserved through oral tradition passed on from generation to generation since these were not consigned to writing for a longtime.

The Vedas are called *Sruti* literature, which signifies that the truth revealed by the learned seers is not merely representation of their own introspection. Individual introspection surely can be subjective in nature. The sages of the Vedas proclaimed that the knowledge communicated by them through the Hymns of the Vedas is not their own discovery but is the one revealed to them by Supreme power without effort. To understand the significance of *Sruti,* we can look at these compositions by learned sages as being made while in higher state of inspiration by none other than God. Inspiration so used for composing the Veda Hymns has human contemplation on one side and God's revelation on the other side. The compositions so made are to be taken as impersonal truth which is eternal, nitya and are verifiable not only by logical reasoning but by self experience as well. The truth so composed has resulted in unique value of these compositions which were as relevant to humanity at the time of their compositions as these are today and are expected to remain equally relevant for all time to come as these touch the basic core of humanity without any restriction of time and space.

The Vedas are not a single literary work like Gita or collections of smaller books written at the same time like *Tripitakas* of Buddhism and Bible for Christians but a whole literature, which got composed over centuries by many contributors and was handed down from generations to generations through oral forms. This literature is not only earlier than that of Greece and Israel but also reveal a high level of civilization among those who composed it as an expression of their gratitude for the powers that they worshipped. The Hymns composed are called *Mantras,* which means 'thinking', or 'formulae' by which the contemplation of the particular God is attempted.

It might be remembered that Vedic age of Indian Civilization formation period is considered as heroic age of our culture. It was here that most basic features of traditional Indian culture took initial shape. It was precisely in this period that many fundamental concepts identified with Hinduism today, saw their fundamental emergence.

A Guru always taught the Vedas to a disciple. Pronunciation (sound made while speaking the words), intonation, rhythm and metre—all of which were very important for hymns. We must salute to those *Brahmins* who have preserved these voluminous *mantras* over centuries and over generations without allowing any variation in these features. In all we have four Vedas namely, *Rig-Veda, Yajur-Veda, Sam-Veda* and *Atharv-Veda*. Now let us briefly look at the contents of all four Vedas:

Rig-Veda

Rig-Veda is by far the earliest evolution of religious consciousness in entire humanity. What we have here is an out pouring of poets who seems mesmerized by the immensity of this universe and never ending mysteries of human life. The composers of Rig Veda see Gods in natural phenomenon of Sun, Moon, Agni, Dayus (sky), Earth, Maruts (winds/storms), Ap (water), Usha (dawn), and Nisha (night). As a continuation, many other Gods where the areas of influence were not very transparent in the beginning were also related to natural phenomenon only. These deities included Indra, Varun, Mitra, Aditi, Visnu, Pusan, the two Asvins, Rudra and Parjanya. The last category of Gods worshipped in Rig-Veda included Gods having abstract qualities. These included Savitr (the life giver), Sradha (dedication) and Manyu (anger). In addition to Gods, Rig Veda also includes poetry for Asuras, which are meant not in any bad sense but influential characters possessing wonderful powers. It was only later that Asuras got identified with things anti-god and much later that these got mentioned as demons.

Varun is a God common to both India and Iran and is supposed to regulate the course of Sun and sequence of seasons—basically keeps the world in order. Indra is worshipped as King of Devas and is invoked during struggling situations to fight on behalf of Devas. Agni is shown as mediator between men and gods. It was understood that whatever is offered to Agni will reach Gods. Similarly, Mitra is the God of light. The Sun is supposed to have three eyes consisting of Mitra, Varun and Agni.

Rig-Veda contains several mythological accounts of the origin of this world and hymns praising Gods and prayers for life and prosperity. These compositions are said to have composed in early Iron Age. There are multiple estimations about the period when this Veda would have been composed. But the excavations on the banks of ancient river *Sarasvati*, which have been conducted after 1990, throw altogether new light on Rig-Veda's compositions. The sacred river *Sarasvati* has now been identified as having originated from Himalayas and flowing through Punjab, Haryana, Rajasthan, Gujarat before meeting the sea at bay of Khambat. New findings also suggest that the river got dried up at around 1900 BC due to unknown but natural reasons.

Having multiple references of Sarasvati all through Rig-Veda clearly suggest that their compositions would have been completed much before any signs of river's drying up, meaning much before 1900 BC. The approximate period by Indian historians for Rig-Veda composition is taken around 3100 BC to 2500 BC. Most of the western historians put up this period at 1500 BC to 1200 BC but that need not be even discussed as their calculations were based on assumptions which were not correct to begin with. Most of their estimates were based on the theory of Aryans being invaders from outside who came to north India from southern steppes mounted on their chariots in about 1500 BC. As per popular Western views Aryans are said to have arrived, pushed Dravidians to South, killed indigenous people, enslaved many other habitants, and composed Rig-Vedas soon after their arrival on Indian soil.

But keeping all controversies surrounding the period of its composition aside, Rig-Veda is certainly the oldest text found anywhere in the world and has no parallel in entire human history. These were composed or edited by various Sages and the names of these learned sages are very much mentioned at the beginning of each new chapter of the printed books available now a days.

The **Aryans:** *Historical Perspective*

As mentioned earlier, historians are divided on the origin of Aryans and all sorts of theories are found to contrast each other's findings. To fully appreciate the background of Aryans composing Rig-Veda, it will be advisable to glance through at Aryans and their area of influence. There are numerous theories about Aryans and their relations with Vedic culture of ancient India.

In Sanskrit, however, the word '*Aryan*' means 'a noble man' and it is taken as a linguistic term rather than indicating to any separate ethnic group. It is generally believed by historians from western World that Aryans were not the original inhabitants of India. Historians are not on single page whether they migrated into India or they invaded India or they are originally from India and spread to rest of the world from India or they were related to Sindhu Sarasvati Civilization which popularly is also called Indus Valley Civilization or Harappan Civilization.

But to say that Rig-Veda composers are from outsiders is completely unpalatable. The strongest argument about this is the shear fact that Rig-Veda talks of almost everything under the sun and its hymns carry numerous references to the life of that time, natural surroundings, social structures, geographic features of its influence area but does not talk of any land other than the land where these are composed. Had the composers come from any other land, just a couple of centuries before the compositions of such voluminous poetry, it is but natural to assume that their compositions would have talked about that other land, their original land, in the same manner as every other immigrant culture has done throughout the human history and continues to do so till this day.

When English people came to US some five hundred years ago, they called the entire area only as New England with name of every village, town and street named after some icon from the parent country and culture. Rig-Veda doesn't talk of anything like this. The kind of intimacy and attachment is shown by composers with physical surroundings and landmarks of the land of compositions, it would be just unimaginable that the composers, counted in large numbers and spanned over few centuries, had their roots in some other land.

Contents and Context of Rig-Veda

Rig-Veda, as it exists today, consists of a total of ten books where book number one and tenth are supposed to be compiled at comparatively later period than the remaining eight books. In totality, the Veda contains 10,521 *mantras* arranged under 1028 hymns. It is said that the material available today is only a small part of the mass volume, which was originally there. The hymns related to praises for the particular Gods appear in adulation and sycophancy and seek blessings for the abundance of cows, sons, and material objects for prosperity. Rig-Veda believes that God is only one but God is called by different people with different names. Regarding the authors and composers, there is a general agreement among experts of the subject that the hyman of Rig-Veda have not been composed by any one person or in any single time period. (Tirth)

In addition to offerings praises for Gods, Rig-Veda also contains poems related to almost all other important aspects of human life of that time like importance of actions for realizing Dharma, and issues like friendships, keeping good company, cooperative approach to work, high morals, commitment to practise brahamacharya, seeking knowledge from wherever available, appreciating importance of parents for giving life, protecting the physical health of the body using *prana* (*Pranayam*), mutual importance of man and women, discussing intelligent people and able administrators, analyzing relation among guru and shishya (teachers and students) etc. The depth of knowledge and impact of its language is so impressive that these look equally relevant even today. It is indeed amazing to find such intricate but critical aspects of human life getting commented at such an early stage of evolution of human civilization and the universality of the comments. Beyond doubt, Rig-Veda is the greatest literature of all times and provides a great feeling for everyone belonging to this culture. (Tirth)

The hymns were composed in Vedic Sanskrit which had great importance for sounds made while speaking out. That version of Sanskrit provided higher focus on sounds of the words to the extent that it was forbidden to be reproduced in writing. Because of this strict focus on the power of words, for a long period of time Rig-Veda was preserved only orally, even until much later when writing had become popular. There were strict guidelines for memorizing it without ever referring to anything written as a text. There were restrictions even for reciting it by those remembering it by heart. For example, anyone who has eaten meat, seen blood, seen a dead body, had sexual intercourse or engaged in writing, was strictly prohibited to recite any portion of Vedas. It is said that unique sound powers of the *mantra* was just beyond any language to comprehend and reproduce.

The Vedas are treated as a revealed text and hence no one was allowed to tinker with the same even in slightest possible manner. There was total ban on non-believers, women, and pariah to learn Vedas with the single objective of avoiding injury to the power of sounds of words and to avoid dilution/pollution to its divine powers. Such exclusive preservation practices ensured that the Vedas were not abused even in right hands. As such, those who learned the Rig-Veda were exclusively male *Brahmins*. As per many Indian historians, these strict codes must have been the reason that elite of that time, involved in composing and preserving the Vedas, got called "Aryans".

A good reading of this Veda will reveal to its reader there was no rigid hereditary system of castes in place. The class system mentioned was based on occupation of the person and a son is commented to have a profession different than his own father. But this picture got changed in subsequent Vedas. In the initial parts of Rig-Veda, one comes across references to just two classes (*varnas*), firstly, the very own of them, *Arya,* and secondly, all the rest called Dasas. But in the later part of the Veda, there is a story about dismembered Primeval Man found by Gods at a sacrifice—his mouth became the priest (*Brahmin*), His arms were the Raja (*Kshatriyas*); his thighs, the commoner (*Vaishyas*) and his feet, the lowest and dirtiest part of his body—the servants (*Shudras*) which was basically to include all other classes.

As per Rig-Veda, people were not classified separately based on their class or practices but also by their social or anti-social behaviour and by their inclinations for addictions also. Indulging in wine drinking, games of dices, sex outside prescribed limits and hunting have been identified as behaviours pulling down any one to lower class irrespective of their origin. These are strong signs to suggest that 'class' of a person was not based by birth or by occupation alone but any one found diluting his personal practices by indulging in prescribed vices, carried the risk of getting his class reduced from higher to lower. This goes to suggest an auto corrective system, which promoted those who followed good practices and punished those violating it. No one need to argue with such dynamic class segregation, which is fair and transparent.

Rig-Veda is a text dominated by men of the world dominated by men and treats women at best as objects. A Vedic man gave equal importance to two of his prized possession, his cattle and his wife. It was only in later portion of Vedas that some importance was given to women, as the wife was required to be present when the husband was to perform a Vedic sacrifice.

Vedas are to be taken as a base on to which many more things were to be added in due course with much wider influence from all inhabitants of the area in which these were composed and preserved. With evolution of time, new ideas and new narratives got added to the basic theme of Vedas, which resulted in new practices involving larger contents and traditions.

On the philosophical level, the Rig-Veda seers admitted their inability to clearly comprehend all the creation of this visible world. They were satisfied looking at these creations as matters of surprise and were contended with the fact that it was not possible for them to be sure of many things which lie so far beyond the human knowledge. All the scientific advancements made until date fail to change the so-called perception of the seers. Even today there are so much more which is yet to be conceived by human capabilities. But they applied logic to conclude that the attributes of creation and governance of this universe could be granted to one single Being. This concept result is Vedas advocating the concept of Monotheism. This monistic emphasis led the Vedic thinkers to look upon a Deity as a different name or aspect of the One Universal God, the Supreme, and looking at a single deity as representing some essential aspect of the divine Being.

The seers of Rig-Veda did not see any disconnect in a person worshipping many deities as they assumed these deities as just a reflection of one and only one God. This unique tradition later became a basic foundation for Hinduism, which consciously provided space to a single worshipper to choose any form for his worship of the God. Rig-Veda also raises the question of human Self and suggested that there remains an unborn part of every human which survives death and which works like a controller of the body during the entire life. This so called unborn aspect was looked as being different from individual soul. In one of the hymn there is a mention that *"two birds live in the single body where one enjoys the fruits of the action of the body while the other is just a passive spectator"*. These concepts were to be further enlarged by subsequent thinkers to evolve in full-fledged doctrines and became foundations of Hinduism as a religion.

Some people also call Rig-Veda as *Mantra* Yoga. The *mantras* of Vedas have been believed to have special power when pronounced using Vedic Sanskrit, a language which was called the language of cosmic mind. The significance of the *mantras* sound effect was beyond any language to capture. Learned teachers will vouch that even Classical Sanskrit failed to capture those sound significance so all other modern languages need not even be mentioned capable of reproducing those magical sound impacts.

In yet another impressive contemplation, Rig-Veda suggested that a human could become a Devta, a Deity, by one's own deeds. Infact, the ultimate objective of the knowledge given by Rig-Veda can be said to encourage each individual soul to become universal soul by way of worship and following a moral life.

At this stage it will not be out of place to look at the Rig-Veda from the perspective of Max Muller, a German born philologist and orientalist who was one of the founders of Western academic field of Indian Studies and an authority on comparative religion, and he said:

> *"As long as man continues to take interest in its history and as long as we collect in libraries and museums the relics of former ages, the first place in that long row of books will belong for ever to Rig-Veda. Without shadow of any doubt, it is but the oldest book of the entire world."*

Other Three Vedas

Yajur-Veda

Yajur-Veda means 'wisdom of sacrificial formula'. It is a liturgical collection and was composed to meet the requirements of ceremonial religion. It practically served as a guidebook to the priests who were to pronounce these prose and *mantras* at sacrificial ceremonies while performing manual part of the sacrifice. Prose was largely to be used for explaining different rituals and *Yajnas* using hymns of Rig-Veda.

There are two main branches of *Yajur-Veda* named *Krishna* and *Shukla*. Each one of these has their own recensions. The recensions under Krishna *Yajur-Veda* are named Taittiriya, Kathak, Maitrayani and Kapisthala. Similarly, the recensions under *Shukla Yajur-Veda* are named Madhyadin, and Kanva.

Dated around BC 1200-1000, additional texts of *Brahmanas* add information on the interpretation and details of their performances at Yagnas. Main events, which are covered with specific *mantras,* dedicated and *vidhi vidhan* mentioned include *Agnihotra, Rajasuya, Ashvamedha, Purushamedha Yajnas*. The well-commented Isha Upanishad is also part of this Veda.

Sam-Veda

Sam-Veda is purely a liturgical collection. If Rig-Veda is to be taken as recital praise of the Gods, Sam-Veda will be called Veda of holy singing. As such, this Veda ranks next to Rig-Veda in terms of sanctity and liturgical importance. The hymns of Sam-Veda are chiefly used for chanting by Priests at the performance of important sacrifices where juice of soma, clarified butter, milk and other items are to be offered to various deities.

The hymns in Sam-Veda are used as musical notes. These are almost completely drawn from Rig-Veda. Hence, these have no separate distinctive lessons of its own. In a way, Sam-Veda is nothing but a reduced version of Rig-Veda. Many people say that if Rig-Veda is a 'word' than Sam-Veda is a 'song for the same word'. Similarly, if Rig-Veda is to be taken as knowledge, Sam-Veda is truly its realization.

The collection is made of complete hymns, part of hymns and detached verses, which are all taken from Rig-Veda and are transposed and rearranged to suit the particular ceremonies where the hymns are supposed to be used. In order that the original hymns of Rig-Veda can be suited for the musical singing, the verses are altered suitably by prolongation, repetition of words/letters, insertion of syllables, etc. Sam-Veda contains melodies or musical chanting and that is why it is called as beginning of Indian musical arrangements. This laid the basis of Indian Classical music getting identified with our ancient religious practices.

Sam-Veda is also representative of the ecstasy of spiritual knowledge and the power of devotion to the Gods. There are three recensions of Sam-Veda: Kauthuma which is popular in Gujarat and most part of north India, Ranayania, which is popular in north Karnataka and Jaiminiya or Jalavakra which is popular among Nambudri *Brahmins* of Kerala.

Dated around BC 1200-1000, this is smallest of all Vedas and is principally based on songs and singing. Many *mantras* contain scientific knowledge which got grasped by scientists over thousands of years later, e.g., rotating earth, shining of moon based on sun light. Many *mantras* also include medical solutions. This Veda is supposed to be meeting point of Gyanyoga, Karmayoga and *Bhakti* yoga.

Atharva-Veda

This is completely different from the other three Vedas detailed above. Atharva-Veda is regarded next to Rig-Veda in terms of importance with respect to history and sociology. The basic spirit of this Veda is quite different from Rig-Veda and the language used also is quite simpler. Sometimes, people say that this is not a Veda as it mainly contains spells and charms prevalent at the time of its composition and basically it depicts the Vedic life as it was prevailing at that time.

Atharva-Veda is a Veda of charms and spells. It teaches the art of sorcery (Jadu Tona). This Veda evolved techniques for curing physical ailments, satisfying various desires, lusts, passions and ambitions. It also provides ways of warding off dangers and omens. Specific *mantras* are provided to teach methods of exorcising and propitiating demons, ghosts and evil spirits.

In addition to magic and spells, it contains *mantras* for miracles, medical treatments, science, and philosophy. Other subjects covered here are geography, space, geology, Ayurveda medicines and practices, surgery, longitivity, child birth. In total there are about 6000 *mantras*, 760 hymns and small portion written as prose as well. This is the last of all four Vedas and more focused on social subjects rather than Gods and religion. Going by contents of this Veda, many people prefer to keep it out of religiously focused literature. But it is a fact that this Veda also has been practised by many Indians for a long time and it certainly add one unique shade to our multicoloured culture.

The antiquity of Atharva-Veda also is pegged to a approximate period of BC 1100-1000. Gods here are reduced to secondary position unlike Rig-Veda. Atharva-Veda also indicates that by its time, the nature worshiping got reduced among Aryans of this time.

Each Veda consists of four parts namely Veda, Brahmanas, Aranyakas and Upanishads.

The *Brahmanas*

The *Brahmanas* are commentaries on the four Vedas detailing the proper ways of performing rituals. Basically, Vedas relied on the truth content while *Brahmanas* proposes infallible power of *mantras* in their correct pronunciations. In other words, content having been taken from Vedas; the focus here is on the process for execution to get complete advantage of the magical powers of the *mantras*.

The *Brahmanas* were very advantageous in the development of later Indian thought and scholarship, including Hindu philosophy, predecessors of Vedanta, law, astronomy, geometry, linguistic, the concept of Karma, or the stages in life such as brahmacharya, grihastha and eventually, *sannyasa*. Some *Brahmanas* contain sections that are Aranyakas or Upanishads in their own right.

The language of the *Brahmanas* is a next stage of Vedic Sanskrit, which is younger than the text of the samhitas (the *mantra* texts of the Vedas proper), but for the most part is older than the texts of the Sutras. Some of the younger *Brahmanas* (such as the Shatapatha *Brahmana*) are estimated to have been written around 6th century BC or late Vedic period. This roughly corresponds to the period of emergence of great maha-jan-padas or kingdoms out of the earlier tribal kingdoms.

The *Brahmanas* got composed during a revolutionary social and intellectual transformation of urbanization post decline of Sindhu Sarasvati civilization. By this time, there was a significant geographical and social shift in the history of India. These texts start to mention the Ganga Yamuna plains of *Doab*, which is an area that is covered in detail in the long poem of Mahabharata. The main cities finding reference in here are Hastinapur, Kashi (capital of Koshala/Videha) and Kaushambhi. The language of *Brahmanas* is bit different than used in Vedas suggesting a good time difference in the composition. The *Brahmanas* basically cite Vedic verses and explain them by describing the circumstances under which those were first created. But many stories retold in here have under gone transformation impacted by the social changes in the interim period. In that context, the *Brahmanas* are a step forward in evolving and continuing the Hinduism constantly borrowing from the past and responding and recreating newer texts incorporating the changes that took place in the actual world.

This was the time when people have started settling down in their well-built houses as against nomad nature in the early Vedic time. Trade has started in through the river routes in north India. Forests and minerals were getting converted into resources. The Vedic people moved from Punjab up to Magadha and in a back flow from east to west area of Gujarat. Agricultural surplus allowed formation of many towns and cities all along the Ganga and Yamuna. The agricultural surplus resulted in a new kind of economic power resulting in higher importance of *Vaishyas* in the social structure. Many also started accumulating notable wealth cutting across the earlier social orders.

More surpluses meant bigger kings, which meant bigger sacrifices, which in turn meant more elaborate rites and celebrations necessitating the focus on vidhi vidhan covered in the *Brahmanas*. The kings also had to spend increasingly larger amounts on maintaining armies and other administrative systems, which were not important earlier. This resulted in squeezing the money available for priests and sacrifices. Henceforth, financial condition of priests were never to be similar to past.

The *Brahmanas* era also witnessed big change in meat eating practices of Hindus. Meat eating is actually linked to non-acceptance of *Ahimsa* which slowly became a basic foundation in area where agriculture grew much better and capable of sustaining human life. Eating meat got accepted only when the meat was from a sacrifice. At this time in history, killing of a cow or bull got equated to expelling the embryo from own wife. This change in meat eating appears to be a result of philosophical considerations, method of livestock breeding, easy use for utilizing the surplus produce from cattle unlike in the past, etc. arising from the urbanization in the basin of Ganga Valley.

Chart Showing Linkage of Vedas with *Brahmanas*, Aranyakas and Upanishads

Veda	Samhita	Brāhmaṇa	Ar̄anyaka	Upanishad
Rig	Shākala	Aitareya Kaụshītāki	Aitareya Kaụshītāki	Aitareya Kaụshītāki
Shukla Yajur	Vājasaneyi m.* Vājasaneyi k.**	Shatapatha		Īṣāvāsya Bṛhadāraṇyaka
Krishna Yajur	Taittirīya Maitrāyaṇīya Kaṭhaka	Taittirīya Maitrāyaṇīya	Taittirīya	Taittirīya Mahānārāyana Ṣvetāṣvatara
Sāma	Jaminīya Rāṇāyaniya Kautuma	Talavakāra Chhāndogya		Kaṭha Kena Chhnādogya
Atharva	Shaunaka Pippalāda	Gopatha		Muṇḍaka Māṇduka Prashna

*m: Mādhyandina. **k: Kāṇva

3

Upanishads: The Philosophical Treatises

Contributing to the Theology of Ancient Hinduism

Forming core spiritual thoughts of Vedanta Hinduism, Upanishads primarily discuss philosophy, meditation and form of God. Literally meaning as mystic teachings—it means, "sitting near the teacher" to learn secret doctrine. It also means Brahm knowledge by which ignorance is loosened or destroyed. Originally, there were around 1200 different Upanishads but later on only about 108 remained available. Upanishads take Vedic learning to highest metaphysical state beyond which is only realm of silence. Upanishads have explained and elaborated on identity of *Brahman*, Jivatma, 'you are that', the quest for unity in diversity and law of Karma. Upanishads characterize universality. Upanishads deal with their subject matter in such details that these are beyond any possible controversy in terms of their principles. All sides of arguments are discussed and deliberated to reach the truth in a unique manner where there is no room for any one to express difference of opinions or ask for evidences and arguments. Truly speaking, these are highest level of philosophy ever conceived by human mind.

Upanishads basically develop the Vedic ideas and symbols and provide them new meanings as a proof of awakening of mind. With the passage of time, old ideas are always reinterpreted in newer lights and with newer explanations. To that extent,

Upanishad are but a natural expansion of Vedic doctrines in so far as these belong to philosophical contents and ignoring Vedic emphasis on rituals and sacrifices as external offerings for pleasing the Gods for seeking personal blessings.

Upanishads are product by groups of mystics embarking on the peaceful conquest of inner space. By the time Upanishads were starting to get compiled at Guru Kuls (forest academies) in north of India, external rituals were getting faded and were getting increasingly replaced by rigorous introspection. The worshippers had been over Vedic rituals as the only route for seeking their divinity. They were no more that focused on directing all their attention on the Devas of Vedas. The focus was certainly changing from external performance of a rite to its interior significance. The entire focus of Upanishads was on the '*Atman*', the Self within, which is supposed to be identical with the '*Brahman*'.

The format of Upanishads is pretty bizarre and full of riddles and hence quite hard to penetrate easily. To a new reader without much background of Indian scriptures, these will sound incredible statements of abstract thinking so difficult to comprehend. It must have been the practice of the day that sages choose to write using as few words as possible to convey the point in view rather than systematic writing like now a day. As prevalent in that period, a debate will follow with arguments and counter arguments being hurled from either side of the debaters but finally the debate will end with one side of contestants falling silent. Their silence leads the reader to probable final position. It was certainly a very unique but very interesting indication of developing a consensus on spiritual matters. Many of these debates have involved influential kings and their priests to indicate the importance these commanded.

The great conclusions of Upanishads cannot be easily understood using the lenses of logic or sense perception. Deep understanding will require long period of meditation training so that the seeker is able to develop total transformation of looking at self and the rest of the world outside. I am taking pain to explain to first time readers to ensure that you do not get discouraged in your efforts to comprehend the meaning in very first or initial efforts. Please remember that there is deepest possible treasure of spiritual knowledge lying beneath our Upanishads and additional patience required for sharpening your understanding will be worth all efforts.

But let us not assume that entire population of that time was equally involved in pursuing studying Vedas or *Brahmanas* or Upanishads. As is always the case, in all times and cultures, during this period also there were only a handful of enlightened spiritually inclined members of academies which were involved in creating new Upanishads. Only those select few were drawn to contemplate and come up with their own renditions of specific aspects of ultimate supreme power governing this universe vis-à-vis human mind. Spirituality, by its very nature does not attract every one as it always required special talent, intelligence level and deep desire to shift focus from externally visible objects of attachment to the internal *Shunya* (vacuum of inside world of a human), it is easy to assume that it was not, and it will never be, for all ordinary people.

Many people even at this point of history were offering rituals and sacrifices in traditional Vedic ways. External symbols are easy to visualize and hence, draw ordinary people. In all times, deeper subjects attract but only a handful of people. What is interesting is to note that the results of their findings effect humanity at large. Certainly, concentrating human mind with its monkey like nature on the core of human of inside would have been as difficult in ancient times as it is today.

Sages of Upanishads were aiming at enhancing spirituality of their students so that they are moved away from carnally oriented thinking. In that process, the sages used to ponder problems of the deepest concerns of the human beings. With to and from communication between the teachers and students, new theories were devised. Idea was to prompt students to respond spiritually for which it was like mandatory for the students to develop spiritual dispositions. With the same purpose in mind, the language was reticence where as few words were used as possible so that the person uses his own contemplation to understand the true meaning hidden behind the words.

The two earliest Upanishads are Brhadarankya and Chandogya. A single author writes neither. These are anthologies of separate texts put together at a later stage by different editors. It might be safely concluded that the process of compiling an Upanishads would have been where a particular new idea was developed by *Brahmin* Teachers originally and discussed among the fellow gurus and disciples at the academy. Later, the revised theme was well debated among other *Brahmins*, kings and learned

Kshatriyas leading to fresh refinements. Finally, after incorporating all the points, final text was getting compiled by lead Guru of the concerned academy. The learned people involved in such debates came from diverse background of social structures and classes. Anyone with right orientation without considering what his class is was welcome to participate in evolution and debates of these ideas. This democratic approach resulted in very cross-cultural contributions bringing out these unique ideas.

This has no parallel in human history which has rather seen continuous violence and hatred for each one's own view point on all matters including theology and spirituality. Growth of spirituality is known to progress in the serene, peaceful and congenial environment where there is no horror of aggression or deprivation or violence among majority of inhabitants.

Ideas of Upanishads were to help us rise beyond the glamour of fleshly life. The authors of Upanishad share with us their own experiences of divine efforts and the successes achieved by them in visualizing the splendours of the unknown. Since there is a minimum level of spiritual awakening being necessary to appreciate these findings, these teachings made more sense only to selected few who have been able to cross a threshold limit of spiritual awakening. Also, these experiences were desired to be well guarded and were to be shared with eligible candidates. Chandyoga Upanishad says that secret doctrines of *Brahman* may be shared by a father only with his elder son or a trusted pupil alone but not with any other person even if that person offers the whole world with all its treasures. The sages were to share these sacred teachings with strict testing about capability and willingness of their pupils.

The theme of Upanishads moves away from Vedic hymns and gets engaged in searching the reality which lies beneath the flux of things—"what is that which being known, everything else becomes known?" Actually, going a step further, there are several indicators in Upanishads which clearly make adverse comment on empty barren ritualistic religion being propagated by *Brahmanas* based on Vedic rituals. The understanding by this time had improved to conclude that undertaking rituals and sacrifices do not lead to liberation but, at best, takes us to the world of Fathers from where one has to come back again to the earth in new life in due course. Also that when all the things already belong to the

God, what is the point in making any offering of the material things? After all, what can be given by a human to a God? Upanishads highlighted one's own self and one's own will as the right offerings to be made to God.

Special mention is required for Yajnavalka who was the personal philosopher of King Janak of Videha who himself is known as leading exponent of emerging spirituality of his time. Yajnavalka is credited to come up with one of the most critical finding ever that each human has an immortal spark at his core, which participated in and was of the same nature as the immortal *Brahman* that sustained and gave life to this cosmos. This was a discovery of great relevance and later became central insight in every major religious tradition. People called it '*Atman*' or 'soul' or 'rooh' but it was established that there is some thing which remains even after the physical body gets destroyed.

During Vedic period, the view was that it is immortal *Brahman* that gave life and sustains to the entire cosmos. New Spirituality of Upanishads focused on *Atman* as an immortal spark at the core of the human person. The ultimate reality was very much permanent and was having everlasting presence in every single human being which can be discovered in the depth of Self "*Atman*".

This means that an enlightened person could experience transcendence by exploring and tuning the mysteries of their own nature rather than by taking part in magical external rituals. As in a dreaming stage during the sleep, one take external world apart and create his own joy, pleasure, delight, fears, pressures etc. But what happens in dreams is only a temporary release similar to orgasm. The moment the person is awakened, the dream gets over and reality takes over. But such joys and pleasures are just momentary and are just like a glimpse or peep of the permanent liberation which is the ultimate aim of all spiritual quests. It is in such an enlightened state of permanence that the sage experiences the *Atman*. Simply put, once a person is able to reach the depth of his own inward world and come across his own Self, he is bound to experience the orgasm like joy constantly without any disruption or fear of ending.

Knowledge of deep inner self is an experience of bliss. This knowledge lay beyond concepts and did not depend upon logical deduction. Logic is meant for a mechanical mind. Contrary to that, bliss is rather an awareness of an inner light within the heart. Before this, the followers of Vedic rituals believed that the Self was perceived by accumulating a stock of perfectly executed sacrifices. But by the time of Upanishads, it was agreed that simple rituals were not enough and that the internal self was possible to be conditioned only by our actions, thoughts and experiences. This is the doctrine which got popular as a new concept and was later called "Karma". In later periods, as we all know, Karma became and continues to be basic tenets of Indian spirituality. It was here in Upanishad stage that Karma was first introduced to Indian philosophy.

The Upanishads were promoting yet another basic theme of Indian spiritual thought of "*Moksha*" (liberation of soul), from painful cycle of life and death. With proper deliberations and taking the internal Self experience to its final stage, *Moksha* was taken as the ultimate goal of spiritual life. It was also realized by sages that *Moksha* couldn't be achieved by external rituals but only by the quest of interior knowledge. The *Atman* is not considered as soul or psyche as Indian spirituality didn't separate body from spirit unlike Christianity rather saw human being as a composite whole.

There is another way of linking Upanishads with Rig-Veda; while Rig-Veda dealt with five elements of which the human body is made of. It suggested that the body dies and get merged into the five elements that it is made of. But Upanishads raised the questions of what happens to the soul? Upanishads constantly talk about "Transmigration", yet other basic tenets of Indian thoughts. Looking to momentary, petty and frivolous existence of human life, some people started feeling that the cycle of life and death need to be broken by getting out of this vicious cycle. These people got engaged in searching for ways to get out of the said cycle. Upanishads offered a way to such people by offering them ways and means of conquest over rebirth by exposing such person with the complete knowledge of *Atman* and following the teachings suggested in Upanishads. This was a big shift as until then, the *Brahmanas* were promising the same thing to every person who had acquired the right knowledge and was performing the rituals in complete manner. It takes years to open up the depths of the Self through silence, meditation and spiritual discipline that leads the aspirant to realize the futility of desiring transient desires and objects. Many more ways of achieving *Moksha* were to be worked upon by later sages who came out with alternate philosophies for this very purpose like *Nyaya, Vaisheshika, Sankhya* and Yoga. All these are shared out in sufficient details under a specific chapter dedicated to Indian Philosophies.

As mentioned earlier that there are about 108 Upanishads available out of a total of about twelve hundred composed initially. But the great thinker of all time, Shankaracharya wrote his detailed commentaries on eleven of these. Relying on his intellectual judgement and theological supreme knowledge, only those eleven Upanishads are considered main Upanishads until present time. The names of these eleven are—Isa, Kena, Katha, Prashna, Mundaka, Mandukya, Taittiriya, Aitareya, Chandogya, Brahadarnakya and Swetashvatara. (Radhakrishnan)

In addition, there are many others Upanishads which are actually more religious than philosophical in their contents. This justifies their classification under *Puranas* and *Tantra* rather than Vedanta. As mentioned earlier, the Upanishads were compiled as a group effort and hence are not attributed to any specific composers but main doctrines of Upanishads are attributed to sages by the names of Aruni, Yajnavalkya, Balaki, Svetaketu, and Sandilya. Most of these are supposed to have been composed during 800 BC to 500 BC period. There is fair amount of certainty for their composition period as Gautama Buddha has been found to rely on some of these during evolving his separate theology. Undoubtedly, these are earliest philosophical compositions of the whole world.

Various Upanishads are related to different Vedic traditions and family lineage but their source of stories are common and all through, these remain tied into a common thread and also remain in communication with each other. Bridging *Brahmanas* and *Upanishads* and overlapping both these are another group of Vedic literature called Aranyakas. As the very name suggests, Aranyakas were composed in forests but dealt more with rituals and much less with metaphysics like Upanishads did.

Dara Shikoh is credited with translation of many Upanishads into Persian language (1656-57) and from Persian these also got translated to Latin and finally reached to the Western world. Upanishad belong to Axial Era named by Karl Jaspers which cover the period of 800 BC to 300 BC, when for the first time and almost simultaneously, mankind in Greece, China and India are said to have questioned the traditional pattern of life and focused to look to the depth of individual soul.

Upanishads are also called "Gyan Khand" of Veda meaning 'knowledge portion' of Vedic scriptures. The famous Brahmsutra is an aphoristic summary of the teachings contained in Upanishads and commentaries prepared by learned thinkers on Brahmsutra forms the basis of all philosophical approaches of Vedic branch. To that extent, Brahmsutra are truly called seeds which can be planted to let grow into full fledged trees with the efforts of a great mind.

My reader may have noticed that I have been constantly mentioning only Indian thoughts and not Hindu thoughts. It is precisely because until this stage of history, there was no separation or segregation in different branches. Jainism and Buddhism alike with their own interpretations also accept Upanishad's teachings equally. This speaks universality of these teachings. The moment we connect these thoughts to Hinduism, there is a risk of limiting their true nature. One must be clear with the real definition of Hinduism (the one which relates to Sanatan Dharma with all its inclusiveness and all pervading moral and social harmony among all elements and living beings of this universe) before proudly identifying Vedas and Upanishads with Hinduism. Clearly, limiting the scope of these infallible scriptures with generally understood Hinduism (being one among Christianity, Islam and likes) will be a great injustice to their universal character.

The Upanishads are undoubtedly great heritage of entire mankind for eternity.

4
Traditions of *Shramana*

This was a non-Vedic movement parallel to but very different from historic religions. It developed in the Upanishad days and soon after that. This is a very important tradition which gave rise to great traditions of South Asia namely Yoga, Buddhism and Jainism. *Shramana* tradition is also responsible for some *nastika* schools of Hindu philosophies such as Charvaka and *Ajivika.* These will be discussed in detail once we reach Indian Philosophies section.

Literary meaning of the word *Shramana* is 'one who strives' or one who exerts himself and performs religious austerities. The term came into existence to denote those monks who got wholeheartedly devoted to pursue enlightenment on a full time basis leaving family and all other relations behind. These were individuals who considered themselves free from any binding of traditions and dedicated to self-experience by going totally independent of society around. They were wanderers and didn't remain at one place for a long time. In a way, these people were in direct competition with Vedic *Brahmins* who owe their allegiance to everything Vedic. Just to reiterate, Vedic *Brahmins,* as of this stage, didn't believe in *Samsara* and were stressing mastery of Veda texts and performing Vedic rituals as a way for liberation.

This tradition evolved in the Magadha area and was certainly influenced by indigenous inhabitants of that area as against Vedanta school, which was from Aryans having significantly higher presence in Punjab, Haryana and western Uttar Pradesh, and decreasing slowly as we travel to east direction until we come to Patliputra.

As against Vedic system which emphasized on sacrifices and rituals for seeking liberation from *samsara, Shramana* opted for the path of achieving liberation by renouncing householder's life, engaging in austerities, meditation and discussions of associated philosophical theories. But many other fundamental theories namely, karma, rebirth, *samsara* and transmigration were accepted by Vedic systems and *Shramana* equally. They did not accept the *Brahmin* authority of Vedic parampara as the media for seeking God; they wish to go there based on personal experience.

Basically, the tradition hinged on the fact that once cycle of rebirth is understood, the goal of human should be to quickly find escape from that cycle and that was said to be possible only by moving away from the world and focus on spiritual activities. The followers of these traditions spent their entire energy on pursuing austerities, meditation and contemplating about associated theories. Mahavira and Gautama both were leaders of their *Shramana* orders together with many other names quoted in Jain and Buddhist literatures who were also engaged in achieving liberation similar to these two enlightened people. But it is not to say that entire *Shramana* traditions were dead after branching out of Buddhism and Jainism. At best, these two thoughts were a good example of the success out of this tradition.

However, going forward, in due course, *Shramana* tradition also experienced evolutionary changes. Riding on the enlightenment of Gautama Buddha, many people opted for Buddhism and became known as Bhikshus. They started living in monasteries. Initially, Buddha recommended monastery living for Bhikshus during rainy season alone but later the arrangement became permanent. For those who followed Jain tradition, wandering also got waned out in due course. Some of remaining *Shramana* who preferred Vedic traditions over Jain and Buddha, joined mainstream Vedic system where, in due course, many of their traditions got absorbed in Hinduism.

Beliefs and main concepts of *Shramana* philosophies and their comparison with the Vedic tradition are as under:

- *Denial of Creator or Omnipresent Gods*: This was single most important point of their independence from Vedic culture who believed in these principles as core of their traditions.
- *Rejection of Vedas as Revealed Texts:* Followers of Vedic traditions believe that Vedas are not composed by human but have been revealed by the creator himself as divine truth. This is the reason that every word included there is

to be accepted as word of God and no alteration/deletion is permitted in Vedic parampara.

- *Affirmation of Concepts like Samsara, Karma, Rebirth, Transmigration and Existence of Soul*: In due course all these principles got absorbed in Hinduism and are defining features of the entire Hindu belief system. For a grown up Hindu as myself, coming to know that all these major concepts were borrowed from other independent source like Shramana is a great revelation. The common sources of these concepts define such a great similarity among Hinduism, Jainism and Buddhism.
- *Affirmation of the Attainment of Moksha through Ahimsa, Renunciation and Austerities:* These concepts were fundamental concepts for both Buddhists and Jains but Hinduism went through a lot of discussions and yes-no situation for accepting *Ahimsa* which was so integral part of their rituals and religious performances. Hinduism took another 400-500 years before finally accepting complete *Ahimsa* as part of efforts for seeking *Moksha*.
- Denial for efficacy of sacrifices and rituals for purification.
- Rejection of the class system and caste system.

Undoubtedly, this important tradition had very critical footprints over emergence of many basic principles of later Hinduism. Its contribution was equally great as of Vedic traditions. Can we imagine Hinduism of today without the concepts of *Samsara* and *Moksha* as both of these are direct contribution of *Shramana* to the ultimate Hindu thoughts.

In due course, *Shramana* traditions also went through evolutionary process and after separation of Buddhism and Jainism, rest of the movement got absorbed and incorporated by *Brahmins* in their own beliefs and practices. It was at this critical juncture in history that Hinduism altogether abandoned the sacrifices of animals and adopted *Ahimsa* as yet another sutra of Sharmana's into Hinduism. The wondering sadhus of that time created a separate place for themselves in the social structure where every householder considered it his obligatory duty to contribute for meeting basic physical needs of these sadhus. But for *Shramana* traditions, renunciation in Hinduism would have remained limited to people in *Vanprashtha* and *Sannyasa Ashramas*. In a way, the present practice of sadhus that we come across living in Akhadas who make regular appearance in large numbers on occasions such as Kumbha melas, are modified extensions of this basic thought of ancient Indian society.

No doubt, modern Hinduism can be called a combination of Vedic and *Shramana* traditions as its present structure of beliefs and philosophies is a unique mix of practices drawn from both the systems. And the very success of both the systems lies in the fact that even normal inhabitants of India who have been materialistic in their quest, have had a long tradition of venerating those who seek the spiritual, and they continue to support them. (Armstrong, Buddha)

5

Harappan Civilization and Vedic India: Two Sides of the Same Coin

The mature Harappan civilization popularly called The Indus Valley Civilization began as early as 6000 BC when inhabitants of the region began to develop a distinct cultural style. It was spread in basin of Sindhu and Sarasvati Rivers. As we may know, river *Sarasvati* later became extinct. Harappa happens to be the first place where remains of this great civilization were first got noticed. Considering the volume and density of findings in other places since then, and considering the fact that the civilizations was well spread between two great rivers of their times, it is only justified to call it "Sindhu Sarasvati Civilization" rather than calling it Indus Valley which is how the Westerns prefer it. But name is just a name and it has no relevance against the substance.

All we know about this heritage is out of excavations starting only in 1920s. As per historians involved with these excavations in India and Pakistan, there are strong conclusions that by 2600 BC itself city-states began to emerge with common, standardized, and shared elements, such as pottery styles, baked bricks, and stone weights in the entire impacted area. Based on these findings, the period of 2600 BC to 1900 BC is taken as "mature period" of this civilization. While the indications of early evolutions of the settlements dates back to 3300 BC and even before.

There was internal trade throughout the civilization consisting of beads, lumber, pottery etc., transported by bullock carts and boats. Items are also found suggesting well-developed trade with far-flung cultures to the east and west. Certain Mesopotamian sites, such as the ancient city of Ur, have yielded materials of Sindhu Sarasvati origin. By 1900 BC there appear signs of distinct regional developments, such as local languages and writing began together with emergence of a broader-based fluid cultural tradition stretching to the plains of the Ganga in north India.

The remains found from excavation sites (over one thousand and still continuing) include many images and objects used in day-to-day life allowing a peep into expected systems of that time. As anywhere else in the world, initial clusters of human settlements came in the fertile silt carried by rivers assisting the people to grow enough foods and facilitating trade and transport. Sindhu Sarasvati valley is said to span over a million kilometers going upto north of what is today called Punjab going down to Lothal sea port and wide enough to include many parts of present Rajasthan, Gujarat, Sindh, Haryana, Punjab and Baluchistan.

The artifacts analyzed from the excavation in this area reveal presence of many seals which include cubical terracotta dice, seals depicting many animals and agriculture tools, stones which were more like weights and many other seals having markings in combination of drawings or designs and figurines. Weapons made of copper and bronze are found in plenty. Also found are things using gold, iron and lead. Their towns were square, had elaborate drainage system, bathing pools, grain storage spaces, play grounds, buildings presumably used for government purposes and had houses of different sizes.

Based on their study of material excavated, experts in related subjects from the world over have indicated that those people grew many types of grains: they spun, wove and dyed wool, and were probably the first to use wheeled transport. The seal depicts animals like bulls, rhinos, elephants, tigers, snakes and crocodiles and some animals which have no parallel at present. In particular, there are seals having figure of a healthy creature having body like a bull with head of a Zebra and having a single horn coming up and going in front.

Another potential continuity between Indus Valley religion and modern Hinduism is the emphasis on the ritual of bathing and personal hygiene. The bathing tank at Mohenjo-Daro suggests a connection with the bathing tanks found at most Hindu temple sites. Similarly, smooth oval and doughnut-shaped stones at Indus Valley sites have led to speculations that these are evidence of early worship of the symbols of male and female generative principles, the *linga* and yoni, respectively, which are widespread in Hinduism even today. Also found are statues and amulets of gods and goddesses and sculptures of people sitting in Yoga postures. All these evidences, clearly provide an undeniable linkages and continuity of Sindhu Sarasvati Civilization with Vedic civilization generally credited to a later period in and around present day Punjab and Western UP.

The most important find for religious purpose is a male God who has features suitable for Shiva with an exposed phallus or may be end of waistband (the seal is just one inch long, hence gives rise to lot of imaginations by various experts.) Also found are many figurines depicting women. What are not found, however, is any recognizable structures which can be safely concluded to be religious building. (Doniger, 2009)

Interesting Findings

Initially, it is not certain as to what brought an end to such a great civilization. Though historians from complete spectrum of opinions believed that floods did eventually bury the remains which got accidentally found during laying of railway tracks during British Raj time. There is numerous mention of a great flood in many subsequent scriptures and one cannot rule out that the flood so mentioned may have been the one which engulfed Indus Valley and covered a great civilization. But then, all religions of the world and basic scriptures do carry reference to a devastating flood which resulted in almost a fresh beginning of the humanity. In any case, there were many indications that clearly prove that the candle of entire Sindhu Sarasvati culture got extinguished rather abruptly.

Major Break-Through

Detailed work carried out by Archeological Survey of India in the basin of Ancient River *Sarasvati* results in rejection of many theories that were earlier getting propagated about Vedic culture being attributed to Aryans and that they were from a different race which was most probably from out of India. Before going further, it is critical to understand about existence of Sarasvati and its course during its hey days. Sarasvati was considered a mythological imagination until recently. But new facts and analysis have come to surface just recently negating those assumptions and Sarasvati need not be considered a myth anymore.

The available evidences conclude strongly that it existed as a great river originating from Himalayas and discharging into the sea at bay of Khambat having its course via present day of Punjab, Haryana, Rajasthan and Gujarat. The existing rivers like Sutlej and Yamuna were its main tributaries. These findings are based on Geological and Hydrological examinations collected in last 50 years. There are overwhelming evidences of Sarasvati as a great river based on remote earth sensing pictures now available from more than one sources. (Chapter, 2012)

These excavations suggest that the spread of human concentration of Indus civilization was to the east of Sindhu with largest concentration being on the banks of Sarasvati in Rajasthan, Haryana and Punjab region. Most of the *Ashramas* of ancient sages were settled on its banks where the Vedas got composed over several centuries. No wonder that Sarasvati is mentioned time and again in Rig-Veda as the main river. In fact, Rig-Veda has over thousand references to samudra (ocean) and talks about dozens of ships and about Sarasvati flowing to Sea. Before few decades, some historians were considering the Vedic reference to Sarasvati as a small river in Afghanistan which ends up in desert area. But references to Sarasvati in Rig-Veda clearly indicate to a big river capable of accommodating ocean going ships. Surely, Vedic composers have no compulsion to talk about a mythical river or exaggerate a small river as a big river. (Vedas, 2012)

The great river came to a slow end by 1900 BC due to changes in tectonic shifts and presumably also due to reduction of water flow from the original source. Experts related to this field confirm the Sarasvati catchment area falling in Punjab as area where active faults are present resulting in lateral and vertical tectonic movements. These movements must have resulted in diversion of streams in distant past. As the most probable reason, one of such heavy impact tectonic shifts must have been responsible for change of course of Yamuna and Sutlej drifting from Sarasvati to Sindhu and Ganga respectively. Good thing is that these are no more assumptions but hard facts backed up by multifaceted evidences like remote sensing imagery. Unfortunately, such evidences were not available to historians earlier when they were guessing about different conclusions. Presently, Government of India has highly technical teams working to identify exact course of Sarasvati in the hope to find higher chances of underground streams on the old river bed.

May be, and I am just guessing, the so called tectonic shift was large enough to disturb the flow of many of these rivers and large scale additional flow of water going to Sindhu, all of a sudden would have become main reason of a big deluge. And drastic reduction of flow in Sarasvati would have forced the habitants to look for alternate sites for their resettlement. Some of them would have gone to northerly direction in Punjab and *Doab* while some from the southern area must have gone down to the banks of Narmada.

Excavations at several places like Dholavira and Lothal which are found to be at the bank of Sarasvati and the material collected are crystal clear that Sarasvati area was integral part of this culture peaking around 2500 BC and coming to a complete end by 1900 BC. Certainty about existence of Sarasvati and its repeated mention in Rig-Veda together with its ending by 1900 BC makes it predate the end of Sarasvati culture. This helps in establishing that Rig-Veda got composed before 1900 BC for sure. This immediately force people to believe that Vedas had been composed at the banks of river *Sarasvati* only and no where else. (Frawley)

The findings of excavations at Dholavira confirm its occupation between 2650 BC and 2100 BC. In addition, ASI has done excavations in about 1200 ancient settlements all along the bank of Sarasvati concluding strongly about its course and mighty size. Excavations at Bet Dwarka also suggest presence of well-developed and flourished human civilization in that part in between 7000 BC and 2500 BC. In a way the plight of historical contributions made by Sarasvati to Indian civilization is similar to the modern India as both of these have Himalayan and glorious past but remain unaware of the same unless being told by others. Both lost their shine over the period while the earlier converted to a desert the other got captured by foreign rulers and got plundered several times.

Predating Vedas to the culmination of Sindu Sarasvati completely results into a 180 degree turn on the so called foreign historian's myth of Rig-Veda being composed by so called Aryans who supposedly invaded north India around 1500 BC, fought with Dravidians, pushed them back to South India and converted other indigenous population as slaves and established their own kingdoms. This theory, we should all remember, has always been a vested interest theory advanced by English people and German historians as it serves their dubious objectives of downplaying Indian culture as not being originally Indian. Afterall, they were ruling India and considered it as their Jagir. Their military triumph over Indian allowed them to think bigger of themselves and allowed their flight of fantasies to conclude what suited them.

There are many other strong arguments to throw the 'Vedas by *Aryan* invaders' theory out of the window. Let us look at few important points mentioned hereunder:

1. There is no reference anywhere in Vedic literature to suggest Aryans as a separate race or people from outside the land. The literal meaning of the word as well as multiple references refer to *Aryan* only and only as "noble" which can be equated to some people being called 'Sir' in English system. So, to begin with, considering Aryans as a separate race is ill founded on wrong understanding of the word itself.
2. Racial types found and analyzed from *Sindhu* Sarasvati to modern times, from North of India and from South of India strongly suggest a strong continuity. There are studies after studies on the point to take away any ambiguity that racial type of Indian habitants underwent any change in last couple of thousand years. Certainly there is no dilution and no major influx of people from outside is plausible.
3. There are many religious signs available in *Sindhu* Sarasvati excavated findings that *Sindhu* Sarasvati and Vedic compositions are surely in communication with each other. The seals, the figurines and the God-like idols and presence of Vedic ritual kunds are all clear proof of the continued relation between Vedic period and *Sindhu* Sarasvati.
4. If Aryans were not originally from India, how come none of their books ever carry a direct or indirect hint to their

original place? It is but a common knowledge that any migrant will always carry memories of their place of origin and will cherish those things for a long time. Vedas don't say a word for any other potential place of their composers. All it says about the place is words like '*Saptasindhu*', '*Brahmvarta*' and '*Aryavarta*'.

5. Aryans are painted to arrive in north India riding on their horse driven chariots. But who can use chariots in hilly terrain of North Western India (read Afghanistan) or in deserts that *Aryan* invasion required? Again, Sindhu Sarasvati excavations have shown sufficient evidence of chariots being in existence and hence their reference in Vedas should not be taken as if chariots are a matter of import. As seen earlier, the evolution of chariots started after initial Rig-Veda hymns have already been composed. To that extent only later part are found having references to chariots. It is like saying why a nuclear bomb was not referred in First World War? Well, precisely because there was no bomb exploded before Second World War.
6. Recent excavation and its findings suggest clear presence of Rig-Vedic people living in India as long ago as 4000 BC. The whole concept of *Aryan* invasion is nothing but a sinister design of narrow ideology of English sponsored and funded German nationalism headed by people like Max Müller who have been proved wrong on so many counts already.
7. One argument goes that India did not have horses while Rig-Veda is very horsy. Again, excavations have shown presence of horses in India even in earlier part of Sindhu Sarasvati. Maybe horses were imported from outside countries but trade had been known to exist in early Sindhu Sarasvati period and arrival of horses in India had surely started and presence of horses in India does not necessitate Aryans arrival.
8. *Aryan* invasion theory suggests that Vedas have been composed in Punjab area where Aryans came and settled from their Central Asian roots. The presence of Sarasvati River in the Rajasthan area which is repeatedly and clearly mentioned in the Vedas itself, comes out the main place where Vedas got composed. It is only after the drying up

of the river that people have moved in north direction to make their settlements. New evidence suggests that much before the sages shifted their base to Punjab and *Doab* area, Rig-Veda has already been composed.

9. Western historians relate Sanskrit as the language having common roots with other Indo European language groups and find Avestian to be immediate family of Sanskrit. Yes, there are strong similarities among Sanskrit, Avestian, Latin and Greek but languages are languages and these have been found travelling from one place to another almost continuously and not necessarily with the people who spoke these languages. With newer evidences available off late, it is proven that Avestian culture emerged 500 to 1000 years after the Vedic culture. Similarity in languages of two different cultures with so much time apart, in fact, goes to prove that language from Indian subcontinent travelled West in pre Sindhu Sarasvati period and may have spread to Euro Asian region in due course—a fact that has been mentioned by Indian scholars even before the Sarasvati excavations results were out in open.
10. Ancient portion of Rig-Veda does not carry reference to either cotton or silver while there are references to copper and gold. This again proves that composition of Vedas happened in period when cotton and silver were still not found and used. This again pushes back composition to before 2000 BC period.

So, there are clear reasons for us to conclude that theory of invasion by Aryans is a complete false theory; that Aryans are not people from out of India but a group of noble people from well within the Indian diaspora of that time; that Sarasvati river got dried much after the period in which earlier Vedas got composed and that the region where Vedas got composed was on the banks of flourishing Sarasvati river; and finally that migration of Aryans to Punjab got compelled by the end of Sarasvati.

Many times, one comes across writers from the West, specially English trying to somehow play down the great heroics of Indian History but undisputed fact acknowledged by the entire world today is that when Sindhu Sarasvati people of Indian subcontinent were building great cities and when the people on this land were composing great literature, people in British were still swinging on trees.

The purpose behind explaining this matter in such detail is because this has very significant impact in analyzing Hinduism as a home grown tradition or something which has come from outside. The question is not important only for pegging the likely period of Rig-Veda's compositions. Origin of Sanskrit, the class system which later gave rise to caste system, philosophies developed from Indian territories are some of the issues which get linked with this base issue. Because, if Aryans were outsiders, all their magical creations will also get credited to foreign lands, than the Dravidians being ethnically different from north Indians will also get established. Then superiority of *Brahmins* and *Kshatriyas* will also get legitimacy. In that case, Sanskrit will definitely belong to Indo European group and an import from outside. Besides, all our scriptures in Sanskrit will get rendered written by outsiders. All other languages originating from Sanskrit will get reduced to piracy. These are all pillars of entire Hinduism and settling this point strongly and conclusively was essential to establish Hinduism with its motherland.

In conclusion of the argument about inseparability of Sarasvati and Vedic culture, I would like to reproduce a portion from writings of V. S. Wakankar (1919-1988), Padmashree award winner and great Indian Archeologist who is known for discoveries of 30,000 years old Bhimbetka rock caves and painting in 1970 and also for tracing the basin of dry river *Sarasvati*:

"(i) Harappan and Pre-Harappan Civilizations developed along ancient Sarasvati and therefore these may be more appropriately described as part of Sarasvati-Indus Civilizations.

(ii) Most of the Rishi Ashrams described in Ramayana and Mahabharata were lined along Sarasvati river.

(iii) Perforated pottery jars and fire altars are found in most of the 1200 settlements excavated along Sarasvati river indicating that civilization which flourished was Vedic.

(iv) Land was fertile and barley etc. were cultivated in the Sarasvati region even 7000 years back and same style of cultivating the fields continues till today in areas like Rajasthan and Haryana.

(v) It is unhistorical and unscientific to say that Vedic Aryans migrated from any other region to India. They belonged to India and compiled Vedas in settlements along Sarasvati river."

Continuity of same culture till date is also founded by the book "The Sarasvati Flows on—the continuity of Indian Culture" written by Dr. B.B. Lal, the retired Director General of Archeological Survey of India. Dr. Lal also was given Padma Bhushan award in 2000 for his meritorious achievements in his field where he also worked on many committees of UNESCO.

So please next time if you come across any reference to Aryans being imported from any place outside India, you should be able to pause and confront your opposition with strong arguments against such lies. Every bit of Vedas and every thing connected with Sanatan Dharma, the great Indian tradition, has germinated very much on Indian soil and every Indian deserves to feel proud of their spectacular, splendid and grand heritage.

6

Unique Hindu Doctrines

Hinduism has no founder and it is a conglomerate of diverse beliefs and traditions. Inspite of this, Hinduism is proud of being World's oldest living religion with the number of its adherents counting over a billion and spreading over all the continents. Hinduism is indeed a diverse system of thoughts and beliefs spanning from Monotheism, Polytheism, Pantheism, Monism and even Atheism. So, it is interesting to know the nature of that strong glue which is able to bind all its followers together and keep them together over centuries; the glue which creates "*Vividhta main ekta*" which translates to "Unity in Diversity".

Here we shall briefly touch specific 'articles of faith', those glues and binding forces that are accepted by most followers of Hinduism. The idea is to put together all those principles and concepts that are common to all the followers of Hinduism. These tenets are the reply to many questions that are generally asked by persons from outside the faith, for example "what makes us Hindu?' or "what do we have that others don't?" or "what is so unique about Hinduism?" or "what is the foundation stone of Hinduism?"

These concepts will keep coming back fairly regularly in many subsequent chapters. A good look at these at this very stage will help us in better understanding and connectivity. To some extent, the study of these tenets in proper details will serve as a crash course about main concepts of Hinduism. While these are defining concepts on one hand, these are also differentiating shades that allows Hinduism to stand out of others in the crowd.

Reincarnation

Hinduism believes in *"punarjanm"*, reincarnation. This is our basic theme and is as old as Hinduism itself. We believe that every soul has a final destination of reuniting with its original and eternal source, the Supreme soul of the universe. However, until such time that perfection is acquired by experiencing pains and pleasures of accumulated karmas and/or by obtaining proper knowledge, a soul will continue reincarnating again and again on the earth. During the process, the soul enters many bodies, assumes many forms and passes through continuous process of births and death. The selection of which body it enters in the next life depends on cumulative karma of all previous births.

Important Hindu scriptures like Bhagwad Gita are full of references for rebirths. In Gita, Lord Krishna can be heard telling Arjuna that:

> *"Arjuna, both you and I were born many times in the past also. You don't remember those births but I do remember all of those as well."*

And it is not that this concept is just a belief. Many of us may have come across examples where a child is said to remember whereabouts from his previous birth. But in most of these cases, the child forgets those memories with advancing of his childhood. Thus, there are evidences that a new birth is in continuation of a previous journey.

The doctrine of reincarnation, known also with other terms like rebirth or transmigration of the soul etc. concerns the rebirth of the soul in a series of physical bodies. It is in India and Greece that the doctrine of rebirth has been most elaborately developed. This doctrine is a central doctrine of the Indian religions and is shared by all the other major religions originating out of India: Hinduism, Buddhism and Jainism alike. All the diverse religious groups and philosophical schools of Hinduism, except that of *Carvaka,* (explained later in detail), believe in reincarnation.

Karma-Samsara

The nature of birth, that is, the condition of the body to which the *atman* gets associated, depends on Karma. Karma signifies action, every sort of action, whether good or bad, meritorious or non-meritorious, religious or worldly. Here, however, karma signifies the moral debit or credit of one's actions. Every action inevitably produces its own fruit, and the subject (actor) has necessarily to experience all the consequences of his own actions. A person's behaviour leads irrevocably to an appropriate reward or punishment commensurate with that behaviour. It is the inevitable law of retribution called 'the law of karma'. It is the 'law of cause and effect' applied to the life of every individual, law according to which every one gathers the fruit of what one has planted.

Under normal human life, the effects of Karmas of a person do not get settled during a single life. Because while he experiences the fruit (which may be delicious, neutral or sour, depending on the quality of accumulated karmas) of previous karma, there are new additions that also need to be experienced. While one settles old fruits, new actions result in new fruits to be experienced/settled later. As a result, the *atman* has to seek association with *sarira* repeatedly. So it is believed that the soul from all eternity is undergoing birth and rebirth due to this inviolable law of karma. This is how the doctrine of the transmigration of the soul gets established.

The entire process of repeated birth and death of the bodies associated by soul is called *Samsara*. *Samsara* implies "to wander or pass through a series of states or conditions". Life, therefore, is not determined or limited to one birth and one death, but is instead a *samsara*; a current, a course, a migration in circle, which is always determined by the law of karma. In short, human life is a *karma-samsara*, a transmigration of the soul according to the inevitable law of retribution. But is there no end? Is there no escape clause? Yes, there is the way out. It is by purifying and refining of one's karma so that there is no further 'debits' and by acquiring right vidya (knowledge) which results in elevating the thoughts, using mind, to a state of consciousness where it becomes aware of its own immortal nature independent of the material body's existence.

> And this, precisely, is summary of the teachings of Hinduism: follow Dharma, acquire positive fruits of your karma, recognize the true nature of Atman and get rid of the Samsara and achieve Moksha.

We, sometimes, come across people who don't find this concept acceptable citing the reason that if few souls eventually seek Vidya and are able to upgrade to next level by achieving *Moksha*, the total number of human being on the planet earth must eventually come down and not go up as is the case in reality. But we cannot talk of only reduction of souls. After all, as per Hinduism, there are many sub-human beings in the process of their evolution getting eligible to get the life of a human being. Consequently, the number of human beings is on the increase. Hinduism also asserts that divinity is equally present in every soul, whether that is in a human or a subhuman body. Otherwise it goes against the idea of God's omnipresence.

Accumulated Karma as the Cause of Reincarnation

According to our ancient concepts, man is composed of two opposing fundamental principles; the soul (*atman*) and the material body (sarira). This can also be explained as 'subtle body' and 'gross or physical body'. The *atman* is eternal, immutable, and indestructible while the body is temporal, created, mutable as well as destructible. The union between *atman* and body is just accidental. Actually, it is a type of imprisonment to *atman* due to ignorance (*avidya*) and karma to which it is associated from all eternity. *Avidya* and karma are two basic presuppositions of Hinduism. They have no end because they did not have a beginning. It is therefore a truth that transcends every intellectual explanation.

When a person dies, his physical body gets merged in the five elements that it is made of while the subtle body which includes mind, intellect, *prana* (vital energy) is said to proceed to other plane. It is said that unfulfilled desires remaining live in the mind result in rebirth as it is only in this physical world that desires have chance to get fulfilled. Further, every birth offers another opportunity for the soul to accumulate good karmas and attain desired Vidya by shedding attachment and seeing through the prism of Ahankara. Eventually, one is expected to reach to the level of spirituality by crossing over all desires.

Life Divided in Four Stages

The division of entire human life span under fours distinct categories is another unique pearl of the necklace called Hinduism.

Named as "*Ashram* Vyavastha" it is a system devised by our revered sages to support the human efforts for achieving the esteemed aims of life. This system is a structure designed to maintain focus of human beings throughout their life span so that right priorities are pursued for a fulfilling life. The stages defined under this system are completely in sync with nature, aging process of the body, social demand and maturity of mind. Basic aim behind this four-step staging is to fix proper orientation of this journey called life towards the search of divine.

Sages have realized that human desires and instincts have strong pressures and take out a lot of energy from his entire life and that unless it is properly guided, there remains a risk of people continuing after worldly desires having no time to pursue other equally pressing obligations. The *Ashram* system works as a system of moral checks and balances, a system for maintaining balance in line with physical changes in the human body. This is yet another unique contribution of Indian sages to the world and has no parallel.

To make the matrix complete, we can also briefly touch upon the four aims of life as propagated by Hinduism. These are Dharma, Artha, Kama and Moksha. The objective of four prescribed *Ashram* system is to inculcate the sense of divinity as we go after hard realities of human life without losing divinity and by continuously holding dharma. As such, this system works as a road map with proper milestones reminding us to change gear as we go along the narrow and intertwined road called life. It tells us as to what are the highest ideals of human life at each stage of life so that we can continue finding balance in our present day requirements and ultimate aim of human life.

Again, these are universal principles and will remain relevant as long as man survives. Of course, with changing environment and time cycles, there may be a need to redefine the dos and don'ts so that the magic of the ageless principles does not get lost. Let us try to understand the Four Stages along with present day context:

First: Brahmacharya Ashram

This exciting first stage is said to start at about eighth year of a person's life and is devoted for learning all types of subjects with underlying conditions of celibacy, strict discipline, chastity and obedience. In ancient times, the sole purpose was to learn the Vedas and other education by remaining at Gurukul (Forest Academy). This stage was supposed to continue up to the age of twenty five years. But it can be taken to extend up to the time that person continues acquiring knowledge and wisdom in his chosen field. Every young man is different and different professions/ subjects require varying lengths of period. So spirit should be given importance over letter. There are also different stages within each subject. Some one pursuing PhD may remain in this stage upto 27-28 and if some one just wishes to finish college, he may come out of this stage at 20. So, depending on individual cases, especially with reference to current social norms, the length of *Ashram* will need to be adjusted but without compromising the desired virtues of celibacy and disciplined life.

The theme is that whatever you wish to learn, and so long as you are engaged in learning, please ensure that:

- Turbulent desires are kept under control lest these start inflicting injuries on your moral and physical health.
- Learn to remain master of senses and sense organs lest you should become enslaved by natural instincts that will prove to be the roadblocks to the process of learning.
- Develop the capacity to remain strictly disciplined to make strong foundation for the achievements during balance period of your life.
- Acquire full knowledge of spiritual practices and live the concept of Dharma as prescribed by our scriptures.

Understanding Brahmacharya as observing celibacy alone is a narrow view. Celibacy is part of discipline that is recommended for a person engaged in acquiring knowledge. It is hardly difficult to assume, even today, that only a student approaching his education with controlled desires and senses and maintaining strict moral discipline alone will achieve his results. The focus here is not only on subject knowledge alone but equally on harmony with morality and spirituality.

A mind not well-trained in this stage of Brahmacharya will remain weak and helpless to resist its worldly tendencies. Strong and purified mind developed in this stage is always going to remain strong foundation for all subsequent stages to overpower anxieties, worries, lack of priorities and lack of balance among conflicting pursuits of entire human life.

Second: Grihastha Ashram

Having obtained complete knowledge in the previous stage, it is expected that by now the soul is fully incarnated. It is now time for using the awakened body and mind to accumulate as many Karma credits as possible. Now is the time to go after natural tendencies of pursuing money, fame and power but without compromising with Dharma. This is also the time to marry and initiate the process of procreation. Two important aims of life namely Artha and Kama need to be pursued and achieved is this stage of life. To do that, one is expected to use his skills for his trade, cater to material needs for all subsequent stages of life, actively serve society, and experience fulfilling narrow objects.

For this stage in life, Vedas recommend daily puja and rituals which are nothing but daily reminders to the person about his final destination so that he/she does not get overwhelmed by worldly concerns and anxieties that they forget the distance to be covered in their balance journey. Religious rituals are to work as regular reminders to let them constantly know that they have many things to do and miles to go.

Again, our scriptures prescribe that everything to be pursued in this stage, has to be under the umbrella of Dharma; because worldly experience makes it easy to forget the difference between right and wrong. Fine, one has to accumulate material wealth to fuel the rest of the journey but be careful not to acquire too many 'debits' for your karma lest your *samsara* should get lengthened rather than shortened.

> Interestingly, the Way shown by Hindu Concepts are Both Practical and Ideal at the Same Time.

But this stage must end by the time one turns fifty years of age. And this is where most of us get into trouble. Needless to say that ignorance binds us to continue this stage without stoppage. It is natural to seek more time than we already got. *The desires of money, fame and power are insatiable and have no limit. One can never get enough of these. But, if you continue pursuing it, it will be at the cost of time recommended for the next stage in life.* In modern life, you hardly come across someone who is ready to exit Grihastha *Ashram* at the turn of fifty. But this is perfectly doable, and I say so with my own live example. All you need is the firm conviction that you must end on time. Further, if one were convinced of it being the right way, surely, he would have planned his actions of last few years in a manner to make it happen. In my personal case, it was possible for me to meet most of deadlines by my fiftieth year and that inspired me to comeout of the career so that I could devote my full time and energy in pursuing the next stage of life. But for the inspiration from this ancient system, this very book may not have been in our hands as I would have been attending some business meeting rather than writing these lines.

Third: Vanprashtha Ashram

When you are through with your worldly obligation for your direct family and immediate society, have scaled the height of your full potential in your profession, are well provided for basic material requirements for your remaining life, have repaid all your debts, then it is time for you to systematically work on making your soul happy. You might ignore or keep your eyes closed but now onwards, you are supposed to work for improving your afterlife. With the understanding of 'Law of Karma', we know that the '*Samsara*' will continue till the 'debits of karma' get neutralized. But it needs to be worked upon. Grihastha *Ashram*, by its very nature of the activities carried out for pursuits of money, power and fame, makes it impossible to earn 'credits of karma'.

Our ancient sages were practical enough to realize the reality of life. Hence, they recommended for *Vanprashtha*. But its meaning in current time has changed. Literally, it means moving on the edge of the society towards forest but the real meaning is dissolution of attachments with worldly relations and giving up the life of luxuries. The knowledge of detachment will refine the enjoyment and enhance spiritual orientation. The best understanding of this stage of life is summarized by Manu Samhita Chapter 6, shloka no 8, which is produced below with present day meaning (*a translation but not a literal translation*):

> *"He should be engaged in regular study, control his senses, keep friendly behaviour with everyone and maintain a tranquil mind*

at all times. He must always give charity as best as he can, should not expect or accept any gifts from others and he should always have mercy for all living beings".

This is the time for silently giving back to society at large with your wisdom and experience. While in this stage of life, one is financially self reliant, physically fit and mentally alert. So, this is the right time to acquire spiritual knowledge, learn how to give up worldly pleasures, spend time in contemplation and meditation while remaining available to guide and educate everyone who is willing and desirous to learn from you. You should bring changes in your food habits and must 'eat to live' and not 'live to eat'. You must stay away from any form of attachment with whatever kind. All types of attachments are known to colour your thoughts and weaken you to see clearly. All the energies at your disposal must be regulated for enhancing spiritual orientation with eyes on attainment of *Moksha*.

To pursue this stage in current perspective, it is not obligatory to move to the edge of the society or go settle in forests but to refrain from attaching yourself in worldly life suitable only for a person in his previous stage of Grihastha. Living in forest but the world, desires, family and friends occupying every second of your thoughts is certainly not having moved to Vanprastha. On the reverse, remaing in the heart of the city but spending time for meditation, yoga or study of scriptures to enhance own spirituality is very much promotion to Vanprastha.

This is the stage where you must condition yourself to lose dominance in every sphere of life. It is a tough call but experience of learned sages is there to prompt us and guide us for experiencing the freedom of giving up. This is the stage to give up everything you have, both good and not so good; donate money as much as you can, keep yourself free to help society by sharing your wealth of wisdom and experience. This is the time to encourage your children to live their life independently and be a guide to them, but only for issues that they bring to your attention. Because now you are not pursuing things for any selfish motive, you will feel a unique satisfaction allowing you to look everything with broader outlook.

You have to live life of a recluse who is supposed to talk less but listen more; who is doing less but experiencing more; who has stopped receiving but enjoys in giving. With minimum possessions and far away from luxuries, you feel happiness only in exploring your own consciousness with whatever means known to you. This is actually the most rewarding stage in life where you are supposed to be at peace with yourself. During Vedic period when many people were opting for this stage regularly, great achievements were accomplished by people living in this stage of life. The composition of Upanishads, the running of forest academies, evolution of defining concepts in theology and philosophies of Hinduism were all the result of these people who went ahead on these uncharted waters and produced some great heritage. Surely, people engaged in accumulating material wealth or enjoying luxuries of life can't be expected to contribute on other fronts.

Some of the unwanted fears and frustrations in our present day society are due to overlooking of this great tradition. Today, most of the people wish to continue with Grihastha ashram till last day of their life. This leads to conflict with next generation and a void on spiritual knowledge working to generate unwanted diseases, anguish, afflictions and distresses.

The stage is to be continued up to the age of seventy-five years. This is a transition stage with ultimate pursuit of God.

Fourth: Sannyasa Ashram

After successful completion of *Vanprashtha* stage of life, the person is expected to become one with universal humanity after dissolving all the ignorance of separate existence. Now, he has nothing to call his own. He is in service of others. He should be completely in control of his own destiny. He rejoices every opportunity of consoling others, motivating others and guiding others for pursuing the Dharma-filled life.

It is wrong to say that he has become useless and all he is doing awaiting death. On the contrary, an elder on the path of Dharma has already lost any fear of death, as he is able to see reality beyond human life. Yes, physical body is deteriorating but the soul is at its best. His discipline, wisdom, spiritual attainments are all helping him to connect with the supreme reality like never before. For his cessation of human body is going to be only just a brief interval after which a new life will await his soul in new life.

It is unfortunate that compulsions of material world rejected a highly commendable system of living life with migration from one stage to another in a seamless manner. Undoubtedly, the price of this rejection is the widespread fears and frustration among various sections of the society where people feel threatened for their position, where no one has time left to pursue spirituality, accumulation of Karmic debits are going unnoticed.

Society Divided in Four Classes

After going over the tradition that got evolved in evolution of all human civilizations, one finds that primitive societies have been highly complicated structures with their own beliefs and codes of social conducts. However, common to all human civilizations, the fundamental needs of the societies were moral and spiritual, military and economics. As leaders in all matters relating to social interactions, Vedic people from India have assigned these roles to different groups.

This classification, as applied under Hinduism from ancient times, divides the society in four separate and distinct classes based on professions. The first and most distinguished of all is *Brahmins,* the second in rank come *Kshatriyas* or *Rajas,* the third are *Vaishyas,* the Landlords and Merchants and fourth and last residual category is called Shudras or Menials.

Brahmins retained the duties of learning and holding virtues and thereby supposed to only undertake priesthood and duties relating to acquiring and preserving knowledge, reading and tutoring others; *Kshatriyas* carry the mantle of being men with courage and bravery and are responsible for military services including all its branches; *Vaishyas* were supposed to carry the responsibility of generating economic resources by engaging in agriculture, trade, industry and cattle breeding. The last category was more of a residual category with the mandate to extend services to above three classes in whatever area they require. These people, responsible for servitude affairs, were called the Shudras. With subsequent developments, yet another category got added to this structure called the Untouchables. Here we have people engaged in handling of human waste, latrines and animal carcase and working with animal hides.

This system has been in vogue ever since later part of Rig-Veda. To begin with, the classification of the caste of each person was based on their individual profession based on the education and skill sets. There are numerous examples in Vedas where a person has a different profession from the family where he was born including some acclaimed sages who contributed the Vedic literature itself. But subsequently, this system got identified as hereditary. This was the beginning of troubles of the faults that are attributed with our caste system.

As shown in the pyramid below, the large chunk of entire population was categorised under Shudras and Untouchables with *Brahmins* being least in proportion and commanding highest position in the social structure followed by *Kshatriyas*. Twice born Group indicate the people entitled to wear *janeu,* the sacred three thread.

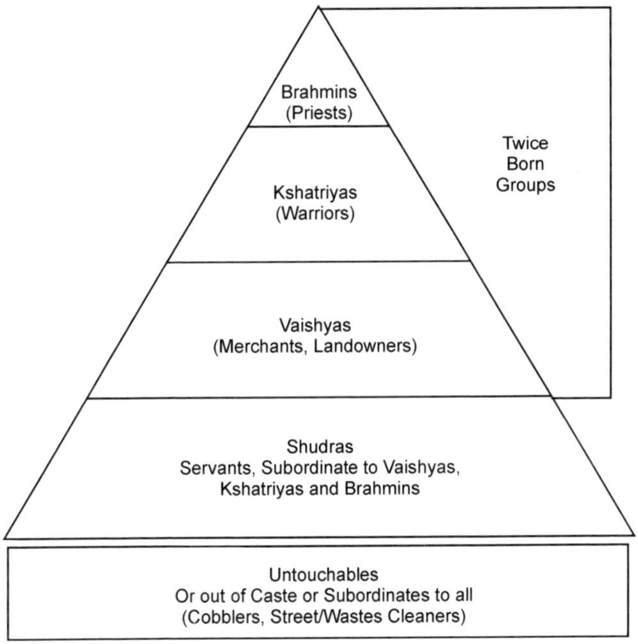

Some people call the 'class segregation' as one of the greatest evil of Indian social structure because this system is held responsible for severe social discrimination and exploitation of lower castes at the hands of people from higher class. It is unfortunate that all over the world, the strong person has been seen to commit atrocities on weaker person. Indian social system has not been an exception of this rule. Over a long period of times, this system has kept a large chunk of Indian population under pressures from the minority of higher classes leading to lack of education, untouchability, lack of social equality, denied access to religious places, commercial exploitation, etc.

More often than not, we come across only bad things about classification in these four classes together with castes and sub-castes arising with increasing number of professions. But there can be another side of this coin as well. I would like to quote from "Hindu Manners, Customs and Ceremonies" (1897) by Abbe J.A. Dubois, a French national who spent a lot of his time in India and is credited to be one of the first Europeans to authoritatively comment on Hindu practices and customs and I quote:

> *"I am persuaded that it is simple and solely due to the distribution of the people into castes that India did not lapse into a state of barbarism, and that she preserved and perfected the arts and sciences of civilizations whilst most other nations of the earth remained in the state of barbarism. I do not consider caste to be free from many drawbacks; but I believe that the resulting advantages, in the case of nations constituted like Hindus, more than outweigh the resulting evils."*

Class segregation assigned each person a profession that was to be pursued from generation to generation forcing people to acquire special expertise that was simply difficult to be copied by others. It is to the credit of our learned social legislators of ancient India that they got so clearly acquainted about the natural character of inhabitants of their times and evolved provisions helping them to cultivate knowledge and skills as per their traits so that no one was burdened with what they were not good and at the same time rigidly imposed professions on even indolent and careless natured inhabitants of the society. Is there any thing objectionable to this doctrine? Probably no.

Now, this is the reality that till the time this class system was working well in Indian system, India was on top of the world in most areas including education, agriculture, industry, literature, sciences, arts and crafts besides all things religious. Keeping aside charges of discrimination and exploitation, this was the system promoting expertise. People segregated by professions were able to achieve proficiencies that allowed higher expertise in their respective crafts. Why were Indian artisans of Silk could weave finer than any one else in the world? Why were Indian Rishis were able to create scriptures better than others in the world? Why were Indian smiths were able to handle all metals better than others in the world? The common answer is the expertise achieved under the class system of ancient India.

The segregation had another remarkable impact. It was only in India that even frequent wars among kingdoms had no impact on economy and culture as only one section of the population was engaged in war while most others remained un-impacted and kept carrying on their professions as business as usual. Elsewhere, war involved each and every young person resulting in wiping out of losing side.

To the credit of Indian system having great cultural and socio-economic progress, other societies of those times were operating largely on tribal system where wars meant inflicting injuries to entire population. In that situation, most people were always preoccupied with fight for basic survival with no focus on developing other professions specially those not directly related with war and its administration.

Sadachar (Critical Virtues)

Hinduism provides great importance to some core virtues that every follower is expected to practice at all times. The scriptures are full with instances where the importance of these virtues has been established as practices for appropriate social behaviour. These are like sanskaras that are interpolated from very childhood so that these are ingrained as second nature for all Hindus.

The following are some of the most important qualities listed in Hindu scriptures. There is no prioritization or grading for these virtues as these as without any compromise in behaviour for all Hindus irrespective of differences in their social status or stage of life or age, caste, class, gender variations, etc. A true follower of this great tradition is generally expected to conduct his life founded in these virtues.

Ahimsa (Non-violence)

In addition to incurring physical injury to all living being, it refers to each and every action or thought which, directly or indirectly, results in harm to others. Besides actions, speaking unkindly to any other human being or even getting a strong thought in the mind aimed at any type of harm to someone, qualifies as Himsa. As commonly understood, non-violence, is only but a very narrow meaning of *Ahimsa.* This concept is further explained in much greater details under the chapter on Yoga.

Sanyam (Mind and Sense Control)

Sanyam will apply to outer and inner self-control of all the sense organs, all the action organs, the subtle organs of mind and intellect. The word 'Sanyam' is composed of the two Sanskrit roots 'sam' and 'yam'. Sam means total and Yam is an important part of Yoga Sutras and is explained in detail under the chapter on Yoga.

In short, it will mean exercising restraints on desires so that the mind remains pure to cultivate and develop positivity. Thus Sanyam will cover the total personality, expression, behaviour; all the dimensions of human nature. Sanyam works at various levels: first the sensorial level, second the mental level, and then at the psychic and spiritual levels. Sanyam, or the process of transformation, applies to each and every expression in life, including behaviour, attitude, speech and thought.

Sahishnuta (Tolerance)

The core meaning of this virtue applies to readiness to bear or to deal with inconveniences in discharging swadharma (individual's own righteous obligation which changes with age and stage in life etc.). It is expected that human life will pose many situations where a person has to go through the hardships. Tolerance provides the strength to be unmindful of all difficulties coming in the way of discharging one's own responsibilities. Of late, this virtue is expanded to mean "sarvadharma sambhaava" the feeling of extending equal respect to the religious faiths of others. The other important phrase clubbed under this virtue is "**Vasudheva** kutumbkam" which literally means the whole earth is our own family. It arises out of our ability to exercise full tolerance for the peace and harmony among the societies in the world. Hinduism believes about the truth that somehow the whole world has to live together like a family. This is the reason why Hindus think that any power in the world, big or small cannot have its way imposed on others.

Atithisatkar (Hospitality)

The very word 'Atithi' means some one who is without any date, who is expected at any time without prior announcement. Offering hospitality to each and every guest is fundamental to Hindu culture and providing food and shelter to a needy stranger was a traditional duty of the householder. The key *mantra* of this virtue is "Atithi Devobhav" meaning that a guest is to be treated as God. It was especially important to extend hospitality towards *Brahmins* and *Sanyasees*. Our scriptures are full with stories regarding the benefits of offering a suitable reception even to an unannounced guest and the sins that accrue from neglecting one's guests. Tradition teaches that, no matter how poor one is, one should always offer three items: sweet words, a sitting place, and refreshments which may be only a glass of water. The flower garland is offered to special guests and dignitaries, as a symbol of welcome and regards.

Karuna (Compassion)

The words used to convey this virtue include *Daya, Karuna, Anukampa, Kripa*, etc. Each of these may be explained to have meanings wider than each other's but in totality these all indicate a concerted effort by a person to extend his shoulder to mitigate the sorrows and difficulties of others. Focus is on treating the sorrows of others at par as one's own misfortune and then helping by taking as much efforts as possible to help the other person to overcome the same. Hinduism looks at compassion both as a value and as an essential attribute present in each human. The virtue of compassion is greatly helpful in creation of an all-inclusive society as it help in appreciating the pains of others and helps them find relief.

Samrakshan (Protection)

Extending full support to some one who comes calling on you in his hour of despair or extending support for some one who is weak to stand for his own rights is considered an essential obligation under Hinduism. This also extends to providing shelter to less fortunate people or even animals that are unable to arrange the same for them. It is under this virtue that one finds Hindu devotees providing or contributing for providing Goshalas or Dharmashalas or Raenbaseras.

Sammaan (Respect)

Here a Hindu is expected to extend his mark of respect to every other living human being depending on the situation. The first of this mark is to greet each other with folded hands. Then it applies for children to bow and touch feet of their elders. Basic idea here is to show dignity, honour, esteem, reverence, deference or submission to the person coming in contact be it elders, be it due to gender, be it due to class, be it due to the person appearing a holy man, be it due to the profession of the person. Special attention is given to a teacher, learned person and elders of the family. The token of respect extends to other living beings like revering cow as mother provider. Respect is also given to things like a book which is not be touched by any portion of feet and always to be handled with respect. The core purpose is to signify uniqueness of the entity in front.

Brahmacharya (Celibacy)

Hinduism provides great importance to following celibacy in all spheres of thoughts, words and deeds. The definition of celibacy does not remain limited only sexual activity alone. While celibacy of thoughts and deeds is recommended all through the life, the sexual activity is permitted only in Grihastha Ashram. In case of Grihastha Ashram also, the sex is advised for reproduction rather than gratification. The sexual conduct of any person even during Grihastha ashram must be well within the boundary of marriage.

Santosha (Contentment)

Contentment is a virtue of remaining happy and satisfied with gratefully accepting whatever material abundance one is bestowed with. On one level, this gets connected to the virtue of doing one's job without expecting any thing in return but on the more important part this feeling gets linked to the happiness in one's life. Contrary to normal belief that money is synonymous with happiness, Hinduism, since the time immemorial, preached the virtue of Santosha as the key to happiness. It strongly provides that contentment leads to relaxation and positivity of attitude. Even scientifically it is proven now that money and happiness are only marginally related while positive attitude and satisfaction are substantially related with overall happiness. The key message here is "*santosham param sukham*" means satisfaction with what you have been given is the foremost pleasure. It is said that Goddess Laxmi of material abundance prefers to stay at the place of the satisfied person.

Swachchhta (Cleanliness)

In Hinduism, cleanliness is yet another important virtue. Swachchhta include abstract state of mind being clean together with a dirt free space. Cleanliness has always been compared next to Godliness and that is why all Hindus must take a bath before entering temples for seeking blessings from their Gods. *Puranas* have included many stories asking for cleaning body before entering the temple. Taking bath is not limited to physical dust alone, for example taking a bath is also practised after visiting a funeral so that the thought process is purified.

It is also linked to social living where all household, work place or public place is to be kept clean all the time. From ancient times, Hindus living in villages can be seen cleaning their open floors with pious cow dung. Cleaning of their homes, particularly well in preparing to celebrate Diwali each year, is believed by Hindus necessary for expecting good luck. Stories also link arrival of Goddess Lakshmi to their abode to stay with clean environment being considered as a precondition.

Sadhana (Meditation)

Sadhana means daily spiritual practice. It is the foundation of all spiritual endeavours. Sadhana is personal and individual spiritual effort. It is the main tool one uses to work on self to seek ways and means to achieve the ultimate purpose of life, *Moksha.* It can be done alone or in a group. Sadhana is whatever you do consistently to clear your own consciousness so you can relate to the infinity within you. Recommended on daily basis, meditation helps in tuning up our nervous system.

There are many practices to choose from and each individual is encouraged to find out his or her best suitable way by experimenting with alternatives available. Best advised time is *Brahma muhurat,* which basically means well before sunrise as the general environment is expected to be quiet, body rested after a good night's sleep and mind comparatively free as the day's pressures of real life issues are still away. But if some one cannot rise early in the morning, any other time of the day may also be selected. Besides being a tool for spirituality seekers, many people are going for it even for instant results of energizing their daily schedule and maintaining positive attitude during tough conditions. Daily meditation goes a long way for enabling the person to remain in charge of his life on all planes and its regular practice is the key to achieving one's own spiritual objectives.

Besides above eleven Virtues, there are few others which also are taken by various schools as main virtues. These will include Curiosity, Diligence, Flexibility, Forgiveness, Gratitude, Honesty, Integrity, Modesty, Simplicity, Tranquility, Truthfulness and Wisdom. These all get mentioned in all Hindu scriptures specially *Puranas* and all Hindu followers are drawn to follow these in their day to day life situation to remain firm in Dharma.

Every Hindu is expected to work on acquiring these virtues until such time that these become their second nature. Hinduism requires proficiency in all of these virtues as indispensable for the spiritual seeker. Knowledge and practice of the truthful and righteous way of living, will lead to the purity and fearlessness that is a prerequisite to the absolute bliss of Self Realization which is the ultimate purpose of every individual soul.

7
Sanskrit: The Language of Hinduism

Sanskrit is undoubtedly the liturgical language of Hinduism since the time early Vedas were composed and continues to be used as a ceremonial language for all things religious throughout all branches of Hinduism. Further, it has been the philosophical language of Hinduism, Buddhism and Jainism. Besides, Sanskrit has been a great scholarly language for literature, scientific work and philosophy of northern India since the beginning and going right into early part of second millennium post CE when it got side stepped by the regional emergence of several other vernacular languages, most of which got evolved only under Sanskrit's own umbrella.

Sanskrit as a language is part of the family having distinct commonality with most other European languages namely Greek, Latin and Norse-Germanic languages (ultimately, these languages contributed for origin of today's French, German, Italian, Spanish, English and all their other off-springs and cousins). Majority of Western language experts from European background indicate it to have originated from a place near Anatolia, Turkey (also called as Asia Minor). But Indian experts always maintained origin of Sanskrit on Indian soil itself. As the immediate family, Sanskrit is also attributed to have family links with Indo-Iranian group of languages being source of languages such as Avestan, Persian, Pashto and Iranian.

The Tree of Languages

This relationship has been established based on structure of alphabets, the arrangement and expression of vowels and consonants, usage of verbs, usage of nouns, reference to genders, similarity in syntax and finally widely shared common words. Experts conclude that so much similarity cannot be attributed to a matter of chance and no one doubts that there was a link between all these languages. However, the difference lies in place of origin. No one from India will ever agree that Sanskrit, the language of our Gods and Vedas is not original to its land of influence.

Many Indian experts argue that common proto languages were not different than proto Dravidian or the one spoken by people from Sindhu Sarasvati Civilization. Understandably, these arguments are not taken seriously by experts from outside India who, on the contrary, hardly find any commonality of Sanskrit with Dravidian languages of Indian subcontinent or with other languages of the region like Chinese, Arabian and Hebrew.

Linguistic similarities in terms of common grammar, vocabulary, verbs, near common words for many objects, similar cluster of Gods etc. are all strong indications that Sanskrit with other European languages have originated, very initially, from a common ground. But having established that Vedic Sanskrit must have flourished to the level of being used for composing Vedic Hymns by 2500 BC, it is only more plausible that view of Indian experts is indeed valid that Sanskrit emerged on Indian lands and must have crossed to other destinations in usual course.

Languages are known to go through a lot of permutations and combinations over short periods as these are known to both influence and get influenced from the developments in their surroundings. One certainly finds many examples where people move on from one language to another under some compelling or comforting situations. Languages move from one place to another both with and without its speakers and such movement is registered over short period of times. Migration of individual scholar, an ambitious warrior or a trading exchange or even a nomadic tribe moving from one place to another is enough to carry a language from its origin to new destination.

If one is to accept, for a moment, the idea that Sanskrit arrived in India from outside, there are immediate questions of how and

The Tree of Languages

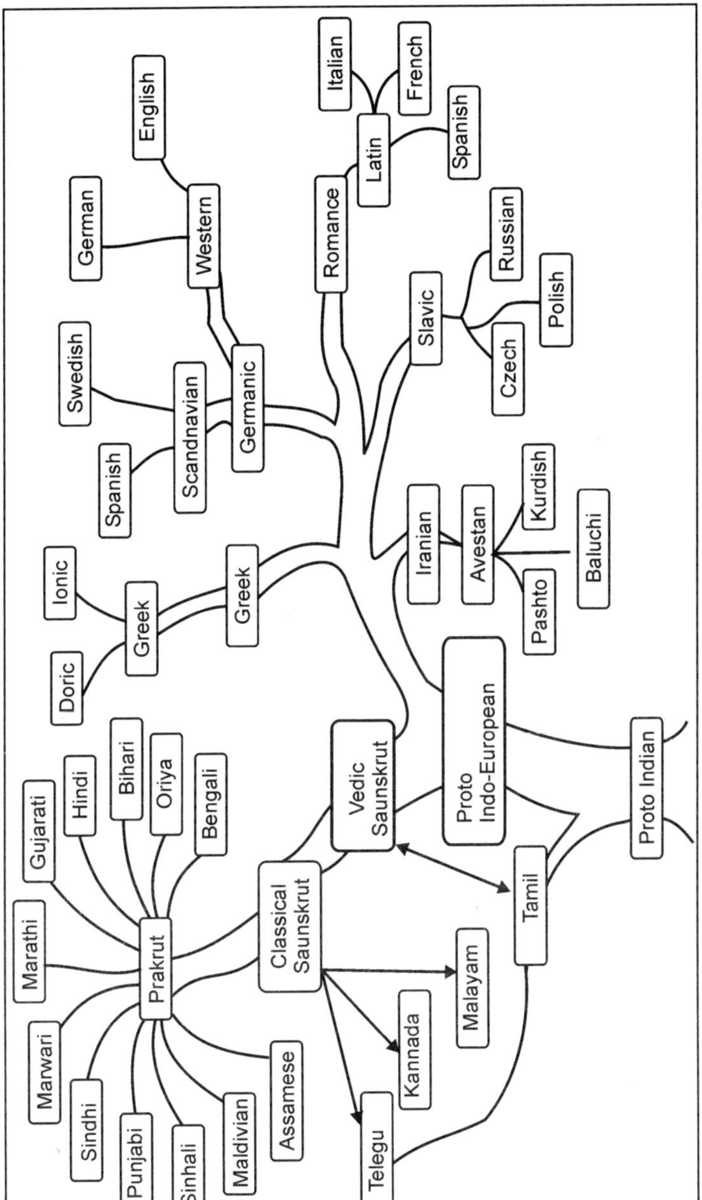

when. Sindhu Sarasvati, which is established to be part of the period when Sanskrit had emerged, refined, spread and used for composing mammoth proportions of compositions, is said to have started before 6000 BC and farming is found to take place ever since. Evidence suggests that around 4500 BC, the settlements of villages and urban areas have already started around Sarasvati River. If this was, by itself, one of the most advanced and prosperous civilization of its time, how come there is possibility of any import of a language into this area from outside? On the contrary, these are perfect credentials for a case of an export.

One of the apparent reasons of western experts identifying originating source of Indo European languages to Anatolia hinges on the findings of archeological ruins of Catal Huyuk in South Central Turkey which indicate about a civilization which would have existed between 7500 BC and 5700 BC with best estimate of its full flourishing at around 6000 BC. But near home, recent excavations in Sindhu Sarasvati Region have also conclusively proved existence of a far more developed civilization than the one found at Catal Huyuk. This again indicates towards stronger reason of Sanskrit having originated at Indian soil itself and all other languages are likely to have emerged from Sanskrit.

The literal meaning of Sanskrit is linked to the root "samskar" i.e. completely formed, refined, advanced and highly elaborated. Thus, Sanskrit means a refined and well-formed language. This goes to suggest that there would have certainly been a language not so refined. Linguists call that group of language as *Prakrit* Language meaning natural language of the inhabitants of the area. It requires small imaginations to visualize the presence of some simpler spoken dialect or a group of dialects from where Sanskrit would have emerged as a superior refinement. So it is not the very first language of its time but refined from many others. Sanskrit has a unique feature of grouping vowels and consonants, detailed coverage of all vowels to represent all types of human sounds and groupings of consonants in neat categories like all dental consonants of t, th, d, dh and n being grouped together. Combinations of k, kh, g, gh, gy and p, ph, b, bh, m are similar other examples of this greatness.

On the other hand even most developed European languages of today have not been able to even segregate vowels and consonants, forget about their sequential classification. Sanskrit has been having its phonetic conditions without any dilution for over five thousand years, no mean feat. The art and science of *Sandhi* and *Sandhi Vichchhad* (combining words and segregating them) is yet another great unmatched feature of Sanskrit since Vedic days. After studying complete and scientific grammatical mathematics of Sanskrit, one can only laugh out on people who try to equate Sanskrit with other languages of its time and conclude that all these originated from some unknown common source. As an Indian I am proud to feel that Sanskrit indeed is first most developed and advanced language of entire humanity and most other languages have their association with Sanskrit either at their origin or during their evolving phase. Partial similarity of such languages with Sanskrit is a clear proof behind such conclusion.

There have been many efforts to decipher the signs found of seals from Sindhu Sarasvati excavations to establish some conclusive link between that period and Vedic Sanskrit used for composing Hymns but without any acceptable success. But this is also a fact that Sanskrit remained a language of words and was transmitted orally for a very long time. Actually, Sanskrit was not to be reduced to writing during Sarasvati period. There are hymns in Rig-Veda clearly prohibiting passing on the secret knowledge of Vedic Hymns to anyone who is not eligible and emphasis was always on preserving phonetics of the *mantras* so that their power was not reduced.

It is universally recognized about Sanskrit that it is one of the most magnificent, the most perfect and wonderfully sufficient literary instrument. It is accepted as the most scientifically constructed language ever. The other adjectives attached with it are sweet and flexible, strong and clearly formed, vibrant and subtle etc. There has always been great importance attached to correct pronunciation for each vowel and consonant and that has not changed a bit over so many thousands of years. On many of these facts, Sanskrit certainly scores over other languages clubbed as part of its family. (Macdonell, 1900)

Sanskrit may not have been used for common parlance or for communication within ordinary folks. Being a language of elite, Sanskrit didn't allow use of slangs or imperfect versions. Undoubtedly, there would have been one or more *Prakrit* languages taking care of common communication. It will be difficult to visualize small children playing in a village corner and speaking

Sanskrit or a house lady instructing her washerman in Sanskrit. Sanskrit was used only by *Brahmin* adults only for liturgical purposes.

And these *Brahmin* males must have been bilingual and maintained normal communication with their parents, wife, children, servants and neighbours on the other side of the road by using other spoken language while using Sanskrit for their composition and other liturgical works. This interaction with other natural or vernacular dialects and languages resulted in expanding Sanskrit on one side and allowing others to peep into Sanskrit on the other side. Many words and traditions found in later writings of Sanskrit literature are a clear proof of inter language interactions.

Unlike other languages of its time, Sanskrit didn't have a script to begin with as it was originally a language only for verbal use. The Vedas' poems composed in the early times were preserved only through oral traditions for over 2000 years. Due to strict emphasis on phonetics/sounds of Vedic hymns, Vedas did not allow to get consigned to writing. Some ancient Sanskrit texts, however, are found in Brahmi script. Brahmi scripts are common to all other Indo European, Dravidian, Tibeto-Burman, Mongolic and Austroasiatic languages and have many versions. The medium for writing was Birch bark and palm leaves. Both of these were very perishable in nature and require rewriting for preservation. Indians have never preferred using leather etc. for it was always considered immoral to handle skin of dead animals for any thing religious.

Stages of Sanskrit: Excellence Refined

Sanskrit can be easily classified into three distinct age groups. To begin with, we have ancient Sanskrit used for composing Vedas, *Brahmanas* and all *Upanishads*. Then comes the Panini version with its own grammar and vocabulary (approximately around 400 BC) called Classical Sanskrit. Bulk of the literature available on date has been written in Classical Sanskrit. The last step in growth of Sanskrit came in early centuries of the first CE millennium when the script got upgraded to Dev Nagri, the grammar got refined and teaching and learning of Sanskrit acquired prime importance. At this time, Sanskrit has also acquired the status of official languages for many kingdoms within the heartland. It was in this period that bulk of the literature got written and is still available partly.

Being a language of elite, all upwardly mobile people engaged in education, in rituals for kings, philosophers, those engaged in trade and commerce and composers were all using Sanskrit. This was probably the time where one has to learn Sanskrit to prove himself in any part of socio economic spectrum. But strict grammar and elite attraction continued to result in a situation where it became the language mainly for writing purpose unlike of other *Prakrit* languages which were used for oral communications.

By this time, writing has become very popular; issues relating to scripts have been settled. Perhaps, it will not be out of place to compare Sanskrit in India around 200 BC-400 CE with the status of English of India of 2000 CE where most all higher education, all legal works, most works in research and every other works for pan Indian appeal uses only English in spite of so many other complete languages available.

We have to remember that the earliest inscription of Ashoka period found have used Prakrit or Pali and not Sanskrit. Ashoka ruled India in 265 BC until 232 BC and he ruled on the largest part of India. Clearly, Mauryan Dynasty did not take Sanskrit as its official language. However, inscriptions found belonging to other periods starting from 150 CE and later have used Sanskrit written in Dev Nagri script in plenty.

Sanskrit has also seen great work by its Grammarians who did excellent job in refining and enriching the language continuously. This has enabled Sanskrit to enlarge its vocabulary matching with developments in other human spheres. As a result, Sanskrit kept growing in its stature as a source to feed most other vernacular in the main land of its influence as well on its peripheries.

Most certainly, Sanskrit has provided major influence over most other vernacular languages that took form in eastern side on India mainly Bangla and Oriya. In fact, due to continuous and ongoing exchange in all spheres of public life between north and south India ever since Gupta dynasty, Sanskrit also started influencing Dravidian languages especially through *Brahmins* in south India also learning and writing in Sanskrit. I read some one comparing influence of Sanskrit on other languages of the subcontinent by comparing it with the way Mahout directs the elephant to move forward and for course correction any time it deviates, off course, Sanskrit occupying the driving seat.

Sir William Jones, an Anglo Welsh philologist and an authority on Indo European languages who lived between 1746 to 1794 and founded Asiatic Society of Bengal said in 1786 during the annual meeting of the society at Calcutta (now Kolkata):

> *"Sanskrit language, whatever be its antiquity, is of a wonderful structure, more perfect than Greek, more copious than Latin and more exquisitely refined than either; yet bearing to both of them a strong affinity, both in the roots and verbs, and in the form of grammar, than could possibly would have been produced by accident; so strong indeed that no philologist could examine them all without believing to have sprung from some common source which perhaps no longer exist ".*

Sanskrit's Literary Treasure: Broad Classification

Great sages of India have been creating literary masterpieces since the Rig-Veda time although the content and emphasis have evolved in line with social changes around. Total volume of such creations was much more than what is currently available. The losses are attributed to lack of proper media for storage of the literature created. Initially, there was no writing of Vedas and *Brahmins* have preserved these only by oral traditions who laboured for generations to carry over the Vedas with sheer memory and recitations. Later, the media for writing was limited to birch bark or palm leafs and these had but very limited self-life. Proper preservation demanded rewriting of the material all the time. We can easily assume the gigantic resources required in terms of writers and material to continuously rewrite literature coming over for centuries along with literature getting created by new generation. As a consequence, substantial portion of earlier literature could not be saved and got vanished.

We will attempt to have a broad look at whatever remained salvaged. In order to get a clear picture, proper classification of the available Sanskrit literature will help in better comprehension. But we must remember that the whole volume available today is composed and compiled over millennium and consists of distinct types. The categorization of such volume itself has its own challenges and that is why there is no consensus among literary circles about a final categorization. But like many other things,

Hinduism doesn't get scared from consensus and multiple categorizations are well accepted as normal. Thus one will always come across situations of marginal overlap and we must be open to live with the fact that as it is with such a great volume of literature, it is next to impossible to fit it in tight categorizations.

Indeed the whole developments of Sanskrit literature has so evolved that overlap is unavoidable. Reader is advised to keep this caution at the back of his/her mind and is better advised to refrain from taking it as a gospel truth. However, some categorization is always better than not having one:

Vedic Literature

Each Veda is divided into two categories namely 'Samhita' which is collection of fundamental hymns composed in verses and '*Brahmanas*' which consist of prose text used for explaining the meaning of the liturgy included in Samhita. Next we have 'Aranyakas' which contain discussions on sophisticated subjects like Maha Vrata and Praan Vidya explaining how one, who follows the Vedic injunctions and performs sacrifices correctly, goes to become god's alike. The last part is 'Upanishads' which we have already seen are philosophical treatises. Upanishads are also called Vedanta which literally means end of period of Vedic texts. So, all the Vedas, *Brahmanas,* Aranyakas and Upanishads put together are called Vedic Literature.

Vedic Literature is generally called "Shruti" which means revealed texts. Many people believe that Vedas have not been composed by human but have been revealed by the Gods. Some people believe that only Vedas were revealed while sages composed *Brahmanas* to Upanishads. But let us be practical and understand that all these are great creations by our great ancestors who were very much human. The true meaning of Shruti is pure preservation of the text, over generations, without any dilution/addition/deletion of even a small vowel. The entire Vedic Literature including Upanishads is having universal approach to entire humanity of all times and have no shade of any religion. The concepts contained in this category are beyond any restriction or limitation. These are expected to guide the humanity until its very end as these contain truth and only truth. The spirituality contained in Upanishads indicate emergence of some of the basic religious concepts of Buddhism, Jainism and Hinduism alike.

Vedanga

Next generation of scripturesis called Vedanga meaning 'limbs of the Vedas'. There are six main disciplines, which are included under Vedanga. The first one is called Nirukta and deals with science of etymology. Second one is called Vyakarna where we have Panini's Astadhyayi, which redefined Sanskrit as Classical Sanskrit, by setting complete rules of total grammar. All subsequent creations used Classical Sanskrit as main language. Thirdly, we have Siksha dealing with phonetics as to how each syllable need to be pronounced with complete psychic effects of the words remaining intact. Fourthly, we have Chhanda Vedanga consisting of science of metres. As per this Vedanga, all syllables are categorized under Guru and Laghu as distinct categories and string of Guru and Laghu sequence is called metre. Several of these metres have been used under different scriptures. Fifth Vedanga is called Jyotisha and deals with all aspects of Astronomy. The very word Jyotish literally refers to science of 'shining objects' and included observations and rules for all celestial bodies. Lastly, we have Kalpa Vedanga dealing with ritual portion of Vedas and detailed out rules for all ceremonies for conducting the rituals in perfect manner so as to secure expected benefits. Kalpa Vedanga was further bifurcated under Srautasutra (categorized under Shruti) and Smartasutra (categorise under *Smriti*) where the earlier part dealt with altar constructions and was called Shulva Sutras while the later one was further divided under Gryhasutras and Dharamsutras.

All the Vedangas put together were first expansion of contents of Vedas for converting each of these matters into independent and specific subjects going forward. So, the origin of all this literature is from Vedas and all these were composed in aphoristic style. Aphorism style resulted in making Vedanga very difficult to comprehend even by people having in-depth education of Sanskrit. Some of the words used in Vedanga are as long as hundred letters. All compositions under this category are called "Sutras" literally meaning 'threads' on which each aphorism is mounted like a pearl to make the complete necklace. The practical translation of Sutra is 'Formulae'. Like every formula require a big explanation to prove the final result contained in it, so are Sutras. One line of Sutra may require a full-fledged chapter to explain the complete meaning. The main objective of sutras was to provide a short survey of the sum of the scattered details, on a particular subject matter, all over the voluminous scriptures inherited from earlier periods.

Most of the times we come across a text whose name ends with the word 'Sutra', we should be able to identify that it will belong to Vedanga; that it would have been composed any time between 500 BC to 100 BC; that the text would be very tough to comprehend; that the text will most likely be first text dedicated to a specific subject matter. The beauty and charm of aphoristic style is unique, as the texts have been composed applying utmost brevity. I read somewhere that the revered composers of sutras were known to experience same delight by saving a short vowel as a *Brahmin* could get on his son's birth. We may all remember that a *Brahmin* is incapable of gaining heaven without a son to perform his funeral rites. So, we can imagine the focus on brevity that would have been applied by the composers. In fact the brevity has resulted at times where different teachers were able to draw different meaning from the same text.

Sutra tradition ended just before end of BC and was replaced by simple verses in poetic style called *Shlokas*. This period is also called the Classical Sanskrit literature period. This period is different than Vedic period in terms of matter, spirit and forms. Vedic period was more on dharma and spirituality while Classical period abundantly developed in all directions of knowledge even when the basic current of Upanishads kept flowing all through this period as well. By this time, the old Deities of the Vedas got sunk to subordinate place except, may be, Indra who was still considered important as chief of warrior's heaven. *Brahma*, Shiva and Vishnu got emerged as main powerful Deities of this period. In addition, there is new creed of minor deities like Kubera and Ganesh and Karttikeya together with new female deities of Shri Laxmi (for beauty, poise and fortune) and Durga/Parvati.

Smriti Literature

Sanskrit literature compiled from around 300 BC to 300 CE is generally grouped under this category. *Smriti* means "memory'. Actually, most of the texts covered under this category are not attributable to a single author. These have evolved from a long discussion in oral traditions and after remaining in public domain for a considerable period of time. Some of these have been produced by forest academies attached to sages with due contribution from outsiders as well. Main texts included here are the two great epics of Mahabharata and Ramayana together with Yoga Sutras, Shiva Sutras, Manusmriti and Devi Mahatmya.

The Bhagvad Gita, although appended to Mahabharata, due to its spiritually rich contents, is included in Shruti category as it is also called 'Gitaupanishad' and for all practical purpose is an Upanishad of Upanishads. Most of the practices of later classical Hinduism are derived from *Smriti* literature. All-important dimensions of worship related matters that are under practice today are directly derived from *Smriti* literature only. Most Hindus regardless of their further divisions into sects, *varnas*, castes follow *Smriti* literature.

Shastras

This category includes elaborated texts composed in metred verses focusing on a single subject at a time. One may say it to be early seeds of specialization on specific subjects. *Shastra* as a word means 'science' but it also got used to denote a 'text book'. Actually, *Shastras* contain a combination of Art, Science, Literature and Instruction Manual, all rolled into one, about the subject matter. The suffix of *Shastra* generally gets identified with subject matter of some kind of technical or specialized knowledge.

Shastras got created with the view of collecting all encompassing knowledge about the subject under a single book; like a compendium. Before *Shastras*, a subject might have been touched by different texts in bits and pieces. The composers of *Shastras* were like mandated to collect all available knowledge on the subject and put it together. In short, all *Shastras* are to be taken as detailed manuals about the specific subject covered therein. Besides covering all important subjects relating to *Dharma*, *Artha* and *Kama*, number of other subjects covered by *Shastras* include Grammar, Architecture, Sculpture, Medicine, Dancing, Fine Arts, Music, Astronomy, Mathematics, Yoga, Astrology, Natural Sciences, *Tantras*, Surgery etc.—practically everything imaginable and much more outside imagination also.

Bhautika Shastra (Physics), *Rasayana Shastra* (Chemistry), *Vastu Shastra* (Architecture), *Shilpa Shastra* (Sculpture), *Artha Shastra*

(Economics and Public Administration) and *Neeti Shastra* (Political Science) are all but few examples of classic literature grouped under this category. The uniqueness of all the *Shastras* remained in their basis of timeless principles. All the principles contained and elaborated by *Shastras* continue to guide future generations for making further advancements in all these sciences for a long time. Such a vast expanse of subjects covered by *Shastras* provides yet another example of Indian advancements in sciences at that time in history.

Puranas

These are prose texts full of mythological stories about the particular deity to whom it is dedicated. *Puranas* puts heaps of praise, appreciation and applaud about the god or goddess it belongs to. The scope of each *Purana* typically start from 'creation of the universe' and all the way upto its destruction where all described as a sole cause of the chosen deity. The stories mentioned highlight role of the chosen god and his unique place in Hindu geography, cosmology and philosophy.

Most of the stories that we would have heard from childhood onward about some god doing this and that and about sages, *apsaras,* curses, tapasyas, fights between gods themselves, *swarga loka,* Narad Muni, *samudra manthan,* boons bestowed and their counters, are all most likely from *Puranas*. These are narrative in nature and got compiled largely in the same manner as the two great epics. These include many *Puranas* like for Agni, Bhagvata, *Brahma, Brahmanada, Narada, Padma, Shivaa, Varuna, Vayu* and *Vishnu*. The *Puranas* are categorized either as per the three *gunas* of *Sattav, Rajas* and *Tamas* or as under gods of *Trimurti* namely, *Brahma, Vishnu* and *Mahesh*. In due course, the *Puranas* are known to have paved way to start of sects within Hinduism. Conversly, sectarian disciples resorted to compile *Purana* for their God in an effort to project him bigger than others around the block.

Nibandha

Later came the Nibandha where one writer picks up a single topic within a broad subject and drew references on that topic from *smriti* literature and *Shastras* to come up a consolidated view and reinterpreting the final guidance in the matter. This part of literature came into vogue only after 500 CE.

Bhasyas (Commentaries)

This was the last category in Sanskrit literature where the writer resorted to provide a new reinterpretation to an earlier text or *Shastra* and basically reinventing the entire concept under changed situation over the period from its first composition/completion. These came into being from around 900 CE onwards. Generally speaking, all commentaries also drew significantly from outside sources and writings by other authors and took up the comparison with reconciling attitude to iron out disagreements and propagating new approach. Many *Shastras* actually got multiple numbers of commentaries.

The chart below provides a quick view of division of Indian Scriptures under *Sruti* and *Smriti* categories. Reader may remember that each *Brahmanas* and Upanishad is identified with a particular Veda and hence have been clubbed under respective Vedas. The classification of scriptures under primary and secondary is yet another way of looking at them for classification purposes.

Just to capture the main scriptures and other critical pieces of Sanskrit literature, we can look at some of the main texts grouped under major heads. It is no comprehensive list as the idea is just to show as examples of the variety of the subjects covered by the great Sanskrit literature which remain preserved from one of the most glorious past of any culture all through the world:

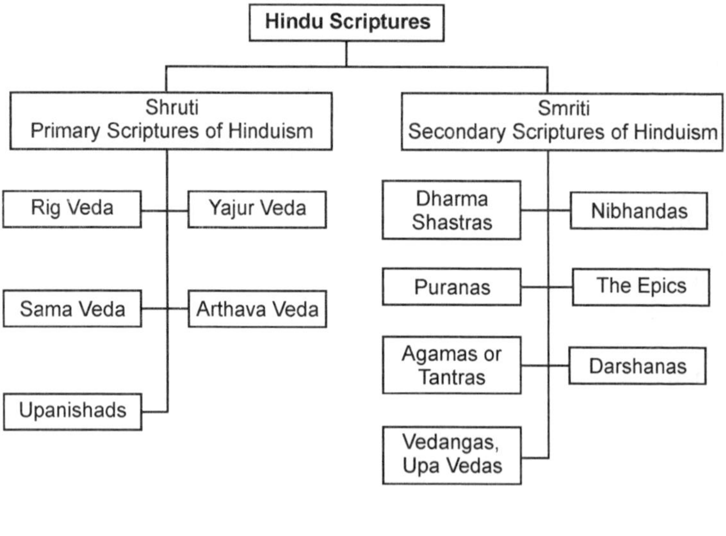

Epics:	Mahabharata, Ramayana
Philosophy:	Yoga Sutra, Brahma Sutra, Nyaya Sutras
Dharama:	Dharma Sutra, Dharma Shastra, Manu Smriti
Grammar:	Mahabhasya, Astadhyayi
Scholarly:	Jyotisha Vedanga, Aryabhatia, Siddhantas, Natya Shastra
Dramas:	Vikramorvasiam, Malavikagnimitram, Abhijnanshakuntlam
Technical Specialisation:	Bhautika S, Rasayana S, Jeeva S, Vastu S, Shila S, Kama S, Neeti S, Artha S, Kama Sutra
Medical:	Charaka Samhita, Sushruta-Samhita, Ashtanga-Hridaya, Ashtanga-Sangraha
Stories:	Panchtantra, Hitopdesha, Vetalu-panchvimsati, Suka Saptati, Katha Sarit Sagara
Puranas:	Agni, Bhagvata, Brahma, Brahmanda, Garuda, Kurma, Linga, Matsya, Narada, Padma, Shiva, Skanda, Varaha, Vayu and Vishnu.

Main Composers of Classical Sanskrit Literature

As already mentioned, going up to *Smriti* and *Puranas*, there is no agreement on the names of the people who can be accredited with the specific compositions of texts remaining available to us. Indian traditions have been very weak in preserving names of the great composers, as such it is rather impossible to identify most of our valuable texts with their composers with certain degree of certainty. Somehow, our ancient sages have not shown any desire to identify their names with their creations, as has been the practice in many other cultures. It is only beginning with Nibandha and Bhasyas that we have a clearer picture about the individuals and their backgrounds. Some of the prominent teachers after 500 CE and beyond who have made immense contribution in continuing Sanskrit literature with time and development are, at random Gaudapada, Govinda Bhagavatpada, Adi Shankara, Vachaspati Mishra, Sureshwaracharya, Padmapadacharya, Hastmalakacharya, Totakachrya, Brahmanand Sarasvati, Madhusudan Sarasvati, Radhakrishnan, Sri Ramkrishna.

Sanskrit's Relation with Hindi

The relationship between these two languages is not as direct and as old as it appears. As already discussed, Sanskrit always had various spoken dialects all through its area of influence. But on the periphery of the main heart land, for example, in Bengal, Orissa, Marathwada and Gujarat, the impact of spoken dialects was much more prominent. This situation resulted in origin of vernacular languages in all these regions with almost direct impact of Sanskrit. But the situation in UP, Bihar, MP and Rajasthan was somewhat different. These areas came in touch with cultural baggage of the invaders right from tenth century CE. The spoken dialects in this area, the Khadi Boli with its variants (which chiefly included Avadhi, Brij, Bundelkhandi), continued absorbing many words and idioms from the territory of foreign rulers and invaders as many of their soldiers and traders, etc. got settled in these areas. By the time of Mughal Empire, the spoken language called "Hindustani" had taken a distinct form with sizable impact of Turkish and Central Asian culture.

In due course, the Hindustani got written both in Arabian script and in Devnagri script. This is how a single spoken language got divided into two distinct written languages called Urdu and Hindi respectively. In addition to commonality of Devnagri being used as script for both Sanskrit and Hindi, the later also borrows grammatical structure of Sanskrit. And as part of bigger family structure, Hindi also draws a lot many words from Sanskrit (like every other languages of India with the exception of Tamil and its three cousins). But a bulk of vocabulary of Hindi is derived from the mix of North Indian dialects and Persian.

The dialectology of Hindi proper is split in several separate groups. On west of north India we have Brij Bhasha, Haryanvi, Rajasthani and Bundelkhandi while on the eastern side we have Awadhi, Bagheli, Bhojpuri, Magadhi and Chhattisgarhi. Similarly, we also come across western version of Hindustani Hindi called Bambaiya Hindi where Marathi influences it. Not far away, one can see it as Dakhini where erstwhile Hyderabad State was using it as Hyderabadi Hindustani. As such, Hindi is somewhat an ambiguous language with many variants. Against this, Sanskrit has always been a single version language with complete grammar and mathematics like discipline preventing any regional influence.

The derivation of Hindi proper from Sanskrit is many stepped and can be looked as under:

- Sanskrit
    - Central Zone Languages
        - Western Zone Languages
            - Hindustani
                - Khariboli
                    - Hindi

The real impetus to Hindi came only after independence in 1947 when Hindi got adopted as a national language. As such, Sanskrit has much less direct impact on Hindi in comparison to its impact on other northern regional languages except that it shares Devnagri as a common script.

Fast Forward

Each of the scriptures mentioned under several categories above is an independent subject matter of a separate book(s) but I wish my readers to get some exposure for some of the main scriptures covering most important objectives of human life. The chapter named "Comments on Major Shastras" covers such comments in desired details.

But before that we should touch base with another important development of this time in terms of emergence of two home grown religions namely Buddhism and Jainism. It is to the credit of these branches that Hinduism will never remain same again. This emergence resulted in lot of churning on many concepts and the crystalisation that followed such churning cemented unique identity of Hinduism as a great heritage of Indian subcontinent.

8

Emergence of Buddhism

Around 600 BC, a lot was happening in India which several writers name a great revolution. Vedic practices were well understood and had been followed for centuries. Like everything else, Vedic rituals have not remained static and offerings to Gods have undergone big change from a simple offering of 'Som Ras' to very elaborate rites. People have been told overtime to believe that the only way to earn merit with powerful Gods is to follow the rites and rituals as prescribed and conducted by learned *Brahmin* Priests on your behalf. A happy and satisfied priest was to help your Gods being happy and blessed for you. But many people have got tired of this and being dissatisfied on many grounds were coming forward to question this status quo.

Prince Gautama, the son of King Suddhodana of Shakyas, having his capital as Kapilvastu, was one such person questioning these traditions.

We have all heard about Gautama who got tired of material life of being a prince and ultimately at the age of twenty-nine years left his kingdom, his beautiful wife, a very young son and all of his family to seek the truth. But nothing happens all at once. He was a born *Kshatriya* and a had good exposure to all Vedic systems of his time, had been married for ten long years, had best of everything that a normal person aspires for. But far from all this, there were many questions that kept coming back to him without clarity about their likely answers.

So, he decided to seek knowledge and went to one *Brahmin* hermit named Alara whose forest academy was not far from his hometown. Later he also joined another ascetic *Brahmin* named Udraka to gain more knowledge and clarity. He spent full six years and learned everything on offer about Hindu philosophies, doctrines, spirituality but he found that his questions have remained unanswered. From there, he left to try penance hoping that it will help him activate his superhuman insight. He is said to have spent another six years with five disciples in attendance and tortured him near to death to seek knowledge pursuing the path of most severe penance. But he still not got what he was looking. Devastated by his yearning for more and more, he got deserted by his fellow disciples and got left all alone. It is as this stage that he is said to have set down under a tree for deep contemplation. At this time, he was also considering going back to his princely life and resume normal life but his heart wanted him to try more. Here he realized that a holy calm life and love towards others were good enough penance for all evils; this is how Self-Culture and Universal Love became the Essence of Buddhism!

He went to Banaras where his old disciples were living at that time and there he shared his new tenets with them. He concluded that based on his self experience, extremes of asceticism or worldly life are to be avoided for a middle way path which opens the eyes and bestows understanding, leads to peace of mind, to higher wisdom and full enlightment—to *Nirvana*.

He explained them four truths about human suffering and all five of them soon converted to be his first followers. Next was a banker's son from Banaras. In about five months of his stay at Banaras he could muster about sixty followers who were all taught with his doctrines and were asked to go in different directions to preach the truth. Soon he got recognized by all levels of society and his fame reached to his home town as well where he got his foster mother and wife and his son also enrolled in his faith who became the first female and only child members of his order.

For next twenty five years, Gautama, the Buddha wandered all through the Gangetic planes preaching piety and holy life to people from all strata of society, poor and rich, good and misguided, high and low without any difference of gender, caste and class. A whole lot of people from women and lower classes were easy converts because it was first time that someone was actually treating them at par and opening doors to them to seek some religious exposure.

He died at the advanced age of eighty and by that time, his order has taken a good shape for keeping the momentum even when he was not around.

The Basic Four Truths Doctrine by Buddha

The First Truth is the 'fact of suffering'. All desires, happiness, sukha (what ever is good), pleasant, right, permanent, joyful, harmonious, satisfying, are all actually the sources of sufferings. People remain engaged seeking pleasures in pursuing for these aims in life but ultimately all of them find that life brings Dukha, just the opposite: frustration, dissatisfaction, incompleteness, sufferings, and sorrows. Buddha realized that life is change and change can never satisfy desire. Hence, everything that changes brings suffering. He concluded that birth, decay, illness, death are all the sufferings that a normal human being is to experience for his daily existence. In addition to these, every person also get sufferings from presence of objects or person that one hates, when he is unable to get the objects of desire, when he tries to cling to people made of five elements, etc. In short, clinging to very existence of the humanity is full of misery and sufferings and therefore, first truth.

The Second Truth is the 'cause of suffering'. It is not life that brings sorrow, but the demand on life. The cause of sorrow is selfish desire: trishna (the thirst for life). Thirst for pleasures, thirst for existence, thirst for prosperity are the examples of thirsts which remain unfulfilled and then lead to thirst for rebirth. Buddha taught that there is no fire like selfish desire. Not a hundred years of experience can extinguish it, for the more you feed it, more it burns.

The Third Truth is that 'suffering that has a cause also has an end'. When there is a complete absence of all passions, when there is a complete destruction of desires then the fire of selfishness is extinguished, the mind is made free from selfish desire, what remains is the state of wakefulness, of peace, of joy, of perfect health, called *Nirvana*.

The Fourth Truth of Buddha is the 'Noble Path of Truth'. He concluded that selfishness can be extinguished by following the eight fold path. The eight steps involved in this path were identified as: 1. Right Understanding, 2. Right Purpose, 3. Right Speech, 4. Right Conduct, 5. Right Occupation, 6. Right Effort, 7. Right Attention, and 8. Right Meditation. If Dharma is a wheel, these eight ways are its spokes, which hold the wheel and help it moving.

Noble Eight-Fold Path

Brief details for these eight-fold path is as under:

Right Understanding: Seeing life as it is—in the midst of change, there is no place to stand firm. Happiness cannot come from anything outside, all things that come into being have to pass away—this understanding is the beginning of wisdom.

Right Purpose: To be willingly thinking that it is in line with life. One should order his life around the Dhamma.

Right Speech, Right Conduct, and Right Occupation: These follow from right purpose. In short these are means to live in harmony with the unity of life.

Right Effort, Right Attention, and Right Meditation: These deal with the mind. Our life is shaped by mind—we become what we think. Right effort is the constant endeavour to train oneself in thought, word and action. Right attention follows from right effort. It simply means keeping the mind where it should be. The wise train the mind to give total attention to one thing at a time, here and now. Right meditation is the means to train the mind. Through meditation, selfish passions will not enter the mind and the mind will grow calm and kind.

The sum and substance of Buddha's teachings is that without entering into any discussion into origin or destiny of men, one should lead a holy life and that will lead him to the Summum Bonum, the highest good. Buddha was said to be not interested in going through complex philosophical issues as he believed that such issues do not help the common person in any way and he wished his followers to remain away from such unwanted intellectual discussions which are nothing but waste of time. He called such questions as improper and preferred to abstain from replying. Once a monk kept pestering him about philosophy, Buddha is said to have told that he was like a wounded man who refused to have treatment until he learned the name of the person who has shot him and what village he came from; he would die before he got his useless information. Buddha wanted to preach a cure for grief, suffering and miseries impacting human here and now (Armstrong, Buddha).

After his death, Buddhism got branched out into two main categories. The first is called Northern Buddhism which got popular in China, Japan, Nepal and Tibet. But this branch of

Buddhism got mixed ceremonies which were never known to Buddha himself. The second is called Southern Buddhism which got spread throughout in Sri Lanka, Burma and Thailand and then came back to south and eastern part of India. Southern Buddhism furnishes most valuable literature of the faith. The most important of these include Suttee Pitaka, Vinaya Pitaka and Abhidamma Pitaka. Suttee Pitaka contains sayings and doings of Gautama himself. He is himself actor and speaker of the doctrines conveyed in his own words. Vinaya Pitaka contains minute rules for monks and nuns who had embraced the holy order for proper conduct and behaviour in Viharas (Monastries). It is said that most of these guidelines have been finalized and got settled during Gautama's own life under his own guidelines. Finally, Abhidamma Pitaka contains investigations on various subjects like conditions of life in different worlds, personal qualities, elements, cause of existence and such other matters pertaining to metaphysics. These were composed mostly after Buddha's death.

In addition to Pitakas, another important scripture called Dhammapada (Dharm-pad in Hindi—the foot prints of Dharma) which is a collection of sayings of Buddha in the form of verses. It is most widely and best known Buddhist scripture. It explains *"Dharma expresses the central law of life that all things and events are part of an indivisible whole. In the human activity, it is the behaviour that is in harmony with the ultimate Unity. Sometimes it is justice, righteousness, fairness, sometimes simply a personal duty, obligations of religion or society. It is also being true to nobility, honour forgiveness, trustfulness, loyalty, compassion, ahimsa."*

If Upanishads are like slides, the Dhammapada is like a field guide. It can't take us there but it can certainly show us the way—tell us about what to look for, warns about missteps, advise about detours, what to avoid. Besides Upanishad and Dhammapada, Gita will qualify to be the third instrument as a map and personal guide book in the journey of exploring the Ultimate. Human beings are not cabin dwellers; born to a life cramped and confined, we are meant to explore to seek to push the limits of our potential. In that journey, the world of senses is just a base camp. The Dhammapada is a map of spiritual journey. One can start from where ever he is. Like on road, our values and aspirations and understanding of life around keep changing as we make progress. (Easwaran)

During the time of Buddha, spiritual seekers were mostly graduates of the forest academies which were very popular around the Upanishad time period. These people turned inward mostly for the same reasons that scientists and adventurers turn outward-not to run away from life but to master it. They yearned to know what is not known yet; to know what human being is, what life is, what death means and can it be conquered. Various Upanishads of the Vedic sages are clearly antecedents of the Buddha's voice.

Meditation Teachings by Buddha

The meditation suggested by Buddha is also different than the one propagated by Hindu philosophy of Yoga. The First Dhyana (Meditation) recommended by Buddha starts with withdrawing attention from all the senses and turning the same inward which he called right attention. Gradually as the quiet settles in, we realize we are in a new world. In this world of consciousness, we cannot look for any landmarks but should rather feel the senses disconnected from the external world and direct the thought process to focus on inward consciousness alone. The mind will try to wander to external world which is but natural. But throughout this first Dhyana, we try to stop the centrifugal force of the thinking process from going outward and to recall the attention back to inward consciousness. In order to attain the concentration which cannot be broken by any sensory attraction (body) or emotional response (mind), we have to work a lot to develop control over senses and also restrict our likes and dislikes in much controlled level. This stage is the first leg in a long journey and itself is a rare achievement. No great flashes of insight come at this stage as it is just but a beginning.

The Second, Dhyana—here the struggle of self mastery over that sector of mind, where lie thoughts, feelings, habits, experiences, that help developing the peculiar individuality of self, moves to a significantly deeper level. Here the quiet of meditation is unassailed by outside world. Distractions can disturb the thread of concentration but not so easily and not so often. Gradually, all distractions start appearing more and more distant. The claims of "I" and "Mine" become smaller and true nature of situations start appearing with clarity. One starts going easily against self will, especially in personal relations. This clarity helps gaining detachment from self-centered conditioning that burden every normal human being. This is swimming against the current.

This is quite a painful process but brings along satisfaction in mastering some of the strongest urges in human personality. Sitting in meditation, at this stage, one descends down step by step into the depth of unconsciousness like a deep sea diver at the bottom of deep sea. The surface seems so far away. Asleep to one's body, thoughts, feelings, desires, separate identity, we are intensely awake in the inner world—deep in unconsciousness, near the very threshold of personality.

Personality Described

Buddha describes personality as a blend of five skandhas or heaps of ingredients—*Rupa* form, *Vedana* sensation, *Samajhana* perception, *Samskar* the focus or impulses of mind and *Vijnan* consciousness. As per Buddha, coming together of these is birth and their breaking apart is death. (Contrary to Vedic thinking, there is no *Atman.*)

Form is merely a wrapper as most important identity of a person is his mind print: his big ego. All these Skandhas are not substances but ever-changing processes. Samskar here means conditioned habit of liking or disliking. These are thoughts, speech or behaviours motivated by the desire to get some experience for oneself. This Skandha prompts action, the Karmas. The last Skandha means appropriation of each unit of experience to a mass of conditioning formed by the past. It is like a river carrying the accumulated Karma of previous thoughts and action.

What we call personality is accumulation of everything one has done, thought and said. It follows wherever one goes. As per Buddha, no one can escape the consequences of one's actions—you can run but not hide. All of us necessarily have Karmic scores to settle.

General: Our life is shaped by our mind, for we become what we think. Normal human being suffers ignorance of thinking 'Self' as permanent. Then he clings to what it wants it to be (real, separate and permanent). From this root ignorance arises *Trishna*—craving for personal satisfaction which is followed by *Dukha*.

The whole theme of Dhammapada is "*our life is shaped by our mind. If we can get hold of the thinking process, through meditation, we can actually redo our personality, remake ourselves. Destructive ways of thinking can be rechanneled; constructive channels can be deepened, all through following eight fold life behaviour and meditation but it requires serious work as irrigators lead water to their fields, as archers make their arrows straight, as carpenters carve wood, the wise shape their lives."*

Selected Clauses from Dhammapada

The idea here is to give a flavour of the simple language with direct meaning and straight understanding being the basis of most ancient Buddhism scriptures. This was a direct contrast to Vedic Sanskrit Sutras popular around the same time which could be comprehended only by best in business. The selection of clauses is just on random basis and interested reader is advised to complete book on Dhammapada for detailed reading.

19. Those recite many scriptures but fail to practise their teachings are like cowherd counting cows belonging to other person.
24. If you meditate earnestly, pure in mind and kind in deeds, leading a disciplined life in harmony with the Dharma, you will glow in glory.
50. Do not give attention to what others do or fail to do; give it to what you do or fail to do.
94. Even the Gods envy the saints whose senses obey them like trained horses and who are free from pride.
124. If you have no wound on your hand, you can touch poison without any harm. No harm comes to those who do not do harm.
133. Speak quietly to everyone and they too will be gentle in their speech. Hard word hurts and comes back to the speaker.
150. Around the bones is built a house, plastered with flesh and blood, in which dwell pride and pretense, old age and death.
185. Do not find faults with others. Be moderate in eating and sleeping and meditate. This sums up the teachings of the Buddha.
202. There is no fire like lust, no sickness like hatred, no sorrow like separateness, no joy like peace.

204. Health is the best gift, contentment is the best wealth, trust the best kinsman, nirvana the greatest joy.

210. Not seeing what is pleasant brings pain; seeing what is unpleasant brings pain. Therefore, go beyond both pleasure and pain.

211. Don't get selfishly attached to anything, for trying to hold on to it will bring you pain. When you have neither likes nor dislikes, you will be free.

219. As your family and friends receive you with joy when you return from a long journey, so will your good deeds receive you when you go from this life to the next.

249. Some give out of faith, others give out of friendship. Do not envy others for the gifts they receive or you will have no peace of mind by day or night.

250. Those who have destroyed the roots of jealousy have peace of mind always.

252. It is easy to see faults of others; we winnow them like chaff (phusa ki taraha fatakna). It is hard to see our own; we hide them like a gambler hides his losing draw.

258. One is not wise because he talks too much. They are wise who are patient and free from hate and fear.

262. Neither pleasant words nor a pretty face can make a person beautiful who is jealous, selfish or deceitful.

280. Now is the time to wakeup when you are young and strong. Those who wait with a weak will and a divided mind, will never find a way to pure wisdom.

281. Guard your thoughts, words and deeds. These three disciplines will speed you along the path to pure wisdom.

286. "I will make this my winter home, have another for monsoon and dwell in a third during the summer." Lost in such fancies, one forgets his final destination.

287. Death comes and carries off a man absorbed in his family as the monsoon flood sweeps away a sleeping village. (height of unpreparedness)

292. Do not fail to do what ought to be done, and do not do what ought not to be done. Otherwise your burden of suffering will grow heavier.

295. The true *Brahmin* has killed mother lust and father self-will; He has killed the king of carnal passions (kamuk

bhavna) and the ego that obstructs him on the path. Such a person is free from sin.

302. It is hard to leave this world and hard to live in it, painful to live with the worldly and painful to be wanderer. Reach the goal; you will wander and suffer no more.

305. Sitting alone, sleeping alone, going about alone, conquering the ego by yourself alone. Abiding joy will be yours when all selfish desires end.

329. If you cannot find a friend who is good, wise and loving, walk alone like a king who has renounced his kingdom or an elephant roaming at will in the forest.

406. That one is a *Brahmin* who is never hostile towards a person who is hostile towards him, who is detached among those who are selfish and at peace among those at war. From whom passion, hatred, arrogance and deceit have fallen away like a mustard seed from the point of a needle.

Concept of Nirvana in Buddhism

Nirvana is not like *Moksha* which is supposed to be available upon death and results in end of the cycle of birth and death. Nirvana does not mean death. It is only the extinction of the special condition of mind which gives rise to *Trishna* for life and for its pleasures which, in turn, continue the cycle of new birth. Speaking conversely, once a person has been able to extinguish his *Trishna* for life and its pleasures from his mind, he will be said to have achieved *Nirvana*. *Nirvana* is something very much attained in this very life. It is the sinless and calm state of mind. It is the freedom from all desires. It is the freedom from all passions. It is the perfect peace of mind. And all this is achievable by any person with continuous and sustained self-culture of his mind. As per Buddha, this is the highest aim of human life and there is nothing beyond ***Nirvana***.

Concept of Boddhisattva

This concept is an interesting part of Buddhism with multiple meanings and explanations surrounding it. Initially, it was referred for Gautama to represent his earlier lives and his own life before he got enlightenment. Later it got used for someone who has started his journey on the path of liberation but he is still not there. It got referred to the time when a person is about to reach the Nirvana stage like someone who is just in the process of reaching the height. Later still it came to denote the monks who have dedicated themselves to become fully enlightened soul and have taken necessary vows to adhere themselves with the requisite life style prescribed by scriptures. Boddhisattva is also called a person who has sacrificed his own Nirvana and has taken vows to help other beings for their relief and liberation.

Branches of Buddhism

Over the centuries after departure of Buddha, the faith had already broken frontiers of the land where it came into existence. Within about six centuries of its inception, Buddhism had expanded across boundaries and soon became one of the main religions in entire Asia. The geographical expansion coupled with passage of time resulted, as elsewhere, in developments of many sects or branches with their own unique features. It developed its own multiple sects and sub sects, different sects worked on their own theologies, geographical diversity also brought it sharp contrasts in the way of worship were conducted. The shapes and systems of places of worship changed from Stupas to Pagodas. These developments in Buddhism are exactly in line with most other religions worldwide. Finally, as we see it today, Buddhism has got three main branches which are briefly touched here:

Mahayana Buddhism

This is the largest branch surviving today accounting for about sixty per cent of followers of Buddhism worldwide. It is also called as path of Boddhisattva. This is the most practised faith in countries like India, China, Japan, Vietnam, Korea, Singapore, Taiwan, Nepal, Sri Lanka, Tibet, Bhutan, Malaysia and Mongolia. This branch considers Buddha as one of the highest Superior Souls or High Being. Their traditions have gone through a lot of geographical impacts and some of their practices are even against the teachings by Buddha himself. For example, this branch worships, including bowing, making offering and chanting to all Buddha and Boddhisattvas.

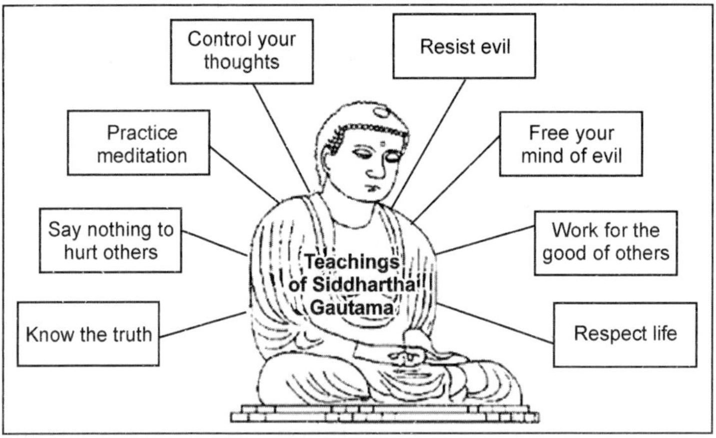

The Eightfold Path

Theravada Buddhism

Its translated meaning is 'Teaching of Elders' and this is the oldest surviving branch of the faith. This is also considered more conservative and the principles followed are more near to what were taught by Buddha himself with not much dilutions and mixing on the way. This branch considers the scriptures as approved at the third Buddhist conference arranged in 250 BC by King Ashoka. Soon after his death, it was first recognized as Sri Lankan lineage as it was in Sri Lanka that its theology and other traditions and practices got final shape. Theravada followers today account for in the approximate of forty per cent.

Vajrayana Buddhism

The last and the smallest of branch of the faith is a complex and multifaceted system. It is suffice to say that, like in Hinduism, this is *Tantra* part of Buddhism and accounts for only a very minuscule number of followers adopting it now. Their practices are full of secrets as applicable to *Tantra* in general.

Buddhism and Hinduism

It is said that an apple doesn't fall far from the tree to which it belongs. There cannot be a better example of this proverb other than effect of Hinduism on Buddhism. Gautama was a devout Hindu by birth and for first thirty-five years of his life. And he had acquired maximum knowledge of Vedic doctrines, rituals, rites, philosophies and every other part of the system called Hinduism. Even at the time that Gautama came up with his new doctrine, there was no love lost, as it was common at that time that thinkers were free to hold their own line of thinking which was different from the main line Vedic system.

So, even after Buddha declared his own faith and started preaching it vigorously and started getting acceptance, it was still taken as an integral and significant part of complex religious character of the subcontinent. At best it was yet another stream of the religious thought. But couple of centuries down the history, situation started to change. When Buddhism started snowballing attracting ever increasing followership, Vedic followers started feeling the heat and started taking it as an active competition and proper lines got drawn as two separate religions called Hinduism and Buddhism. Their comparative position on key tenets is as under:

- Hinduism accepts *Brahman* and *Atman* under the Vedic supremacy principles while Buddhism does not believe in these concepts.
- Hindus believe in four aims of life namely, Dharma, Artha, Kama and *Moksha* while Buddhism believes only in Dharma and revised *moksha* called Nirvana.
- Both believed in Gods but their relative importance in Buddhism is rather low as it keeps human enlightenment higher than seeking blessings from Gods.
- Hinduism believes in *Atman* as the centre point of human existence which remains same over the births until the *Samsara* remains. But Buddhism believes in transmigration without accepting the theory of soul.
- Hinduism believes in four classes and four *ashramas* for humans while Buddhism does not segregate among humans based on caste creed or castes. But there is enough evidence to suggest his marked preference for *Brahmins* whom he considered as higher in spiritual quest.
- Buddha's distinguishing among persons was based on their learning and wisdom unlike Hinduism where it is by birth.

- Buddha spoke against Vedic rites and advised a benevolent life and conquest over passions and desires.
- Buddha strongly recommended retirement from the world as the most efficacious means of achieving aims of life. This is what started the famous monastic system. But Hinduism accepts most people to aim for renunciation only after having fulfilling their obligations to society by living through the Grihasth *ashram*.
- Hinduism accepted teachings of Upanishads as the basis of their philosophy but Buddha believed in Upanishads partly as for him what remained supreme in life was only Holy Life.
- Actually, Buddha accepted bulk of Hindu pantheon of the day but with necessary modifications in line with his cardinal idea.
- But truth, compassion, non-violence are areas where there is complete agreement between both the faiths. On the whole, there are more common grounds than the differences.

9

Jainism

King of Magadha was blessed with his second son in 497 BC who was named Vardhmana Jnatrputra and ultimately got known by the name of 'Mahavira' with literal meaning as 'Great Warrior'. Although he was *Kshatriya* and a prince and a very great physique with all the qualities that can be ascribed with a great warrior but the fight he fought and won was not the usual fight with an enemy. He fought with his own passions and desires to overcome the penances required to achieve higher state of spiritual knowledge so as to achieve his liberation. All the princely luxuries and comforts were not good enough for him to continue his normal life even after living that life for thirty long years and at that time he decided to abandon everything and opt for the life of a renouncer. He had also decided to fight his own battle and obtain enlightenment with his own efforts and not through a learned teacher as was the tradition in those times.

For long period of twelve and half years he wandered from one place to another in entire gangetic planes as a bhikshu practising hardest possible austerities. He deprived himself of food and shelter and even clothes so as to expedite the process of getting the enlightenment in a fast forward manner. He wanted to release his true self from the constraint of the body to achieve inner control. Finally at the age of forty-two, he achieved his liberation and acquired unique knowledge which gave him capacity to simultaneously perceive reality of all the levels and every dimension of time and space.

He called this state as kevala which is an experience which can only be experienced and not described. In this state there is a harmony with everything around and no room for any differentiation. Later he shared it with his followers saying that there is nothing to compare it with. It is beyond words, sound, form, soul, heaven or anything like that. But he had shown confidence that anyone else following the regime recommended by him, will be able to attain the said state and become a Jina. This is how his followers were called as Jains.

Jains believe that Mahavira was in fact the twenty fourth and last of Jina, also called tirthankers. The first of the series of Jinas was Rishabhdev who helped in emerging first picture of Jinas by opposing the illogical rituals of primitive Aryans. The time line of this dates back to early Vedic period. Rishabhdev pursued purity of worship and liberation through personal restraints and conduct. In addition, there is a long list of such great souls each of whom had conquered their liberation pursuing the path of disciplined cultivation of knowledge and control over bodily passions of all kinds. Mahavira is said to be the last in series and is revered as founder of this thought called Jainism.

Teachings of Mahavira

The summary of sustained teachings of Mahavira to his followers over the long years of his preaching can be briefly described here:

- Anger destroys love, pride puts an end to modesty, and deceit takes away friends, while greed destroys everything.
- He who wants happiness, must fight with all the enemies within himself. There is no use fighting external things. Who conquers himself is mightier than the person conquering on the battleground.
- Every soul is the architect on one's own life. Each person is the cause of his misery and happiness.
- Layman commits sins for the sake of his dears without realizing that when the time comes to repay for such conducts, he alone will be responsible and suffer painful punishments.
- Every person has to defend himself from seven sins, namely; drinking, cheating, eating meat, stealing, and relation with prostitutes, hunting animals and mis-advance with other's wife.

- Every person must always remain conscious for non-violence, self-restraints and penance. Self-purification is the purpose of penance that in turn, is the most effective way for destroying unwanted human instincts.

But the single most important doctrine of Mahavira is certainly non-violence against every living being. But his concept of living being was not limited only to human and animals or such being but extended right up to water, plants, fire, air and even stones. As per Mahavira, living being included everything but in different forms of the eternal matter that is constantly changing. It has come to its current state based on its past karmas. Also, that all beings share the same nature and must be shown equitable respect and courtesy. The equality of the tiniest and the largest is unique characteristic of Jainism with no parallel.

It is said that you are more likely to develop hatred for something that you have been using for long rather than a person who is not a user of that thing. Similar thing happened with many *Kshatriyas* of Mahavira time who understood the importance of following non-violence as taught by Mahavira. They were the first to adopt the faith and many of them who were still in military duties and could not give up the same, agreed to do so as soon as possible with them in future. Following the ascetic way of life taught by Mahavira, new followers started getting respect from warriors who were already fighting their internal conflict similar to Arjuna in Mahabharata.

It rather became a craze to get glory for self and family to achieve success by turning to be an ascetic renouncer because it was no cakewalk and required firm determination and astute ruthlessness which were, as it is, the hallmark of a true *Kshatriya*. Slowly-slowly the following increased and the community started getting formed in different parts of the Gangetic planes and west of India. A community so formed was called 'Gana'. His doctrine started finding followers and many of them were people in high places including kings and chief of armies. He wandered from place to place for 35 long years to popularize his doctrines and finally left his physical body in 425BC at the age of seventy two years.

His religion is now called Jainism. As on date it qualifies to be called one of the earliest living religions in entire human history.

It is high on asceticism and put a great deal of emphasis on ethical conducts, personal purity for liberation of individual soul.

Following non-violence of that nature was always going to remain a fundamental principle of Jainism. They were also to believe in non-stealing, truth in speech and maintaining perfect celibacy, the other three components of Yam as prescribed by Yoga philosophy of Hinduism. But non-violence was to be the most critical religious duty for all early Jinas and all other practices were supposed to have no impact if there was a violation of non-violence. Not only that, the scope of non-violence was also now enlarged like never before. A Jain was supposed to acquire perfect empathy with every living creature. He must develop the knowledge that every living being including the stones, as discussed before, are capable of feeling pain as a human and do not wish to suffer pain exactly like we do. This deep awareness at a profound level was to bring that empathy which Mahavira was talking about. A quote from one of the important Jain scripture will bring this point home;

> "All breathing, existing, living, sentient creatures, should not be slain, nor treated with violence, nor abused, nor tormented, nor driven away. This is the pure, unchangeable eternal law, which the enlightened ones who know have proclaimed"

So, the violence included saying bad words (abuse) or simply by physical and mental suffering (tormented) or by lack of empathy (driving away); means that non-violence was to be practised in smallest details of all their life. This is the reason that Mahavira suggested the life of renouncer as he knew well that living a normal material life create enormous opportunities for committing acts of violence on a daily basis. Speaking also is a source of violence, so he advocated as less speaking as possible; every time to use soft tone and words; and if truth was to harm any creature, they were advised to keep quiet. Similarly, the scope for stealing was not only to resist owning anything more than normal requirements but to refrain from owning any material thing.

People following these practices soon reported positive benefits in terms of change of their attitudes in seeing the world and their surroundings in new light of empathy and coexistence. Soon the practices got extending to other unspoken areas like not plucking a fruit from the tree but to wait until it falls on the ground of its own, to be careful while walking on grass to avoid crushing of any insect, not to walk in darkness lest is an act of violence in unknown state, to drink only filtered water, becoming careful and take every step with full awareness of the surroundings. This new found awareness was said to lead the follower to gain 'compassion' for all other living beings.

For people of the time, this concept must have been totally revealing against the prevalent practice of animal sacrifices of Vedic rituals. Later thinkers of the faith also developed their own full-fledged philosophy and wrote many scriptures but, similar to Hinduism, most of their scriptures and thinkers also got lost during famines of those periods.

In terms of philosophy, Jainism did not believe in God as creator. They believed that every form consist of atoms which is the smallest of matter. Matter can be perceived by senses. In addition, there is a lot of energies including but not limited to cohesion, magnetism, electricity. Jains believed that all the matters and energies interplay under set rules for their respective creation, preservation and destruction and operation of these laws don't require presence of any God. They believed in Jeevatma (same as Vedic *Atman*) but not in Permatma (same as Vedic *Brahman*). Jains considered Jeevatma, the soul, also as an aspect of matter.

They believe in *karma,* similar to Hindus.

Later the Jains got divided in two main sects namely Swetambers and Digambers. As the name suggests, Swetambers use white colour clothes and are suppose to follow lineage of Acharya Stulibhadra Suri who is credited with compilation of Jain *Agamas* which is their key scripture. On the other hand, Digambers go without clothes and they reject the authority of Jain *Agama* and all they carry is a broom made out of fallen feathers of Peacocks. They follow the way of Acharya Kundakunda.

Jains have made immense contribution in all spheres of social life since ancient times in India. To begin with, they are major absorbers of the *Shramana* thoughts, an alternate thought process to Vedic since beginning, the other being the Buddhism. They made immense contributions in many scriptures on Indian soil. Perhaps even bigger contribution they made is to promote vernacular languages even when Vedic scriptures were getting composed mainly using Sanskrit. The languages in particular owing lot of contributions from Jain writers are Hindi, Gujarati, Kannada, Tamil and Telugu.

They constructed many temples, caves temples, temple cities and many stupas. Some of the great examples are Marble Temple-Mount Abu, Ranakpur-Mewar, Parsvnath Temple-Khajuraho, Temple cities at Girnar and Palitana in Gujarat, Sammed in Bihar, Sonagiri in Bundelkhand and Muktagiri in Vidharbha. Some of the great Caves temples of Jains are at Badami-Bijapur, Karnataka and Ellora in Maharashtra. Their sculptures are marvelous examples of beautiful ornamental details, minutely carved decorations at pillars, ceilings, doorways and panels.

But after about 1000 years of its establishments and having achieved great heights, the difficulty of following such a tight walk tradition lost its shine. In due course, its followers left for softer options offered by Buddhism and Hinduism who promised a simple way for liberation. Today only about six million followers are reported for this great tradition.

10

Hinduism during Mauryan Empire

Famous Mauryan dynasty originated from Magadha in eastern India is credited for a rule of 137 years between 322BC to 185BC, a period of great happenings for the social, economic, political and religious developments in Indian subcontinent. Chandragupta established it with the help of Chanakya by overthrowing Nanda dynasty. It was a time when Alexander's appointed satrap Seleucus was losing hold of western India to many smaller size clans. Chandragupta took advantage of this situation and advanced rapidly to western area and significantly expanded his empire right up to Arabian Sea.

It became the largest empire of the whole world of that time and the largest ever on Indian subcontinent and covered the regions of Hindu Kush (Afghanistan), Indus Valley (Pakistan), Bengal, and Himalaya to down south (excluding Tamil Nadu, part of Andhra/ Karnataka and Kerala). Having established the systems recommended and perfected by Chanakya, the empire is credited with efficient systems for tax collection, administration, internal security, and security of borders. This facilitated exponential growth in internal and external trade, agriculture and economics as also in arts and crafts. With the exception of Kalinga war, this period enjoyed peaceful periods filled with social harmony, religious transformation and expansion of sciences and knowledge. There was all round peace and prosperity, urbanization was going along fine, newer professions were evolving.

Over 1700 years had passed since the compositions of Rig-Veda and around 700 years since the composition of older *Brahmanas*. During all these years, pure Vedic rituals have gone in background and were practised by a small proportion of the society due to falling belief in effectiveness of rituals for securing final liberation. Another big reason of rituals getting non attractive was reduced knowledge and dedication required to carry out these practices in recommended way of elaboration. On the other hand, '*Brahman*' of Upanishads was faceless and considered too far away by common man and beyond reach. But several, rather wrong practices like class segregation, treatment to women in general, untouchability for people from lowest caste, violence to animals, were resulting in keeping a large part of population on the periphery of religious systems. It was a fit ground for people to lose interest or for many people to turn indifferent to Vedic practices. Both Jainism and Buddhism had taken roots under these conditions but were still in initial stage.

All religious thoughts were getting due acceptance with their own practitioners. Many people were freely experiencing hopping over from one ideology to another. Dharma Gurus were busy promoting each one's own line of ideology by continuously moving from one place to another in the empire. The emperors of this dynasty are not known to have very strong association with Vedic religion and were more interested to follow mono orthodox sects. Jain thinkers who actually got their entry into South through his army influenced Chandragupta very much. Ashoka's father, Bindusar Gupta was known to favour Ajivakas while King Ashoka followed his own recipe which was closer to Buddhism but not one hundred per cent identical. He is said to, however, move much closer to actual Buddhism during advancing stage of his life. Incidentally, his brother named Vitashoka had actually been a strict Buddhist as he renunciated his royal background and preferred a life of Monk following teachings of the Buddha. (Armstrong, Great Transformation, The Beginning of Our Religious Traditions)

Ashoka started stone edicts which were nothing but the best of advertising and media promotion that could have been achieved by the state at that point in history. His edicts grew in content and direction over the years. These edicts are by far the loudest actual non-controversial historical facts about India of that time other than the oral and documented *Shruti* and *Smriti* literature.

Writings on these edicts are neither Buddhist Dhamma (the word Dharma as written in Pali, the language of Buddha) nor Vedic Dharma but is a broader code of human behaviour. The values advised for following were universal in character like honesty, truthfulness, compassion, obedience, mercy, and benevolence. In summary, these writings recommended people to go for maximizing good deeds and minimizing faults. Incidentally, promoters of Sanatan Hindu Dharma will later on adopt most of these values. Actually, these values are applauded by all known religions of the world.

Let us look at the contents of his 11th Rock Edict:

> *"...(one should do) good behaviours towards slaves and servants, obedience to mother and father, generosity towards friends and acquaintances and towards Brahmins and renouncers and abstaining from killing living beings. Father, son, brother, master, friend, acquaintance, relatives and neighbours should say "this is good, this we should also do" By doing such act, there is gain in this world and in the next. There is infinite merit through the gift of "dhamma" "*

King Ashoka founded many hospitals (including hospitals for animals-certainly a first for the whole world), ensured free supply of medicines, planted trees along the roads, got the water wells dug for villages not having access to river water, got rest houses constructed at bigger roads for stay of travellers, got drinking water points operated at pilgrimage sites and initiated many such other public conveniences throughout his empire. This is indeed the idealistic empire reflected in perfect world of "*Ram Rajya*" so highly praised towards the end in Ramayana.

Coming back to edicts, there are a total of 19 rock edicts and nine pillar edicts found across India, Nepal, Pakistan and Afghanistan. Interestingly, Iranian artisans carried out stone carving for many of these edicts. These edicts also had carvings for bulls and elephants, which is like a continuation from Sindhu Sarasvati Culture. Love of the King for animals has been exhibited in the writings advising public to exercise refrain from killing animals as he himself did. Conspicuous absence is for any text out of Vedas or rituals and any reference to caste or class; a complete disconnect with Vedic tradition. One obvious reason is that the dynasty originated and flourished in Magadha where Vedic traditions were never so strong as these were in the hinterland of Ganga Yamuna. It is not to say that Vedic traditions had not reached to that part in east of India. These have certainly reached but history suggests that the basic mood of society from Magadha was more inclined towards Buddhism ideals rather than Vedic ideals.

He addressed issues of Buddhism in the presence of Buddhists. He also held third Buddhist council at Patliputra, his capital. But there is nothing to say that he didn't talk about Hinduism amidst Hindu thinkers. His dhamma (not to be identified with Buddhist dhamma) was to support all religious thoughts. Perhaps it will not be out of place to brand him a real secular ruler. If his mention is found more in Buddhist literature it is because they were engaged in documenting everything about their religion and were better financed and organized for documenting. Hinduism on the other hand, never had documenting as their strong point. Actually, Hinduism was still not around. What were there were Vedic systems and we have already discussed about its pathetic condition at that time.

But soon after death of King Ashoka in 232 BC, India directly entered in its dark age where one does not come across any document or evidence of happenings until the time when Gupta Dynasty took roots in 320 CE. In the interim period of chaos, many socio political changes took place in and around India. Regional kingdoms of smaller sizes came in existence in North, East and Central India. Greek invaders of Bactria took control of Afghanistan right upto the seashore down south. Then came Iranian and Central Asian fighters in the same territory held by Bactria. The impact of these foreigners was felt culturally more on non-Vedic people as Vedic people treated them unclean and maintained their distance. During 200 BC to 200 AD, India saw Jainism and Buddhism going to its peak and achieving deepest reach in the society and maximum following. Since, both these faiths were evolving out of the total social spectrum, whatever they gained was at the cost of Hinduism.

Resurrection of Classical Hinduism

Popularity gained by Buddhism and Jainism, must have been the pressing situation culminating in resurrection of classical

Hinduism and forcing it to reinvent itself to address aspirations of common man. By this time, Hinduism had made its move from Vedic rituals to worship of main Gods comprising trinity of *Brahma,* Vishnu, Mahesh together with personal Ishta devas such as Ganesha and Durga, Laxmi, Parvati and Sarasvati, etc. Competing sects of Hindus gained very fast popularity as colourful deities of Gods installed in various temples attracted commoner much closely than purity of *mantra* in difficult Sanskrit verses which had become so difficult to comprehend. Diverse people of India, evolving under cultural baggage of the past, would also have enjoyed the freedom of worshipping various Gods with human forms, in direct contrast of faceless *Brahman,* which they found much closer to them. This process has been experienced in many other civilizations as well that every time one type of Gods failed to respond to public perceptions, Gods underwent a radical change. In any case, religious movements are found to succeed in compelling circumstances when there are perceptions of something missing from the lives of followers.

Around this time, Indian Religion had changed to become theistic as people started inventing extravagant temples and colourful deities and processions. Regular pilgrimages started for seeking blessings from brilliantly crafted and decorated deities with multiple images of God. By this time, the Indian culture had almost completed its shift from *mantra* to statues.

Some Gods got popular with different names and different forms to ensure easy identification with populace of a particular part or social group or cultural background. But Shiva and Vishnu came out most popular Gods having wider disciples. This can be safely concluded as emergence of less developed faiths of masses after submerging of the religion of elite, the classical Vedic system of *Brahman* achievable only either by highly elaborate ritual systems to be performed by select priests or by even more learned Rishis and Yogis practising conquering the Self by meditating inward.

Coupled with sectarian period, rituals also got simplified and ultimately got to the point where just saying a single word "Aum" and thinking about the proposed activity, the householder was able to complete his rituals without losing the expected benefits. Looks like that even all *Brahmins* were unable to comprehend the intricacies of *Brahmanas* and they would have, intelligent as they always were, promoted the simplified sacrificial rituals to suit the requirements and capabilities of common householder. This flexibility of Hinduism to allow reinvention and continuous adaptability to changing scenario is by far the most important feature of Hinduism helping it to survive as long as it has.

Development of regional kingdoms throughout the territories, later called India, also resulted in churning where earlier language, philosophies and dominance of Vedic period lost supremacy. This was also the period of invasions in India. Greeks (Yavanas), Scythians (Shakas), Bactrians, Parthians continued entering India from North West. All these invaders were called barbarians or unclean (mlecchas).

This period is also known for rich cultural integration. Chaos is known to throw unexpected solutions. Throughout the world, such periods have inspired scholars to pool their combined knowledge together against common enemy to preserve their culture for future generations. Especially in religious and social context, chaotic situation is feared only by orthodox and considered as creative opportunity by unorthodox. As such, this period saw a lot of work done for arts and literature. Icons like Buddhist Stupas at Amravati containing stone carvings depicting everyday life is a good example together with some great literature composed during this period.

Arrival of Kushans from central Asia and their penetration right up to Varanasi in the east, resulted in their empire between 78 to 144 CE. King Kanishka (112-144 CE), who was a Buddha follower himself, gave boost to allure conversions to Buddhism. He got biggest stupa constructed at Peshawar as his state capital. But Kushans were also supportive of other religions and are known to have used deities of Hindus, Zoroastrian and Bactrian for minting their coins. This is the time when maximum work got carried out relating to Buddhist part of the carvings at caves located at Bhaja, Karle, Nasik, Ajanta, Ellora which were largely Buddhist sites. Buddhism and Jainism were still competing with Hinduism but peacefully.

11
Comments on Major Shastras

The period of Gautama Buddha and Mauryan Empire was the historical background in which both epics of Mahabharata and Ramayana together with major *Shastras* got composed. The *Shastras*, for the first time, talked about all aspects of full life of a human. The very nature of this literature was different from Vedic literature in terms of matter, spirit, language and forms. Vedic literature was largely liturgical or philosophical while from now onward, the theme will get abundantly developed in all directions of human life. Most important *Shastras* requiring specific discussions cover all-important subjects of Dharma, Artha and Pleasure by the names of '*Dharma Shastra*', '*Artha Shastra*' and '*Kama Shastra*'. Others that could also be included are *Charak Samhita* covering the entire gamut of *Ayurveda, Vastu* and *Shilpa Shastra*, etc. Let us touch upon the main three *Shastras* one by one.

Dharma Shastra

These *Shastras* are primarily focused on *Brahmins* who are creators, consumers and administrators of these texts. Subject matter is Dharma and focus is to let a *Brahmin* know as to how he should conduct himself during his entire lifetime. Dharma principles of these texts are generally accepted by Buddhists and Jains alike but with varying interpretations (strong view about *Ahimsa* being the single most divergent point of difference).

The basic Sutras forming part of these *Shastras* are by Appastamba, Gautama, Baudhayana and Vashishtha which, like a guide book, mentioned dos and don'ts for all stages of life of a human, duties of kings, judicial matters and personal conduct like diet, penance, daily oblations, funerals, offences, etc. These are prime texts establishing authority for *varna vyavastha, asrama vyavastha,* principles of *dharma* and law of karma. In total eighteen *Shastras* are included under '*Dharma Shastra*' but most important of these are:

1. Manu Smriti (200 BC to 200 CE),
2. Yajnavalkya Smriti (200 to 500 CE), and
3. Narada Smriti (100 BC to 400 CE).

Manu is called the fore father of entire human race and crediting *Manu Smriti* (also called Manav Dharma Shastra) to his name suggest that it was not composed by a single author and must have been compiled by various contributors over a good long period of time. *Manu Smriti* details out very elaborate and clear laws, rules and codes of conduct to be applied to an individual, whole community and entire kingdoms. That is why *Manu Smriti* can be called a foundation of Hindu Social Law.

There are a total of twelve chapters each contributed to different subject matter which include what to eat, whom to meet and avoid, roles of different classes under the caste system, responsibilities of person at different stages of life, how to control woman, duties of a King to properly govern his kingdom, etc. Details included for what 'not to do' include people to be avoided from personal contact, people excluded from teaching Veda, women not to be married with, people not to be invited for specific ceremony, people whose food is not to be eaten, people who do not qualify to be a witness, sons getting disqualified from inheritance, mixed castes to be excluded from social contacts, crimes resulting in getting one's own class degraded.

Manu Smriti was also making a big shift in positioning women completely as subordinate to man from her earlier position of being subservient. Manu is known for his harshness towards women like never before. Provision after provision carry very adverse comments about their lustfulness and Manu (all other composers of the text included) makes it look like wherever women get an opportunity, some bad thing is about to happen. He blames them for having a nature to seduce the men in this world. He goes to the extent of advising wise men not to sit alone with even their mother, daughter or sister saying that carnal desires are very strong and such company can lead to temptations. *Manu Smriti* also provides for number of points for types of women to marry and not to marry and provisions relating to inter class marriages with most provisions favouring higher classes and suppressing the lower classes. It is quite saddening but it contains many derogatory views about women for modern times.

But it would not be correct that all the provisions were mandatory for all concerned; there were many other materials that were accepted as proper guide to social traditions of their areas of influence. However, British rulers adopted *Manu Smriti* as applicable social code to govern Hindus in their raj as people like Robert Clive and Lord Macaulay came to conclusion that it would help them make Hindus subjugate.

Manu also writes a lot about addictions and its dangers. One of his paragraphs completely sums up Hindu's continued thought about addictions:

> "All ten *vyasans* arising out of lust/desire end up badly—hunting, gambling, sleeping during day, malicious gossip, women, drunkenness, singing, dancing and aimless wandering...drinking, gambling, women and hunting, in that order, are universally addictive, each vice is more serious than the one that follows ".

Manu Smriti's highlight was establishing supremacy of *Brahmins,* sanctity to caste system, treating women under strict vigil and lower status to Dalits. It is unfortunate that some of these tendencies can still be traced in modern Hinduism, which is still struggling for providing proper respect to women and true equality to all Hindus alike.

Artha Shastra

Artha Shastra comprises of detailed literature on statecraft, economic policies, military strategies, and bureaucratic framework for administering the kingdom and taxation policies for welfare of people. Some people assign the authorship to Kautilya and many other say that Kautilya is same as Chanakya, the scholar of Takshashila and minister of Chandargupt Maurya. But the kingdom referred in Artha Shastra is much smaller in size than the Maurya Empire had. Many policies perfected by Gupta period get written here. So, it should not be hard to assume that Chanakya was not the composer; his policies and doctrines, however, have been well borrowed and explained in Artha Shastra.

Artha Shastra discusses the theory and principles of governing a state in very direct and street-smart ways and keeps out statecraft out of bounds of morality or reasonability. Like it advises the ruler to use any and every means at his disposal to achieve his goal without bothering any morality attached as a king's action require no moral sanction. Similarly, it suggests that a ruler should always treat his next-door kingdom as his enemy and should make friendship with his another enemy to keep him in check.

It talks about realism and not idealism as a tool to manage economics. Therefore it proclaims that:

> "Wealth will slip away from that childish man who constantly consults the stars: the only (guiding) star of wealth is wealth itself; what can the stars of the sky do? Man, without wealth, does not get it even after a hundred attempts. Just as elephants are needed to catch elephants, so does wealth capture more wealth."

The subject matter is approached very directly and practically. For example, it advises the ruler as to what kind of people should be used to spy on the enemy's military, keep close eye on the activities of crown prince lest he falls for bad company or how to keep a close vigil on checking any premature ambition of his sons before they are able to plan anything silly against the king. It considers economics and foreign policy as a zero sum game. It is all about real politics as it says that keeping check on the corruption by people within the government is like 'discovering how much water is drunk by the fish in a pond'.

In addition to matters of statecraft, it also comments on social codes like kind of marriages, list of vices (lust, anger, greed, conceit, arrogance and foolhardiness). Many of these concepts reflect the mood of *Manu Smriti*, especially when it comes to social norms and class system. But the view point on all such issues also stamped being focused on head of states.

In the same spirit, Artha Shastra invokes worship of Brihaspati and Shukra who were earlier non descript teachers of Gods and Antigods for the subjects of Science and Politics. Before Artha Shastra, the only place having some passing reference to these Gurus also appears is Mahabharata. The very need of such a *Shastra* was new to Gupta period as the subjects of Politics were never under direct scanner in Indian thoughts before that time.

Keeping in line with most of the earlier scriptures, Artha Shastra also provides prime of place to *Brahmins* in all matters relating to administration of states. *Brahmins* influence on Indian societies was too strong to ignore as they were considered intellectual and strategic elite of the entire society. Their mere presence in large proportions in matters of state administration was said to provide a good marriage between Dharma and Artha; another preference for realism over idealism. In fact, Artha Shastra advocated extending many exemptions like payment of taxes and access to state resources for elite *Brahmins*.

It also carries some references to foreign invasions which happened post Gupta dynasty only. Some of the policies mentioned have guided successive rulers in past and are relevant even today. Considering all factors, it is safe to assume that it is a compilation of number of earlier texts written by several authors, and in all probability, Chanakya would have been one of the source as a Professor of Economics at Takshashila.

But soon after the composition of this *Shastra*, the configuration of society and kingdoms would have gone substantial changes rendering the popularity of this *Shastra* next to nothing. It is because of this reason that Artha Shastra went into long oblivion before it got rediscovered about two hundred years ago. But clearly, some of the points touched upon in this document are relevant for practising real politics even today albeit in much more diplomatic manner.

Kama Shastra

The subject of human passions (sexual passions included) has been dealt by most human civilizations in varying proportions. Indian civilization also has not been an exception to this rule. Like the other *Shastra* on different subjects, here again, we find many great works covering this subject in great details. The main compositions under this subject are:

1. *Ratirahsya* by Kukkoha,
2. *Panchasakya* (also called by alternate name of Jyotirisha) by Vaschitorma,
3. *Smara Pradipa* by Gunakara,
4. *Ratimanjari* (Garland of Love) by Jayadeva,
5. *Kok Shastra/Kam Shastra* by Bhanudatta, and
6. *Anaga Ranga* (Stage of Love) by Kullianmull.

The length of these books range from 400 verses to 1200 verses. Jyotirisha is best known for the famous sixty-four positions as well as first genuine book on various teachings on music as a science. The first book, *Ratirahsya* contains, among other issues, categorization of women in four distinct types, namely, Padmini, Chitrini, Shankini and Hastini. The description of each of these goes quite into details. Just for reference, let us look at description of the first type, Padmini:

> *"She is in whom the following sign and symptoms appear—is called Padmini; her face is pleasing as the full moon, her body well clothed with flesh, is soft as the mustard flower, her skin is fine, tender and fair as the yellow lotus. Her eyes are bright and beautiful, well cut and having red corners. Her bosom is hard, full and high; she has good neck; her nose is straight and lovely shaped and three folds of wrinkle cross her middle-about the umbilical region. Her yoni resembles as the opening lotus bud and her love seed is perfumed like the lily that has newly burst. She walks with swan like gait and her voice is low and musical as the note of Kokila bird, she delights in white garments, in fine jewels and rich dress. She eats little, sleeps lightly and being as respectful and religious as she is clever and courteous, she is ever anxious to worship and to enjoy the conversation of Brahmins. Such, then is the Padmini (Lotus Woman).*

The details are numerous and the subject matter has been dealt with, at the same time, as science and art. But the most popular book on the subject certainly the most talked about book on erotica and certainly considered a manual of everything sexual is *Kama Sutra* by Vatsyayan. But it will be interesting to note that *Kama Sutra* had remained in oblivion for most part of its existence. It so happened that some researcher was studying Ananga Ranga and was curious to find many references made to a name called Vatya as an expert or an authority on the subject.

While undertaking search on his works, all main libraries in Mumbai, Kolkata, Jaipur and Varanasi were checked and separate texts were traced attributed on the same title. Later, with the help of a Sanskrit expert, the texts were combined with the help of 'Jayamangla' a commentary on *Kama Sutra* by keeping what matched in more than one text and ignoring what didn't. What we have today, under the Kama Shastra dedicated to Vatsyayan, consists of around 1200 shlokas divided into parts, parts divided into chapters into paragraphs, which is more of a redaction than the original.

Interestingly, Vatsyayan is his family name and his first name is not even known. During the composition of *Kama Sutras*, Vatsyayan was leading the life of a religious student at Banaras and was in full contemplation of his *Ishta deva*. The book is basically an encyclopedia or compendium or a full-fledged thesis on all matters related to passion of love and sex. This work is not to be taken as an instrument of satisfying desires at all. On the contrary it is like walking through the gigantic maze of an activity, which is supposed to come to humans naturally as hunger to all living beings. But after reading this book, one may get surprised as to how little he/she knew about this subject. The book also declares right in the beginning that success will come only to that person who attends to the main objectives in life in the priority of Dharma, Artha and Kama without becoming slaves of his passions. (Burton, 1883)

Similar to Dharma Shastra and Artha Shastra, Kama Shastra is also grounded to the entire subject with practical orientation and provides detailed guidance to the populace to attain enjoyment and fulfillment. Again, it is not to be taken as the very first composition of its kind as Vatsyayan is found referring to around ten previous authors on the subject and borrows from their concepts and findings exactly in the same manner in which today's researcher quotes from other earlier sources to lend credence to his work.

Interestingly, *Kama Sutra* ignores any reference to social classes and all it necessitates to go for the enjoyment is money. Also, *Kama Sutra* advocated meat eating as a normal part of ordinary human life while *Dharma Shastra* recommends eating meat only under specified situations. *Kama Sutra* deals with all aspects of human sexual behaviour. Written in prose, it has many poems also inserted in between. It is wrong to take it as a sex manual as considered by many in the West. On the contrary, *Kama Sutra* deals with ideas for a virtuous and satisfied/blessed life by discussing nature of love, family life and aspects relating to normal pleasure oriented faculties of human life.

Regarding the period of its composition, one major reference is traced to a king who ruled around 100 CE giving an indication that it is surely composed after that period. Taking other such references and the style of language and comments about social systems, experts conclude that *Kama Sutra* would have been composed around 300 CE.

Let us now look at some important parts of this book. We begin with very definition of *Kama*, as explained in the second part as:

> *"It is enjoyment of appropriate object by the five senses of hearing, feeling, seeing, tasting and smelling, assisted by the mind and soul. The ingredient in this is a peculiar contact between sense organ and its object and the consciousness of pleasure which arises from that contact is called Kama"*

In its true approach as a detailed compendium, *Kama Sutra* lists out arts that are desired to be studied together with *Kama*. The composers of *Kama Sutra* prescribe obtaining perfection in many arts to perfect art of *Kama* and this shows their level of thinking. The Arts requiring perfection by a lady aiming success in *Kama* and as mentioned in the original serial are—singing, playing musical instrument, dancing, combining the previous three arts together, drawing/writing, tattooing, adorning idols, arranging beds and flowers around bed, colouring teeth garments and hair, fixing stained glasses, making beds with arranging cushions for comfort and reclining, playing music with water filled glass, storing waters in reservoirs, making trimming and decorating pictures, making rosaries necklaces and garlands, making of various kind of turbans, stage playing, ear ornament arts, art of perfuming and odours and several such other arts totaling to sixty four categories. Main of the other arts listed includes solving riddles, mimicry, carpentry, architecture, and knowledge of gold and silver coins, calligraphy, mental exercises, composing poems, gambling and knowledge of rules of the society. A lady who was well versed in all these arts was called "Ganika" who enjoyed a high place in society and was respected by kings and praised by learned men. How is anyone to conclude that *Kama Sutra* is all about sex?

In a series of many such detailed listings, there are list of signs from woman which are to be taken by men as signs of rejections (list of 24 points), list of men who generally obtain success with women (total of 24 types), types of women who can be gained easily (total of 41), list of excuses which can be deployed by a woman to get money out of his man (list of 27) and list of ways to get rid of unwanted man by a woman (list of 28 points). These are just a few examples of the great details in which the book has covered its subject matter. Again, looking at this book just as a guide to sexual positions is but demeaning. Finally, the *Kama Sutra* compares the passion with an uncontrolled horse. It says that people engaged in this lust pay no attention about its dangers. But in the next line itself it says,

> *"However, to guard against such dangers, do read Kama Sutra and use your own head (intelligence)."*

12
The Mahabharata and Ramayana

Historical Perspective of the Period of their Compositions

The period of 300 BC to 300 CE has been very defining period for Hinduism. The period saw a complete circle of rise and fall of great empire followed by a period of chaos where a lot of disintegration and consolidations emerged and vanished with little stability. But the good thing is that actual happenings of this period are well documented, well recorded and can be corroborated even with independent sources from within and outside Indian subcontinent. Besides literature, also available are inscriptions, coins, monuments, etc. to support the reliability of the historical facts. There are also reports from Greek and Chinese visitors along with their impressions to carve out a rather independent analysis. I say so because when you read about a single incident in Buddhist, Jain or Hindu books, many times you sense conflicting views because, after all, these were competing faiths eyeing a common audience and partisan views can't be ruled out especially when you have been holding one of the three local faiths dearer to you for most part of your life. But comments from out of the country visitors can easily be taken as non-partition and from a different impartial angle. This certainly helps in having better informed understanding about the subject matter.

Mahapadma Nanda, a barber by birth, founded first non-Kshatriya dynasty and waged war with many Kshatriya kingdoms.

Chandragupta Maurya, himself a *Vaishya*, took over from him with the help of Kautilya, a *Brahmin* by birth. A potter, *Shudra* by class, based in Varanasi, has become one of the richest businessmen of his time. Later Pushyamitra, a *Brahmin* commander of army took control of Gupta Dynasty and formed his own Shunga Dynasty. The scene is just to highlight that traditional views of clear segregation of class provided by Vedas have lost boundaries by this time and social structures were in shambles, traditional rituals and sacrifices had lost major attraction with the populace, Buddhism and Jainism were spreading through the length and width of the country; a lot of churning was taking place in entire social spectrum of the country.

Brahmins had accumulated a lot of land holdings out of regular donations received for their work as priests conducting royal rituals or as members of the courts or as teachers and philosophers or gifts by kings. Most of these lands required manual hands for cultivating or mending, which could be secured only from lower class which has been, until so far, kept out from social structures. *Brahmins* were desperate to lure working class people to work at their lands. Buddhism was on the rise in acceptance as Dalits and woman had, for the first time, some mainstream religion, which was ready to take them in its strides. Since no one was promoting Hinduism, many landowners, merchants, high officials, common artisans had started joining either Jainism or Buddhism. The decline in popularity of Vedic culture was slow to begin with but, by now, it had reached the do or die situation.

Hinduism also saw some dilution in its strict past practices and again started allowing woman to participate in rituals. Some *Shastras* of the time actually recommended conducting many rituals only with spouse—some relaxation but still a far cry. *Artha Shastra* may not have been composed as yet but one of its principles that every kingdom on your border is your enemy was already in practice. For peace to exist, presence of a major force is must. If there is no central powerful authority, smaller forces feel threatened all the time and remain active in consolidating their position leading to a general psychic causing the smaller kingdoms remaining engaged in wars with their neighbouring states almost regularly. This doctrine has remained relevant in all cultures and at all times.

Just to recapitulate the scenario, economy and trade were flourishing, professions were competing, widened economic divide was bigger than ever, urban rural divide was also on the rise, all three home grown faiths were competing for political patronage and donations, Vishnu and Shiva had emerged as bigger Gods pushing animal sacrifice and rituals to back ground, society was churning with political configurations, Patliputra had emerged a critical centre for controlling trade, minerals, forest products, agriculture products as well as largest education centre in the world, Greek forces had retracted but had left behind many traders at Gandhar who were expanding trade with India and China.

It was under this background that the long poems of Mahabharata and Ramayana got composed. Both these epics of Hindus, all the way from that time onwards, contain enormous number of morality based stories serving as perfect example to let people learn how to live and conduct themselves under various testing situations of real life. These were aimed for laymen who were always sensitive about their religious duties, householder's duty as well as wish to achieve salvation without taking the route of renunciation. Unlike other *Shastras* composed around that period (and addressed needs of elite groups engaged in higher level learning), these epics were in narrative form and their messages, morals and lessons are simpler enough to be comprehended by a common man. As many people were still not so well educated, such people understood these poems simply by listening from others. Further, these were in form of small sub-stories helping people to better connect with these as against abstract way of older religious literature.

Both these long poems mark major transition from *Shruti* literature to *Smriti* literature. Both these got initiated for the benefit of warriors on the battleground. During war days, the warriors retired in the evenings and had a lot of time for nursing their wounds, taking massaging for relaxation and drinking dining to get rejuvenated for next battle.Warriors also had a lot of time during the peace days when they were simply travelling or camping or practising their martial arts. The people reported to popularize these stories among warriors as well as others, initially, were charioteers who use to play double roles as confidante, friend, motivator, and critique for their masters. Like caddies role at Golf courses where many of them tend to pick up finer points of the trade and become proficient for applying all ground rules and extending expert's advise to the players, many charioteers found the stories and sub stories of these epics as best media for conveying the points to the warriors they served.

Post wars, these people would do the same in peace time and entertain villagers or at festival celebrations. Later still, the *Brahmins* took over the reciting and improvising of these poems. *Brahmins*, who were also officiating at sacrifices, pilgrimage routes and at shrines, contributed towards the spreading popularity of these poems to far off places. These routes and shrines were the points attracting sufficiently large audience having a good mix from different parts of the subcontinent. As the medium was very catchy, language simple and incidences reflecting real life incidents, the plots were gaining popularity like forest fire. The main plots were completely fictional but these were so well packaged with names of the cities, geographical details, gods, Vedic stories all woven to make look as absolute real stories. The broader themes were 'good winning over evil', 'pleasant over unpleasant' and 'dharma winning over adharma'.

All said and done, no one can take away the fact that these epics have served Hindus very well by inculcating deep sense of reverence, devotion and commitment to the path of righteousness and belief and interest in life beyond. By personifying many characters and personalities, the events highlighted helped the reader or listeners for easier comprehension and prompted them to develop sense of differentiating between right and wrong, between good and evil and between appropriate and inappropriate.

Broadly speaking the basic teachings advocated in these poems are similar to those mentioned by *Dharma Shastras* of Hindus but the packaging and presentation is entirely different. In addition, the poetic medium necessitated and facilitated use of many idioms and arguments which, already familiar to the masses, appealed them instantly and gained acceptance of public at large.

Now let us dwell upon these poems one by one.

Mahabharata

Most definitely the longest poem of the world, the Sanskrit version credited to Vyasa Muni, contains about 75000 verse, three million words and about 15 times in size to Hebrew Bible. But the whole of the material available under the title is very fluid as hundreds of different versions, in different languages, giving different importance to characters, incidents and arguments are found in different parts of the country. The number just multiplies once the verbal versions are also get added. Many commentators, for this reason, call it a work in process.

Let us recall the Mahabharata serial being shown some 25 years back on Indian TV on every Sunday morning bringing the entire nation to halt for one hour. It used to start proclaiming

> *"main samay huin. mera janm samay ke saath hua.......main pichhale yug main tha, ees yug main hoon aur aanewale yug main bhi rahunga......"*

Which actually means that unlimited in age and space, time is eternal and infinite. Poets have told it before, telling it now and will also tell it in future ... meaning that multiplicity and multi-versions are integral part of the story and very well accepted since the very beginning.

It is historical narrations having a very loose main plot with so many sub plots getting discussed that the main story needs to be recollected, sometimes with efforts. A number of sub stories are remotely linked to the plot and looks like an after thought forced in an attempt to establish connectivity with some past incident or character or for justifying/providing credence to actions of the main actors of main plot. The focus is to show that every normal living person has weaknesses and limitations and is prone to deviate from the right path recommended for him by *Shastras*. Undoubtedly, this argument is certainly to point to the holes in the teachings and efficacy of Buddhism and Jainism who were engaged in teaching non-violence and idealism at that very time of history. The Mahabharata deals with innumerable testing conditions where it is practically difficult for a normal person to survive without making some twists and turns to the established virtuous behaviour. As far as the main plot goes, it is but a fight of succession within the family where situations take complex turns and forces group of claimants to stand before each other leading to violent confrontation. This is a very common situation and most people were simply able to relate to either sides looking to get bigger size of the cake.

The sub stories would have certainly been initiated in oral tradition, as was a common tradition of that time. After some acceptance and liking, the same would have induced writers to consign the portions into writings. Such writings were again giving rise to more verbal popularization and so on. The iterations of verbal and writing would have remained continued for generations with each contributor adding carved pieces and polished gemstones and widening the mosaic in all directions. We will later see the same pattern being followed for scripting another great volume of scriptures, the *Puranas*. Looking to the large volume of material under discussion, surely, no single author would have lived long enough to put it all together.

This was yet another beautiful example of people who have remained in conversation with each other over generations, knew each other well, had full empathy for others, adopting sub plots from other contributors and than building over such borrowed plots, bringing even silent partners to be part of conversation, listen to every new situation in social life and come forward with new solutions without losing connection with the set of traditions and constantly holding on the main plot. Are we not reminded instantly of Wikipedia? Indeed, the way final shape of Mahabharata has been floating in the history, Wikipedia seems to be based exactly on that very pattern with the exception that contributions in Wikipedia are only written whereas Mahabharata absorbed contributions both in written and verbal forms. Another feature of Mahabharata is liberal absorption of numerous recycled Vedic incidents with newer adaptations.

Multi dimensions of the main story allowed enough space for the new contributors to bring in hybrid narratives. The strong cultural traditions supported the integrity of the text, which allowed the rubbish getting thrown out, and good material being absorbed in the main text. The ground rules for making contributions would have been restricted to simple points like supremacy and infallibility of Vedic injunctions. While one could reinterpret the Vedic stories or provide an extension to that but no one could counter or go against the basic spirit which has been included any where in Vedic literature. In spite of this, there are few contradictions remaining in the final product but it is safe to take such situations as genuine irresolvable issues beyond the capacity of composers reflecting internal dilemma of human nature.

Reflecting prevailing social condition, Mahabharata provides many references where key characters are shown justifying violence. At one place Arjuna tells Yudhishthira after being questioned for an unwanted killing—

> *"people honour many gods who are killers. Rudra has resorted to killings and so is the case with Skanda, Indra, Agni, Varuna, Yama. I don't see anyone in this world with non-violence."*

These sentiments seem building an argument against total non-violence promoted by Buddhism at around that very time in history. Then we got Gita. This appears a very smart move by *Brahmin* redactors to insert a text that accepted political violence of the real world as an inevitable truth ... and in a way projects Hinduism as more practical faith in comparison to Jainism or Buddhism. The insertion of Gita in the centre of the battle-field is like a direct confrontation with others as to what they will say now?

Taking as a direct borrowing from life of King Ashoka who was really torn between pursuing violence or shunning it altogether (post Kalinga war), the core story of Mahabharata is woven around the dilemma between violence and non-violence. Surely, Hinduism was under pressure to find faults with the complete non-violent doctrine of Buddhism being highlighted at the same point in history. Mahabharata composers need to be complimented for bringing in lots of twists and turns to justify wars occasionally as aunavoidable/inevitable compromise. Surely, real politics and competing kings could not be expected to opt for non-violence completely. But to the credit of this great plot that Mahabharata does not indicate to any one squarely responsible for frequent violence.

Now let us look at some other important points. Many Hindus may not believe that immediately but look at the similarity of the character of Yudhishthira being a replica of Ashoka. King Ashoka who ruled between 269 BC and 233 BC belong to the period just around beginning of circulation of Mahabharata's plot. Undoubtedly, the character of Yudhishthira represents many shades of actual life of King Ashoka. Actually, there are several other parallels between the text of this epic and Ashoka's edicts which cannot be ignored. In any case, writers always had the real life situations reflecting in their writings and a great personality like King Ashoka, who had so significant influence over the society of that time could not have skipped out of their attention.

The dialogues of Arjuna and Krishna at the battlefield expressing his doubts about the war also draw a parallel with dilemma of King Ashoka post Kalinga war. It is like directly advocating the need of violence for the warriors. Bringing in the argument about the soul not getting killed is but a lame duck ploy of authors to cover up the deep disgust against killing prevailing in the general mood of the public at that time. Krishna's answers are also rather abstract and complex. The fact of the matter is that composers are bringing in best out of them to justify violence which is actually against the common man's own perception at that time in the history.

All said and done, Gita is to be considered only for its philosophical context. Its language, its content and quality of teachings could not have happened in the midst of a battle field with millions of soldiers standing lined up waiting for the dialogue between one warrior and his charioteer to get over. Personally, I am inclined to agree with the people holding view that Gita must have been an independent book by itself which either could not get popular of its own or its composers preferred it to piggy ride on the popularity of Mahabharata to get more eyeballs or earholes for that matter and decided to throw it in as a part of War Story of Mahabharata.

At this moment, let us draw some light on the plot of the famous poem.

A fisherman catches a fish, finds a baby girl in her belly and raises her as her daughter—she is Satyawati. A sage seduces her while crossing over the river and impregnates her—the son so born is named Vyasa, the attributed composer of the long poem. He gets abandoned on an island of the river. Illustrious king Shantanu saw Ganga, the river at her own bank and impressed with her beauty, proposes her to marry him. The river Ganga agrees to his proposal. They start living happily but every time she delivers a child, she offers the child to river's current. When Shantanu finally questions her after the eighth child, she leaves the child behind and goes back to be the river. Their eighth child is Bhisma. King Shantanu later falls for Satyawati, gets married, have a son who is married to Ambika and Ambalika but dies without having a child.

To continue the lineage, Satyawati invites her abandoned son Vyas (ugly and unusual physical features and fishy smell) to father children with widows of her deceased second son. In the process of unwanted love making, Ambika keeps her eyes closed to avoid seeing ugly Vyas and gets a blind son, Dhritarashtra. During a repeat of this effort, Ambalika, second wife turns pale and gives birth to a weak child with pale complexion and that is how Pandu is born.

Not satisfied with the results, Satyawati invites Vyas again who is sent to Ambika a second time but she is not willing to go through the ordeal again and, to avoid her own embarrassment, orders her maid to switch place with her. The maid goes through the ordeal with pleasure and makes Vyas very happy and so is born Vidur, the only normal child out of all the efforts. But he is born to a lower class through a dispensable and stand-in maid and so he becomes ineligible to become a *Kshatriya* king. As one can see, Vyas is instrumental in bringing all characters to life and also gets credited as the composer—it is like a single person credited for being producer, brings the main actors into existence (both literally and figuratively), director, writer, narrator and lyricist of a mega movie all by himself.

Going forward, Dhritrastra gets married to Gandhari and together they are blessed with one hundred sons. Actually, Gandhari delivered a still lump after two years of pregnancy. But Vyasa cut that lump into hundred pieces and each of that pieces was put in *ghee* (refined butter) filled jar for two more years before the boys were taken out of the jars. Who says that surrogacy is already fully developed; the science of procreation has a long way to go before catching up with the imaginations of composers of Mahabharata.

The weak and pale boy is named Pandu and gets married to Kunti and Madri. To make the matters worse, he is also cursed to die no sooner he makes love to any woman. Fortunately, Kunti knows the art of seeking pregnancy with divine Gods as she is shown having already tried her boon or knowledge during her younger days when she mistakenly invoked Surya who, in spite of her refusal makes her maiden mother of a son. For protecting her respect and name and for coming out of the shame of being unwedded mother, she is shown to desert the child by flowing in the river. A charioteer and his wife ultimately raise this boy. They name him Karna.

With need of the hour (plight of Pandu) and guided by past experience, Kunti separately invokes *Dharma, Vayu* and *Indra* to be blessed with sons named Yudhishthira, Bhima and Arjuna respectively. She also shares her secret art with Madri who invites Aswins (twin brothers) in pair and was blessed with twins who are named Nakula and Sahadeva. Interestingly, all these Gods are not to become fathers in their divine life (due to some curse). But Mahabharata allows them this possibility. The combination of 'curse' and 'boon' work like trump cards and are always available to be used by composers everytime they get stuck in a tight situation. In addition of helping the receiver to come clean of tight situations, the mythological expansion of any such boon gives further sub stories to expand the ever stretching mosaic of mythological literature of this period. The proverb of "one things leads to another" is not sufficient and needs to be changed to "one thing leads to many others".

The number of events of seductions, forced sex, sex among human and animal, surrogating, illegal impregnation, pre wedlock child birth, inter racial sex, etc., in addition to greed for power and wealth, again goes to indicate the troubled social situations of that time. Any literary creation is known to reflect the prevailing chaos on the social stage of the time of its creation and our Mahabharta is no exception to that rule.

The addition of Draupadi brings more twist to the interesting beginning. She emerged during the *yajna* performed by Drupada to avenge his defeat at the hands of Arjuna on behalf of Drona. She is described as divinely beautiful girl with shiny black locks, shiny nails, soft eyes lashes, swelling breasts, shapely thighs and a compelling complexion ... the story goes that in her previous life she desired fourteen qualities in her husband from Lord Shiva. And since even God Shiva was unable to find all those qualities in one single person, she is blessed to have five husbands, who among all of them do possess the fourteen virtues desired by Draupadi. But to save her from being polyandry, she is blessed with a boon to have her virginity restored after every sexual encounter. She comes out a lady of her own mind as she dares to remind Karna, at her *Swayamwara* when Karna also gets up to take aim at the eye of the moving fish by seeing its shadow in the oil below, of being a son of charioteer and stops him from trying his luck and thus picks up a life time animosity with him.

Again reflecting social customs of those days, Mahabharata shows many women having multiple partners, inside or outside the marital bliss. And it was not the women alone as many men also have been described as having multiple partners. All the Pandavas, except the eldest, have wives other than Draupadi. Arjuna has three. This goes to suggest that in that time of the history, at least in *Kshatriyas*, polygamy was common.

I don't wish to narrate too much for the main story is well known. Thanks to non-stop screening of many TV serials by the same name and many other movies which still get immense viewership and regularly bind people to the TV sets in most Hindu households or movie halls, as the case may be. But I must share a few of the many injustice stories contained therein.

Most dramatic figure of entire Mahabharata, of course, is Krishna Vasudeva. He is Lord Vishnu incarnated in human form and is shown to have descended to the earth to establish the Dharma and ensure Right and Virtues winning over Wrong and Bad deeds. He meets Pandavas at the time of Draupadi's marriage and starts working as their advisor almost instantaneously. He arranges situation wherein Arjuna marries his sister and finally Krishna is shown as a mentor and charioteer of Arjuna all through the war days. Interestingly, the character of Krishna is portrayed as some one who on one hand is trying to avoid war and let the peace has its chance while on the other hand he is shown at several instances as someone very eager to see that war is not avoided and some one who uses Pandavas as his human instruments for fulfilling that desire.

Tragically, the Epic paints Lord Krishna as an active agent for carrying out many clever strategies which result in killing of Bhisma, Drona as well as Karna, each of whom were supreme commander of Duryodhana's army. Krishna is shown convincing time and again that these methods are just and fine and necessitated by the circumstances at hand, an argument for a very short term view on situations which is diametrically opposite to the teachings of Sanatan Dharma. This will allow many wrongs to get justified in later Hinduism. Basic idea of the composers was that assuming a perfect human being, as suggested by Buddha or Mahavira, is incomplete and real life situations required a vicious and flexible character like Krishna to help his followers.

This ethical gap remained unresolved well until the end of war where both sides can be held responsible for committing numerous violations of established social laws. As an effort of recovering from ugly situation, Bhisma is shown teaching morality from his death bed including duties and responsibilities of a good king which among other things, justifies violence of war, the ambiguity of righteousness in normal circumstances and the corrective practice of *Moksha* that transcends the opposite forces of good vs. bad, right vs. wrong and pleasant vs. unpleasant. It is a different matter that his real life has many instances where he failed to practise what he preached.

Beside the main plot, there are ample stories involving just and not so just actions at the hands of many characters of the main plot. One such tale of injustice is of Ekalavya, son of a Nishad chieftain. He self learned archery and excelled in his art to the extent that both Drona and Arjuna got scared of his powers. As the story goes, Drona demanded 'guru dakshina' of his right thumb to ensure that the poor guy can never stand in competition with Arjuna. Drona, a seasoned and learned *Brahmin* is clearly at fault of being partisan. Why should he demand a tuition fee when in reality there was never a tuition given? How Arjuna is to be remembered as a great archer of all times if he gets scared from a self trained jungle prince?

The reason is that Eklavya is a man with great commitment, clean heart, full of benevolence and a clear consciousness but he is from a lower class of society. Just because he is a Nishad, higher-class people can manipulate him without many tears being shed for him. If this was indeed the accepted social norm at that time, no wonder Hinduism is blamed for suppressing lower classes at the pleasure of higher classes. It is a different matter that the society had to pay a great price in later centuries when the entire society got weakened and allowed the external invaders to come in and loot the treasures.

Now comes the million-dollar question. How many Indians think that Mahabharata is a work of pure fiction and how many believe it to be a stone solid reality? Most people I have come across say that it can't be a fiction altogether as we still have so many evidences to connect with remains and remnants of the actual fight at Kurukshetra. Actually, we have been trained all our life to believe it to be an actual story forcing us to look other way every time situation presents itself to the contrary. Yes, there was Yaduvanshi King Krishna who ruled from Dwarka. Yes, Dwarka has been since found as a coastal city in west Gujarat. Yes, Bharata was a Rig-Vedic clan ruling in and around present day Kurukshetra and there are records that royal race of Kurus were related to Bharatas. The name of Purus is also there in history but not as the relative of Kurus and not originating the way, Mahabharta tells us to be. Surely, there would have been war among competing cousins for establishing supremacy and surely, there were other influential kingdoms like Panchala, Yadus, Tritsus, Gandhar, Mujavats, Magadh, Aryas and many of these were indeed grouped against each other. And their capitals are indeed have have had names as mentioned in the epic but that does not mean that the entire story is real. Infact Bharatas are regarded very high even in *Brahmanas* and have been presented as models of correct conduct.

But that is the beauty of the great plot that it incorporated so many physical symbols, stories and landscapes and its weaving together is so powerful that a pure work of fiction continues to spellbind most Indians and many more outside as a historic reality. But can we ignore literature of Buddhists and Jinas (which do mention all important actual events of the period to which Mahabharta belongs because that history is shared by Hinduism, Buddhism and Jainism as a common heritage) which carry no mention of Kurus and Purus or Krishna? Leaving aside literature of other religions, even all other Vedic scriptures came into being in the interim period of the event of Mahabharata and its compositions, carry no mention of any clues which can be taken as a secondary evidence of any reality to the events mentioned in the epic.

In yet another twist and bringing the Dharma back to life, the end of the story is very disgusting. Many years after the war Dhritrastra, Gandhari and Kunti see the end of their lives in forest as sanyasis, Krishna's unruly clan kills each other and he himself leaves his body in a secluded place. After learning all this, the Pandavas decide to embark great journey by walking to polar mountains in north until they get dead drop one by one including Draupadi. Finally, Yudhishthira is all alone with a dog that followed him all through his journey right up to the gates of heaven. In the final twist of the tale, the dog is shown to be reincarnated God of Dharma who is accepted at heaven along with the Yudhishthira.

Moral of the story is that we should be happy to get what we are blessed with. Aiming for something belonging to others is full of devastating risk of losing everything we have. Also, that we should always seek the help and guidance of God and make him partner in all our endeavours. Let the God be always on our side—except him nothing is permanent. Duryodhana believed that he was his own master and that he owns power and resources to deal with his enemies. If we look around, we will certainly find people who will resort to any means to achieve success and popularity—they don't believe in God or believe that their actions can go unnoticed by the Supreme. Such people have scant respect for relationship, family, traditions and values. They see only money, power, fame and wealth. They will hardly assign credit to others or appreciate contribution by others. Another most important learning from Mahabharta, clearly, is the risk of gambling under any situation. It took away all the wisdom from some one like Yudhishthira, forget about a common soul. Surely, gambling can never produce a winner; ultimately, all the people involved in gambling are destined to be losers.

But Mahabharata deserves the credit of being brutally honest about the human being so frail as it does not shy away from highlighting follies of human characters without any effort to hide or by putting that under the lid. It is for this reason that many people are against study of this great epic lest there is a fight in the family. But most Indians are trained to take it as a scripture and we are genetically tuned to look aside whenever there is a negative side characterized by its characters.

Ramayana

The basic plot of the second epic Ramayana offers models in Dharma. As a main character, Rama is shown as '*Maryada Purushotam*', an ideal role model perfectly founding his entire life as a symbol of *dharma*. He comes out as a perfect child, perfect boy, perfect son, perfect brother, ideal husband, a great warrior and finally a responsible ruler. The female lead of Sita is also depicted as an ideal wife worthy of being emulated by all Hindu women. An epic of about 24000 couplets grouped under a total of seven *Khands* (Chapters), is expected to have been completed and consigned to written text by about 200 CE after having remaining in circulation for about 400 years in total.

Ramayana continues to be told, retold, translated many times ever since. Ramayana has been performed in dance, drama, puppet show, songs, TV serials, movies over last two thousand years and no other story can ever come close to it as a performing media. It is not even required to mention the base story as every child in India can put all major events of Ramayana together in right sequence without a flicker of the eyelids.

There are various versions of when it might have started and how it shaped to the final book. But looking to some disagreements in the text, it is logical to conclude that a single author did not compose it. In order to remain under focus, we will restrict ourselves only on Sanskrit based version credited to Valmiki. Many other vesions have brought in a lot of localisations and are not worth commenting. This argument, unfortunately, applies equally to *Ram-Charit-Manas* by Tulsidas.

According to some estimates, Ramayana got evolved in four distinct phases. In the first phase, before 8th Century BC, it was just a heroic sonnet detailing war between Rama and Ravana. In the second phase, it turned to a smaller size epic under the title *Paulastya Vadh* and continued to be war dominated. The third phase of second to sixth chapters evolved much later which provided a web of story around the war beginning with Rama's exile and culminating right upto killing of Ravana. This entire phase takes Rama more as a normal human with all its good and not so good parts of nature. The last and final phases are said to be addition of the first and last chapters at around 200 CE when the entire divinity gets added to Rama as reincarnation of Vishnu. (Sonawani)

This evolution has genuine appeal to be true even when one tries to analyze it from the quality of language used, interface between humanity and divinity, description of surroundings covered, comments on social set ups deciphered, etc. In addition, the historical background of those times and impacts and counter impacts of competing faiths of the times, also leave their footprint on the expansion of the epic as we see it today.

The poem claims that Rama's administration is as best as it can ever be and the concept of '*Rama Rajya*' continues to be the scale for comparing performance of each and every ruling system. As an ideal state for all its citizens, it is a situation where rains come on proper time, farmers are able to produce abundant grains and other products for all the populace, skies are clear, people are healthy and happy, cities and villages enjoy sufficient population, no living creature get ever sick, no one commits any violation of dharma in private or public sphere, no one dies unnatural death, there are no enemies on the border ... everything is just as ideal as it can be assumed.

This is what we have heard and believed all our life. But if one starts actualizing the real issues on merits and keeping the divinity aside, the description of some key social issues and treatment provided to some key characters in the *Ramayana* by Valmiki does not sound as great. One may come across many not so bright shades as well. Let us try to look upon some of these, with complete open mind, to bring the sensibility and reality to surface even if it may be contrary to what we have felt until now.

To begin with, there are inconsistencies in the story in interplay between mortal and immortal. The character of Rama generally behaves as an immortal and is aware of the purpose of his coming to the earth as an incarnation but there are instances that the character forgets that and start acting just like an ordinary being. As a patch up, Brahma ji is shown reminding him about that to ensure that story doesn't deviate from the path. Of course, it is not difficult to visualize the reason once we understand how the story got evolved through verbal versions over a long period of time. In any text, when you have miscellaneous contributors, some inconsistencies are but natural. These get explained by the fact that entire divinity issue has been added in the text later and by authors who were certainly not the people who had composed the main body.

Actually, the whole concept of incarnation is a bridge between beliefs of Upanishads that each human being is a direct manifestation of supreme *Brahman* on one side. On the other side, we have ideal, complete in all respects but still human like Gods of sectarian period. And going by stories, it is not that Vishnu is the only God who came to earth in human disguise. There are stories where other Gods like Shiva and Indra have all been coming to earth to live like a normal human but those stories could never get as popular as Ramayana and Mahabharata.

Second inconsistency is the beginning where Valmiki inquires from Narada about any person who is most virtuous, valiant, religious, truthful and able to cause terror even among Devas. To which Narada tells Valmiki about Rama of Ikshvaku clan who is an ideal person. It is at that time that Valmiki requests Narada to narrate his deeds and being obliged by Narada, later Valmiki composed Ramayana in lyrical form. Now if Valmiki does not even know about Rama and his deeds, how come he is shown as his contemporary and even receives Sita post her expulsion? (Sonawani)

Avatar is also a Hindu answer to Gautama Buddha and Mahavira. Again, around this time in history, Hinduism has come under pressure of redefining itself. Because of sizeable presence of competing faiths, this was first time that one has to come up with arguments as to how your religion is stronger, realistic, holistic, popular and expansive than the others around the block. So Rama and Krishna got evolved as Hindu Gods with human forms to stand against Buddha and Jaina by becoming human with direct line of divinity, drawing their power from Vishnu (who by this time has become greater than Gods of Vedas) and grounded in humanity.

The fact that both the epics have evolved in Northern India where Lord Vishnu and its sectarian presence was dominant, the Vishnu emerged as main characters leaving behind Shiva who could not get equal representation in these epics. Let us also remember that the entire concept of *Avatars* of Vishnu were yet to be emerged. *Avatars* got popular only around the *Puranas* got composed which was couple of hundred years after final shapes of the epics was complete.

One marked feature of Ramayana is bad light in which women have been depicted. Be it Kaikeyi, Shurpnakha, Manthara (the maid with the hump) and including Sita. Kaikkeyi is like most selfish queen one can ever have who exploits her sexual hold over king to make him fall in her crooked line. Humpy maid Manthara is shown in poor light as a continuation of the curse that she would have been carrying from earlier lives. One comes across many instances in Indian scriptures where physical disability is shown as an effect of wrong karmas carried forward from previous births. Shurpnakha has a license to be insulted and demeaned as she is but a lady ogress. But worst of all is the situation of Sita. She gets into tight situation more than once and has to suffer repeated tests for proving her chastity. One does not come across situations where any male character is also asked to go through similar stereotype ordeals (Doniger, 2009).

First, Ravana forcibly kidnaps Sita against her will (It is unfortunate but the crimes like forcibly conducted abductions of females that we talk as ills of our present day society have existed even in the past). Secondly, Rama doubts her morality for having lived in other person's house for a long time. This is like treating her as an object. Sita is forced to explain that even a thought of any other person has never entered her mind. But after not being believed, she gets frustrated and runs to commits suicide by throwing herself in the fire. Efforts have been made to convert her attempted suicide as a 'Fire Test' but why there is a need of any test to begin with? When was that Hindu scriptures were doubting male promiscuousness? As the story goes, Agni herself lifts her from the fire and brings her to Rama's lap saying that she is absolutely pure. Based on assurance of Agni, Rama accepts the situation and allows her to remain in his life. This was soon after arriving from Lanka with all the war having been fought over Sita.

Later, Rama makes love to her for many days but as he has engaged in sensual indulgence, there must be atonement. He doubts her himself publically and is totally unconcerned about her sufferings. Sita is thrown out of the palace and she has nowhere to go. Finally she reaches the *Ashrama* of Valmiki and seeks shelter and refuge for living incognito. The situation is controlled only by divine direct interaction as none other than Shiva appears in her dream in the form of Dasharatha and consoles her not to worry for being thrown out by Rama and that it will be best in her own interest to prove her purity and the test will make her famous over all other women ever (Doniger, 2009).

Finally, when identity of Luv and Kush gets revealed and Sita is recalled to the palace where she hands over the children to Rama and vanishes into the earth forever. This is like an after thought of the composers to cement a more acceptable departure of Sita. It may sound strange to believers but all through both the epics, no one seems to worry about infidel males but all females are shown as potential infidel. One is bound to feel so sorry for our women to have been treated so badly all through our history. May be there are a couple of shlokas asking people to worship women as Goddesses but surely no one seems going down that lane in the main epics or in most other literature that we say that we are so blessed with.

But to the credit Sita's character, she protests every time she is shortchanged and doesn't take things lying down. Looks like there has been social yearning for such poor treatment to women around the time Ramayana is under completion. She is shown protesting when Rama doesn't want to take her while proceeding on forest service. While in the forest, she questions Rama as to why he is carrying arms while wearing dress of a renouncer. Rama is shown to come up with not so convincing answer that 'well, it for your own safety and that many animals in forest may also need protection'; a lame excuse to a valid objection. This kind of double speak is surely an effort of face saving on part of learned composers. It is yet another example of raising a query in anticipation and providing best possible answer to salvage the situation.

Actually, Sita is a Goddess even from previous birth. Don't forget, she was also not born from any human womb similar to Draupadi of Mahabharata. She is incarnation of mother earth, a Vedic Goddess. Her past galore has not been highlighted lest she comes out a more established character in comparison to Rama who, as an incarnate of Vishnu, is only as stronger as Vishnu himself. And during the composing of Ramayana, Vishnu is still in the making. It is a situation where two people meet on staircase; one who is climbing up (Rama) and the other one pulled down (Sita) (Doniger, 2009).

Incidentally, the end scene enacted for Sita's final departure where she merged back into mother earth, is completely duplicated from a popular story existing in Vedas involving *apsara* Urvashi. In that story also Urvashi is cursed to spend time on earth as mortal with King Pururava but only until she meets both her lover and offspring at the same time. To that extent, the Sita's character is another recycled example like many others.

The episode involving golden deer Maricha is again a reminder that any one engaged in known human weaknesses, like hunting, will lose control on his sense of judgement and will have to face costly consequences. The scene starting with the deer sighting going upto kidnapping is full of nonstop high end dramatics. It starts with ladylove for exotic objects and instant desire to possess what she likes, then the vulnerability for hunting and chasing the kill without considering consequences. This is followed with distrust by the sister-in-law doubting younger brother not going after his elder brother for his lust for her. Soon comes the dramatics of Laxmana rekha, earliest image of a laser rays loaded with explosives. Incidentally, we do not seem to have something to match of that device until today. Then we have illusion expert

Ravana appearing as a sanyasi asking for alms followed by tricky kidnapping and use of Puspak Vimana, the most modern sci-fi gadget of its time which, in terms of flight of imagination will beat any other gadget ever invented in best of James Bond movies (corrected with time, of course).

Treatment meted out to Bali where Rama kills him behind his back is yet another disturbing sub story of Ramayana bringing in more disrepute to entire culture. It is difficult to find an answer to a simple question of why Bali was so killed. He was elder and he was completely fit to be the king being elder of the two. It is Sugrive who took the kingdom in his absence and, as their tradition went, also his wife. Bali just took it back with force. Rama should not have sided Sugrive going by normal Dharma. Actually, in one of the weak moment for Rama's character, Bali asks him straight about why he killed him in that fashion. The only answer Rama could come up with is *"after all you are only a monkey and kings are God in human form. And that every sage also sometimes kills animal in hunting and hidden traps are permitted to be used for wild animals."* The explanation is unable to gather enough strength behind a poor argument. Undoubtedly, human dharma was violated forever.

But it is not to say that there are no instances or high moral examples. No, there are numerous such examples guiding the path of humanity for many centuries in future. My limited objective in mentioning some negative looking instances is just to prove that these are but just fictions, bigger and better fiction, but, at the end of the day, a fiction. So, let us treat it just like that. No, there are no strong historical evidences to suggest that Ramayana is a depiction of some real historical events.

But Ramayana's evaluation as a poetry will deserve full appreciation. It's a great piece of literature. It remains focused on the main theme where main actors are not far from narrations, an absolute opposite of Mahabharata. The enemy is shown as a foreigner. I suspect that Lanka was chosen as the destination because the entire island had already converted to Buddhism by that time. The friends are of different species. Unfortunately, it is injustice to Tamil speaking people as their territory is shown inhabited only with monkeys and bears. Ramayana composers would have done better if they had shown South Indian habitants also as normal human beings. So what if more people from South India were inclined for Shaivism rather than Vaishnavism but ignoring their presence shows indifferent and insensitive attitude for people who are little away from your core constituency, the northern India.

Another glaring attempt in Ramayana is to promote Vedic rituals (may be an attempt to bring back the lost glory of Vedic *yajnas*) as Rama is shown extending protection to many *Brahmin* priests engaged in Vedic *Yajnas* both during his young time as well during stay in forest. There are people having opinion that Ramayana dwells on the idea of showing conflict between Vedic on one side and Non Vedic Shaivaites on the other hand. Ravana, the villain, is shown as a great devotee of Lord Shiva. Now Shaivism certainly must have been in infancy stage in South India by the time Ramayana was taking final shape and an effort of nipping the bud looks all-probable.

However, core of the story remains firm about good winning over evil. Unlike Mahabharata, Ramayana produces a clear winner. One also must admit that in comparison to Mahabharata, Ramayana deals with lesser *Dharma Sankats*. It constantly showscase Rama as a 'Maryada Purushotam'. It also throws great examples on several social issues like how to have respects in sibling relations, how to differentiate between right and wrong, how to respect parents and sacrifices own comforts for the sake of keeping their words, how to keep promise made even when it is miserably difficult, how to avoid company of bad counsel, how to fight for protection of weak even at the cost of your life, how should we avoid getting swayed by glittering of attractive objects of desire, how to trust friends even from other species etc.

It is primarily because of such social issues getting highlighted that Ramayana in not seen just as a monument of literature but as an integral core of Hindu values and ideals. All through the modern history, Ramayana has been kept in great reverence that just reading or hearing part of it is said to be enough for washing one's sins and a mere rendering of Rama's name is taken as a sufficient cause of liberation. No other scripture, any where in the world, is known to have such great impact on so many people at the same point of time and for so many long years.

Bhagvad Gita and Its Teachings

First thing first; Gita should not be taken as a part of Mahabharata, the epic. It is but an "Upanishad of Upanishads". It deserves to be treated only on philosophical level. The only reason of the composers to add it with Mahabharata is to ensure much larger access to the audience and there they succeed completely. But for its fitment with overall setting of the scene at Kurukshetra, it would not attract so much attention for its philosophical contents as it finally could. It is an apparent truth that the struggle being discussed between Arjuna and Krishna is actually a war constantly going on within man between the tendencies of good and evil, the tendency of ignorance and knowledge, the tussles between disillusion and reality.

Why Upanishad of Upanishads? It is because each Upanishad is taken as a single shot of a distant reality from a particular angle. It talks about the ultimate reality and how to understand and appreciate that reality from the place from where the shot is being taken. But Gita talks progressively of several shots at a time and in such a way that the onlooker, irrespective of his varying level of spiritual inclination, will surely recognize one or the other shot and exclaim that yes, he has seen the reality from his own angle. This ability to engage almost everyone in one or the other path recommended by it, provides Gita with its universal recognition not received by any other Upanishad or any other single School of Philosophy ever. No wonder, it is the scripture translated maximum number of times and in maximum number of languages over almost two thousand years (Easwaran).

In order to understand Gita with better assurance of comprehension, it is essential to grasp some of the basic concepts in adequate details. These include concepts like *Brahman, Atman,* Dharma, Law of Karma, *Samsara,* Maya, and *Moksha* as these shall be liberally used while commenting on the specific teachings from Gita. So a quick word will refresh the reader's understanding of these basic Hindu tenets.

Brahman is the Supreme Being without any form, name, space or any such other feature known to mankind. But it is the cause of everything else. *Atman,* in short, is the divine core of every human being and a part of *Brahman*. Dharma coming from root 'Dhri' is that which supports—supports from within, the virtue of integrity, that establish and maintains harmony within entire creation so as to avoid chaos. Karma gets repeated in Gita so many times, simply means action. But Law of Karma refers to a basic Hindu concept meaning that every event is both a cause and effect. It says that every act is a result of some karma in the past and every act will have new consequences and will induce karma later and so on.... and on. Now, karma is not merely a physical act but includes any mental thought as well. Our sages concluded that relationship between a mental thought and action is not merely accidental but an established relationship where thoughts work as seeds to grow and induce action.

Second part of the Law of Karma says that whatever you do, its results will come back to you sooner than later. Now there may not be anything to prove this in black and white but we know inside our hearts that every time some thing bad happens with us, we try making it linked to something that we may have done in the past. It comes to us naturally because unconsciously we know that there is a correlation. Now just apply the principle inversely. This relation implies that we got some control over the result in terms of our past actions. Hence, we know what to expect in future by working on our actions and thoughts of today.

But unfortunately, more often than not, we related the fruits of today with karma of yesterday but not so much to the opposite. To make this possibility to work in reverse, we need Dharma which will persuade the individual to work in harmony, without any narrow self-interest but for welfare of the universe as a whole.

Finally, so long as the accumulated balance of karma remains in negative, the person has to keep coming back in life after life until and unless the debt is settled in totality by sustaining pains and pleasures. Once settled, the person qualifies for graduating to next level of liberation. This process of coming back to next life after death is called *Samsara,* the cycle of death and life. In West, due to their poor understanding with our logics, they brand it as incarnation or rebirth and laugh it out as impossibility.

Gita offers something or the other for every kind of spiritual aspirant. And this is the precise reason that it gets quoted by all since the time it ever came in public domain. Some one can say that Gita is having contradiction or that it leads to confusion but nothing can be far from truth. Gita is not an academic work of Philosophy but a poetic and practical text and refers to *Sankhya,* the world of mind and matter with three *gunas* of *Sattva, Rajas* and *Tamas* quite in detail. But unlike any other text of Philosophy, what it does is that it starts from the first step of the ladder and provide enlightenment in baby steps with one step at a time and takes the aspirant to the final destination by providing comprehensive tour of all possible ways to reach the final truth. (Easwaran)

During the second chapter itself, Krishna is shown to arouse Arjuna from his despair and sets him on the way of Self-realization. Arjuna is a man of action and is forced to ask questions about life and death. Here Krishna touches all themes and reminds Arjuna about his immortal nature who finally and formally ask Krishna to become his guru. The gist of his teachings to Arjuna, for this chapter, is nicely captured in the following verses:

> *"When you keep thinking about sense objects, attachment comes. Attachment breeds desire, the lust of possession that burns to anger. Anger clouds judgement; you no longer remember your past mistakes. Lost is the power to choose between wise and unwise and your life is utter waste.* (2:62-63)

Gita's central teaching is that one can become free by giving up selfish attachments to material things or attachment with people. Point to be noted is that focus is not material things or people but on giving up selfish attachments. Gita doesn't ask us to stop enjoying material comforts per se but to stop hanging on to selfish enjoyment. Neither it promotes inaction. In Chapter 3, Krishna encourages Arjuna that karma cannot be avoided and he must act out of duty selflessly as a way of going out of the maze of cause and effect. In other words, it asks renunciation of selfishness from all our thoughts, words and actions. And to engage in *Nishkama Karma* i.e. work without selfish desire.

Teachings of Gita call upon humanity to reserve the power of detaching from everything beloved; however much the soul may might yearn for it and whatever may be the pangs of misery one may feel in giving up this attachment. The focus is on power or ability to get over any thing as the weak people have no place in this life or the life after. Weakness leads to slavery and all kinds of misery: physical and mental. Habit of attachment is said to bring miseries involving family, friends, work and intellectual faculties. Gita suggests the ability to detach at will as the power of enjoyment. That man alone gets the best of nature who has the power of attaching to a thing with all his energy together with the power of detaching when he so decides. Gita does not aspire for a man who never loves any thing, who is not soft hearted, who is not sympathetic as such a person will be like a wall. It asks a person to have equal power of attaching and detaching at will.

Some people find faults with such Indian teachings saying that Hinduism teaches desire less action and go to the extent of holding this attitude responsible for many miseries being faced by the subcontinent in recent times. But such conclusions are wrong because these teachings do not suggest working without desires. Hinduism, on the contrary accepts desires as fuel of life and nothing can be achieved without a strong desire. The point to appreciate is 'selfless desire' or 'desire without selfish motive'. The selfish feeling keeps us away from real Self. If it is selfish, it can't be in harmony with the universe. Conversely, if it is good for all and it does no harm to anyone, this will never be 'selfish'. In addition to master selfish desires, it is also said to be necessary to subdue possessions and egocentricity.

Another important dilemma of most human beings gets discussed in Chapter 4. While Krishna is eager to grant Arjuna knowledge of higher spiritual truth or wish to show him a mystical vision, Arjuna is grappled with immediate issues and simply wants to know way of getting out of his present difficulties relating to his family tragedy and conflicts and is shown in a state of mind where higher teachings don't register. This is a situation most of us can empathise with directly and squarely. Later Krishna reminds him of his many earlier births that Arjuna does not remember. This is in a way reminder to all of us that what appears our immediate priority, may not be so and that we should not compromise long term for the sake of short term. By now Krishna is no more a normal human being but is raised to a divine nature and as an aspect of Lord Vishnu, a form that he will remain all through the remaining book. At the end of Chapter 4, there is new introduction of path of spiritual wisdom.

Chapter 6, which is one of the most intriguing chapter of Gita, deals with what is a true Yogi and appears to, without saying so, find faults with some other religious movements in vogue, and so highlight the path of spiritual wisdom by declaring supremacy of the meditation founded in God itself with unwavering faith:

"Meditation is superior to severe asceticism and the path of knowledge. It is also superior to selfless service. May you attain the goal of meditation, Oh Arjuna. Even among the people who

meditate, those man and woman who worship me with perfect faith; completely absorbed in me, is the most firmly established Yogi." (6:46-47)

Gita is also called a textbook of the supreme science of Yoga and the beauty again is that it does expose a person with all types of Yogas. Gita's teachings resolve around tension between Dharma, *Bhakti* and *Moksha*. When Arjuna is not feeling satisfied from Krishna's discourse on Gyan and Karma, he is offered a third alternative of Devotion. Gita's contribution is to work as a bridge for bringing together varying paths of Karma, Gyan and Surrender at the same pedestal. Since followers of each of these paths believed their preferred way as superior to others, if not the only path to salvation, it was like mandatory to rope in all the ways with equal importance lest the harmony get disturbed or any one feels left out. As a smart move to manoeuvre the complicated puzzle, Arjuna is freed from the consequences of his actions by acting in devotion to Krishna who is exhibited as a God having both *Nirguna* and *Saguna* characteristics. (Easwaran)

By Chapter 9, Krishna is shown replacing himself with many other Gods and Goddesses usual to Hindu pantheon as Krishna is said to have contained all those individual aspects within himself. And proclaims that it is Krishna and Krishna alone who should be worshipped. He takes over the ever-pervading mantle of being a God, a refuge, complete support, only true friend. These are first initial seeds of *Bhakti*, which was to flourish in due course in full-blown manner. This chapter also reveals more compassionate nature of Krishna by showing that *Bhakti* of Krishna is far more potent than observances of Vedic rituals or worship of any other God. Finally, Arjuna is exhorted that to attain eternal immortal state, he must have total devotion to Krishna.

"*What ever you do, make it an offering to me—the food you eat, the sacrifices you make, the help you extend, even the sufferings that you go through. In this way you will be freed from the bondage of karma, and from its results both pleasant and painful. Then, firm in renunciation and yoga, with your heart free, you will come to me.*" (9:27-28)

So, what is important to truly comprehend Gita is to go deep in the true meaning of all "words" and "concepts represented by those words". For example, *Nishkama Karma* does not mean good work or free work or work of charity. These are subtle concepts for finer understanding and mental state of the doer makes the difference. If we were to do a job which can give a large benefit to others and, incidentally, we also stand to gain, it is still *Nishkama karma*. But if you do the same job with desire of your gain being the driving force, it will get classified as selfish. Logic is simple to understand: an action without the motive of benefit to self will purify the mind and vice versa.

This also comes out as a smart move to outpace Buddhists attitude to Nirvana, the Gita's *Nishkama* focus just on action and not its results. What it propagates is that so long as you are doing something within the ambit of your swadharma and you are not attached with the fruits of such action, you don't lose the salvation. This ends up as a very smart way allowing a person to continue leading a material life with a spiritual mind and still remain available to the calls of his profession without compromising salvation. In other words, one can do anything but so long as the attitude is of a renuncient, you still don't lose your claim to salvation—a middle of the road approach and an easy escape from the conflicting zone.

One of the highly discussed lines of Gita is where it says

"Karmanye Vadhikaraste, Ma phaleshou kada chana
Ma Karma Phala Hetur Bhurmatey Sangostva Akarmani" (2:47)

Which means:

"You have right to work but never to the fruit of such work. You should not engage in action for the sake of reward nor should you long for inaction. Perform Arjuna, as a man established within yourself, without selfish attachments and alike in success and defeat."

We can easily correlate this doctrine with our work place experience. The focus here is to give up attachment with results of what we do. Many times we get attached in desiring that the work in our hand must result in the way that we wish or desire. That feeling, at times, prompts us to seek some unwanted actions and results in our sadness if the results are not as desired. Now if we were to do our job with non-attached attitude, with pure motive and adopt means in accordance with Dharma, will it really matter if the result of that work was a success or failure? Irrespective of the result, will our courage, confidence, capability will get shaken? Once we have given our best, do the failure break sour heart, will it make us depressing ever? No, it can't be so.

On the contrary let us try recollecting any work that we may have done with selfish motives and ask us an honest question. Did we enjoy doing that job? So, let us try taking this doctrine in our work life and we will surely be a better person. Gita says that the attachment to karma is pleasant at first but bitter like poison at the end. In the last section of the verse, Krishna asks Arjuna not to consider inaction as he wanted to leave the battle field and go away to forest. Inaction or escape from action is not the solution. From all sides, the option recommended is only work but without attaching self with results of actions.

Another beautiful concept explained in detail, like nowhere else, is the concept of '*Shraddha*'. Unfortunately there is no apt word in English to convey the complete meaning of *Shraddha*. The nearest word will be faith. *Shraddha* entails every belief we hold deep without possibility of any need for even questioning its logic. This is a bundle of all those values in our system that provides colour to our perceptions for things that we come across. *Shraddha* unfortunately governs our thought process even without we coming to know about it. Because of its criticality, Gita says that a person is what is his *Shraddha*. Even Christianity believes that a person is what he thinks in his heart. It is not what we wish it to be but what we deem worth having. Because what we value more is what we try going after. That is how, *Shraddha* guides our actions and ultimately determines our destiny.

So Gita provides explanation as what is right *Shraddha,* which is total faith in spiritual laws, in the unity of life with God, acceptance that divine is present in every ordinary person in equal proportions. And to put it differently, wrong *Shraddha* is thinking existence is all about life, that happiness is best pursued by following self interests. (Easwaran)

Finally Gita ends at right note by offering a choice to Arjuna. Having exposed Arjuna to a detailed differentiation of normal self with the real Self, explaining the relationship between thoughts and action, teaching the laws of karma, prompting him to leave everything on God, teaching the *marga* (road) of *Bhakti* and exposing him to the way of *Raja Yoga* and *Gyana Yoga*, prompting him to have right *Shraddha*, finally Krishna asks Arjuna:

> *"...now Arjuna, reflect on these words and then do as you choose"*
> 18:63

This brings to surface the option of choices that each one of us faces in our daily life. After all, the longest battle going ever since is the battle within every human where the twin halves of human nature are constantly fighting with each other. Humans, like Arjuna, have no choice but to fight, to act. The only choice a man has is to choose which side to fight for.

Gita makes us in charge of our own destiny as captains of our own ships and masters of our own souls. It guides us to all possible ways and warns us with possible hurdles but at the end of the journey, as master of the ship, we alone will be responsible for all the results.

13

Emergence of Caste System in Hinduism

Gita's teachings of swadharma also became focal point for establishing the system of caste. Increase in the number of professions also increased the need of categorizing them under established class system of *Brahmin* or *Kshatriya* or *Vaishya* or *Shudra*. Main four-class segregation originally perceived and practised in the past was unable to bind people together without caste factor being brought in. To begin with the whole premise of class segregation was linked to professions pursued. But during interim period, the number of professions has multiplied many folds. Further, the geographical expansion of people has brought new factors linked with languages and regions into play. People pursuing similar professions and belonging to same region and speaking same language started feeling natural affinity. This genuine evolution resulted in emergence of castes under the main class segregation. People from same class but different castes found themselves clubbed together.

Then there were new categories of people who were now getting integrated with the existing social structures. On one hand, this category included invaders like Shakas and Kushans and on the other hand there were people like Nishads as well as other tribals and people earlier sitting on the fringe of society but now knocking at the door seeking entry. Sub categorization under caste enabled such new groups entering in mainstream of society to get clubbed under already existing four-class super structure. Interesting point to note is that absorption of new people in new castes was in all classes including *Kshatriyas* with the sole exception of *Brahmins*. Since *Brahmins* have been in charge of approving social categorizations, they smartly ensured that there was no dilution to their own class. So, *Brahmins* excused themselves from any new addition to their class.

Largest amount of additions happened under *Shudras* as the big chunk of people getting absorbed came from so called 'neech' and 'mleccha' castes (people from hills, tribals, forests and other unclean people from alien origins). *Kshatriyas* got only a handful of castes who were warriors from other regions or some small groups who already owned kingdoms of small states. Large addition to *Shudras* did not matter much as it was already a class excluded from Vedic rituals and they were surviving with their own Gods and rituals. It was as this time that the pyramid of classes got complete with large proportion of population placed at the bottom of the pyramid, *Vaishyas* sitting next with lower proportions. That was followed by *Kshatriyas* reducing the proportions even further. *Brahmins* were happily sitting at the top with least proportion of their own. But they were commanding the driver's seat for administering the entire social structure by framing the rules of the game and than by sitting as judges of the references brought forward by all others.

Again King Ashoka disturbed the puzzle by promoting a new dhamma. His dharma was something different than the Buddhism but it was called so because Pali as language was common to both Ashoka and Gautama. Ashoka's dhamma was called 'sadharana' which means general in nature and applied to all right thinking people without making and distinction based on sects or castes.

Mahabharata on its part promotes and suffocates the '*Verna Vyavastha*' per se. There are references where sages are discussing class system and link class with colour saying that "*Brahmins* are fair, *Kshatriyas* are ruddy, *Vaishyas* are sallow and *Shudras* are dark complexion people". Probably this is first time that skin colour (read racism in today's context) got added into the already complex jigsaw puzzle of Hinduism. Some intelligent writers later justified this by linking this colourorisation to the base shades of the famous *Gunas* of Vedic Hinduism. Just a quick catch up that *Sattva* is identified with white colour, *rajas* with red and *tamas* with black. The colour saffron is attached with the transcendent spirit and that is why all people engaged in pursuing salvation of spirit are found wearing clothes in this shade to this day.

There is a very interesting story explained in Mahabharata is an interesting read. It goes as:

> *If different colours distinguish classes among the four classes, how is it that there is a mix of colours among all classes? Desire, anger, fear, greed, sorrow, worry, hunger and exhaustion affect all of us. How then are the classes distinguished? Sweat, urine, faeces, phlegm, mucus, and blood flow out of all our bodies. How then are the classes distinguished? And how can you tell one class from another among all the species (jati) of the countless creatures, moving and still, that has such various colours? The sages replied: "Actually, there is no difference between the classes; this whole universe is made of Brahman. But when the creator emitted it long ago, actions/karmas divided in into classes. Those Brahmins who were fond of enjoying pleasures, quick to anger and impetuous in their affections, abandoned their own dharma and became Kshatriyas, with red bodies. Those who took up herding cattle and engaged in plowing, and did not follow their own dharma, became yellow Vaishyas. And those were greedy and fond of violence and lies, living on all sort of activities, fallen from purity, became black. And that's how these actions/karmas split off the Brahmins into a different class, for there was never any interruption of their dharma and their sacrificial rituals* (12.181.5-14)

At one place in Gita, Krishna also tells Arjuna "*it is better to do your own duty poorly then another's duty well.*" This is the same language used by Manu also for erecting firm partitions for crossovers in each other's obligation of professions. In this way Arjuna was dissuaded not to think about giving up violence as he was a *Kshatriya* and violence was his usual swa-dharma. One tends to see through the safer situation of *Brahmins* whose duties consist of only perpetual moral duties where there is no confrontation between 'swa-dharma' and 'Sanatan Dharma' or 'sadharana dhamma'.

The class system is known to exist in many other cultures and regions but in India it got further categorized into *Jati* (caste) and their sub categorizations. The term *Jati* appears in almost all Indian languages and is related to the idea of lineage or kinship group. There are perhaps more than 3000 *jatis* in India and there is no one all-Indian system of ranking them in order of status. Yet in each local area *jati* ranking exists and is very much related to purity and pollution. Each *jati* has some unique job, but not everyone in the *jati* necessarily performs it. A *jati* is identified in a local setting by whom its members will accept food and water from and to which *jati* its members will give food and water. People will try to marry their sons and daughters to members of their own *jati* and will give their major loyalty to their own *jati*. A *jati* will usually be organized into a *biradari* (a brotherhood), and this organization carries out the business and oversees the working of the *jati* and has the power to exclude an offender from the *jati*.

A *jati* can improve its position in the class system by advancing economically and emulating social groups with money and power. At the same time, a *jati* can also move up in the caste hierarchy. Mobility in the caste system has been termed "Sanskritization" by the scholar M.N. Srinivas. To gain position in this process, a lower *jati* copies the habits and behaviour patterns of the dominant *jati* in the area. This may mean a lower *jati* will change its name to one of a higher *jati*, adopt vegetarianism, observe more orthodox religious practices, build a temple, and treat its women in a more conservative way. The type of emulation will depend on the habits of the dominant *jati* being copied. If the *jati* can gain acceptance for its new name, new history, and new status, it will then marry its daughters to members of the *jati* in which it is seeking to gain membership. In due course of time the new position on the social scale will be solidified and accepted by other *jatis*. (Society)

All said and done, Caste system continues to have a powerful presence in every Hindu's life. The mobility across caste continues to be extremely low and is to be taken more as an exception. We can call it undesirable or with what ever name but designations of castes overshadows each and every other distinctions namely, religious, sectarian, regional, linguistic.

14
Golden Period of Indian Civilisation

If the period of 200 BC to turn of the millennium is termed as a period of consolidation, the next period of around five hundred years is acclaimed as the Golden Period of Indian Civilization. The area outside India was having presence of dynasties such as of The Achaemenids, Parthians, Sakas and Kushans and India had seen good presence of Maurayan Dynasty. All these contemporaries have developed similar characteristics of complex empires evident in good administration, professional armies, effective communications and political stability together with by and large tolerance of multiple religious faiths of the populace.

India once again saw emergence of a very effective and successful dynasty in the form of Guptas ruling in between 320 to 550 CE and produced many great rulers like Chander Gupta I, Samudra Gupta, Rama Gupta and Chander Gupta II (also known as Chandragupta Vikramaditya—the sun of power), Kumar Gupta. The beginning of the dynasty has marriages within other great ruling families at its base (marital alliances) but once it was established, the first few rulers pursued highly aggressive expansion policy in all directions. At the height of this dynasty, the empire spanned from river Sindhu to Bay of Bengal in one direction and from Himalayan Mountains to Deccan Plateau on the other direction. Most of the well known Kings of this dynasty are credited with some major inclusions in their territories to the extent that at the time of Vikramaditya, this empire had become the most powerful in the world by completely liquidating forces of Sakas, Mlecchas, Kambojas, Yavans, Tusharas and Hunas. It was the time when Roman Empire was on the way down. Vikramaditya also created his second capital at Ujjain to ensure that his empire is better managed from the centre of the geographic spread of his empire.

Samudra Gupta was a great lover of arts and literature besides being a strategist military leader. A firm believer of Hinduism, and is known to be worshipping God Vishnu and as a true Hindu with inclusivity, he is the one who allowed Sri Lankan Buddhist King to make the famous monastery at Bodh Gaya. These were not only great warriors and consolidated their boundaries by winning over many local kingdoms; they also expanded the boundary of their rule outside traditional Indian subcontinent. Besides, they were known as people giving a lot of encouragements to all forms of arts, literature, religion, natural sciences, music, paintings, sculpturing. All these developments resulted in good opportunities for cultural and economic exchanges across empires ranging from Romans on one side and China on the other side.

Peace, Prosperity and Stability of this period enabled fantastic progress of scientific, literary, religious and artistic endeavours. As happens in most historical periods with such environments, extensive discoveries got achieved by numerous contributors in all diverse fields of Science, Technology, Engineering, arts, dialects, languages, literatures, yoga, astronomy, mathematics, theology, philosophy and what not. All these elements got crystallized into Indian Culture and greatly contributed for evolving the Hinduism that we are left to this day. Undoubtedly, there is no other period in history of such great progress on all these fronts.

Sanskrit got recognized as major languages for the official work of the kingdom and for most compositions in religious spheres, major *Shastras* got compiled, both epics got reduced to their final shapes, number of tenets got fully absorbed in breadth and length of the society, the personal Gods in the shape of Vishnu and Shiva evolved, people started idol worships replacing Vedic rites as symbol of religion, the castes got enlarged with the influx of major chunk under, the early *Puranas* got started giving rise to yet another type of mythology laden bulky scriptures meeting alternating aspirations from different parts of the country. So much got done during these five hundred years. Hinduism underwent a great transformation as it made its switch towards temple based religion.

This period is credited for producing some great explorers of different branches of learning. The great astronomer and mathematician, Varahmihira whose treatise named Pancha-Siddhantika made great contribution in expanding scientific knowledge of his time. Other great luminaries of this time included, just to mention few names at random, Kalidasa, Aryabhatta, Vishnu Sharma and Vatsyayana. Kalidas is also known as the best dramatist and romantic composer of all times. It was the brightest spot in Indian history for Hindu Religious and Intellectual resurgence. Besides, it was a great time for developments of magnificent architecture, sculpture and paintings. The main accomplishments of this period are summarized as under:

- Concept of zero and introduction of decimal numeral system which changed the face of mathematics for all time to come.
- Establishing movement of earth around the Sun, Solar and Lunar eclipses got established.
- Sushruta Samhita, a great redaction of all major concepts of *Ayurveda* medicines got composed in this period along with a very innovative chapter on surgery, yet another first transformation in medical science.
- Chaturanga, the game which is now known as "Chess" got devised in this period based on tactics perfected as war game involving tactical advancement or retrieving of infantry, cavalry, elephants and chariots. Military conquests of this dynasty prove beyond doubt that Indian system of fighting wars was the best in class.
- *Kama Sutra*, the literature of every aspect of human sexual behaviour got composed during this time.
- The fundamental discovery that earth is not flat but round and rotates around its own axis got initiated in this very period.
- Discovery that moon does not have its own light but shines due to reflection of sunlight also got established in this period.
- Large size Hindu deity, Buddha statues and Jain Tirthankar statues got stone carved in this period from big centres at Mathura and Gandhar.

- Caves of Ajanta, Ellora and Elephanta came up during late Gupta period.
- Dashavatara Vishnu temple at Deogarh, Parvati temple at Nachna, Kuthara and brick built Lakshmana temple at the banks of Mahanadi at Sirpur and Varsha sculptures in the rock cut cave at Udayagiri all came up in this period.
- The early *Puranas* started taking their final shape during this period.
- The system of minting Gold, Silver and Copper coins started first time showing India as the prolific minter with advanced progress in metallurgical sciences.

These examples are not to be taken as stray cases of sparks but as the examples of all-round advancement in all knowledge fields. India had never seen such great intellectual advancements. Even diplomatically, this was the best time of history as Guptas are known to have harmonious trade and cultural relations with all powers in the west and with Sri Lanka, Burma, Malaysia and China on the east.

But all good things must end too. The nomadic groups of Huns started invading the country from central Asia. While their initial attempts got failed, the Gupta Dynasty could not eventually recover back from the losses of facing Huns. After the decline of Gupta Dynasty, India again saw disintegration under numerous regional and smaller kingdoms, which ultimately resulted in decreased collective power to stand against aggressions from foreign lands.

With end of Gupta dynasty, the shining Sun of Indian intellectual advancements went for sunset followed by a very long, dark, oppressive night where Indians went through a long period of nightmare, condensation and trampling forced under foreign invaders.

15 Yoga: The Spiritual Connect of Hinduism

The seals excavated from Sindhu Sarasvati sites showing Rishis sitting in yogic postures suggest emergence of Yoga and Rig-Veda is intertwined. The practice of Tapas (sitting in deep contemplation) finds its mention in Vedas and *Brahmanas* at many places. Needless to say that Yoga has been around with Hinduism even before concepts like spirituality and religion came to exist. Our revered sages of ancient times, people who composed Vedas and subsequent scriptures have realized the importance of silencing human mind in an effort to focus on deeper depths of the mind in a serene quietness and away from subjective distortions.

They have realized that all human beings universally come across experiences that touch all of them in similar measures. And that basic questions like 1. Am I a good person? 2. Why do I suffer? 3. How am I connected to the world around me and what is my position therein? 4. Things happen in particular ways but why? 5. How can I live my life in best possible manner? This realization of existence of a divine light deep inside the human heart and the realization that the same light also exists in everyone else, became the base of universal inclusivity of Hinduism which make it stand taller than most other human thoughts throughout the long human history.

These initial thoughts later got developed into separate subject called Spirituality. The Indian way of practising these essential human understandings with the objective of gaining mastery by mind over body and emotional self with a purpose to win over the human desires is what we call Yoga. Simply put, it is the unique combination of physical and spiritual experience. The feeling of Spirituality is known to possess a person at any stage and may get kick start under numerous influences and need not be connected necessarily to any religious feelings or matters of faith. So, yearning for Spirituality is independent of religious affiliations. But Hinduism has never seen this experience as external to religious manifestations.

Hinduism has been using this urge be taken as a way of life aimed at the individual finding his relationship to the external world and invocate him to find his own truth. This desire to go to the real self-Truth has been the hallmark of Hinduism thought and is responsible for higher achievements. It will not be any exaggeration to say that Hinduism is the fruit of highest intellectual and spiritual development of our great ancestors with array of Rishis and Munis.

At this stage we can also realize that religious ideas, the way we apply this term now a days, must be better based on scientific methods and disciplined observation—the same techniques which are used by all Scientists to come up with new discoveries which are known to transform our lives so much. If a process is so successful in one stream, why not replicate the same in another field. After all, most people earlier believed that world was flat but changed their conviction, even by going against their religious faith, that world is indeed round and spinning rather than stationery. So, if the religious ideas are totally based on faith and beliefs alone, there is possibility of mistaken understandings. Religion is fine and so is all the worship that we undertake but should the individual also seek rationale as what is the science of his religion? Should he not direct his thoughts inwardly to seek answers to many of the religious questions and longings within their own spiritual nature? Yoga is the answer to these questions and much more.

Yoga practitioners of antiquity have realized right in the beginning that human mind needs to be silenced as a prerequisite for accurately reflecting objective reality without its own subjective distortions. Yoga was not to create that reality but it was to prepare the human mind to be capable of apprehending it by assisting it to transform from prevailing noises, clustered thoughts, crowded views and its natural monkey like nature to a still position where it is disconnected to not only physical body but to that intellect plain which gives rise to newer thoughts every split of seconds. Just for an example, Carl G Jung, an eminent Psychologist and Psychiatrist who founded 'analytical psychology' and a prolific writer on many subjects from Switzerland, described Yoga as "one of the greatest thing the human mind has ever created."

Yoga practices have been developed over a long period of hundreds of years and finally got compiled by Mahrishi Patanjali as *Yoga Sutra* in the first century AD. Again, Patanjali is not the inventor of Yoga but only somebody who consigned the ancient practices into writing and should be credited as a compiler or redactor. Patanjali listed five distinct impulses, *vrittis*, that slave the normal human mind, namely, Ignorance, Ego, Passion, Disgust and Lure for transient life. These impulses surface and resurface one after the other in inexhaustible and uncontrolled energy. Since, these are basic part of human nature; one cannot win over these simply by study or understanding. Human being is deeply conditioned by *Vasana* (lust) and just having knowledge of it is not enough. Simply said, 'Yoga is the science of mounting a constant pressure on the unconscious mind to bring it under control and to behave as directed such that it must follow your command like under a servant master relationship.' But mind being a monkey, this situation is possible only after establishing a perfect balance among body, psychic, through strenuous practices of long drawn process and use of human intellect.

Nature is supposed to contain gross manifestations (effects) and subtle (causes) perceptions. The gross can be easily perceived by senses. The practice of Yoga will lead to the acquisitions of more subtle perceptions. All orthodox Indian philosophy has liberation of the soul as a single goal of humanity. One of the main Philosophy emphasized on acquiring knowledge while other focused on right rituals and meditation as the way forward. But many renouncers found, in practice, liberation of soul only through study and meditation extremely difficult. The forces of visible material world with all its desires and passions held human beings in such a powerful grip that tougher measures were required to aim for *Moksha*. The most effective and most practised method devised to achieve that goal is called "Raja Yoga".

The Raja Yoga

The science of *Raja Yoga* proposes to put before humanity a practical and scientifically worked out method of reaching this truth. All other scientific pursuits in any field require the laboratory to experiment and instruments. The laboratory used in *Raja Yoga* is the mind itself and it is also used as an instrument and as an equipment for observation. The power of attention when properly guided and directed towards the internal world, will analyze the mind. But turning the mind inside and stopping it from going out and then to concentrate all its power and finally throw those powers on the mind itself, is very difficult proposition. The only solace is that it is certainly not impossible as so many people are there who have made progress on their journey on this road in past and present alike.

Unlike basic sciences, the prophetic religions are supposed to be based on personal experiences of their respective founders. It is understood to be difficult and, at times, impossible to get such experiences repeated by others. That is why, today, the preachers tell us to just to follow the religions based on faith without asking questions. But Yoga is the science teaching us how to get these perceptions/experiences by any human at any point of time. Logically speaking, there is no point in following a religion if you are personally unable to feel that experience yourself. But logic certainly does not apply to all religions. Not having experienced your own truth is comparable to having a soul inside you but never having a feel for it well within yourself.

As per Vedas:

> *"... than alone all doubts vanish, all darkness get scattered when a person has grasped the truth, realized it and felt it in his heart of hearts".*

What is the use of such knowledge? Well it will take away all our miseries. Every misery comes from fear or from an unsatisfied desire ... for example, if you know that you are a soul and a soul never dies, you will have no fear of death. Once you are aware that you have become perfect and far above attachments and desires, you stop having desires. If you stop having desires, surely there can't remain unfulfilled desires. Let us be clear that desires can be only curtailed and never fulfilled. Because every time you try fulfilling one desire, newer desires are bound to crop up without any end.... Let us see how *Raja Yoga* helps in that direction.

The final goal of *Raja Yoga*'s all combined teachings is how to concentrate the mind, then how to discover inner most recesses of our own mind, then how to generalize their contents and form our own conclusions. As truth requires no prop to stand, the study of *Raja Yoga* requires no faith or belief. So it is quite universal in its approach and equally suitable for every age group or religion basis or gender or regional background person.

Human body and mind are very well connected. If one gets disturbed, the other also gets impacted. With vast majority of humanity, the mind is largely under the control of body. (That situation brings them nearer to animals that also have little developed minds. Have we not seen them doing all the things that a human does for self or family except that they don't have the power of reasoning)? But before any attempt to control the mind, one is ought to sufficiently control the body. Here is the use of all the '*asanas*' recommended for practising for a long period of time before one tries to graduate to higher level of pursuing the Yoga. All one gets out of pursuing all sorts of *asanas* is to manage control of mind over body. But that is only a small fraction of Yoga or just a baby step towards the long journey of Yoga. This explanation is just to preempt some of the readers who may be equating practice of *asanas* with Yoga. No, Yoga *asanas* are not for helping you get a muscular body. One should never forget that one who does opt for violent exercises, carry the risk of living shorter. People using their brains rather than their muscles, generally live much longer.

As per *Raja Yoga*, the external world is but the gross form of the internal. The internal envisaged world, the subtler world, is the cause while external world is effect. Once the man is able to control his internal, he will get the whole external nature under his control. You must have heard that every big reality first takes shape in the mind of its designer. Similarly, a person seeking advantage from Yoga must first firm up his mind with a clear dream of what needs to be achieved. After all, if your drawing is not firm, what kind of construction you can expect physically.

In religion, as much as in all other matters, one is advised to discard everything that weakens the person and adopt what strengthens him. One should not have anything to do with any such idea or concept or ritual that tends to make you less strong. Mysteries and andh-*bhakti* or such other illogical points weakens the human brain, so we are better advised to stay away from believing anything illogical or something that doesn't make sense to us. Another word of caution about extremes, an aspirant for Yoga practices must avoid the extreme of luxury as well as austerity. He must neither observe fast too much nor torture his flesh. He who sleeps too much or works too much or he who does no work, none of these people can ultimately be a Yogi. So, bringing harmony in all actions and establishing our life style without going into extremes is a precondition for expected results. Further, it has been seen that in human society, too much wealth or too much poverty is a great impediment for the higher attempt for spiritual quest. It is, more often than not that the greats of the world come from middle of the strata.

Steps to Achieve Final Goal

Contrary to general expectation, Yoga is not simply sitting in few absurd postures and achieves proficiency in sitting in some postures where many others are not able to hold their body. It is much more. Having a very narrow view on Yoga is a criminal waste and far from the complete system. It is a step-by-step journey to be learned only by practising. Simply getting knowledge of all the steps doesn't help in any way. Let us understand the steps needed for climbing one at a time and the journey must begin from the first step to avoid the risk of crash landing. Each stage is desired to be perfected first before going for the next step. Any one jumping from one to another or not qualifying step one before working on step two will never get expected results.

The whole process of *Raja Yoga* is divided into eight steps, named:

1. *Yama,*
2. *Niyam,*
3. *Asana,*
4. *Prayanam,*
5. *Pratyahara* (restraint of senses from their objects),
6. *Dharana* (fixing the mind on a single spot, concentration, *ekagrata*),

7. *Dhyana*, meditation, and finally
8. *Samadhi*.

The texts suggest that each stage requires rigorous work spreading over years. So, any time one comes across someone promising quick results under the disguise of Yoga, is surely not to be relied. But we have a situation where it is difficult to find so much of spare time for going through the process step by step but the gains at the end are simply attractive. This dichotomy is the reason behind that people find difficult to let go Yoga advantages so easily. It is to bridge this gap that numerous commercialized versions are available all through the world promising instant Yoga advantages. But, the real Yoga is not open for fast forward mode. Neither there is room for some quick-fix solution or short cuts.

Let us now talk about each step in some detail:

Following *Yam* and *Niyam* are basic but essential preparation for Yoga. The aspirant is required to strictly follow the prescribed *Yama* (prohibitions) which include

1. *Practising Ahimsa*—Killing of animals or incurring physical injury to some one will be but a limited meaning of *Ahimsa.* Unfortunately, English languages (like many other languages of the world) do not have a word to express the real power of *Ahimsa.* It refers to each and every action or thought which, directly or indirectly, result in harm of any living being. Besides actions, even speaking unkindly to any other human being or even getting a strong thought in the mind aimed at any type of harm to someone, will get qualifies as Himsa. As we have seen earlier, both action and thought are of equal importance throughout Indian systems. Following *Ahimsa* will include avoiding non injury to all, not causing pain to any one, having feeling of compassion towards all living creatures, following practice of forgivingness, having peace and equanimity towards self and others, abstaining from eating animal meats, avoiding actions of all types of cruelty including for animals and other living beings. (V.)

2. *Forbidden to Steal*—means prohibition to grab whatever one wants and whenever he wants. Having any tendency of pilferage or for lifting any thing in excess of minimum required for basic living. A person should be satisfied in basic requirement of food and shelter being met without any grudge or objection. Contentment with minimum resources for minimum requirements

is the point being talked here; not only the kind of stealing to be reported to police. The idea here is to develop a feeling of happiness by accepting one's life situations and conditions, what ever they are, and by developing the attitude of contentment so that one is not always engaged in piling up more and more. By practising this prohibition, we shall get relaxation of mind, a feel of peace; a distinct form of happiness.

3. *Must not Speak a Lie—"Satyam vada"* the categorical statement coming out of the Upanishads makes it beyond any qualifications. At the same time, speaking truth must meet twin conditions of being necessary and kind. In other words, it means that one must speak kindly and only when necessary and must speak truth and only truth and nothing but truth, at all times and not even attempting any kind of distortion or addition or subtraction. Speaking truth at all times leads to purity of speech which then will lead to purity of mind. Thinking deep, one does realize that speaking truth is a natural to humanity but we have got habituated to move away from this on some or the other loose pretext. But every time a lie is spoken, there is a burden on soul and by abstaining from speaking we take a step towards our natural self. Truth is known to require strength and courage.

4. *Total Abstaining from Sex and Intoxication*—for preserving physical and mental powers and enhancing will power, this prohibition goes a long way. Ancient Yogis claimed that of all the energies of human body, the highest is called "ojas". This is stored up in the brain. A person having higher ojas is certainly more intellectual and spiritual. The power used during sex, when properly controlled, gets converted to ojas. So only a chaste man can make ojas rise and stored in brain. This is why chastity is considered highest human virtue among all religious orders in the whole world and Hinduism is not the only one advocating this great virtue.

Similarly, intoxication weakens the power of judgement and comes out as absence of will power. Both these traits shall be required in abundance when we pursue further steps on our way up.

Another word of caution! And this caution is applicable for all four points equally forcefully. All the four points in discussion above call for total abstaining. One can not talk about how many times are ok or how much is not ok. No, the matter is absolutely clear. Either one observes the prohibition or he doesn't. There is a no mid way.

As a second step, and only upon complete success over the first step of following Yam, the aspirant must be able to follow *Niyam* for mastering over bodily and psychic disciplines. These include:

1. *Complete Bodily and Mental Purity*: This requires periodical baths, restricted eating, eating on time, getting regular exercises, sufficient amount of sleep, following schedules regularly, etc. The focus here is on being clean and disciplined.
2. *Contentment:* Being satisfied with life in totality. Contentment enables one to enjoy the peace of mind which will work on stress levels of the heart and mind will be handy for regulating the thought process in later stages. The mind of a person who is not contented, remains pursued on objects of unfulfilled desires and that will create road-blocks on the way of seeking spiritual gains.
3. *Austerities:* Fasting, penances, observing Dharma (behaving kindly and courteously to everyone no matter what is going inside the heart).
4. *Studying Holy Scriptures and Repetition of AUM:* Indian scriptures are full of knowledge on all human aspects. Regular reading of these scriptures has been known to provide encouragement to spirituality seekers for thousands of years. And regular rendering sound of *"Aum"* also is a symbolic move for showing complete faith in all Vedic literature. It is not to be taken as an abstract word. So any where one comes across mention of chanting *"Aum"*, it implies, following everything mentioned in the Vedas and Upanishads.
5. *Complete Surrender of your Individuality to Personal God:* This *Niyam* requires us to surrender our complete existence to Eshwar meaning complete abandoning to the will of the Supreme. The merits of this surrender have been dealt in detail during our discussion on Gita where Krishna is heard encouraging Arjuna to leave everything to God. The firm belief of complete surrender to Supreme is desired to bring us nearer to God.

Yam and *Niyam* combined are basically moral training; it is only based on the continued practice of these that further practice of Yoga will succeed. The dedication of aspirant in following these preparatory conditions goes to test and prove his spiritual ambition. Success in these is known to lead the practitioner to be a different kind of human being with a radical moral transformation.

Yoga aspirant has to leave his unenlightened self behind, abandon *Ahamkara* and behave as if their soul is already liberated. Over a period of time, by sheer dent of practice, these ethical disciplines are to become second nature. No progress can be expected unless the above-mentioned controls are exercised and psychological transformation is achieved.

At this stage, and only after the teacher is satisfied that the aspirant has mastered the Yam and *Niyam*, he allows the successful aspirant to start the first *Asana*. Sitting in crossed leg position for hours together, motionless with back, neck and head upward, the Yoga aspirant is supposed to learn to severe the link between his mind and his senses. *Asanas* include a series of exercises, physical and mental, to be gone through on daily basis until the higher states are reached.

Different sages developed different postures over long years spanning centuries just to innovate their own tools that helped them in aiming for severance of mind from sense organs. In the process, some *Asanas* also got identified with providing direct indirect benefits for the physical fitness of internal organs of the body just as a bye-product. Yoga was never developed with physical health at the centre—for that, our sages had devised *Ayurveda.*

One is allowed to find his own comfortable posture to continuously sit for long hours except that spinal column should remain erect in line with neck and head. After sitting, one has to purify the nerves by using techniques like '*Anulomvilom*', '*bhastrika*' and '*Kapalbhanti*'... according to one's own capacity. These may be practised four times everyday at dawn, midday, evening and midnight. Keeping body healthy and strong is a precondition for ensuring obstruction free *asanas*.

It may have come as a new learning altogether. Because until now, we may not have understood the tough preparation originally designed for getting permissions for sitting for the first *Asana*. But once we apply the logic that Yoga is not so much to do with the body but the mind and consciousness, we start appreciating importance of the ground rules of physically challenging *Yama* and *Niyam*. This also helps us in realizing the gap in real Yoga and 'Instant Yoga' being served all around. Body is important but only in limited capacity. *Body is the vehicle of soul where the mind is navigational tool.* Of course, you need a good vehicle to reach your destination trouble free but once you reach the destination (and if you know that you are not going back) you park the vehicle in a parking lot and soon forget everything about it completely. The destination, here, is liberation of soul.

As a next step of the ladder, the aspirant learns to regulate his breathing for inflicting even greater attack on one's subconscious self. Respiration by nature is a fundamental and automatic sequence in every living being. But for pursuing *Pranayam,* one has to learn to breathe more and more slowly with longer and longer pauses in between. *Prana* is the force that is setting the whole engine of our body into motion. The most obvious manifestation of *Prana* is breath. Entering through the breath will enable us to find out about the subtle forces, the nerve currents that are moving all over the body. It is by controlling these nerves that one hopes to control the body. Finally, we shall try controlling the mind also.

As a practical suggestion, you should get used to carryout a pre-*pranayam* routine where you take deep breath and throw it out for couple of times. Then take it in with one nostril and throw it out slowly through the other nostril and repeat the same sequence using other nostril. Initially, you may experience that you are unable to breathe deep enough or are unable to fill your lungs full enough, take it as natural. This practice will correct this tendency soon.

The person dedicating himself to practise Yoga should try *Pranayam* minimum two times every day, in morning as well as in evening. And, undertaking all these steps with unstoppable regularity is the key. Doing it only when you have time and skipping on other occasions will result in skipping of success also.

One should better have a special room/place kept exclusively for conducting *Pranayam*. It is like mandatory to enter the identified space with completely clean body and mind. You can also place flowers in this room, burn incense, no quarrel, and no anger and have no unholy thought in that room. To the extent possible, the entry to such a place should be restricted only for like-minded people. Basically, one has to create this special space as one's own temple. And once there, *the aspirant should pray for seeking knowledge and clarity; prayer for seeking anything else will always qualify as selfish.*

Pranayam literally means control of *Prana* which has a much wider meaning than breath. *Prana* is infinite, omnipresent manifesting power of this universe. Everything called energy or force is evolved from *Prana* including gravitational and magnetic forces. Every action by the body, as nerve current or as a thought, is all manifestation of *Prana*. The sum total of all forces in the universe, mental or physical, when resolved back to their original state is called *Prana*. Controlling *Prana* is the end and aim of *Pranayam*. I am highlighting the point here with the idea of bringing the point home that there are several words in our Sanskrit that a language like English fails to convey even a small fraction of that. *Prana* vs Breath is one such example.

> *"He who has controlled the Prana has controlled his own mind and all other minds that exist. He has controlled his body and all other bodies that exist, because Prana is the generalized manifestation of force."*

The *Prana* is the vital force in everything. Thought is the finest and highest action of *Prana*. Thoughts are at different planes—instinctive thoughts (like reflex to hit a mosquito if it bites), the conscious thought (based on reasoning, judging, looking at pros and cons) and finally the super conscious thoughts. All thoughts are part of *Prana*.

Initial success of *Pranayam* shall be visible within few months of concentrated work e.g. expression of one's face should look better, calmness should be visible, voice quality should have improved—and the whole of nature will begin to change and one's own source book of knowledge will open out.

All actions, internal as well as external, occur when the mind joins itself to certain centres, called organs. Hence, nothing wrong or unwanted will be done if the mind remains under control. Is it possible? Yes, actually this control is also possible by another person. That is what precisely hypnotic tricks are all about. But such involuntary controls results in disastrous consequences as it uses lots of energy from the mind that is getting controlled externally. *Pratyahara*, meaning "gathering towards" implies that a person has succeeded in attaching/detaching/controlling his mind to or from the centres at will. Once this stage is achieved, one can indeed say that person has become man from the earlier position of being a machine. And this is certainly a long step towards real 'Freedom'.

How hard is it to control the mind? Human mind is just like a monkey, incessantly active by its own nature, than it gets drunk on desires, thus increasing the turbulence even further. After the desire, there is a further sting of scorpion called jealousy and last of all demons that enter the mind is demon of pride. So... first of all sit for a while and let the mind run on. Give it long rein and let it wander where ever it wishes to. Don't get astonished thinking that such bad thoughts can entre your mind. It is normal, it can happen with anyone. Once you practise sitting in *Asana* over a good period, the number of thoughts entering the mind will gradually reduce, and in few more months, these will become fewer than before, until at last the mind will be under perfect control. This controlling and not allowing it to join with organs is "*Pratyahara*". One has to be prepared for a long journey, as it is not going to happen so easily.

Having mastered *Pratyahara*, next thing to work on is *Dharana* also called *Ekagrata*, one pointed concentration. Aim is direct concentration on a single object or idea or even body organ in an uninterrupted manner. Important thing is to put away any emotion or association or distractions that try to invariably rush into the mind. Finally, when the Chitta or mind stuff, is confined and limited exclusively to a certain specific point, it is *Dharana/Ekagrata* achieved.

The Yoga aspirant must always practise, should try to live alone as much as possible; the companionship is a distraction of mind. He should not speak much or work much for the same reason. The biggest advantage of Yoga is that it tones down nervous excitement, brings calmness and enables human to see things more clearly. Temperament will improve positively and so will be the health and voice/sound.

One should give up all argumentation as it only throws the mind off its balance. Talking does not help in realizing things of subtle planes, so give up all vain talks. Also give up the desire for nibbling on one idea after another. To ensure full success, take up only one idea. Make it your life—think, dream and live only that one idea.

Let the brain, muscles, nerves be fully focused on that very idea with all their capabilities and energies.

Having followed all above steps of *Raja Yoga,* one comes to Dhyana, meditation. When the mind has been fully trained to remain fixed on a certain internal or external idea/action/thought for as long as desired by the Yogi, it is called Dhyana. Having reached this stage, the master Yogi thus sinks deeply into his inner world and away from ordinary consciousness that he enters the state called "*Samadhi*", trance. In this stage he is able to control his psychic life and he becomes *Abhedya,* impervious, invulnerable for his own condition. At this stage, hot, cold, hunger and sleep, etc. are no more personal concerns.

Pranayam throws out all impurities of the body. By *Dharana,* all impurities of the mind get thrown out and by *Pratyahara,* all impurities of attachment meet the same result. Finally, when *Samadhi* gets achieved, one reaches the stage where everything that hides the lordship of the Soul is taken off.

Finally, in *Raja Yoga,* the Yoga of Meditation, Gita teaches how to discipline the mind and senses until the mind process is suspended in complete emptiness and merging in the Self. Later, especially after arrival of *Bhagvad Gita,* some other types of Yoga also got recognition. These were said to have same ultimate purpose taking a different route to reach the ultimate goal. Let us briefly talk about these as well.

Karma Yoga (The Yoga of Action)

Many earlier philosophies encouraged seeker to leave the Sansar and go in search of truth to a Guru or some forest academy. But Gita presented yet another way and called it "*Karma* Yoga". It suggests work to be carried out without any attachment to the work itself or desire of results—like *Nishkama Karma.* Under *Karma Yoga,* one is asked to dissolve his body mind identity by connecting with whole of life and dedicating yourself in service of others without any attachment and without expecting anything in return.

This allowed normal people to continue engaged in normal activities as householders without losing their claim for liberation. It was a good reply to both Buddhism and Jainism which encouraged its followers to leave behind everything and pursue liberation as a single-minded activity. One can imagine a situation of the society if all able bodied people decide to hang their boots and start pursuing *Moksha* following the ascetic life. That is certainly no practical situation for the universe to continue.

Simply put, Karma Yoga is a path of doing the right thing, of following one's own swa-dharma and accepting destiny as it comes. One, who discharges his duty without getting attached to results of his work and adopts right means, is a Karma Yogi. To drop the doer from the action is Karma Yoga. To see one self as a divine tool and to be happy to offer the results of his actions to the divine is following karma yoga. (Peter Marchand)

Bhakti Yoga (The Yoga of Devotion)

In recognition of the general mood of thinkers of its time, Gita explains *Bhakti* as a mode of total surrender to the chosen God. Point is mere knowledge of scriptures can't lead to *Moksha*. One has to have Gyan, Karma and *Bhakti*. This way Gita, again, opened vast potential for normal householders engaged largely in their chorus to seek *Moksha* in the easiest of all and quickest possible way. No wonder, *Bhakti* was later to become such a great movement and attracted substantially large number of followers that the earlier recommended paths of knowledge could have never dreamt of.

By exposing a seeker to *Bhakti* Yoga, the same goal is taught to be achieved by identifying with their God in love and devotion by completely devoting one's own identity to his chosen Ishta Deva. This is by and large the only path followed by Islam and Christianity. Here your love for your God allows you to close your mind and just follow the path shown without looking anywhere or applying any logic.

Bhakti will be discussed in more detail later.

Gyan Yoga (The Yoga of Knowledge)

The word knowledge taken here does not apply in intellectual form of the word but the knowledge of *Atman* and *Brahman*. This is the path of wisdom and direct experience of *Brahman* as the ultimate reality. It renounces both desire and action. But it is understood to be very steep and difficult to practise. Throughout the long history of mankind only a select and elite group has been able to proceed on this path.

While under *Bhakti* the devotee follows the promptings of his heart, in case of *Gyan* Yoga he uses the power of mind to discriminate the real from unreal. The aspirant here is supposed to use his will and discrimination to get out of the normal attached identity with body and mind until he realizes the real Self.

In conclusion, it can be said that all four schools need to be blended in appropriate proportions. Any single school looks incomplete without others. So, aspirants are advised to follow all schools to ensure full advantages.

In addition to above four distinct schools, we also come across some other forms of Yoga: the prominent among those are *Tantra, Mantra* and *Hath Yoga*. We will have a good look at *Tantra* and *Mantra* under the topic 'Sects of Hinduism' but we still need to touch base with *Hath Yoga*. Hath is part of *Tantra* Yoga which puts all concentration on step number three and four of Astanga Yoga or *Raja Yoga*. It is actually a short cut process to avoid other steps with the aim of quickly reaching the last step. *Hath Yoga* focuses on postures and breath control to energize the subtle nadies.

There is one more important point in there to understand with reference to Yoga practitioners. And it relates to the knowledge that the final benefit will not arrive all of a sudden. Yoga requires a lot of efforts and a lot of practice. Regularity is the key to success; half an hour per day in not equal to three and half hour on Sunday. But consolation is that some advantage is assured every time one sits for practising Yoga. It is not that if we are not able to reach to the destination, there will be no gains. There is proportional advantage related to the degree of our progress. Spiritual peace and power is expected to flow towards practitioner in the same proportion that he loses his individuality. Yoga trains a person to consciously suppress individuality by proper physical, mental, moral and spiritual development.

16
Composition of Puranas

Historical Perspective at the Time of Writings of *Puranas*

This was a time when Chandra Gupta II (376-415 CE) inherited a big empire from his father, Samudra Gupta in north of the country. Pallavas, Pandyas and Cholas who were still busy settling issues with each other dominated South India. First Chinese visitor named Fa Hsien had visited India and wrote extensively allowing a better peep into the social spectrum of India of that time.

Gupta court has been known for its "Nav Ratnas" who included genius from all walks of life including Science, Maths and Astronomy. Astronomers like Aryabhatta and Varahamihira and Mathematicians like Brahmgupta who gave Zero to the world by propagating the theory that the number remaining after a number is subtracted from itself is zero, were also belonging to this court. The great Sanskrit play writer and poet, Kalidasa also belonged to the same empire. In general, the empire was supportive of all issues of creativity and innovation. Guptas were first to make Sanskrit as their official court language.

But soon after fall of Gupta dynasty at the hands of Huns, Buddhism also faced a lot of hostility and oppressions from new rulers. Lot many practising monks got killed and several monasteries also got destroyed. This was probably first such religion based oppression on Indian soil.

Returning back to religious stage for Hindus, Vishnu as God has been only scantly mentioned in Rig-Veda. He is associated with qualities of saviour par excellence who was always ready to come down from his comforts in Swarga Loka to help suffering humanity. After all, he is known as the God who is involved in creation and preservation of this earth and is known to having supported this earth upon his shoulders. His image was always of benevolence and protection of human being. His marriage to Goddess Laxmi which also became much more important in that time than ever before, resulted in his enhanced image as a superior God pushing Indra to the background and being remembered and worshipped only as a God of Rains.

The other God of sectarian popularization, Shiva evolved out of terrifying Rudra of Rig-Veda. Shiva is supposed to have been worshipped by Sindhu Sarasvati Culture people even before Rig-Veda got composed. Shiva comes out as a God of extremes—frightening as well as gracious. He is not afraid of violence, sometimes on small issues, but is also known as a source of great happiness. He is known as protector of all performing arts, icon of salvation and immortality. Shiva is creator and destroyer at the same time. He is a commoner as well as siddh Yogi. People trapped in complexities of seeking spiritualism amidst involvement of a householder with attachments with worldly things and family, find Shiva as someone much closer to them than other Gods.

This complex interplay of this time with Hindus in North and Hindus in South vs Buddhism vs Jainism going right upto village level is the background for start of writing of a new kind of literature called *Puranas*. This literature is more relaxed and writings under this corpus are neither attentive nor too much concerned about accuracy or detailing when compared to classical Sanskrit literature composed until that time. And one may call it a "Pulp fiction" of India.

But they represent a very large volume of writings. And it is to their credit that the Gods worshipped till today had been installed in their pedestal through lot many stories mentioned and repeated with different versions in *Puranas*. It is to the credit of *Puranas* that all forms of worship were brought together under one particular system. Another great turn that was provided to Hinduism of all times, the inclusion of and Women qualifying for salvation through worship was also due to *Puranas*. *Puranas* alone unlocked the door for both tribals and other castes as well and placed them on the lowest rung of social structure.

Socio-Cultural Background

It will be very interesting to understand the socio cultural conditions which resulted in emergence of *Puranas* which lead to Puranic Hinduism to take deep roots to the extent that a large part of Hinduism as ordinarily understood today is shaped out by *Puranas*. We have discussed earlier that *Brahmins* have consolidated their position over time by taking over priestly duties once the rituals became very sophisticated. They projected themselves as essential agent to secure spiritual and religious merits. We might have heard stories where a rich goldsmith becomes Dharmamurti in his next life after he donated all his property to *Brahmins* at his great *Yajna* or a rich prostitute named Lilavati attains Shivaloka by donating a hillock to a poor *Brahmin*.

Riding on such stories and general belief that donations to *Brahmins* is sure way of accumulating karmas credits, lot many land was accumulating with *Brahmins* and Temples. These land grants are said to contribute towards Indian Feudalism of this time. Land needed additional hands for its mending. This necessitated diversion of lower rung population from other vocations to agriculture. That made it mandatory to absorb them in mainstream of religion by adding them to the lowest rung of existing social structure of class. Women got added to ward off expansion of Buddhism. The problem was that those excluded until now had already developed their worship practices which were idol based. Some of them were worshipping animals or different form of Goddesses.

It was at this time that Hindu practices came up with various *Avatars* of Vishnu and other Gods. This expansion allowed absorption of gods of newly added smaller communities of Shudras into mainstream either as an *Avatar* of a chief God or as their junior partner. In order to absorb their practices, the recognized worship methods also got added. That is how we have nine different types of worships until now. These were 1. *Shravanam* (by listening); 2. *Kirtanam* (by devotional group singing); 3. Smaranam (reciting name repeatedly); 4. *Pada Sevanam* (sharing feast offered to God); 5. *Dasyam* (rendering self to God like a slave); 6. *Archanam* (worship by offering flowers, incense); 7. *Vandanam* (praying earnestly); 8. *Sakhyam* (worship in form of a friend); and 9. *Atmasamarpan* (total surrender of one's life to serve God). Each one of these practices was actually practised by one or the other smaller community which got absorbed into main stream. So the polytheism and idol worship got added to Hinduism together with switching from complicated rituals to simpler ways of *Bhakti Marga* (Gadkari, 1996).

The legends and myths relating to different *Yugas* also got added by *Puranas*. Before *Puranas* one does not come across mention of *Yugas* as separate mythological time periods. In a smart move by the *Purana* composers, they linked various popular salvation practices to *Yugas*. *Puranas* mention that the way for achieving spiritual salvation in the *Sat Yuga* was through meditation, the *Treta Yuga* by *Yajnas*, the *Dwapar Yuga* by reciting sacred *mantras* while the *Kali Yuga* was by repeating name of God Vishnu with full devotion.

At the time of *Puranas*, the Hindu religion has gone out of hands of *Brahmins* and any one could take up writing *Puranas* or contribute in specific *Puranas* without any class restriction. The composers came up with stories after stories to drive home various points to cement absorption of minor communities in mainstream. For example, in Mahabharta Anushasan Parva saying "Even a *Shudra* having a good heart, liberal mind and clean character can become a Yogi" or *Brahma Purana* saying that "...a *chandal* wins over a demon by his *bhakti* for Vishnu and both of them achieve salvation" or in *Bhagvadgita* Srikrishna telling Parth that "Even *Vaishya, Shudra* women or others born of sin can achieve salvation by taking refuge in me" or showing Valmiki, the robber as author of Ramayana or showing *Vyasa,* the son of a fisher women as author of Mahabharata were few such steps which would have been unthinkable until the time of *Manu Smriti*. (Gadkari, 1996)

Another commonality among most *Puranas* is having separate chapters on *Kali Yuga*. All the *Puranas* talk about collapsing of old social systems and big tumbling down of most social codes relating to relatives, family and women. This indicates towards big impact of mixing of Shudras into the social structure on well established and strict social codes of the past.

Numbers and Classifications

There are about 18 *Puranas* and large number of sub *Purana* (*Upa Purana*) dedicated to different Gods and other subject matters.

The eighteen major *Puranas* are the *Brahma, Padma, Vishnu, Shiva, Linga, Garuda, Narada, Bhagavata, Agni, Skanda,*

Bhavisya, Brahma-vaivarta, Markandeya, Vamana, Varaha, Matsya, Kurma and *Brahmanda Puranas*.

The *Brahma Purana* consists of 10,000 verses, the *Padma Purana* of 55,000 verses, *Sri Vishnu Purana* of 23,000 verses, the *Shiva Purana* of 24,000 verses, *Srimad-Bhagavatam* of 18,000 verses. The *Narada Purana* has 25,000 verses, the *Markandeya Purana* 9,000 verses, the Agni *Purana* 15,400 verses, the *Bhavisya Purana* 14,500 verses, the *Brahma-vaivarta Purana* 18,000 verses, the *Linga Purana* 11,000 verses, the *Varaha Purana* contains 24,000 verses, the *Skanda Purana* 81,100 verses, the *Vamana Purana* 10,000, the *Kurma Purana* 17,000, the *Matsya Purana* 14,000, the *Garuda Purana* 19,000 and the *Brahmanda Purana* 12,000. Thus the total number of verses in all the *Puranas* is 400,000 strong.

Language and Content

Puranas are easy Sanskrit texts addressing religious aspirations of all classes following mythological stories and events. The stories told and elaborated here contain substantial local content in terms of rituals, practices, geography, and instructions about worship. These are not very comprehensive or based on complete thinking of *Shastras* and were compiled in bulk with lots of repetition of stories and instances which are just vaguely grounded to something said in the *Sruti* literature. *Puranas* allowed play of imaginations going to infinite levels. *Puranas*, meaning "ancient", are actually compendiums of myths and rituals shown in continuity of past.

Composers wrote these with a lot of focus on 'our own' God, our own pilgrimage, our own river, our own people, our own customs and festivals and our own Heros. I read somewhere those composers of *Purana's* believed that "it is our world and this is the whole world" and most parts of the voluminous literature is coloured with such localizations.

Hinduism Goes Out of Hands of Brahmins

The localization resulted in mammoth expansion of beliefs and Brahmins had no option but to accept the entire range to accommodate each belief by submerging strict orthodoxy applied in the past. Interestingly, *Brahmins* were not the main writers of *Puranas* as writers from other classes took lead in this literature.

This resulted in loosening of the grip that *Brahmins* commanded until now on all Vedic and Hindu writings in general and in conducting rituals in particular but not now. *Brahmins* were sidelined, as most of the rituals mentioned in these *Puranas* didn't necessarily required presence of *Brahmin* Priests.

For the first time in the history, Hindu religion percolated down and became accessible to all its practitioners from all classes and *Brahmin* sieve could not hold it under tight thumb as in the past. Another interesting point about *Puranas* is that these are not strictly for one or more Gods alone. Many temples and towns also got their *Purana* and in vernacular. *Puranas* have a separate category called '*Sthala Purana*' which, as the very name suggest, are for specific places only.

Shiva and Vishnu Calling Shots

Main gods covered in *Puranas* are Shiva and Vishnu. *Brahma* has been given very small space for worshippers throughout Hinduism and *Puranas* are no exception to the rule. Actually speaking, the so called *Trimurti* of Hinduism consisting of Brahma, Vishnu and Mahesh seems more like a matching game with Christianity where there is a trinity consisting of Holy Spirit, Holy Father and Holy Son. In practice as well in most Hindu scriptures, *Vishnu* and *Shiva* are their own preservers and destroyers. Especially for the followers of both Shiva and Vishnu, their Gods are complete Gods and they don't consider it as a faith that their God is only for creation or sustaining or destroying as the concept of *Trimurti* bases itself on.

And one more important point not to miss is that by this time Vedic Rituals had been completely replaced by Puranic rituals. Meaning thereby that since the Vedic days, Hinduism as a religion got completely transformed with only key philosophical concepts of *samsara*, karma, *moksha* continuing but all visible practices of rituals which were once backbone of Vedic dharma, all sacrifices, all Gods named in Vedas got transformed or pushed to back stage.

The compilation of *Puranas* also got carried out on the lines of epics and a lot of oral to writing continued for over centuries. Actually, the discussion if Mahabharata is an epic or a *Purana* continues without any conclusion. Many writers actually treat Mahabharata just another *Purana*. This is corroborated by the fact that they contain references and counter references for events and characters and outcomes of one into another. At the time of epics only few cross-references are found but in *Puranas,* there are hundreds and hundreds of cross references. As per one estimate, the period of compilations of few important *Puranas* is shown against their names below to highlight how long these have been in discussions before taking their present form:

- *Brahamanda* (350 to 950 CE)
- *Markandeya* (250 to 550 CE)
- *Matsya* (250 to 500 CE)
- *Padma* (750 o 1000 CE)
- *Shiva* (750 to 1350 CE)
- *Skanda* (700 to 1150 CE)
- *Vamana* (450 to 900 CE)

Let us look at a reproduction of some random excerpts from *Shiva Purana* to get some flavour of the nature of writings and the pattern of showing the chosen God of the particular *Purana* as bigger than all others combined:

> *"First of all, Sage Shaunak expressed his desire to Sutji about knowing the means, which could help a man in this era of Kali to attainment lord Shiva, by cleansing all the impurities of his mind and rectifying his inherent demonic tendencies. Sutji then described about Shiva Mahapuran—the supreme of all the puranas, which was narrated by Lord Shiva himself and which was later on retold by Sage Vyas with the permission of Maharshi Sanatkumar, for the benediction of common man. Sutji said, "By understanding the mysteries of Shiva Mahapuran and singing its praises, a man attains greater virtues than that which could be attained by being charitable or by the performance of all the 'yagyas''. Contemplating on the subject matters of Shivmahapuran give auspicious fruits just like a 'Kalpa-taru' (A mythological tree which fulfills all the wishes).*
>
> *"Once while travelling lord Brahma reached the abode of Lord Vishnu. He saw Lord Vishnu resting on Shesh-Nag and being attended by Garuda and other attendants. When Brahmaji saw that Vishnu did not get up to receive him, he became very angry. Very soon, verbal duel erupted between them. It became so severe that a battle was fought between them, which continued for a very*

long time. All the deities arrived from the heaven to watch the battle. They became very worried when they saw no sign of battle coming to an end. They decided to go to Lord Shiva, to seek his help "Lord Shiva became very angry with Brahmaji. He proceeded to punish Brahmaji for his falsehood. Lord Vishnu requested Lord Shiva to spare the life of Brahmaji. Lord Shiva became pleased with Vishnuji and accorded him the same status as that of his own."

Let me also share a story from *Vishnu Purana* which, in Hinduism, is very well quoted story of evolution of the living beings:

Parashara said, "Maitreya, let me tell you about how Brahma performed the act of creation."

Brahma is merely part of Narayana. And Narayana is Vishnu. Nara means water and ayana means resting-place. When the earlier creation was destroyed, the world was full of water and Vishnu slept on the water. That is the reason why he is called Narayana. Narayana saw that there was water all around and desired to create the world. He, therefore, adopted the form of a boar (varaha) and went all the way down to the underworld. There the earth saluted him and asked him to rescue her from the underworld. Upon haring the earth's request, Vishnu in his form of a boar began to roar. He used his tusks to lift up the earth from the underworld. Then he carefully placed the earth on the waters. The earth floated on the oceans like a huge boat. Vishnu levelled out the earth and placed the mountains in their proper places. The earth was divided into seven regions or dvipas.

After that came the question of creating the beings. There were four types of beings that Brahma created through the powers of his mind. The first were the demons or asuras, they came out of Brahma's thighs. Next came the gods or devas, they emerged from Brahma's mouth. From Brahma's sides there were created the ancestors or pitris. And the humans came out the last. Many other things were created.

After that Brahma was both hungry and angry. The demons of hunger took form and wanted to eat up Brahma, their creator. There were some among them who did not want to eat their creator, but wanted to protect (raksha) him. They came to be known as rakshas. And those who wanted to eat him came to be known as yakshas. When Brahma saw these undesirable creatures, the hairs on his head fell off and grew up and stood up again. From these hairs were born the snakes. The gandharvas were born. They were known as gandharvas because they sing.

Many other things were created. From Brahma's age were created the birds, from his chest sheep and from his mouth goats. From his stomach and sides there came out cattle and from his feet horses, elephants, deer and camels. Plants sprouted from the hair on Brahma's body.

There were four classes of humans that were created, the brahmins, the kshatriyas, the vaishyas and the shudras. The brahmins came out of Brahma's mouth, the kshatriyas from his chest, the vaishyas from his thighs and the shudras from his feet.

Let me also share the full version of the story about *Samudra Manthan* included in *Vishnu Purana*. This must have been heard or read many time before but a quick read will show the *masala* material included to draw the point home that all devas have been enjoying good life in *Deva Loka* only due to blessings of Lord Vishnu. The simplicity of narrations, and connectivity with everything said or written in the past together with faith of worshippers made *Puranas* the most remembered source of all mythological stories on Hinduism.

"There was a sage called Durvasa who was descended from Mahadeva. Once upon a time, Durvasa was wandering around the world. And in the hands of a pretty woman he saw a beautiful and fragrant garland. Durvasa wanted the woman to give him the garland, which she gladly did. Durvasa placed the garland on his head and continued to roam around the world. Who should he then run into but Indra, the king of the gods? There were other gods with Indra and Indra was seated on his elephant, Airavata. Durvasa picked up the garland and threw it at Indra. Having caught the garland, Indra placed it on the head of his elephant. Airavata got surprised at the pleasant smell that was coming from his head and he raised his trunk to get a better sniff. In the process, the garland fell off his head and onto the ground.

Durvasa was very angry. He thought that Indra had insulted him. He had not even bothered to thank Durvasa for the garland. And instead of placing the garland on his own head, he had seen it fit to place the garland on the head of an elephant. From which place it had fallen off onto the ground. Durvasa therefore got ready to curse Indra. By then, Indra had realized his mistake. He got off the elephant, fell at Durvasa's feet and begged that he might be forgiven. But Durvasa was not like the other sages; he refused to be pacified. And so he cursed Indra. What was the curse? That Lakshmi should disappear from Indra's abode. (Lakshmi, you may know, is the goddess of wealth and prosperity and associated with Vishnu but not from the beginning. It is Puranic stories like this which were responsible for creating many new equations among all the characters of Hindu mythology)

When Indra returned to where he lived in Amaravati, he found the place to be deserted and dilapilated. Lakshmi had left. The plants were dying. The sages were not performing sacrifices. People had become selfish. It was not simply Amaravati that had become like this. Indra ruled over all the three worlds. And in all the three worlds this was precisely what had happened.

The demons never liked the gods and were forever trying to fight with them. They now discovered that the gods were less powerful and less well protected. So they attacked the gods and gave them a good thrashing. What were the poor gods to do? They elected the god Agni as their leader and fled to Brahma for refuge and help. (Devas have been projected as a bunch of jokers, good for nothing stuff who are not able to manage any situation and are made to run to either of the main Gods—what a downfall for Indra from all powerful in Vedas) Brahma told them that he was unable to help them himself; they should seek help from Vishnu. On the northern shores of the great ocean the gods assembled and began to pray.

How could Vishnu ignore such prayers? He manifested himself before the gods and gave them the following advice. The gods should meet the demons and have a temporary truce. Both sides should get together and prepare to churn the great ocean. Before the churning, herbs were to be thrown into the ocean. The mountain Mandara was to be used as the churner and the great snake Vasuki as the rope for churning. It was expected that amrita (a drink that made one immortal) would come out of the ocean as a result of the churning. And the gods should promise the demons that this amrita would be equally shared out among the two sides and make them stronger. The promise of the amrita would make sure that the demons took part in the churning. This was nothing but an empty promise. Vishnu hastened to assure the gods that he would ensure that the demons got none of the amrita.

This the demons did not know, they gladly agreed to the churning. Herbs were hurled into the ocean and the churning began. The gods grasped Vasuki's tail and the demons its head. In fact, it was Vishnu who asked the demons to grasp the head of the snake. Flames and smoke belched out of the mouth of the snake and made the demons suffer. The gases that came out of the snake's mouth went up into the sky and formed clouds. These clouds were driven towards the tail and poured down as soothing rain on the gods who had grasped the tail. On what was the huge mountain Mandara to be balanced? The solution was again provided by Vishnu. Vishnu adopted the form of a gigantic turtle on which the mountain could be placed.

Thus the churning went on. And wonderful were the things that emerged out of the ocean as a result of the churning. The first to come out was the cow Surabhi, worshipped by the gods. Next the goddess Varuni emerged. Followed by the fragrant tree known as Parijata. Out came the apsaras *(dancers of heaven). And the moon, which Mahadeva accepted as an adornment for his head. (starting this Purana, all painters of Shiva started putting the moon on every depiction involving Shiva). There were bad things as well. The poison that came out was accepted by the snakes. And dressed all in white, the god Dhanvantari came out with the pot of amrita in his hands. At the sight of the amrita, the gods, the demons and the sages were delighted. But there was more to come. There emerged a lotus flower with the shining form of the goddess Lakshmi. She held another lotus in her hand.*

As a height of variations in narration, please see below the summary of the same Poison as included in *Shiva Purana:*

But before Amrita could be recovered, Halahala ("the most vicious and venomous poison of universe") was produced, which started killing both sides. As no one could bear the poisonous fumes emitted by the poison, both Devas and Asuras began to collapse due to asphyxiation. They ran for help to Brahma, who looked to Vishnu for advice. Vishnu said that only Shiva could digest the deadly poison. So both parties went to Kailasha and prayed to Lord Shiva for help. Shiva chose to consume the poison and thus drank it. His wife Parvati, alarmed, stopped it in his throat with her hands, thus earning him the name Vishkanttha (the one who held poison in his throat). He was later saved by the mahavidya (Tara) who is also a form of Parvati. The poison made his throat turn blue;

hence, he is also known as Nîlakantha (the one with a blue throat).
Story continued: The sages began to chant hymns in front of her. The gandharvas sang, the apsaras *danced. Rivers like the Ganga arrived so the Lakshmi could have a bath. There are eight elephants who protect the eight directions. These elephants took clear water from golden vessels and bathed the goddess. The ocean gave her a garland of lotus flowers which would not fade. Vishvakarma provided the jewels. Thus bathed, dressed, jewelled and garlanded, Lakshmi embraced Vishnu. Since the demons did not like Vishnu, this meant that Lakshmi had forsaken the demons. And Lakshmi smiled upon the gods. The demons did manage to get hold of the pot of amrita. But Vishnu adopted a female form to trick the demons of the amrita and give it to the gods.*
The gods drank the amrita and attacked the demons with swords. The amrita had made the gods strong and the demons were not match for them. Their armies scattered and they fled into the underworld. The gods were delighted. They bowed before Vishnu and continued to rule over heaven. The Sun went back to its old path across the sky. So did the stars. Indra ascended his throne and ruled over the three worlds, after having prayed to Lakshmi.

All other *Puranas* also equally project their chosen God as supreme and provide for story after story how the God prevailed in most testing situations. Besides those identified with the main heroes of *Puranas*, Lord Shiva and Vishnu, other *Puranas* are *Agni, Bhagvata, Brahma, Garuda, linga, Markandeya* (focus on Shakti Goddess), *Vayu* (focus is again Shiva), *Varaha* (all *Vishnu avatars* and Durga), *Padma* (focus on Bhagwat Gita), *Narada* (focus on *Vedas* and Vedanga), *Matsya* (focus of Vishnu incarnation by the same name).

The sole purpose behind reproduction of above quoted stories is to excite the readers towards mythological aspects of the *Puranas*. While they had redefined external symbols of worship and have aerated the whole range of Hindu Gods, the fact remains that Puranic Hinduism is truth less religion with nominal connectivity with the real Hinduism of universality and spiritualism. The intelligent reader is encouraged to see through the unrealistic mythologies surrounding *Puranas* and other practices of worship evolved thereafter including the endless Gods with their *avatars*. Even by mistake also, the great religion of Hinduism should not be reduced or limited to Gods and methods of worship alone.

17
Sects of Hinduism

Every time one talk about Hinduism, statement like 'Hinduism is not a religion but a way of life, having multiple beliefs, customs and traditions' keep coming back in one or the other form. Hinduism indeed is a Conglomeration of many intertwined mix of smaller religious groups where each member group believes in some shared concepts along with many unique traditions, beliefs and practices. Some differences have been there since ever while many variations developed over a period of time. For almost over last two thousand years, sectarianism has been an integral part of culture at Indian subcontinent.

Yes, Hinduism has many sects within its fold. But the great thing about Hinduism is that all sects coexist with complete harmony with each other and there is complete acceptance of others' beliefs and traditions. Most are expected to have heard Hinduism being referred as "Unity in Diversity". But study of Hindu sects and their extremely tangent traditions will help seeing that diversity unity discussion in a new light. These sects are quite different from each other but have comfortably remained under this big umbrella of Hinduism without any history of violent confrontation that is so common with other popular religions of our times. It is again to the credit of all pervading inclusive approach embedded in Hinduism with deep roots that even sharply dividing identity of separate sects has not erected any walls. This is the strength and true meaning of "Unity in Diversity".

Rig-Veda has a very famous line "*Ekam Sat Viprah Bahudha Vadanti*" which translates to '*Truth is one; sages call it by various names*'. This saying truly represents Sects of Hinduism. It is very liberal, tolerant, flexible and catholic in its views and traditions. Different sects of Hinduism are just like different gemstones of a single ornament called Hinduism. It is said that there are various types of minds and temperaments. If so, there is a need for different types of faiths. This open-minded acceptance of every kind of faith in God is but a cardinal tenet of Hinduism. Many of us would have heard Krishna telling Arjuna in Gita:

> *"Howsoever Men approach me, even so I do welcome them. For the path taken by Men from everyside is mine."*

Normally, the meaning of Sect and Cult are not very far but of late, the cult is believed to denote a much narrow view where there is intolerance for every person outside the cult. We must understand that Hinduism never had any problem among the followers of different cults. They have grown peacefully intertwined with each. Basically, the beginning and end destination of the journey are identical among all Hindu sects. All one can find are some difference of opinions about the way to reach that commonly shared destination. Their paths cross each other almost regularly and they share many resting places and shelters on the way. So, study of sects in Hinduism is but an academic exercise. Sectarianism has been initiated around the turn of BC CE time period as evidences are found suggesting that 2nd Century CE onwards all the kings in large part of subcontinent had started following one or the other popular sects.

Traditionally, Hinduism is said to have five sects namely Shaivism, Vishnuism, Shaktism, Bramanism and Tantraism but in modern time that will not be enough because it is not possible to segregate and identify every Hindu strictly identified with any one of them. Over the period, larger proportion of Hindus have broken the walls built around their sects and have embraced a much wider, all-inclusive pluralism. Let us call this new category as the "Popular Hindu Sect". Today, by far, Popular Hinduism has more followers than all other sects combined. Followers here believe in best of all practices from all sects and worship many Gods all at once. For them, individual God is nothing but a specific manifestation of the Almighty and they don't believe in any one of them being superior or inferior to other.

Brief description of traditional sects is provided here under:

Shaivism

Followers of Shiva believe him to be 'All in All': a creator, preserver and destroyer; independent of any other God. They are more attracted to asceticism then adherents. It was first time in *Svetasvatara* Upanishad (400 BC to 200 BC) (Wikipedia) that emphasis was changed from *Brahman* to personal Ishvara who is said to be manifested *Brahman*. This Upanishad was the first hint of theist in character and identified Supreme *Brahman* with Rudra. Shaivism saw rapid expansion in 200 CE to 500 CE periods starting from South India and going up to all parts of the subcontinent. The volumes of Puranic literature, through singing, writing and reading, fuelled this expansion further. Shaivites believe in '*Vairagya*' more than others.

Many prominent rulers of ancient India such as the Kushans, the Guptas, the Barasivas, the Satavahanas and the Cholas were ardent worshippers of Shiva. The Barasivas played an important role in preserving many ancient traditions of Shaivism, at a time when Buddhism was on the rise. Apart from the Indian subcontinent, Shiva was also worshipped in other parts of the world such as Nepal, Sri Lanka, Malaysia, Singapore, Cambodia and Indonesia.(V)

There are many sub-sects with in Shaivism. While they all acknowledge Lord Shiva as the Supreme Deity, they differ from one another in respect of other details such as the modes of worship, nature of *Brahman*, the nature of individual soul, the relationship between the two, the nature of reality and the means to liberation. These schools of Shaivism primarily fall under one of the three schools of Hindu philosophy, namely *Advaita* (monism), *Vishishtadvaita* (qualified monism) and *Dvaita* (*dualism*). Of the few sects that survived the vicissitudes of time, the following five are the most prominent; 1. Pashupata Shaivism, 2. Kashmiri Shaivism, 3. Siddha Shaivism, 4. Gorakhnatha Shaivism, and lastly 5. Vira Shaivism which have their own pockets of influence in different parts of India. (V) Practitioners apply *tilak* on forehead with three horizontal strips for unique identification.

Main places of worships are called *Jyotirlingas* which are situated at 1. Somnath-Veraval, 2. Mahakaleshwar-Ujjain, 3. Omkareshwar-near Indore, 4. Kedar Nath-Uttarakhand, 5. Kashi Vishwanath-Benaras, 6. Rameshwar-Rameshwaram,

7. Nageshwara-Dwarka, 8. Trymbhkareshwar-Nashik, 9. Bhimashanker-Pune, 10. Grihshneshwar-Ellora, 11. Vaidyanath-Parali-Maharashtra, 12. Malikarjuna-Srisailam.

Pashupatinath at Kathmandu, Nepal is another big place for Shiva devotees and that temple is counted as half *Jyotirlinga* with other half being Kedar Nath. Kashi Visawanath at Benaras is considered one of the holiest places and is mentioned as one of the Padal Petra in *Thevaaram* (the famous Tamil poetry for praises of Shiva).

Vaishnavism

Vishnu followers give total importance to Vishnu and all his incarnations. Vishnu followers are generally non-ascetic and are mainly dualistic. Vaishnavism is very rich in saints, temples and scriptures. Most important incarnations for worship are Lord Rama and Lord Krishna, the heroes of great epics. Followers of Vishnu believe in *Bhakti* and *Bhakti* Yoga as tool for final salvation. This sect draws their influence from Upanishads, Bhagwat Gita, Padma *Purana*, Vishnu *Purana* and Bhagwad *Purana*. There are many other sub sects within Vaishnavism. Most ancient of all sub-sects is called Sri Sampradaya popularized by Ramanuja Acharya. They worship Lord Vishnu and Laxmi in all their incarnations. Vallabhacharins, another sect has its major followings in Maharashtra, Gujarat and Central India. These followers are seen worshiping Lord Krishna as "Bal Gopala" which covers his life from infancy to the age of twelve years. Similarly, we have Chaitanyas in Odisha who worship Lord Krishna as Supreme Being. In addition we have the Madhavas and many more and still growing.

Vaishnavites apply *tilak* on forehead in vertical strips with shape of the strips being different for different sub sects. In modern times, this sect has had seen vast expansion on foreign soils as well with ISKCON and Hare Krishna Movement being the prime example.

Major sages known to have promoted this sect are Ramanujacharya, Madhavacharya, Nimbarkacharya, Vallabhacharya, Surdass, Tulsidas, Eknath, Chaitanya Mahaprabhu and Tyagraja, etc. They draw direct lineage from Vedic Brahminism. As a result this has been most popular sect in Hinduism until Mughal raj. Main pilgrimage for Vaishnavites are Guruvayur

Temple, Sri Rangam, Vrindavan, Mathura, Ayodhya, Tirupati, Pandharpur, Puri, Mayapur, Nathdwara and Dwarka.

Shaktism

Starting with Vedas, one has not seen much to talk about Goddesses except some wives of Gods. Characters of Draupadi and Sita, in the great epics, were the first signs of some significant presence of women in religious horizon of Hinduism. Most Sanskrit texts have referred them merely as Devis having much lower positioning in terms of power and scope. So, it is to the credit of *Puranas* that Hindus started giving higher respect to Goddesses than before, if not the same status as Gods.

Devi Mahatmya, a long story included in *Markandeya Purana* is by far the first step for showing high and glorified women Shakti having divine power equal or better than some Gods. Eventually, Goddesses got divided into two categories, Goddesses of Breasts (who are wives of main Gods like Laxmi, Parvati, Sarasvati, etc.) and Goddesses of Tooth, the fierce killer with plenty of uncontrolled power, generally celibate and without having children of their own but protecting her followers from all difficulties as a mother. Maa Durga, Maa Kali, Maa Bhawani falling under this category. (Doniger, 2009)

Shaktism is worshipped in Tantrik practices where the Goddesses worshipped are Chandika and Ambika, etc. Like other sects, Shaktism also has got sub sects. Largest schools of Shakti are Sri Kula (Family of Sri) practised in South India and Kali Kula (family of Kali) practised in East and North India. This sect of Hinduism is an exception to the whole world as there is no other example in any other religious liturgical history having such a complete female oriented system.

It is alleged that practising Shaktism leads only to *Siddhis* (occult power) and *Bhukti* (material enjoyment) while practising Shaivism or Vaishnavism leads to *Moksha*, the spiritual liberation.

Tantraism

Followers of *Tantra* from the start involved higher classes, women and low caste people. They actually didn't follow normal Hindu class segregation and argued that there are only two classes; male and female. Accordingly, women play equal role in their rituals. The tradition started as a parallel to Vedic system with the difference that they believed individual Sadhana as a route to salvation without going out of the world. So, *Tantra* followers don't give up worldly pleasures to seek union with their Gods. But over the centuries, many practices entered the sect vitiating the original *Tantra* to an altogether different sect. Later followers had no concern how they look and extremes of them are called "*Aghoris*" referring to people having nothing as horrible. As a sect, *Tantra* followers had their own texts, rituals, myths, art forms, *mantras* and yantras as well as their own Gods and Goddesses. Much of *Tantrik* ritual take place in remote areas away from public view as this practice is individualistic against group practices of Vedic followers.

It looks like later *Tantra* got more attracted to meet natural traditions of some of the Shudras and other cursed people who were forbidden by the Vedas. Such people formalized their own doctrines.

Basic *mantras* of *Tantra*, available to both ascetics and householders, promised Bhog and *Siddhis* on way to Nirvana. They, thus, aimed for best of both the worlds and their recommended path is '*bhukti* to *mukti*' or from '*bhoksa* to *moksha*' best translated as "sensual delight to spiritual flight".

Their rituals are based around madira, mansa, matsya, mudra (like the one used in hand position or a dance position) and maithuna (which included sexual or menstrual discharge). Some tantric rituals involved women both as sexual partners but to say that *Tantra* was in any way had some gender preference will be wrong. In the main Tantrik ceremony the male invokes Shiva and accompanying women partner invokes the Shakti Goddess to enter her body. During the intercourse, their sexual fluids unite and generate unusual power to activate the *Kundalini* that travels up their spine by energizing all the *Chakras* to finally help experiencing the ultimate bliss and complete enlightenment.

There are many other Yogic kriyas and practices that also suggest ways and means of activating the *Kundalini* and reaching the so called bliss without resorting to union of male and female. But *Tantra* assumes in ritual sex to achieve the same purpose. Somehow, the current impression of *Tantra* appears that it is for low caste people who were at home with all kinds of impurities and had no bounds of social behaviour and used human skulls as their begging bowls, lived and prayed with corpses in cremation grounds, drank alcohol and ate meats of all varieties.

Mostly, they worship ascetic rupa of Shiva and fierce rupa of Shakti. In any case, *Tantras* was never ever a mainstream sizable follower's sect. It has been written and discussed with its illogical but fascinating practices where the forbidden activities are allowed under so called umbrella of an established and highly regarded religion like Hinduism.

Brahamanism

Also called Smartha Tradition, this sect is dominated largely by *Brahmins* who are dedicated to *Smriti*. They are basically liberal followers and non-sectarian in nature. Their path continues to be grounded in philosophical, meditative path emphasizing man's oneness with God through understanding. They are like purist of the past and continue recognizing the *Brahman* of Upanishads as the highest principle in the universe that pervades all of existence.

As per one writer, all *Brahmins* who specialized in Karma kand and who followed Vedas and *Shastras* came to be known as Smarthas. No wonder, these are more orthodox and follow traditional Hindu denominations observing strict rules and regulations. As an extension of their lineage, their philosophical basis rests on *Mimansa* and *Vedanta*.

Great thinker Adi Shankara is credited with regeneration of this tradition. It was his lifelong untiring efforts that he brought all Vedic communities together under one umbrella and revived the great tradition. In a cleansing effort, he removed all non-*Smriti* elements that had crept into Hinduism over the period. To bring all other sects also together he established that worshipping different deities is compatible with Vedas and not contradictory as all Gods so worshipped are but different manifestations of only one *Nirguna Brahman*. Following this, *Shiva, Vishnu, Shakti* all got added to the worship by the followers of this sect also.

Adi Shankara established the non-dual interpretation of Upanishads as a touchstone of a revised Smartha tradition by bringing together Adaivta and Smartha as a solution to varied and sometimes conflicting devotional practices. Thus one could worship and practise either of Vishnu, Shiva, Durga, Surya or Ganesha as one's own *Isht Devta*.

The Sringeri Sharada Monastery founded by Adi Shankarachrya in Karnatka is still the main centre for this tradition.

Under this tradition, Supreme reality *Brahman* transcends all forms of personal deity. God can be taken as *Saguna* or *Nirguna* i.e. *Sakar* or *Nirakar*. As *Saguna*, God exhibits qualities such as infinite nature and characteristics such as love, compassion, justice. As *Nirguna*, God is understood as pure consciousness totally unconnected with matter as experienced by humanity. We will take these matters in detail when we discuss Philosophies.

As regular Puja rituals, the temples made by followers of this tradition, especially during medieval time, one finds all the deities worshipped. The normal arrangement is that principal deity is placed in the centre surrounded by smaller shrines containing residual deities. Going forward to modern times, most temples built follow this very arrangement.

This sect also believes in *Ashrama* system of Hinduism where different sets of rules are prescribed for different stages of human life where a person graduates from *Brahmacharya* to *Grihastha* to *Vanprashtha* to *Sannyasa* depending upon his age, maturity, mental disposition, qualification and spiritual bent. These rules transposed and amended to modern time life style, are still very relevant and guide many seekers to decide their own way forward.

In modern times, Vivekananda and Dr. S. Radhakrishnan are two great teachers and followers of this tradition. Undoubtedly, as a good luck to Hinduism, the enlightened individuals appeared on horizon and took the responsibility of refining and reviving basic Hinduism at regular intervals. They allowed Hinduism to stand strong in facing a long competition from other homegrown religions. These people included ascetics, yogis, religious scholars, priests, teachers, intellectuals, authors, commentators, kings and other influential persons from different walks of social life. They kept the process of making it relevant and pushing the orthodoxy at bay.

Hinduism gained a lot from such individuals. Not being a religion, in the ordinary sense and bound by no creed or dogmas, it assimilated a wide range of thoughts and established a firm foundation upon which it got strength to stand firm for a long time in history. Hinduism is indeed comparable to a Banyan tree where branches return to the ground and become roots and trunks. These roots soon grow into another tree such that eventually you have a forest of banyan trees without being able to know or without being feeling the necessity to know the original roots.

Because of its flexibility and openness for accepting new streams with open arms, Hinduism has been rated as one of the most popular religions attracting whole host of new followers as against most other religions where one gets to follow it more by birth in the family than own personal attitude for the values of the religion. As a result, there are many new sectarian movements with varying success holding the flag of keeping it relevant for our future generations. These are:

- The Swamy Narayan Movement
- The Radhasoamy Movement
- The Ramakrishna Mission
- The Meher Baba Movement
- The Self Realisation Fellowship
- The Self Revelation Church of Absolute Monism
- The Brahma Kumaris
- The Church of Shaiva Siddhanta
- The Satya Sai Baba Society
- The Muttapan Tevyam
- The Ananda Marga
- The Transcedental Meditation
- The Tantri Spiritualism
- The Hare Krishna Movement (ISKCON)
- The Echanakar Movement
- The Osho Movement
- The Krishnamurthy Foundation
- The Auroville Movement of Aurobindo and Mother
- The Mother Meera Movement
- The Sahaj Yoga Movement of Maa Nirmala Devi
- The Mata Amritanandamayi Mission

18 Purusharthas in Hinduism

The vision of God is evident through his manifested creations. His world is filled up with the abundance of material and spiritual beings and energies. A common man is rightfully busy seeking correct guidance for his actions and thoughts such that there is appropriate harmony and balance in natural desires, organ sensory fulfillments and pursuits of ultimate liberation from the so-called Mayajal. *Purusharthas* means "Aims of Human Life". Hinduism provides great value and provides a clear path to its followers by showing them the aims of life with proper prioritization and sequencing.

Purushartha serve as right pointers in the life of a human being. The word *Purusha* is used here as an individual soul or Self in its purest form. And the meaning of the word Artha used here is Purpose or Objective. Man is also a God in his microcosmic aspect. God always maintains a perfect harmony in balancing the blissful coexistence of the entire universe clearly maintaining set rules. Therefore he should also emulate the God and manifest the same reality in his own little world. So, it is like an obligatory duty of every human to first understand and then pursue these aims in order to serve the purpose for which he has been created and sent to this life in this universe.

As per basic tenets of Hinduism, man, as an aspect of God itself, exists in relationship with God like a reflection in the mirror that is somewhat different but inseparable. Veiled in him is the true Self under influence of *Prakriti*. The purpose of his life at earth is to follow the Dharma of God and achieve *Moksha,* liberation from *Ahamkara,* false self by leading a balanced life in which both material comforts and human passion have their own place and legitimacy. The four chief aims of human life suggested by Hinduism are:

(a) *Dharma,*
(b) *Artha,*
(c) *Kama,* and
(d) *Moksha.*

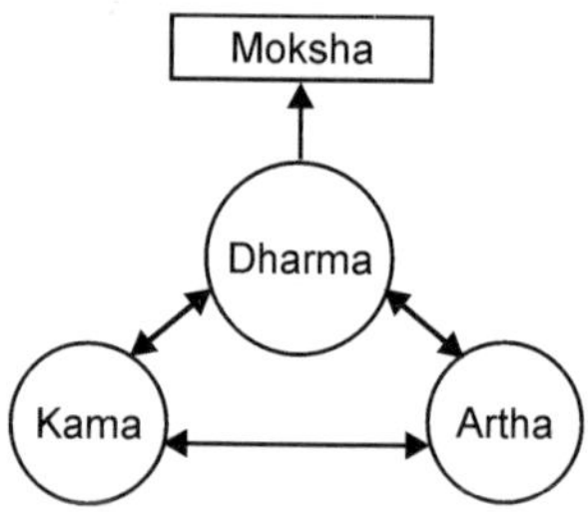

Every individual in Hindu Society is expected to work hard to achieve these four objectives of life with detachment, without any expectation and as a sacrificial offering to the God. Depending upon his attitude, sincerity and dedication applied to pursue these; these goals either set him free or entangle him deeper with the allurement of human life.

A true understanding of these aims will certainly help us prioritise our efforts of normal day life and will give us a sense of purpose, inspiration for working hard together with sense of duty and fulfillment. Many of us also come across this question from within as what should we strive for at our current stage of life. We are always looking for some one showing us the right direction at every stage of our life journey. These aims are designed to meet just that basic human requirement.

Even before understanding individual objectives in detail, it should be clearly understood that it is just not recommended to jump over to the final goal by skipping other goals on the way. It is strongly argued that due experience of all aims of early life is essentially desired to help realize the ultimate aim of liberation. Unless we have gone through *Kama* and *Artha,* it will not be possible for us to appreciate as to what is the thing from which we need to seek liberation from in the first place. Unless a normal householder goes through the householder's life with all its problems, challenges, sufferings and other such experiences, he will not be able to feel the sincere desire for liberation. The real life actual experiences coupled with his own intellect and knowledge actually drives his sincere efforts for pursuing comparatively hard pursuit for liberation.

Also, each one of us must avoid self negation which will be rightly construed as running away and escapism rather than liberation. The life desires are proper opportunities to bring about balance, richness, complexities and opportunities as a role on a big stage called cosmic drama of immense proportions wherein the person gets through his self initiatives, self controls, self efforts and self motivation alone.

Now let us focus on each of these pious aims:

Very First Aim of Life—Dharma

As a word, Dharma is used in almost all eastern religions but it means many things to many people and almost impossible for understanding it in well-defined limits set by any combination of words. English words like duty, faith, religion, righteousness, sacred law, justice, ethical obligations and morality are but unable to completely comprehend the true gist of Dharma as meant in Vedic traditions. In Hinduism, more accepted definition of Dharma can be taken as

> *"Obligatory duty as prescribed by Vedas expected to be performed by an individual in accordance with the rules prescribed with relation to his age, caste, capability, capacity and profession without any desire, preference or attachment with the result of such act."*

The fact is that Dharma is much more of a concept rather than a single word and must be understood accordingly. Being a common origin from *Dhri* (same as used in *Dharti*), it will also cover all obligations for protecting everything on this earth and its equilibrium. In broader terms, it is the secret glue and binding force upholding and regulating the entire creation just as the law of gravity upholds the entire material universe.

Dharma is to taken as a divine constitution that defines individual roles and responsibilities in the social and moral contexts. It is supposed to be sacred, inviolable and pervasive. It is the one that an individual undertakes in harmony with divine injunctions and his own sense of morality and justice. But as this world is full of Maya and Bhram, it is not so easy to comprehend what is appropriate and most of us will feel pressure of going through '*Dharma Sankat*' at many times in our life. It is for this very precise reason that our Acharyas and Gurus have recommended study of scriptures under the able guidance of well qualified Gurus, who alone can help us to accurately and safely navigate through the tough terrains of Dharma Granthas.

As a personal experience, I wish to share that absence of a Guru can result in some detours resulting in some additional time and energy required to sort out initial hiccups. But once you have gone through first reading of scriptures like *Law of Manu, Bhagavad Gita, Vedas, Upanishads* with proper commentaries, an individual with normal level of intelligence will be able to perfectly navigate himself with perfect understanding of Dharma with reasonable clarity. This point is just to allay fears that if we are not able to have access to a Guru, we are not capable of seeking right pursuits of Vedic knowledge or knowledge of Hindu thoughts and beliefs.

Applying the meaning of Dharma just to denote a religion is but a very limited view of Dharma in its Vedic background. It is much later that the word "Dharma" came to be used as Religion. Just to recall, for thousands of years of ancient Indian history, there was never a need to define Religion in separate boundaries. It was possible for any one to hold different faiths or worship different Gods without being differentiated under Religions. So, even at the cost of repetition, Dharma is much wider than Religion and must be understood accordingly.

Second Aim of Life—Artha

With meaning equal to wealth and prosperity, it is recognized as quite essential for the overall happiness and well being of any individual living worldly life. It is well recognized that none of our duties can be fulfilled without wealth being around. It is considered as second most important aim in Hinduism and it recommends seeking wealth to uphold Dharma and help family and society to help achieve their goals.

Another way to define it as an aim in life is to say that Artha is working for and achieving success in terms of wealth and power. Various forms of Artha can be briefly classified as under. The sequence is not accidental but a well-defined prioritization:

- *Inner Wealth*: Positive mindset, self respect, internal peace;
- *Physical Wealth*: Ability and capacity to undertake all physical acts with vigour;
- *Family Wealth*: Well knit family and circle of friends and other personal community;
- *Professional Wealth*: Actualizing highest potential by reaching at pinnacle of pursued profession by attaining everything possible to attain;
- *Economic Wealth*: Money or everything convertible to money, freedom to acquire things required for pursuing what one really likes and generally to be used for making life easier.

Contrary to general understanding, especially one propagated by foreign commentators of Hinduism, it does not glorify poverty although it advocated austerity, simplicity and detachment for everything material. And to its credit, for most part of its glorious past, the entire region of Indian subcontinent which is the land where Hinduism has evolved and pervades, has been well known for its riches until the time when its riches itself became the attraction of foreign invaders of all types of people from Arab, Central Asia, Mongolia as well as Europe. So, anyone connecting Hinduism with poverty is suffering from a lack of vision and nothing else. Hinduism has never considered the desire for wealth as bad but greed is certainly considered so. Selfless desire for creating and preserving wealth is highly recommended.

But one more critical point needs to be understood in sufficient clarity and that is the difference between Sanskrit words '*Artha*' and '*Anartha*' the two opposing terms linked with each other. Hinduism recommends but only righteously acquired wealth as the constituted meaning of Artha. Any part of wealth acquired by foul means or dubious methods is considered *Anartha* which is not only looked with disdain, but also which is synonymous with 'bad omen'. So, wealth is not the recommended wealth unless its means of acquisition are as per accepted norms of right Dharma.

Wealth is taken as divine energy. Abundance of this divine energy is nowhere objected or held undesirable. Actually, one comes across many *Veda Mantras* where oblations are made to various Gods for bestowing wealth. Hence, aiming for wealth is virtue. Creating it and collecting it for family and society is not sinful. But taking something belonging to someone else is certainly sinful. So, one must have clean and clear means of acquiring wealth to be on right side of this virtue.

In addition, Hinduism also emphasizes that being poor or rich should be taken just as an experience without getting attached to it. So, one should become indifferent to comforts/discomforts or having/not having of life caused by it. What is advocated is moderation and balance in pursuits of both material and spiritual goals of one's life. Most modern thinker of our time, Vivekananda has said:

> *"Religion is never for a person with empty stomach. If a person is struggling with survival needs, he cannot focus or appreciate any religious teachings."*

Third Aim of Life—Kama

Before going in detail, it is imperative to clearly apprehend the real meaning of this word, which has been generally twisted to denote only a small portion of its true meaning. Generally speaking it is understood as carnal desire. But that is not the correct understanding. 'Kama' actually means the enjoyment of legitimate desires with the help of honestly acquired wealth. Kama is also said to include producing and enjoyment of art, music, dance, drama, literature and poetry. So, all human desires of good things in life constitute Kama. This will include building a grand house, good conveyance, and good food, pampering of body, enjoying a mushaai'ra or throwing a great party as well as meeting carnal desires. Kama is also said to include producing and enjoyment of art, music, dance, drama, literature and poetry. It is thus religiously praiseworthy to take part, to support, or just to appreciate any form of pleasure. However, in terms of taking it as an objective of life, the caveat of use of honestly acquired wealth and the activity itself being within the gambit of Dharma is equally important.

Hinduism, together with Buddhism considers 'Kama' as root cause of human suffering. Hence, detachment from sense objects, specially, sex is advocated as a way out from these sufferings. As per some interpretations in Hinduism, it can either be means of liberation and happiness or a great hindrance and cause of suffering, depending on how we approach it. In any case one has to overcome it ultimately to achieve salvation. It can be either done by abstaining from it or by indulging in it. The former is the way of Vedanta and the later is the way of *Tantra*. The first is the way of suppression while the second is the way of expression. The fact that *Tantras* have finally vanished from most part of Hindu thoughts, we should bury the expression of sexual powers as a means of liberation through the Tantrik way and side with Vedanta thoughts of the way through suppression.

Generally speaking, Hinduism does not object to sex so long as it is not in conflict with the principle of Dharma and is used for the purpose of procreation, perpetuation of family and social order within the well established boundaries set in traditions, social norms and scriptures. Sexual activity is part of social obligation and should not be indulged for seeking pleasure. But sexual desire has been well understood as the ultimate in all basic human desires and unless it is overcome, one cannot overcome the Maya and ultimately one has to overcome it for seeking liberation as the final aim of life.

The Puranic time is full of many stories portraying Gods and Goddesses as oversexed objects with even Gods finding it hard to resist beautiful *Apsaras*. But the real Vedantic Hinduism has had very clear views on this aspect and side stories better be ignored by intelligent readers and seekers as undesirable diversions which will ultimately delay reaching our final destination.

Final Aim of Human Life—Moksha

Pursuits of Dharma regulate the life to keep an individual on the right path. While pursuits of Artha and Kama add to his worldly experience and impart valuable lessons of life. The pursuit of the final and most important aim in human life of *Moksha* is to be pursued for liberation and leading to the world of *Brahman*. Following Dharma starts in early student life and continues all through. Pursuing the twin aims of *Artha* and *Kama* are reserved for the householder stage. Finally, seeking *Moksha* is considered as most important among all aims of life and is recommended to start only after seeking experiences of all other three aims. This is the only aim to be followed all through *Vanprashtha* and *Sannyasa Ashramas*.

Moksha is both *Purushartha* and *Parmartha*. It actually means absence of '*moh, maya* or *bhram*'. Bhram is caused by the inter play of three *gunas,* the activity of senses and attachment with the desire of sense objects. Liberation is achieved when quality of '*Sat*' is increased by suppressing that of '*Rajas*' and '*Tamas*' and overcoming the desire of sense objects by detachment, self control and completely surrendering one's all actions to God. This is achievable only by following the path of *Gyan, Karm, Bhakti* and *Tyag*.

These aims ensure that we do not neglect our obligations of human life at every stage, become obsessed with any one aim at the cost of other, maintain happiness and balance in human life, cater to both material and spiritual aspirations in right priority and proportions.

It is well accepted that the achievement of Artha and Karma must come before the final quest for spiritual salvation. A person must enjoy in some measure what worldly life has to offer, pay off debts to society and contribute one's bit in maintaining a healthy communal life before turning away from the transient world and attaching himself to the changeless Reality that lies veiled beyond material existence, which alone can give everlasting joy.

In the times that the Hindu society gave proper emphasis on these aims and such other traditions, it grew to its maturity and became rich, splendid and unique. It reached its pinnacle in culture and civilization; it developed great literature, science, arts, crafts and industry. It also laid inspired basis of wonderful spiritual philosophies. But in due course came degradation on all cherished values. Old time integral harmony among various aims gave way to higher focus on *Kama* and *Artha* at the cost of Dharma. But even so, some strong basis of the old knowledge did remain and kept alive the hopes of the people even in the darkest days of Hinduism. That is why Hinduism alone, out of all ancient civilizations, still exists today having lived an unbroken continuous collective life.

The quest for *Moksha* and its value as the highest goal of human life had not been understood even among most Hindus nor widely taught. The tendency amongst spiritual aspirants to have disdained and lack of meaningful involvement in society still exists. On the other hand very tiny number of householders, even today, are able to come out from Kama and Artha to pursue *Moksha* with total dedication.

19

Beginning of *Murti Puja* (Idol Worship)

Vedas and Upanishad have created *Brahman* the supreme. But in due course of time that God had become very remote and people felt he is no more approachable. They needed a God who can watch over them, guide them for good and punish for wrongdoing. History suggests that whenever one God fails to deliver, people get ready to create another God. This is something they always do and will continue doing so. When one religious idea ceases to work for them, it is immediately replaced. (Armstrong, 1993)

This is what happened in Hinduism too. Following the popularization of *Puranas* and process of sectarianism, Vedic divinities no more met common person's aspiration of connecting with the Supreme and achieve salvation. The Upanishad's *Brahman,* which was formless and without attributes, was felt to be so far away and hence, neither available nor achievable. Human mind with its limitations, finds it difficult to comprehend God in absolute. (This experience is Universal in nature and true for all times in History). People were yearning for a system where they can directly connect with their Ishta Deva and establish their own contact without the need of any intermediary. But Vedic approach was collective in nature and conducting *yajna* required specialization of priests. *Yajnas* were very elaborate and only very rich people can afford their arrangements. By the beginning of Common Era, *Yajnas* were getting conducted only by kings and aristocrats.

Emergence of Krishna and Rama through the epics and emergence of *Puranas* has shown that Gods like Shiva and Vishnu could also be visualized in human form. Worship of Gods in such visible forms was sure to help them visualize the incomprehensible divinity in form and with attributes. A common worshipper still believed in Vedic ideals and power of *mantras* never was under question. What was missing was the form to easily identify with. The *Brahman* without form was no more cutting ice.

The situation of that time will be well understood by a story narrated in Vishnu *Purana* which deals with this 'formless' or 'with form' dilemma. It correlated the form of God that a common man loves with the formless by an example of playing flute. It says; the air that fills in the lungs of the player, the air that flows through the bamboo of flute, and the air that flies out of the holes of the flute are but different aspects of the same air that fills the whole space. But it is the specific vibrations, the modalities and the pattern of relation of the air that flows in and out of the flute that creates the sweetness of the melodious musical notes. Meaning that omnipresent God being there everywhere does not help in a seeker identifying with the same but once the seeker can see him in some form with his own eyes, the essence can be better grasped through human ingenuity, imagination and devotion.

In addition to imagining their God in a form, the common man was yearning for a direct relation with the object of their worship. They also felt need for a God who can be loved, respected, be submitted to and even feared of. The wanted a God who can be approached during pressing situations of life and who can be relied to extend His support and provide his blessings, who could protect the good and punish the evil. Devotees wanted to pray for happiness and enjoyment in this world rather than the life after. And all this was desired without losing the aim of salvation. People needed something concrete, simple, and yet attractive to worship and to address their prayers. They were looking for seeking the divine with the help of Deity and other forms whose shape is symbolic.

It was in this background that *Tantra* tradition got revived with desired variations.

Tantra had been intimately related with Vedas but had remained dormant for a very long period. While Vedas primarily focused on true knowledge as the source seek to liberate, *Tantra* believed that mere knowledge is not enough. *Tantra* had said that mere mention or understanding of "lamp" is not enough to dispel the darkness. They had believed that prime essence of liberation is the actual, direct experience i.e. "*Sakshatkar*" with the Supreme. Truth had to be realized and brought into one's experience and that was not possible unless there was a definite, determined and sustained action to attain one's ideal of truth. This determined action was called "*Sadhana Kriya*" in Sanskrit. *Tantra* followers maintained that rituals of sacrifices performed routinely in daily life are rather shallow but "Sadhana", on the other hand, is a spiritual discipline. They promised that if their system were followed, the seeker would achieve *Siddhi*. (Rao)

With due progress over centuries, *Tantra* practitioners have expanded their practices to include *mantras*, *yantras* (postures and gestures), offerings of flowers and incense, *pranayama*. The *Tantra* was promising its followers *Bhukti* and *Mukti* i.e. wellbeing in this world and liberation from the *samsara*. The core faith of their ideology is the conviction that the worshipper will get united with the worshipped. *Tantra* is also known for another key ideology that liberation can be achieved by common householders and not by denial of the worldly pleasures but by sustained discipline and practice. In the context of its time, the *Tantra* approach was more open and radical. It also overlooked the artificial restrictions of Vedic system in terms of gender and class segregation. Actually, *Tantra* was always open for women and men alike.

Every idea has to wait for its time to flourish. Time for many concepts of *Tantras* had arrived. *Tantra* recognized the urge of natural human desires and admitted the ever-ongoing conflict between flesh and spirit. Surely, these ideals of *Tantra* were earlier not acceptable to orthodox followers of Vedic tradition who always had distanced themselves from *Tantra* branding it a cult and non-Vedic wisdom; but things change with time.

Tantra followers didn't thought so ever since beginning. They acknowledged Vedas of great antiquity and revered them highly. It never claimed itself to be opposing any *Shastra*, used the Vedic *mantras* with vigour. So, all said and done, the worship practices of *Tantra* started getting popular support of all and sundry. Here come the Temples and Deities ....

To summarize, the living religion of Hindus, beginning first centuries of Common Era, worship practices of an Ishta Deva in the form of a chosen Deity of the God of personal choice established in homes or temples. This worship of the *Ishta Deva* could be of Vishnu, Shiva, Kul Devi, Kul Devta. A Devta who had most appeal to his *Upasak* (devotee) is named *Ishta Deva*. And it could have taken any shape (like Vishnu represented by a simple *saligram* or Shiva by a *Linga*) or any other *pratima* (physical form) or even a picture. Ordinary worshippers made images using perishable material not surviving for long. Later other materials like stones and metals got used, a practice which continues even today.

Vast majority of human beings are weak minded. Presence of a physical object helped these people to attain *Ekagrata* (one pointedness) of mind and purity of heart. Once the devotee was able to raise his level of understanding and can see the divine presence every where and in every thing, he/she was free to worship without any particular object as well.

In due course of time, images of Vishnu with His *Avatars*, images of Shiva and Shakti became more popular fuelled by sectarian growth throughout India. Such idols started getting established at homes and temples and eventually, this form of worship became popular leaving only a few, mostly *Brahmins*, continuing with Vedic rituals and *yajnas*.

Speaking philosophically, an Idol is just an external symbol of God for worship—it is just a reminder of God's presence. It is a material image igniting a mental form of God in devotee's mind. It makes achieving steadiness of mind easier, especially for the beginners. All forms, in general, are all alike and are merely a different manifestation of same Almighty God. Any one trying to show one superior to other will only be reflecting his ignorance and nothing else.

Idols are not idle fantasies but aid that channel devotee's attention towards God. Through an idol, the devotee feels the presence of his God in his vicinity. As a direct symbol, an idol made of stone, wood or metal or any other material, for a devotee, bears the mark of his Lord, something sacred and holy, and something eternal. Its worship is just a beginning of religious process. Next stage of worship comes with recitation of *mantras*. The next stage of mental worship, the best of all stages called 'Meditation on Absolute' follow that. So these different ways are like different ladders available to be used for that ultimate purpose of all—to raise the consciousness to a level where the Devotee feels the overpowering union with His God.

Hindu traditions are like kind mother. A mother helps her child to stand up, to hold on, to take first step and finally to run as fast as feasible. Hinduism, with all its variations and multiplicities of ways for a single destination, provides its followers its guidance and motivation right until the aspirant follower attains its due destination. But it works as a strict mother who will always hold her child in due care and will show the alternate ways without forcing or without any barricading to force you go only in the direction she feels right. Alternate Hindu practices of worship hold hands of the aspirant by encouraging them to climb up taking one step at a time until such time that *Nirvikalp Samadhi* (stage of super consciousness) is achieved.

20

Evolution of Temples and Allied Practices

Beginning of *Murti Puja,* riding on the inclusion of several minority communities, soon started giving impetus to establishment of Temples. We could also get some hints of temple worship in the epics as well where some mention starts coming giving descriptions of existence of images of deities and practice of invocating the gods and their worships. But let us be clear, in the very beginning, that temple does not merely means a place having one or more deities of various Gods and people visiting these places just for Murti Puja.

The local word for temple is "*Mandir*" which literally means "a place where human mind becomes still and soul floats free". It was only later that use of temples as a place for meditation or a serene and quite environment allowing the devotee to concentrate for connecting with his God, decreased to just symbolic while the use of the place for making offerings to and establishing eye contact with the deity became more popular. It may be attributed to increasing population that, at present, only few temples remain suitable for attempting meditation in quietness as most places are crowded and well frequented by a large number of devotees.

Regarding the evolution of Temples, it is also expected with larger acceptance that *Yajna Shalas* used for conducting Vedic havanas have gradually mutated to emerge as temples in a slow process and under the counter influence of Buddhist stupas which have certainly marked their beginning before full fledged temples arrived on the scene. By the epic period, the cults of devotion had started having their wide spread influence and are said to contribute for slow emergence of places of worship which took forms of temples as we know them today. The very first presence of proper size temples are generally traced back to Gupta Dynasty, the golden period of Hinduism, where we come across with earliest temples at Sanchi, near Jabalpur, Madhya Pradesh, Bhumara in MP, Nachna in Rajasthan and Deogarh near Jhansi in Uttar Pradesh.

Further, under logical influence of sectarian progress, the temples also evolved with distinct mark of regional and sectarian evolutions in North and South of India. This is evident from distinct style of curvilinear towers of 'Nagara' style in initial temples in North India to truncated pyramid style of 'Dravidian' style used in South India and finally, in style named 'Vesara' which came out as a combination of both styles. (*A Brief History of Hindu Temples,* 2000)

With the need for worship of a Deity well settled, next evolution must have lead to other related questions like how to put it all together—how to house the images of deities, what kind of place should be selected, what should be the architecture plans, what should be the size of such places, how to create idols, how to worship different deities, etc. It was to address all such questions that got addressed by emergence of new form of literature called the *Agamas*.

Agamas are a set of ancient texts originated initially in oral traditions and subsequently consigned to writings over a long period of time beginning around 600 CE. Final versions of these texts came out as complete guides for temple worship addressing all aspects of constructions, worship practices, worship methodologies, instructions for people identified for carrying all activities of a temple. *Agama* had its roots in the 'Kalpa Sutras' which were to guide daily life and conduct of the people affiliated with the Vedic rituals during ancient times. Kalpa Sutras have touched upon prescribing *vidhi vidhana* (holy procedure) for domestic rituals, formal *yajnas*, mathematical calculation for construction of *Vedi* and specifications of implements used. Soon, these were to be reinvented to respond changed social requirement, a process one sees so often in every connected practice and tradition in Hinduism.

First qualified text on design of temple can be traced to Brihat Samhita composed by Varahamihira sometimes around 560 CE who was a great astronomer, mathematician, astrologer from Ujjain and was one of the Navratnas of the court of Yashowardhan Vikramaditya of Malwa. This text came out with comprehensive calculations involving all these elite subjects to decide the most suited architecture for a temple of God. That is why most temples have complete square mandala formation, four gates with one on side, incorporating radial balance technique to facilitate a strong structure and congenial atmosphere for meditation, worship and sacred space.

Following temple culture, scholars started working on *Agama Shastra* to address all the issues relating to temple construction and operations, in the true nature that *Shastras* are known for. One *Agama* text will always consist of four parts dealing with knowledge, meditation, rituals and ways of worship. This fourfold classification with similar details is also common to Buddhism and Jainism. It is hard to assume for a normal Hindu like me myself that Hindu temples are largely a catching game response by Hinduism to Buddhism and Jainism as construction of Buddhist Stupas had started earlier and, facilitated the need for temples in Hinduism.

Each of these four parts has both external and internal interpretations. External part talks about ways of doing things while internal talks about spiritual significance of the rituals performed. The parts relating to Rituals and ways of worship pertain to worship in temples and hence occupy major space of these texts. Also included are training manuals meant for performing priests, their induction into temple service, worship attitudes, details of occasional celebrations or festivals, etc.

Pulled by the sectarian preferences, the *Agamas* also had to branch out into each sect. Each sect and its sub sect had specific Deity with specific characteristics, and hence, each of these required a separate *Agama* text providing uniqueness of their own sect/sub sect. As a result, there are 28 *Shaiva Agamas, 77 Shaktas* and 215 *Vaishnava Agamas* and another large number of sub *Agamas*. Then, there are exclusive *Agamas* in Tamil prescribing similar requirements of temples in South India with their unique flavour.

Regarding Temple constructions, *Agama* texts forge special relationship with *Shilpa Shastra* to deal with all aspects of architecture, design and even material of construction. Besides *Shilpa Shastra,* the text require the temple architecture to combine principles of Yoga, Astrology, and consideration for sacred geography of the proposed location for temple construction. Also are prescribed principles of Vaastu Shilpa in terms of dimensions, proportions, air circulation, agni sthana, location of temple pond, directions and size for entrances along with lighting considerations. Similar considerations apply to building the Deity. They are very particular and maintain that a temple is to be built for a Deity and not the other way around. So, no work can start unless one already has the Deity.

There are substantial differences in architecture, customs and rituals in Temples in different parts of the country largely due to applicability of unique characteristics of the sects and sub sects combinations concerned.

So finally we have a yet another mix of traditions drawn from different periods, different ideologies, different philosophies, some continued, some forgotten, some brought back from past, some repackaged, some borrowed, some revived, some consigned. It is to the credit of this development that temple worship is completing nearly two thousand years in India. In spite of so many changes have happened on all fronts of personal and social life, political and economic, but the temple based idol worship facilitated by *Agama* texts starting early centuries of the first millennium, is still going great and providing followers same experience of connection with their Ishta Deva. Great!!!!

Forms and Types of Hindu Temples

India in general legged behind European culture in terms of construction of expansive, impressive and long lasting structures at public places. Construction of temples is no exception to this rule. Whole of Vedic culture is in total contrast with building construction. On one hand, we had Sindhu Sarasvati Civilization which, in 3000 BC, has been found to have use of baked bricks in construction of most of its buildings and offers first peek into structured urbanization any where in the world, the entire Vedic period between 1500 BC to 500 BC is identified in making only a *Yajna Vedi* as any sign of systematic construction. Forget city clusters, parn kutir for sages and mud house for the poor were good enough for most inhabitants.

No wonder that even around 300 CE, a period associated with earliest humble beginning of temple constructions, perishable material of wood and clay bricks was used. Stone became a preferred material of construction only in third generation. Second generation belongs to cave temples or temples carved out of cliff or cut out of rocks. Different temples have been known to adapt to different regional beliefs that had different deities; some times exclusively or with others, incorporating yet another example of 'Unity in Diversity".

To begin with temple complexes came up much beyond usual sacred and secular space of worships. Besides worships, the temples became places for marking festivals, celebrating music and dance forms of arts, commemorate marriages and births and such other significant social life events. Temples have been known to even solemnize successions of Hindu kingdoms. Like all-purpose community centres, initial temples were to address most collective social events. Later, this trend got more concentrated in South Indian temples as North India started temples as largely religious centres focusing on unique construction art, sculptures, carvings and themes.

All five cosmic elements were incorporated in temples as recognition of their presence in creating and maintaining this world order. Besides, we have had representations of both feminine and masculine deities representing their togetherness for regeneration. Also focused was presence of sounds and smells with all eternal nothingness of space. The idea of arranging all these elements in special manner was to create an ambiance of sacredness, life, worship, spirituality and divinity. Step by step, temples came to be associated as structured spaces with unique arts, carvings, display of pictures linked to aims of life, decoration of deities, empty space for deeper human contemplations and facilities for purification of one's mind. The whole experience came to trigger a process of self-realization with all the divine presence of the Gods and its manifestations.

Temples started to take two forms–a house or a palace. The first one is simply a good enough place for human dwellings and is used largely by the devotee to *Bhakti* to establish personal and direct communion with his Ishta Deity. The whole setting is as if the Deity is on visit to the devotee's place and is to be taken care and provided for exactly as an esteemed guest. It is usual to see such devotees attending the Deity for bath, food, change of clothes, sleeping and waking time attendance, etc. Such temples are largely housed within houses but many going in public spaces as well. Second form of temples are of Palace category and are of bigger scale, having areas to accommodate large number of people's congregation, are elaborate on construction designs and styles and normally cater to more than one deity. These are like separate institutions by themselves and employ full time people including priests, decorators, administration, maintenance crew, kitchen staff, accountants and what not. These institutions run based on donations and gifts offered by visiting devotees, general public as well as one or more wealthy family from rulers or business people. Some of these temples have been flooded by donations and offerings including jewels and precious metals going in tons and have been the attraction of foreign aggressors providing next to nothing security and holding on riches of generations. But donations and monetary offerings are ingrained in Hindu thoughts as easy way of earning blessings of the deity and facilitation for final liberation. All Hindus, therefore, can be seen making these offerings each and every time they visit temples on pilgrimages or even on day-to-day basis for normal worships.

Major Temples of India

Let us look at some main initial temple complexes in India to get a good feel about the evolution of these inseparable parts of our proud past. A good read of the section will take the reader through for developments in different parts of the country and briefly touching about applicable socio-religious factors. Attempt is again to put all these temple/temple complexes in order of their emergence.

Elephanta Caves Complex

To begin with we have Elephanta caves temple near Mumbai carved sometimes around 700 to 800 CE. It is not known with full clarity as who undertook the excavation in these natural caves. It is because Konkan, as a state at that time, was but a small kingdom and could not be assumed to undertake and finance such gigantic excavation and sculpting in hard rocks. There are several stories as to probable powers that may have undertaken such a work from the Maurayan rulers of Konkan to Badami based Chalukyas. But these are mere propositions based on financial capability and clout of probable rulers of the time when these caves were sculpted. There is a network of caves where the first and larger group has five Hindu caves while the second and much smaller group has two Buddhist caves. This is a Shiva temple with *Trimurti* figure showing all three faces of Shiva. Also seen are Nataraja and Ardhanareeshwar forms of Shiva.

Ellora Caves Complex

Then we have Kailashnath temple of Shiva at Ellora starting carving sometime around 750 CE and continued for over 300 years. The two-kilometre area complex is completely carved out by chiseling out extra material from the rocks leaving behind magnificent sculpted figures of Shiva and Parvati, *linga* and bull Nandi in various postures. Even the three story high columned arcade is completely sculpted out. All of thirty four caves represent epitome of Indian rock cut architecture and consist of twelve Buddhist caves, seventeen Hindu caves and remaining five being Jain caves. With Dravidian sculpture forms, the effort was to recreate Mount Kailasha, the permanent mythological abode of Lord Shiva. It is said to be a beautiful example of striking proportions, fine workmanship and ornamentation sculpture. The temples also have many Vaishnavism deities on one side of the complex. Also depicted is Durga with the scene of killing Mahishasur. These caves are great examples of religious harmony prevailing among all homegrown religions where due importance was given to all three. The cave sculptures, constructed largely by Chalukya and Rashtrakula kings belong to an era where Buddhism has started its decline while Hinduism has started reasserting itself.

Khajuraho Complex

Next in line will be the stone temples at Khajuraho in North east of Madhya Pradesh, the area dominated by strong kingdoms of Chandella Dynasty at Bundelkhand. The 'Nagara' style temples are reported to have been built in 900 to 1150 CE. The total complex is said to have about 85 temples of largely Hindu and some Jain temples spread over twenty kilometres of vast area, are having very intricate erotic sculptures. The images of these temples are irrefutable evidence suggesting very strong sectarian worship in vogue at that point. Going by the sculptures on the outer walls of the temple complex, one finds carvings of couple in erotic embrace and in maithuna figures which gives an impression that the King was a *Tantra* follower. Also on carving list are many war related material like decorated elephants, horses, weaponry and warriors so as to make a strong military statement about the strength of Kings of the area. It is not difficult to appreciate, as the construction was all state funded and military power enabled continuity of rule. Undoubtedly, seeking spirituality without military power had not worked for any King. These temples came under destruction attack from Sikandar Lodhi in 1495 but their remote locations came handy to ward off continued destruction spree by subsequent Muslim aggressors of many hues.

Konark Sun Temple

Tantra is again at full bloom at Sun Temple of Konark, Bhubaneshwar. This complex was constructed in 1240-60 and is decorated with magnificent large stone wheels with intricate carvings. The outer walls of this temple also include erotic scenes to celebrate the beauty and to gather up all sensual thoughts so that the worshipper doesn't carry those corrupted thoughts any further. (This explanation fails to cut ice with many readers but this is the nearest one goes in justifying *Kama Sutra* poses on the walls of a temple). Interestingly, figures of stunning female beauties were also carved in many Buddhist Stupas in the shape of Yakshis and Yakshinis and gorgeous *Apsaras*. The main deity is showing Nar Simha worshipping Durga and Jagannath (another Vishnu incarnation) but dedicated to worship Sun. Incidentally, Sun is a Vedic God for energizing the universe.

Temples of South India

Next in line of discussions are major temples from South India. Most of these have some very unique characteristics much in variation from temples in North India. To begin with, more than place of worship, temples in South came up as places for all community activities. All public functions, which were in past conducted within courts of the Kings, got shifted to new temple complexes. As is the case everywhere, temples were constructed by the kings and were a proof of kingdom's economic and political prosperity and political power. So, they started becoming bigger and better as if all the kingdoms were in competition to each other.

Typically speaking, they have a large monumental tower at the very entrance with gorgeous and stylish designs, called *gopuram*. These got started by Pallavas and Pandyas as a dominant style statement and to hide the interior shrines for worship. Depending on the expanse of the temple, many have more than one outer precincts and as many *gopurams*. As south Indian temples had always been more orthodox, at many temples the access to the sanctum is restricted to only priests, kings and few others. South India certainly boasts for having some of the largest Hindu temples in the whole world. Pallavas built many temples like Meenakshi in Kanchipuram, their seat of power including Shore Temple at Mamallapuram. Pandya's best examples are the temples in Madurai area. Cholas created their imprints on temples like Nataraja Temple at Chidambaram and Sri Ranganathaswamy at Srirangam and at many other temples at Cholapuram. The temple at Brihadeshvara at Thanjavur, which is one of the largest temples in India, is yet another example of great architecture of Chola kingdoms.

North Indian Temples and Foreign Aggressors

To the contrast of South India, North Indian temples have been simpler, smaller and focused more on to worship than community activities. The restrictions are far and few and most people are allowed access right upto Deity darshan. Typically, the *Garbha Griha* houses the main Deity and in front we have large hall for facilitating congregation of devotees coming for Darshan and making their offerings. Most temples of North India got attacked one or many times from the stream of aggressors over many centuries for looting all the precious stones and jewels. Actually, till that time, temples used to be working like banks having non stop offerings from devotees. Being religious places, no one cared for security for protection from aggressors. So, looting temples had become a fun time activity for the aggressors with a lot of kill without any opposition.

Until the rise of West, India was undoubtedly the richest country in the world helped by its conducive climate and fertile soil. No wonder that its riches made it an irresistible target of the Mongols and their descendants who had gathered military powers and took to looting of India as a profitable profession.

Beginning with Mahmud of Ghazani, herds of aggressors from 11th to 16th century have been using the same method of entering India via Punjab and looting the temples of all their wealth and in many cases also destroying temples and converting them to Mosques. Some of these were also religious fanatics who had double purpose of attacking Hindu temples. Mahmud of Ghazani was, however, no religious proselytizer and his objectives were only and only economic and political. He is known to have made seventeen aggressions on India before he died in 1030 CE of malaria at the age of 59. His sixteenth aggression involving famous Somnath Temple of Gujarat is reported to have provided him huge catch of loot, which was twenty times bigger than his first aggression. And by that time he had opened the floodgates for many of his direct and indirect descendants to pursue the easy way for making huge riches of looting Hindu Temples.

Most temples in South escaped these aggressions simply because they were deep down of the country and most of these foreign aggressors never had the patience of reaching there or the strategic peninsular geography prevented these people to take risk of getting trapped.

Over last couple of hundred years, there is mushrooming of temples in all parts of the country with states like Tamil Nadu, Gujarat leading the pack. Besides, Cities like Delhi and Mumbai saw many temples getting constructed with the process continuing even in current periods. State like Rajashthan and Gujarat are also famous for their Jain temples with great stone carving work attracting lot many tourists from all parts of the whole world. Increasingly, temples have been associated with a place where God may be approached and where divine knowledge can be discovered. Once again we have scenario where many temples are getting richer once again as was the case during the glorious past.

21

Daily Rituals, Rites, *Yajnas* and *Japas*

Like some other religions, in due course of time, symbolism has crept in Hindu practices also where many followers start providing great importance to symbolic art of their religion in terms of its Rituals, Rites, *Yajnas* and Recitations. All these are taken as outward expressions of ideas intellectually held and emotionally felt. These rituals are concerned with the expressions of these ideas and feelings, specifically called religious. Ultimately, these are all tools and means by which mind is purified and transformed. These are instruments where consciousness of the devotee is shaped into forms of experiences that are taught by holy scriptures. Let us briefly touch these.

Vedic Fire Ceremonies

Called by various names like *yajna*, havan, homa or agnihotra, it consisted of a continued sacrificial fire, invocations of one or more divinities, placing offerings of ghee, samgree and grains into the flame while Vedic Hymns are recited. Vedic fire ceremonies are known to have been held from antiquity of Vedas or even earlier. These were held during auspicious astrological moments in the hope that the patron conducting these *Yajnas* will be blessed by the Gods with abundance of fortune, cattle, healthy life and male progeny together with all possible material benefits as also for removing obstacles from their way. Fire has been treated in Hinduism as a medium of establishing contact with the desired

Gods and all offerings to fire are to be treated as direct offering to the God invoked. These were to be carried in the presence of elders and well-wishers and the ceremony was to be followed with distribution of gifts and charities as per financial position of the patron.

The rationale behind these *yajnas* was to sanctify the life of a householder and to provide it a spiritual touch. Initially, people themselves conducted these ceremonies but later, due to increased sophistication and complexities of Vedic *mantras*, these were to be conducted only with the help of an experienced and qualified pujari (priest). Still later, these got more elaborate and were conducted only by kings or aristocrats. The elaboration involved, took these away from the reach of common man. Movements like *Arya Samaj* have brought in larger focus back on havans by keeping the elaborations away and making efforts to encourage individuals to carry out these rituals independently without losing many benefits. One can come across many families holding havans on important events in their life and inviting family and friends and experiencing unexplainable feelings of realizing the strong influence of Vedic *Mantras* recited in that environment.

Daily Rituals

Every *Brahmin* is supposed to undertake worship of gods at every junction of the day and night called '*Sandhya Upasana*'. The activities prescribed for this daily ritual begin with having taken bath as a token of physical self-purification. Offering of water to Sun God follows bath with recitation of '*Gayatri Mantra*' from the depth of the heart. After water offering to the Sun God one is required to sprinkle water over own face and touch various parts of body with wet finger. Idea is to pray for removal of obstructing negative forces and obtain control over demons of anger, lust and greed.

Besides Sandya Upasana, the daily rituals include offerings to the Gods, offerings to all living beings, to departed souls, showing hospitality to others and continuous remembrance of God through recitation of the Vedas or other holy scriptures. These activities are intended to bring in a lot of merit to the being by bestowing illumination, mental peace and grace. Prescribed as *Nityakarma* (daily obligation), these are like mandatory for every Hindu wearing *Janeu*, the sacred three-thread mala.

Sanskaras (Sacraments)

Hindu followers are also advised by traditions to celebrate rites related to marking the passing of various stages in human life. These start from the stage where 'would be parents' decide to seek the child and go right upto the death of the person. The major sanskaras prevailing to this day include one for seeking pregnancy, after three and six months of pregnancy, after the child birth, for assigning the name of the child, after six months of the child for feeding grain first time, after one year for his first hair cutting, at six to eight years when he is sent to his Guru for study, after completing his study, at the time of his marriage, at the time of starting third (*Vanprashtha Ashram*) and fourth stages of life (*Sannyasa Ashram*) and finally, after the death of the person (kriya karma). In short, all stages from conception to cremation get covered.

The objectives of these rites at each stage are different and are intended to add different colours to a picture called human life. To begin with, it is to seek good impression on the embryo, then for proper growth of the baby in mother's womb, for healthy birth, etc. The ritual at the age of 6 to 8 while being sent for education is called '*Yagyopaveet*' or '*Upanayana*' and is celebrated as an important ceremony. This is taken as a beginning of next stage in life and also as a second birth; a spiritual birth of the child. Sacred thread consisting of three strands knotted together is offered to the child who is soon to be sent to his Guru for starting his 'Brahmacharya' stage of life. The three threads (*janeu*)are to help the boy to exercise triple control over his mind, speech and body so that all his thoughts, his words and his actions are aimed solely at attaining perfect knowledge in his chosen field. Next big occasion is of marriage well known to all.

Finally, at the time of death of the physical body, the last rite of *Antyesthi* is held. This includes consigning the body to flames as the best use of a dead body. The soul is supposed to remain cling to the body (on account of attachment) until it is fully destroyed. Burning the body is to help the soul travel from 'Pret Loka' to 'Pitri Loka'. Left out bones are to be inmersed in a river or some other water body. People, who can afford, also take these to offer to Ganga at Hardwar or Varanasi as Ganga is known to be capable of washing sins or bad *karmas* of human at any stage of their life.

Regular Jap (Chanting) of "Aum"

Chanting of *AUM* has paramount importance all through Hinduism. Invariably, all the prayers from Vedic times start with "AUM". This word is much more powerful than the three letters that make it. "AUM" not only carries three distinct sounds but the pronunciation of the word generates the fourth sound of vibrations. This vibration is said to be essence of all other sounds in the Universe. Even with all the scientific discoveries in so many fields, the vibrations created by AUM are not repeatable in any other combination of words in any other language of the world. It is hard to comprehend the levels of insight of our great ancestors who left us such proud heritage.

So, chanting of "AUM" is said to produce a strong vibration inside the human being which resonates with the universal vibration and this helps us in elevating our mind from every day mundane matters to the true Self. Many Hindu practitioners can be seen chanting of this strong word with or without external aids. Many people do it with a mala of beads; some do it by counting on fingers while many others just chant it by itself.

Regular chanting of the word "AUM" is also reported to result in several other health related benefits like slowing down the nervous system, calming the mind from pressures, making the mind ready for meditations etc. May be it is because of such multiple benefits that chanting of "AUM" is one of the few practices which have survived many thousands of years and have continued holding its importance from Vedic time to this day.

Outward Symbols in Hinduism

Hinduism of modern time has continued providing importance to external symbols as continuity since Vedic period. Over the periods in History, the symbols have also seen improvisation keeping in line with developments in its surrounding environment. Let us briefly look at the main external symbols and the logic or reference related to each.

To begin with, we have *tilak*. It is to be taken as a mark of auspiciousness together with cultic identity. Initially, the *tilak* was to be applied in the middle of forehead at the place of 'the third eye'. The sandal paste, which was the ideal material for *tilak*, was supposed to have medicinal benefit of calming the heat generated during concentrating the mind in meditation. The soothing nature of sandal was to nullify the negative energy. Later, Vaishnavites and Shaivaites started their own separate styles to add the *tilak* to denote their cult and sub cult identity. In line with that, Shiva followers use '*bhasm*' to apply horizontal lines while Vishnu followers use vertical lines using sandal paste. Similarly, followers of Shakti apply *kumkum*. In all cases, having the *tilak* works as an invocation by the person that "*may my eye of intuition open and guide me with the right perception of this world*". This feeling is to get renewed every time one applies the *Tilak*.

Invocating small prayer before every meal comes as second symbol. Here the devotee sprinkle little water around the plate with food and make an offering to all five types of '*pranas*' and lastly to the *Brahman* residing inside, his physical body, as a mark of accepting the food for the body. Hinduism considers food not for its taste or elaboration but as an offering for well being of this physical body made out of five elements. Having '*Shika*' (choti) and wearing '*janeu*' are another symbols starting from the student life of Hindu boys. These are intended for achieving self-discipline, generate noble thoughts and help in controlling passions. More prevalent in Vaishnavites, these also appear to be symbolic continuity with full-fledged asceticism of Shaivaites.

Having '*mundan*' (shaving the head except 'shikha') is another such symbol used frequently by many followers. Shaving of head is associated with sacrifice of attachments with this world. It denotes that the person having mundan has moved on from the normal attractions of this world and has decided to pursue spiritual ambitions by sacrificing desires for sensual objects and thoughts. Mundan by a person out side student life also denote that the person has given up being part of specific "four stages of life" and have decided to directly engage himself for attaining '*Moksha*' as the sole purpose of remaining life.

Use of Lights, Dhupam, camphor, sandal paste and ringing of bells are other well known symbols associated with Hindu worship system in general. Lighting of 'diyas' by burning ghee or oil is to dispel human ignorance in the same way as light removes the darkness. The Lamp shown at the cover of this book may also be taken as reinforcement of this very logic. Dhupam denotes worship for all pervading God where the spread of scented smoke reflects the presence of God and his creative powers. The scent is to help remove all *vasanas* from human thought by purifying it and working on the generation of good thoughts. Melting of camphor and its burning is identified with quick melting of individual ego under the influence of flame of 'self realization' without even leaving its residue ash. Applying sandal paste is to remind the being of maintaining patience even under testing times and replacing the urge for outbursts out of pressure to calmness of sandal fragrance. Lastly, ringing bells are to create rippled vibrations of sounds to ward off external sounds and to make the mind focused inward for concentration and meditation.

The sign of '*Swastika*' is yet another highly used symbol in Hinduism. Infact, it is considered as auspicious by Hindus as Cross for Christians. The very name combination of three words namely '*su*' meaning good or well, '*asti*' meaning being and '*ka*' which is used in Sanskrit to intensify the verbal meaning of the subject. The combined meaning comes out as 'this that is auspicious'. The symbol has been now traced back all the way to Sindhu Sarasvati Civilization where many seals are found having swastiks imprints. Since the ancient time, *swastika* sign has been used by all Indian origin religions as a symbol of auspiciousness. The four sides are taken as showing energy flowing to all four directions or as four faces of Brahma, the creator. Many people also relate its importance to '*Purusharthas*' the four aims of human life. May be it is the power of this sign that it is used, with little variations, in most parts of Asia and Europe and some parts of Africa as well with universal meaning of its association with the auspiciousness.

Suffice to say that Hinduism has moved over to token symbolism under practices influenced by its sects and also as absorbing symbolic ideas from other faiths from India and abroad. But like all symbols, these are just to create separate identity for outsiders for easy recongnition. Beyond the tokenism and gesticulation, these external symbols do not have much relevance and their limited role is to reflect the core values of the faith.

22
Indian Philosophies

Generally speaking, Philosophy is a western word, which mainly relies on intellectual pursuit. The corresponding Indian word is 'Darsana' which relies on direct vision of truths (experienced by ancient sages of India) and pure *Buddhi* (reasoning). It will not be out of place to say that ancient India has led the entire world in developing philosophical traditions much before people in other cultures, Greece included, even started thinking about it. The antiquity of Indian Philosophies will become clear by quoting Abbe Dubois, a French national who spent his life time studying Indian cultural and customs in 20th Century.

> *"There can be no doubt that Philosophy flourished in India before it had been as much as thought of in Greece. Of what account, in truth, was the learning of Greece, of what account her system of polity, until Pythagoras, Lycurgus, and other famous Greek travellers, animated by the desire of educating themselves, studied the manners and customs of Asiatic peoples, and borrowed from the Hindus especially, many percepts and doctrines?"*

But let us deal with the first question first. What is Philosophy? Is it something like the one preached by quick fix preachers and trainers as "a kind of recipe for happiness and fulfillment", or is it all about some "not understandable mystical riddle"? Some times we also come across some people making very complexly intertwined statements claiming those to be their philosophy of life. The reality is not so, certainly not so. It is a full-fledged and well developed stream like all other Sciences and is equally heart-warming and satisfying once it is clearly comprehended.

Let us have a look at basic questions common to all investigation:

- What is the nature of the universe?
- What is the nature of God?
- What is the nature of soul and what is its destiny?
- What are the laws of soul's life?

Philosophy deals with concepts exactly as Science deals with functions or natural rules. As Science has many sub sections like Physics, Chemistry, Biology, Botany, etc., Philosophy also has its sub systems as under:

- *Logic:* This section deals with study of all techniques of evaluating claims or statements being true or false. It also deals to decipher about reasoning being good or not good.
- *Metaphysics:* This deals with very fundamental questions about what exists and what doesn't exist, For example, a question like is mind a physical? If it is not physical, how does it interact with other physical organs like hands or eyes? Does God exist? Is it perfect? Before that, what is perfection?
- *Epistemology:* How do we acquire knowledge? What all can we know? How to know whatever we can know?
- *Ethics:* What is right to do? What is best to do? What we ought to do? What is wrong? Why is it wrong?

The basic idea to touch on the basics of these parts is to prepare the reader for going through something difficult but exciting. Actually, like study of Science, Philosophy also aims at discovering truth. It is in this background that we will look at Indian Religious Philosophy as a discovery of truth for key investigation points listed above. And, again like Science, there is nothing final. Each attempt is like a work in process because whatever is known by today, more can get added later. Idea at all time is to refine the theories in light with new ideas, new progress and new findings new techniques.

I mention Indian Philosophies and not Hindu Philosophy. It is because fundamental Philosophies have been said to evolve to concrete levels even before Buddhism and Jainism branched out as separate religions with some variations from the other schools evolved until then.

A small note of caution—understanding Philosophy is tedious and difficult since issues are abstract in nature. So, please read this section slowly and carefully. Don't get disheartened if first few readings come out boring and going over the top. It is absolutely expected and there may be many sentences that may require repetitive reading for a good comprehension. But, once you are over at least two points will be very clear.

We will understand the fundamental concepts refined by our ancestors so many years in history which will help us comprehend many subsequent developments in our religious and personal evolution process. Secondly, it will make us proud that our ancestors had scaled to the pinnacle of these understandings centuries before any other civilization or culture could dream of.

Categorisation of Indian Philosophical Schools

There are two broad Schools called Astika and *Nastika* but Astika here does not mean "theist" neither *Nastika* implies with "atheist" as understood in common parlance. For the purpose of this classification, someone who accepts the authority of Vedas as infallible and considers it supreme revealed scriptures is to be called Astika. On the other side, anyone not accepting Vedas as supreme and revealed scriptures got branded as *Nastika*.

- *Astika* Schools: The initial number of schools under this category (and hence integrated ultimately as part of Hinduism as a religion) are: 1. *Sankhya* 2. Yoga, 3. Nyaya, 4. *Vaisheshika,* 5. *Mimansa* and 6. *Vedanta.* (I wish it were possible to use Sanskrit font to make these words reveal their true inherent meaning)
- *Nastika* Schools: These included Charvaka, a very interesting school that is very identical to the current materialistic philosophy for many people in West, *Ajivika,* Jainism and Buddhism.

Let us try understanding these one by one:

Sankhya Philosophy

Sankhya means "number" or "perfect knowledge". It was one of the first attempts to present Indian Philosophy in a cohesive, comprehensive and persuasive method. Founding of *Sankhya* is credited to ancient Sage Kapila (around 800 BC). Unlike in Vedas and Upanishads (where one come across hints and indirect references or at best speculations about God, Human spirit and *Brahma* and such other abstract subjects relating to universe and its origin etc.), *Sankhya* is concerned with *Pramana* (proof), care to define its terms involving consistent systems and not merely intuitions. *Sankhya* is the first system to study human consciousness. Its main objective was how to understand various forms of human experience with objective world. This analysis was to be with reference to consciousness of a human being, as a subject in detail, without bringing in any idealism as to what it should be or emotional fundamentals—purely a discrete study.

To put whole concept of *Sankhya* simply, this universe consists of *Prakriti* (matter) and *Purusha* (consciousness). Jiva (spirit) is a state where *Purusha* is bounded with *Prakriti* through the glue of desire, and, end of this bondage is *Moksha*. Surely, detailed understanding of these concepts will take some serious efforts. Let us look at these one by one.

Purusha is the transcendental Self (pure consciousness) and *Prakriti* accounts for whatever is physical and visible in this world. Let *Prakriti* not be understood 'material nature' which maybe the very obvious meaning coming to an Indian reader based on the reading of *Prakriti* as a word. Let us try in another way. Our world is filled with objects. Objects are made of compounds. Compounds are made of molecules. Molecules are made of atoms. Atoms are made of particles. Particles are made of a subtler substratum. While one evolves out of the other, all of these levels of reality coexist and interact with one another. '*Prakriti*' is the primordial state of matter, even prior to matter as we know it in the physical sense. *Prakriti* manifests as the three *gunas* and the other evolutes (*Gandhi*).

Sankhya's *Prakriti* is root cause of the manifested world. It is something accounting for everything physical and made out of a proportionate mixing of three *Gunas* (normal meaning is quality or nature but here used as a constituent) called *Sattva, Rajas* and

Tamas. Let us try understanding these *Gunas* in a bit detail for understanding for future:

- *Sattva*: Represents poise, fineness, lightness, illumination, joy and happiness.
- *Rajas*: Represents dynamism, activity, excitation and pain
- *Tamas*: Represents inertia, obstruction, ignorance and inaction.

So, any physical item or event is a manifestation of evolution of *Prakriti*. It is imbalance in these *Gunas* that result in creation of twenty-three identified constituents that include *Buddhi* (intellect), *Ahamkara* (ego) and *Manas* (mind). So, we have to remember that as per *Sankhya,* these three qualities in a human being are part of *Prakriti*.

Let us understand the sequence of these 23 constituents—first is *Buddhi* (mind), *Buddhi* gives rise to *Ahamkara,* Ego (ego here means specific features leading to specific individuality). From *Ahamkara* comes five subtle elements and two sets of organs. The subtle elements are shabd, sparsh, roop, ras, gandh. Set of organs is external (sense organs and action organs totaling to ten) and internal (mind). From subtle elements are produced five gross elements (*akash, vayu, tejas, apas* water, *prithvi*.)

Better way to understand the interplay between *Prakriti* and *Purusha* is that the first is experienced and the second is experiencer.

At the next twist, soul is a fusion of *Purusha* and *Prakriti* where soul is unrestricted by its physical body. *Samsara,* the bondage (the cycle of death and rebirth) is said to arise when *Purusha* mistakenly is unable to discriminate itself from *Ahamkara*. (*Ahamkara* is part of *Prakriti* but *Purusha* mistake it to be itself). So, the *Samsara* continues until the time this ignorance persists. The moment *Purusha* develops knowledge and ability to discriminate the difference between itself and *Prakriti,* the Jiva is called liberated (means *Moksha* attained). *Sankhya* relied on 'Viveka', the intuitive discrimination for a being to guide his *Buddhi* to differentiate between *Purusha* and *Prakriti*

As per *Sankhya,* at the beginning of the Universe, before the living creatures came into being, the *Prakriti* with its three *Gunas* coexisted in the primal matter. But the presence of *Purusha* disturbed the equilibrium and that initiated the process of Utapatti (emanation). The first category emerging after original unity was *Buddhi*. *Buddhi*, if properly developed, could still bring enlightenment. Hence, it was considered very close to *Purusha*. But in any unintelligent human being, the *Buddhi* remains clouded by the gross elements of this world which is its undeveloped state.

Next category to emerge was *Ahamkara*, ego. All other creatures emanated from *Ahamkara* including Gods, human, animals, plants and such other insensate things. This *Ahamkara* is identified as main source of human problems because *Ahamkara* is responsible for transmitting different *Gunas* in varying proportions among human beings. Those beings that were having dominance of *Sattva*, became devas and holy men. *Rajas* was dominant in normal humans and *Tamas* dominance being became animals.

But most importantly, the sense of ego trapped us in the false self which was far away from *Purusha*, the pure consciousness. I think…I want….I wish…I fear…. The "I" in all these statements is actually not *Purusha* but *Ahamkara*, the ego. This *Ahamkara* on which we lavish so much of attention and energy is actually transient for a limited time. This ignorance of taking it as permanent is rectified by renouncers using meditation and study. And…once this clarity is achieved of pure consciousness, the *Moksha* is achieved. The point to carry home is that 'ego' is not our real self.

There is another important part of *Sankhya* school relating to 'cause and effect'. *Sankhya* believes that the 'effect' exist in 'cause' in un-manifested form before it gets revealed (a plant has its base in its seed). The effect is always related to its cause. If it was not so, an effect should have been possible from every cause (any plant can come out of any seed). Based on this logic, it builds that the world would not have come suddenly in a miraculous way by the order or wish of some God or creator. *Sankhya* is of the opinion that the world evolved through a creative process stretched over various phases of changes and transformations. This process of evolution is guided, directed and monitored by inherent tendencies of substances characterized by the combinations of *Gunas*. It further believes that there is no God but there are many Jivatmas.

To summarise, *Purusha*, due to ignorance, identifies itself with *Buddhi* and *Ahamkara* which are products of *Prakriti*. This results in continuance of *Samsara*. When, with the use of Viveka, human being brings clarity that *Purusha* is not bound, Self is no longer subject to transmigration and absolute freedom arises. Also, *Sankhya* as a philosophy is mainly devoted to theoretical problems and touching upon practical problems. But our next school of Yoga is mainly devoted to practical problems while touching on theoretical problems.

Yoga Philosophy

While *Sankhya* is called 'theoretical', Yoga Philosophy is called 'practical'. Yoga is supposed to be a twin of *Sankhya* school as they both start and end at the same street. The only difference these two schools have is the process of achieving the clarity of the ignorance that *Purusha* needs to differentiate itself from *Prakriti.* Yoga philosophy is credited to Maharishi Patanjali with approximate period of around 150 BC and assumes a personal God who controls the process of periodic creation and dissolution and is omniscient and omnipotent.

Yoga philosophy is based on the idea that if man wants to understand his place in nature and be happy and progressive; he must aim at that physical, psychological and moral development which will enable him to pry into the depth of nature. He must observe, think and act; he must live, love and progress and his development on all three planes must be simultaneous. As discussed earlier, *Sankhya* school aims at achieving that isolation through systematically segregating consciousness from everything such that at the end of the process, pure consciousness is all that is left. Yoga achieves that very purpose using the celebrated Ashtanga process of *Yam, Niyam, Asana,* and *Pranayam* to *Samadhi* (entire process has been discussed separately under the chapter relating to Yoga) (Gandhi).

In short, Yoga traverses the same street as that of *Sankhya* and allows a detour use of 'tapas' and 'swadhyaya'. Yoga is largely preoccupied with refining human psyche, human nature, human body and its entire constitution to understand and explore the inner core by strict disciplining of the body and mind.

Fast forward to 1100 CE...and we find that both these schools are unable to attract attention from thinkers anymore. After that these schools lost their pride of place as the main schools. While Yoga continued to be pursued and progressed for its use for disciplining the body and mind, it lost its relevance as a school of Indian Philosophy.

Nyaya (Logical Reasoning) Philosophy

This philosophy is ascribed to Aksapada Gautama (2nd century CE) and is detailed in Nyaya Sutras containing five chapters. Nyaya deals with logic, the process of reasoning. This philosophy considers doubt as a prerequisite for any logical inquiry. This goes to the credit of Nyaya that all subsequent philosophers use this mechanism to prove their point. This school is also called 'Tark Vidya' (argumentative knowledge) as it makes detailed use of arguments. In its analysis, it logically takes up validity or invalidity of factual knowledge so as to reach the final Truth.

Nyaya is said to be under-studied due to highly technical terminology that scares the novice. It is also called empirical realism as against Vedanta following transcendental idealism. The brief summary of the five chapters is as under:

- Chapter 1: It defines sixteen categories of knowledge which lead to liberation.
- Chapter 2: Examination of doubt, the *pramanas* of refutation of objection against four *pramanas*.
- Chapter 3: Examination of soul, material, body, sense and their objects.
- Chapter 4: Examination of *pravritti, dosha, pretyabhava, phala, dukh, apavarya.*
- Chapter 5: Discussions of various kind of futility

This school considers God as the operative cause of creation, maintenance as well as destruction. It believes that the world doesn't get created out of nothing or by itself but the creation takes place out of eternal elements namely, space, time, mind and soul. Nyaya considers world as real and made out of minute atoms that are not capable of any further division.

The crux of this philosophy is the proposition that in order to obtain the summum bonum (ultimate, singular and overriding aim which is ought to be pursued by each human being) one must acquire the valid knowledge of the truth. This knowledge will drive away miseries, cycle of birth, mundane existence, faults and false knowledge ... and the result will be *Moksha,* the liberation.

Let us now try to understand the propositions of this school. Please don't get scared with the details. You will have better understanding of the whole once you have gone through the same few times over.

Ok, to begin with we have following three objects starting with Sanskrit word 'Pra' which means correct knowledge of any object arrived at based on reasoning:

1. *Pramata* (*pramatr*), the subject, the knower
2. *Pramana*, the means of obtaining the knowledge
3. Prameya, the object, the knowable

The knower is simple to understand. *Pramana* consists of four types given below.

1. *Pratyaksha*—Direct based on perception
2. *Anumana*—Inference based
3. *Upamana*—Based on comparison
4. *Shabda*—Based on testimony

Pratyaksha Pramana is further bifurcated in three categories of Laukik, Alaukik, Bahya which means ordinary, extraordinary and external respectively. Going further, Laukik *Pratyaksha* Praman can be of two types—Nirvikalp and Savikalp which means indeterminate and determinate. Similarly, Alaukik *Pratyaksha Pramana* can be had with three different bases i.e. Samanya Lakshan (perception of class) or *Gyan Lakshan* (based on association) or Yogaja Lakshan (based on intuitive perception).

On the other hand, Prameya, the object of knowledge, is comprised of twelve types. Four of these make physical world—air, fire, water and earth. Next two are involved as object of knowledge but are not physical in nature—soul and mind. After that we have Time and Space which are non material in nature but belong to physical world. Next we have Akash that is a physical substance but is not connected with the cause of production of the physical world. And finally, the twelfth component called Body which the direct object that is used for experiencing the external physical world through mind and senses.

For getting guided to final liberation, and after understanding *Pramana* and Prameya as discussed in above paragraphs, we are told that another fourteen categories are to be applied for processing a point to be evaluated to reach the correct knowledge:

1. *Doubt—Sanshaya;* a state in which mind wavers due to confusion
2. *Purpose—Prayojna;* motive for discussing the point. May be it is only presumed and not fully understood. But it must be established before hand.
3. *Examples—Drastanta;* use of illustration to highlight a common fact
4. *Doctrine—Siddhanta;* demonstrated conclusion of an argument, an undisputed truth
5. *Constituents of inference—Avayava;* components or parts of a logical argument
6. *Hypothetical argument—Tark,* persuasive reasoning
7. *Ascertainment—Nirnaya;* conclusions, final deductions
8. *Discussion—Vaad;* proposition
9. *Wrangling*—Counter argument
10. *Irrational Reasoning—Vitanda,* destructive criticism
11. *Fallacy—Hetvabhasa;* fallacious reasoning
12. *Unfair reply—Chhala;* deceitful disputation
13. *Futility—Jati;* logic based on false similarity
14. *Grounds for defeat—Nigrasthana;* putting an end to arguments beyond doubt

Right perception is to be taken as source of right knowledge. Knowledge itself can be of two different types—*anubhav* and *smirti* (experience and memory) and both of these can be both valid (prama) and invalid (aprama).

Finally, Nyaya proclaims that cognitions and conscious states of mind arise in soul when it is related to mind, mind is related to senses, and senses are related to the external world. The soul is to be known with anumana as it is not physical and one's own soul can be perceived only on the basis of mental perception while the soul of other person can only be perceived by inference. The person who obtains valid knowledge of external world, its relationship with the mind and self will enjoy liberation. Also concluded is the fact that liberation will never be possible unless the identity of the soul with the body is given up.

Vaisheshika Philosophy

Vaisheshika as a school is as old as Buddhism and Jainism. It explains the nature of the world under seven categories namely *Dravya,*

Karma, Samanya (universal), *Vishesh* (exclusive), *Amavaya* (inherence) and *Abhava* (non existent). There is nothing in the whole universe that is outside these categories. This philosophy is attributed to Rishi Kanaad of 3rd century BC. His concept of *Dravya* (object) consisted of an atomic cosmology of nine elements. Four of these elements are material in nature namely earth, water, fire and air while rest five, namely, space, time, ether, mind and soul are abstract elements. As per this theory all the material objects are made with combination of these elements alone.

Gunas (qualities) here are divided into twenty four which are *roop, ras, gandh, sparsh, sankhya, pariman, prathkyat* (individuality), *sanyog, vibhag, pratav* (priority), *apratav, sukh, dukh, icchha, dvesh, pryatna, gurutva, dravyatva* (fluidity), *sneh, sanskara, dharma, adharma, shabda, intellect*. Karma here means a direct physical action including throwing up or down, picking up, squeezing, contraction, and motion. The next element of categories, Samanya is of either higher category or lower category. Similarly, Vishesha is bifurcated into infinite nature, as each atom is separate from other. So, there is infinite individuality.

As per *Vaisheshika*, every object has something 'samanya' and something 'vishesh'. The portal under which 'samanya' and 'vishesh' qualities or energies are able to exist together is called 'Dravya' (substance). These qualities are separate entities and hence need to be classified separately as *Gunas* and *Karmas*. As per this philosophy, *Samnya* or *Vishesh Gunas* do not exist without a padartha—so there is an intimate relationship among them. This relationship is called 'samvay' (perpetual intimate relation).

With reference to cause and effect, *Vaisheshika* suggests that every effect is fresh creation or a new beginning as against *Sankhya*, which said that, every effect is connected to the cause itself. This system accepts an 'Ishwara' as the efficient cause of the world while eternal atoms are material cause of the world. Another marked specialty of *Vaisheshika* is its belief that consciousness is accidental i.e., when it gets attached to a body then only consciousness is acquired. Further that soul develops attachment with body due to ignorance—it identifies itself with body and mind.

Atoms of *Prathvi, Jal, Tejas* and *Vayu* are eternal and *Vaisheshika* supports that the universe is created of these four elements. And they believe that having only atoms was not necessary, there must be somebody to fit them in separate shapes and sizes, and hence, there has to be a creator. Rest of the *Dravyas* from *Akash* to *Manas* are eternal and all these except mind are all pervading – existing everywhere. But manas (mind) is atomic and connected with *Atma* (soul). When Atma gets related to manas, knowledge is the result. Gyana is a special category of Atma but it is *Manas* which receives the sensation of pleasure or pain. The different sense organs are only the instruments of knowledge. When, by the grace of God, the Atma acquires the right knowledge of things, all miseries vanish and the supreme bliss, *Moksha* follows.

Mimamsa (Critical Inquiry) Philosophy

It is probably the earliest of all philosophies and is related to *Karma Kand* part of the Vedas. Also called *Purva Mimamsa*, this philosophy aims to provide rules for interpretations of Vedas and provides philosophical justifications for rituals presented therein. The philosophy is based on *Mimamsa Sutra* by Gemini of 4th century BC.

The central tenets of Mimamsa are ritualism, anti asceticism and anti mysticism. The aim is elucidation of dharma understood as a set of ritual obligations and prerogatives to be performed as prescribed by Vedas. This dharma is limited to the meaning of virtue or morality. It is said that rituals, if properly performed, maintain harmony of universe and further personal goals. Since with simply perception and reasoning, one can't know dharma, one must depend on revelations of the Vedas that are eternal and infallible. Gemini almost guaranteed the sacrifice life in heaven after death. In continuation of the past tradition with little changed, he advised that while women can sacrifice but Shudras were still kept out.

While Nyaya School distinguished only four methods of knowledge perceptions, namely *pratyaksha*, anumana, upamana and shabda, Mimamsa added another two to make them total six. The new addition is 'Arthapatti' (hypothesis) and 'Abhava' (knowledge by negation). Later on, this method of Arthapatti became very common with Science streams as it is based on the principle that "something already observed would have been impossible without the hypothesis". The concept of Abhava also is very interesting; it suggests that both known and unknown factors are to be taken together to reach to final knowledge. So, when the other five methods from *Pratyaksha* to Arthapatti were not able to operate, the resultant is called Abhava.

Some people do not consider this school as a full-fledged philosophy because it takes power of *mantras* as power of God. The entire knowledge here is derived purely based on verbal recognition of the words as contained in the Vedas. Historically, the school took shape when Buddhism and Upanishads were marginalizing Vedic sacrifices. This school tried demonstrating validity of Vedic texts by rigid formulation of rules and for their right interpretations.

Vedanta Philosophy

Also called *Uttar Mimamsa*, this school is based on *Vedanta Sutras* (also called *Brahma Sutras*) and came into existence during 500 BC to 200 BC. The sutras are written in very terse style and allow scholars to search multiple meanings and conclusions. In the process of commenting and finding new meanings to the Sutras, philosophers have founded varying schools of this philosophy. But most notable of these are 1. Adi Shankara (8th Century CE) named *"Advaita"* (Non Dualism), 2. Ramanuja (11th century CE) named *'Vishishta Advaita'* (Qualified Non Dualism) and 3. Madhva (12th century CE) named *'Dvaita'* (Dualism).

The meaning of Vedanta, as the name signifies, is end of Vedas but in reality it refers to period of Upanishads. So, Vedanta school of philosophy is basically philosophy of Upanishads that reads through the lenses of unity of *Atman* and *Brahman*. This school basically assumes the material world consisting of *'avidya'* and *'maya'* where even death is but only maya.

The basic difference here with the other schools is that they believed that God and the Universe are two different substances while *Advaita* believes both were the same substance.

The concept developed by Shankara states that the eternal Self is *Atman* and universal Self is *Brahman*. The world is made of categories of space, time and cause. These categories are not self contained, self-consistent or self regulated. Hence, they point to existence of something unalterable, something.... Absolute. As per Shankara, *Brahman* is that Absolute and which enables the empirical world to exist by itself. It is ignorance that affects our whole empirical being. This ignorance can get removed only after realizing the truth. Shankara concludes that the highest representation of *Brahman* is *Ishwara* or *Saguna Brahman*. But the *Nirguna Brahman* transcends this and is the basis of manifested world.

Vishishta Advaita of Ramanuja is said to be a combination of *Sankhya, Yoga* and *Advaita* schools. He advocates that the highest status of *Brahman* that can be humanly realized is only the *Saguna Brahman* or the God with Qualities. Ramanuja took exception to Shankara's *Nirguna Brahman* saying that it is something hypothetical as it is beyond experience. Thus his way of realizing the Absolute is by symbology with devotion. The combination of *Saguna* form and devotion brought this school close to *Bhakti* as a dominant theme of his philosophy. Ramanuja further said that consciousness and *Brahman* are not identical rather consciousness is just an attribute of *Brahman*. Since mind can only understand symbols and images, there is no point in discussing the abstract.

As per Ramanuja, *Brahman, Atman* and *Jagat* are different and eternal and at the same time inseparable. *Brahman* is related to the other two as soul to body...all three together form an organic whole. Conclusion of this philosophy is that Absolute and manifestations are two aspects of the same Reality, therefore, *Brahman* is qualified by the Universe and the living beings.

Madhva's theory is an improvement over Ramanuja and states that there is no interdependence among *Brahman, Atman* and *Jagat*—all three are simply independent and eternal.

Let us look at the whole Vedanta principles in a summary. In all apparently individual forms of existence what is present is one indivisible *Brahman*. But owing to particular adjuncts into these forms, the form appears broken up and different from each other—into a multiplicity of intellectual on sensitive principles, the Jeevatma. The reality in all these *Atmans* is universal *Brahman*, the aggregate of individualizing body organs and mental functions, which is in our ordinary experience separate and project as different *Atmans*, is due to Maya and hence unreal.

The non-enlightened soul is unable to look through and beyond Maya, which like a veil hides it from its true nature. Instead of recognizing itself *Brahman*, the soul identifies itself with *upadhi*, the given name under the influence of Maya and thus looks for its true self in the body, in the sense organs and manas.

Incidentally, Maya is a principle of illusion, the non-definable cause owing to which, there seems to exist a material world

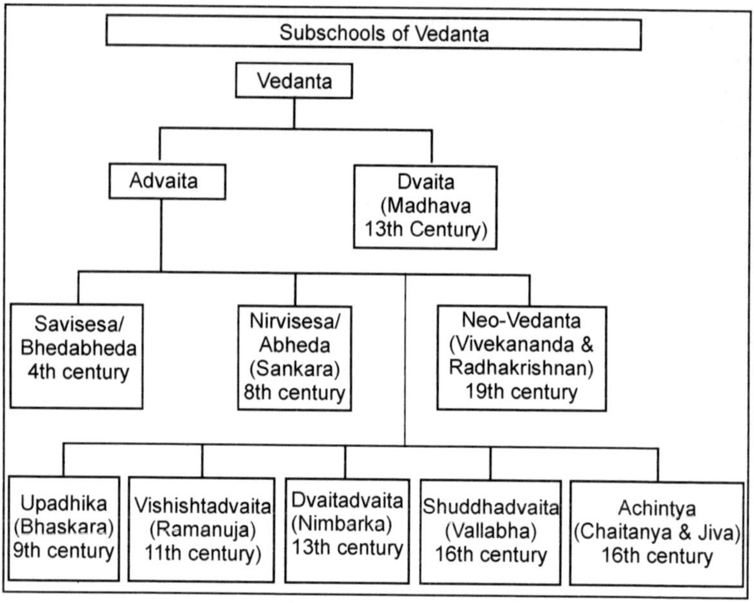

comprehending distinct individual existence. Its association with Maya enables the *Brahman* to project the appearance of the world. In simple world, Maya is Shakti of *Brahman*.Through its actions in this situation, the soul burdens itself with merits as well as demerits and the consequences of these actions have to be borne or enjoyed in series of future embodied existence. It is the Lord, who as dispenser allots that body to which the individual soul is entitled based on its previous actions—and so the process continues.

Vivekananda, the great philosopher of recent times, said that it is foolish to attempt to prove that the whole of Vedas and Upanishads as Dualistic or Non Dualistic as they are both. They are but different conceptions leading to final conclusions and that both *Dualism* and Monism are necessary for the evolution of the mind.

All said and done, Vedas and Upanishads begin with the premises that there is something deeper than what is perceived by senses and mind. The way to discover that hidden is only through mind. Life is a psychic journey and the only means available for this journey is our own mind. So, we must become aware of our own infinite dimension not in an egotistical sense but in a universal sense. Because when the mind crosses over the intellect and the ego, it attains oneness with the Self, the *Atman*.

But the opponents of Non Dualism of Adi Shankara had a strong argument that if both *Atman* and *Brahman* are one, one cannot love God or worship God because he himself is God. Probably, the compulsions of *Bhakti* period where normal worshipper was dying to have a God visible to him must have been the background of such opponents.

Charvaka Philosophy

This is a school of materialism or rationalism that denies surviving soul and refutes transmigration. This is also an ancient school and predates both Buddhism and Jainism. Meaning of this Sanskrit word is "sweet talk". This is also called Lokayata School. Lokayata means "those of the world."

Charvaka was originally a Brahminic thought which denied the concept of life after death. It believed that there is nothing called 'Parloka', the world beyond. In this sense, Charvaka stands totally separate as all three, Vedic, Buddhism and Jainism thoughts have a common sharing and belief about rebirth, karmic distribution and existence of Parloka.

Charvaka believed on *Pratyaksha Pramana* (direct perception) through sense organs as the only knowledge that is duly verifiable by all and is completely beyond dispute. In addition, this school also accepted Anuman but to the extent that it is based on experience. Like, if one sees smoke in the distance, one can conclude that there must be fire. But no Anuman can be accepted for matters like soul or God or other world. After all, who has ever seen that?

And since the school accepted only direct perception as the truth, they believed only in four eternal elements namely, earth, water, fire and air. It refused to consider the fifth element of Akash. On the same basis, it refused to recognize soul or *atman* as a surviving entity, simply because its existence is out of perception. The school also did not accept consciousness as part of body. Instead, they held that consciousness is a user of body. And since it uses it, it can't be a part of the body. They compared consciousness with other situations like happiness or intoxication, which are both functions of the body but can't be said to be part of the body

The school is also known for rather radical views about the pain and miseries being a reality as advocated by most other philosophical schools discussed above. Charvaka argued that fine there is pain but it advocated human beings to go after pleasures. Pleasure was advised to be pursued even if there was some pain in the process. Let the pain be there but don't worry for anything other than pleasures, was their *mantra*.

Charvaka took pleasures as the precedent to everything else. There is a shloka in Sanskrit about their philosophy which suggest "Consume (as food) ghee as much as you can and if you cannot arrange it for yourself, borrow from others but enjoy ghee". Consuming Ghee, in the times when the shloka was composed, must be the ultimate pleasure or equivalent to current time 'masti' or 'having a good time'. Basically they recommended not letting the pleasure go in hope of future pains.

Their belief was rather simple—there is no heaven, there is nothing called final liberation, nothing like a soul, or other world. Whatever exists is in front of you and what is not here is nowhere. They claimed rationality, clear-headedness, no superstitions, no point in going for meaningless rituals and sacrifices or intellectual dishonesty of making unnecessary tall claims.

On the flip side, this school lacked sense of vision and any ideal to inspire future generations. Such ideas may look very practical for a moment but the reality will soon catch up. Such principles are not able to provide a balance in life or can't bring out any long-term vision. Yes, there is certainly a shock value attached to such ideas but only for a momentary pause. The school also lacked depth as it didn't elaborate important matters like human obligations for social life, how to deal with conflict of interest situations, etc. No wonder, some writers have called it Marx of old time.

Ajivika Philosophy

This is a school that has since died completely and whatever is known about it is all from secondary sources of Buddhism and Jain scriptures. But at some time in history, it must have been very popular as King Bindusar, father of King Ashoka, was a follower of this school for later part of his life. Its prominent teacher is said to be Makkhali Gosala, a man of very humble background, born in a cowshed and hence the name. As the name suggest, the followers of this school were living down the life (reverse of Jivika). But to the credit of Gosala, he is said to have been in direct touch with Mahavira for several years before the two parted ways due to some basic differences on the doctrine.

Ajivika is a school of naked wandering ascetics who believed in karma, fatalism and extreme passivity. They followed the doctrine of abstaining from action to avoid accumulation of 'karma'. They relied heavily on fate as a predetermined will of God. So, they believed that whatever happens in life should be allowed without any interruption or willfull intentional action to the contrary. It promoted the human surrender to the flow of life on course of a predetermined will of God. Their concept may be aptly explained by the famous dialogue of a Hindi film "*Jab jab jo jo hota hai, tab tab vo sab hone doe* (whatever happens, let is happen whenever it happens)" as a complete crux of this philosophy. They are known to be non-theistic as well as against any class systems of the Vedic society.

Based on other second hand information in terms of their practices for meditation (by hanging from a tree like a bat), living naked (like the monks of Digambar Jains), life of ascetic, focus on dance and music for arousing consciousness indicate toward their following some sort of ancient Shaivism practices.

But later, the school got completely disintegrated without any footprints in later part of the history. Some of their practices, for sure, would have absorbed by other religions as was always happening during the entire journey of thoughts getting refined, mixed, reshaped, renamed as a process of churning.

Buddhist Philosophy

Buddhism is woven around the doctrine of four noble truths, namely 1. Life is full of sufferings. 2. The thirst for life and its pleasures is the cause of sufferings. 3. The extinction of the thirst for life is the cessation of sufferings. 4. Such extinction can be brought by a holy life.

There is a special simplicity in everything related to Buddhism and the field of philosophy is no exception to this. The Buddha discouraged his followers from indulging in intellectual disputation for its own sake, which is fruitless, and distracting from true awakening. Nevertheless, the delivered sayings of the Buddha contain a philosophical component, in its teachings on the working of the mind, and its criticisms of the philosophies of his contemporaries.

According to the scriptures, during his lifetime the Buddha remained silent when asked several metaphysical questions. These included issues such as whether the universe is eternal or non-eternal or whether it is finite or infinite, the unity or separation of the body and the self, the complete inexistence of a person after Nirvana and death, and others.

Buddha believed in Gods since they were part of his cultural heritage (being a born Hindu) but he did not believe much in Gods as a help to mankind for getting out of their miseries. Neither he denied Gods but he placed the ultimate reality of Nirvana as higher than Gods. Buddhism doesn't need the presence of God to experience bliss or a sense of transcendence in meditation. They consider such state to be natural to humanity. Instead of relying on Gods, Buddha advised his disciples to save themselves.

Buddhism focuses on objective reality but not the one riddled with logical proof but the one that can be achieved by anyone who seriously tried to live life as suggested by Buddha. Yes, Karma bound people need tools to come out from endless cycle of rebirth into a series of painful lives. But if people can reform their egoistic attitude, they could change their destiny.

When asked if a person who has attained nirvana lived after death, Buddha dismissed the question as improper. It was like asking what direction a flame went after it got put off. Buddha held that rituals, theology or belief set of a person is not important. These could sound interesting but lacked the power of taking him to final significance. In his opinion, the only thing that counted was living life with good Dharma in spite of the fact that they could not express it in logical term.

Jain Philosophy

The distinguishing features of Jain philosophy are its belief about independent existence of soul and matter, absence of a supreme divine creator/preserver/destroyer, potency of karma, eternal and uncreated universe, a strong emphasis on non-violence, accent on relativity and multiple facets of truth, and morality and ethics based on liberation of soul. Jain philosophy attempts to explain the rationale of being, the nature of the Universe and its constituents, the nature of bondage and the means to achieve liberation.

Jainism has often been described as an ascetic movement for its strong emphasis on self-control, austerities and renunciation. It has also been called a model of philosophical liberalism for its insistence that truth is relative and multifaceted and for its willingness to accommodate all possible view-points of the rival philosophies. It strongly upholds the individualistic nature of soul and personal responsibility for one's decisions; and that self-reliance and individual efforts alone are responsible for one's liberation.

There are infinite independent souls. These are categorized into two—liberated and non-liberated. Infinite knowledge, perception and bliss are the intrinsic qualities of a soul. These qualities are fully enjoyed unhindered by liberated souls. But non-liberated souls are obscured by karma forcing it into karmic bondage. This bondage results in a continuous co-habitation of the soul with the body. Thus, an embodied non-liberated soul is found in four planes—heavens, hells, humans and animal world in a never-ending cycle of births and deaths known as *samsara*. The soul is in bondage since the beginning of the universe. However, it is possible to achieve liberation through rational perception, rational knowledge and rational conduct. (Gandhi)

Some writers note that Jain ontology is both realist and dualist metaphysics. It is realist in the sense that knowledge of ultimate reality does not exclude the reality of the existing world; the enlightened world view includes the knowledge of particulars and the world continues to be real even after the liberation. It is dualist in that the two prime categories of substance, soul and matter, are mutually exclusive.

Jain metaphysics is based on seven (sometimes nine, with subcategories) truths or fundamental principles also known as tattva, which are an attempt to explain the nature and solution to the human predicament.

Certainly, the philosophy for Jains is very elaborate and deep. But basic tenets are not far from the Hindu schools except that they did not accept authority of Vedas.

Undoubtedly, several of these independent philosophies developed within Indian boundaries before anywhere else and clearly bear the evidence of high speculative powers of human minds from this pious soil. In yet another greatness of Sanskrit literature that one can trace every step of evolution of human wisdom overarching religious and philosophical progress for entire mankind.

23

Emergence of Islam from Arabia

The extreme climate at Arabia around 500 CE was as tough as it is today. The area was completely dominated by tribes who had their own sets of values and religious traditions. Most people lived nomadic hard life where basic survival itself was always a challenge. It was a domain of nomadic bedu, with occasional settlements where they could find water, cultivation, trading and some cultic centres.

Before prosperity of Mecca, local tribes were engaged in constant struggle with each other for securing for their people whatever little was available there; each day was a struggle for survival. Life could not be thought outside one's own tribe. The working of tribes has some unique features like a pack of wolves. They always remain together and fight the enemy jointly and all get share of their loot. Sure there are chiefs and ordinary people within a tribe but everybody is taken care by donations and grants by other members of the tribe who can afford. (Rodwell)

The ethics for punishments were also unique for an Arabian Tribe where killing any one member of the opposite tribe could revenge loss of a member of the tribe; it is not the person who is guilty but the entire tribe. Each tribe was own government by itself and there was nothing comparable to current systems where you have a central authority and independent police etc. for fixing and punishing offenders. In a tribe's scenario, the head of the tribe has his authority only until his clan is supportive of him but once he loses that respect, he can get overthrown by a new contender. Every individual or clan was as strong as his tribe as no other entity can have separate existence outside his tribe. Any time a chief of a tribe failed to retaliate for loss of life or property of any of his members; soon there will be a loss of respect for his entire clan and anyone from outside would be free to kill its members with impunity. Justice had to be immediate and response to each event of violence has to be at least equal if not bigger. These conditions were perfect platform for constant violence among the tribes with no end in sight.

To take care of communal spirit of the people under such conditions, Arabians have evolved an ideology called 'muruwah' which took care of their religious aspirations, whatever little they had. There were very many deities who were worshipped by Arabs at their shrines but there was no developed mythology or philosophy or anything which could be compared to a full-scale religion. They hardly had any sense of what happens after death and instead believed in fate. Their poetry of that time makes it clear that their basic belief was that fate ruled their destiny and sooner or later fate will bring death. In a social set up with so much of deprivation, mortality, illiteracy, malnutrition and rampant violence, it was but obvious that people start believing only in their fate.

It has been seen in other context also that progress relating to mind and hearts could take place only on a full stomach. In a contrasting situation, ancient India had made such strong strides for developing spirituality and literature because human survival was never an issue. All season rivers have created a very fertile basin where a simple scratch of soil allowed a farmer to grow what ever seed were sown. The dense forest cover and an excellent climate ensured a comfortable life for all the inhabitants. These conditions of Sindhu Sarasvati Civilization are certainly a big reason for allowing our sages to achieve highest possible climb for human minds.

Pre-Islamic Arabia

Coming back to Arabia of before 500 CE, muruwah had far greater significance in terms of all aspects of social, religious and spiritual lives of the tribal populace and included characteristics like manliness, courage in battle, patience, endurance in sufferings and above all absolute dedication to one's tribe. It required a person to follow dictate of his chief without any questioning and to go all the way to avenge any actual or perceived wrong committed against his tribe and specially protect its vulnerable members like women and infants. Muruwah principles may sound very brutal apparently but there are plus points not to be ignored. For example, it encouraged indifference to material possessions and encouraged deep and strong egalitarian values.

But times change and so does the comparative importance of doctrines. Arab by now was surrounded by well settled and prospering mini empires in North-Western Syrian area was controlled by Ghassanids, Arab Vassals of the Byzantines while the North East by the Lakhmids of Al Hira (presently called Iraq) who were under control of Persia. Peninsula Arab was also coming to know of modern developments in all directions. The members of Mecca tribes also accompanied merchants to Syria and Iraq and were not left untouched with the prosperity and civilization growth in those areas. Muruwah was certainly not able to provide answers to the new questions thrown out by new situations.

Arabians were also very unhappy that Prophets of Jews and Christians had already visited them with their holy books but their High God, al-Lah has not favoured them with a prophet or scripture. The people of Mecca were so proud to have the cubical shaped black stone shrine at Kabah but they had still not been blessed with a face and book. People from entire peninsula for pilgrimage frequented Kabah. The tradition of non-violence in the sanctuary and sacred area around the shrine offered tremendous opportunity to all and sundry to carry out their trade and commercial activity without fear for violence. Hashims were a poor clan of Quraysh tribe of Mecca which was the main tribe having control over Mecca.

But between 500 to 600 CE, conditions saw some changes. The trade route from Mecca to northern Arabia increased like never before. This converted Mecca as one of the most important human settlements in entire Arab. They now started enjoying material success and had enough food and other comforts and a different kind of life of luxuries. Mecca slowly emerged as an important trade and banking centre. Trade included wines from Syria and Persia; weapons, spices, textiles and spears from India; slaves from Africa. Caravans used to move between Yemen and Syria and Mecca was a crucial stay point for the same. Mecca soon was also visited by many people for pilgrimage. But prosperity of Mecca had lead to materialism and Quraysh now got richer more than they ever imagined or worked for. But this development simultaneously weakened the tribal ethos of communal bond and taking care of weak and poor exactly in similar ways as material success impacts social life anywhere else.

Newly arrived money from the increased business in their town resulted in their lifestyles pushing back their original tribal values. Tribe was no more first, now the priority started going to individual me and myself. This resulted in clans start fighting with each other for a bigger piece of cake. This is the time when Muhammad, (born in 570 CE) himself a small Hashim merchant started worrying about the falling ethics of Quraysh people and slowly got convinced that unless the Quraysh were to get an altogether new communal bond at the centre of their lives and change their greedy and selfish ways, they will soon meet their moral, political and physical doom.

He was not literate and nothing much is known about his first forty years of life. But surely he had no exposure to hardcore religion or scriptures or philosophies but was a pious man. He got married to a rich widow, Khadija and they had several children but only one daughter named Fatima survived. As the year went by, Muhammad turned more and more towards monotheistic meditation, as was the common practice in his area. He used to take his family every year in Ramadan to a nearby mountain for a spiritual retreat. It was just a common practice among many people to visit shrines, spend time praying their High God and distribute alms and foods to needy people as per their capacity. He may not have been a successful merchant but he was a man with exceptional talents. He knew that many Jews and Christians who come in contact with Arabs makes fun of their not being blessed with own theology or a Prophet who could convey directly what their High God wish to tell them.

Finally, one day Muhammad was torn from sleep and was directed by an angel Gabriel and ordered to "Recite" to the people the message sent by al-Lah for his people. And in spite of his repeated denial and expressed inability to do so, the angel enveloped him and squeezed tightly and forced him to accept his command. He was completely terrified with this experience and shared his shock with his wife who consoled him hard to suggest that he was a pious man who cared for his traditions and his people and that no one will harm him just for nothing. They consulted their relative who convinced them that this is a revelation from the God and that Muhammad has been identified as a prophet for becoming a divine envoy to Arabs. It is said that it was years later that Muhammad got himself convinced about it and started preaching to his Quraysh people and progressively started creating a scripture for Arabs in their own language.

Between 610 and 632 until the death of Muhammad, he was visited by Angel Gabriel without any periodicity many times and prompted him to recite various Ayats to his people. Unlike any other example in the history, Qur'an has been revealed to Muhammad bit-by-bit, line-by-line and verse by verse over a period of twenty two long years. The process of this creation was very tormenting for Muhammad who is reported to get gripped by spasm and sweat ran down even on colder days. The unbearable pain forced him to take his head in between his knees, a meditative position that was usually taken by mystics of that area.

But for first many years, Muhammad did not know much about revelations made by earlier Prophets to the Jews and Christians so, surely, it cannot be called a repeat experience. Little did he realize during these revelations that he was not only redefining the future religions of his people but also that he is creating one of the finest religious scriptures in human history.

There are no firm ideas as to the exact sequence of the revelations as the Qur'an available for our use is a re-sequenced document with bigger Ayats taken in the beginning and smaller toward the end. But many people believe that the content and horizon of revelations progressively expanded. For example, in the beginning, it was directly addressed only to local people for matters of urgent requirements. But later, the scope covered larger width of humanity and became more universal. The benefit of long years gave him ample opportunity to cover wide range of issues ranging from basic survival to fights and conflicts to inter faith comparisons and spiritual and philosophical matters with Arabians at the focus. Over the years, God's revelations also included befitting replies to the critics of Muhammad and acted more like a running commentary.

The Qur'an as a Piece of Fine Literature

For Muslims, it is the word of God revealed in Arabic by angel Gabriel to Prophet Muhammad for entire mankind. For them, it is final expressions from God and there was to be no more Prophet after Muhammad. As it is, Arabic is a very difficult language and it is almost impossible to bring out the forceful meaning once translated into any other language. It is a prose but people familiar with the language maintain that somehow Qur'an prose carry force of conviction, which would have been expected only out of wonderfully crafted poetry. It is crucial to know that its text was always intended to be read aloud. Even today, with all the changes happened in the world, Qur'an, for its full impact to pass on to the audience, is still advised to be read aloud.

Its recitation to a good crowd brings out its features that are impossible to be felt if one decides to just read it silently. This is how Muhammad revealed it to begin with. Best of translation takes away this beauty from Qur'an. It consists of 114 chapters of varying length that are called suras. It was an oral text but soon got consigned to writing within lifetime of Muhammad. Another striking feature of Qur'an is its rhetorical focus using the assonance to round off verses.

Central Theme of Qur'an

To begin with, it is belief in one God, the merciful God who alone is creator of Heaven and Earth and all things and beings therein and whose omnipotence is to be seen in everywhere in his Signs. Secondly, God had sent a series of believing prophets to their people over the ages, all conveying the same message. Muhammad is supposed to be the last such prophet in the series and he has been sent to Arabians with his message also conveyed only in Arabic. (Rodwell)

Daily prayers (*solat*) and alms giving (*zakat*) are two other important pillars of Islam. Interestingly, there is no mention of praying five times a day. Later during his stay at Medina, fasting during the pious month of Ramadan and pilgrimage (hajj) for every capable Muslim was also added as additional pillars of Islam.

Muhammad was actually not aware that a great religion is going to take shape based on his revelations. He maintained that he is not saying anything new and that he was simply repeating the knowledge that has been with his people for a long time already. Initially, he was not interested to the plight of people outside Quraysh. Neither he planned for developing any theology as, with his background, assuming that he knew about theology let alone create a new one, was a difficult proposition. He also did not harbour any political aspirations and was only interested in Quraysh being guided by his al-Lah to come out of their dire situation and become alive to their core tribal values. His people already knew about their God, he considered his work only to remind them not to forget Him and his gratitude. This was in this respect that he asked his converts to show their physical gesture of surrender by bowing before al-Lah every day. Initially, the Quraysh were very offended to bow like slaves.

Islam technically means that Muslims are duty bound to create a just and equitable society. It promoted distribution of wealth by regular donations and considered stockpiling of fortune as wrong. Thus daily worship and regular donations became two pillars of Islam. Islam maintained that God can be viewed only through his natural creations which needed to be observed with lot of attentions and with lots of curiosity. This tenet later gave a big boost to successive generations who excelled in the field of natural sciences.

Worship of a Single God

Subsequent to this, Islam has maintained that the Muslims would surrender to God alone and would not succumb to the false objects of worship—be they deities or values—espoused by Quraysh. In fact, to put any trust in any other being other than God is considered as one of the greatest sins in Islam. Islam maintains *"there is no deity but al-Lah, the creator of heaven and earth, who alone can save man and send him the spiritual and physical sustenance that he needs"*. This was a result of Muhammad's personal experience as he knew that only a single object of worship will have the power to integrate his people and his society. Qur'an sees God as Absolute and that is why it addresses Him with ninety-nine names or attributes. Ultimately it became the first pillar of Islam. It is called Shahadah, the Muslim profession of faith that *"I bear witness that there is no God but al-Lah and that Muhammad is his Messenger"*.

Islam's Attitude Towards Other Religions

Islam as professed by Muhammad accepted the existing religions of Jews and Christians and he never encouraged people from other religion to convert to Islam. Somehow, very few people from outside Islamic world would believe that tolerance is a basic tenet of pure Islam. Qur'an maintained that whatever has been spoken to others by their Gods, we are fine with that. As per Qur'an, Muslims have to be intolerant to injustice even if it by your own people or your seniors or even rulers. The Qur'an does not seem to condemn other religious traditions as false or incomplete and believes that every new Prophet brings more clarity and continuity.

There are several suras that speak about the religious practices and people of Jews and Christians. These suras came subsequent to Muhammad having shifted his base to Medina where three Jewish tribes were already settled with two Arabian clans. During his stay at Medina, Muhammad came in contact with believers of other religions and it was based on his interactions with people from Jews and Christians that he developed his understanding of these religions in a detailed manner. Infact, in order to bring Islam closer to Judaism, there was a time when he even asked his Muslims to worship in the direction of Jerusalem, allowed them to marry Jew ladies and observe holiday on Jew's Day of Atonement. But all that changed later when the Jews of Medina worked against his political survival. His rejection by the Jews was a big disappointment in his life. Later he asked his Muslims to face Mecca again for their daily worship.

But there is nothing in Qur'an about Hinduism or Buddhism that were also equally strong religions at that point in history. But it is purely because Muhammad was neither aware about these religions and nor his interest covered any other person outside his own tribes. But looking to his reactions to other religious thoughts known to him, he would have shown great respect to the religions of east and would have spoken about them also in his revelations.

Violence and Islam

It's true that Muhammad had to participate in wars but those were for the survival of his family and early converts. Historical facts clearly suggest that he neither initiated those bloody confrontations nor participated in those wars with the idea of expanding territory or enhancing his resources or reputation. He did participate in wars but because he was forced into it by others. While subsequent reality of the Muslim world, wars have been used very regularly and entire expansion of Islam as a religion rides over military success achieved by its early followers but Muhammad's action or words or teachings were never expansionists or violent in nature. Islam, through Qur'an justifies only one type of war and that in self-defense. Aggression was strictly forbidden. In order to limit the agony related to war, once the war there, it was advised that the war should be finished quickly. And as soon as the enemy surrendered or called for peace, Muslims were advised to end hostilities and work for terms of truce. Actually, going by scripture alone, one will find more violence in Bible than in Qur'an.

The often quoted reference of 'Jihad' is made out as if it means 'Holy War'. That is completely ill founded. Literal meaning of *Jihad* reads as 'putting God's will in practice'. Considering the conditions in which Islam took shape, no one could have imagined to keep brutal wars out of sight or discussions. Wars were around all the time. Therefore, Islam accepted the reality of a cruel world but called upon all Muslims to additionally prepare on all fronts like social, spiritual, economic and intellectual. Reforming one's own heart and society was considered a bigger 'jihad' while war with enemy only a small jihad. Muhammad's acceptance of wars as inevitable and his dislike for war can be appreciated from the fact that Qur'an called for retaliation to be in proportion to the act of enemy. A person having place for violence in his heart would not have cared to caution retaliatory action also to be pursued with restraint. A measured retaliation will draw comparison with Krishna telling Arjuna in Gita to fight as his swa-dharma. Islam forbids any fight except in self-defense that means unless attacked by some other force. And it is not only that Muhammad only prescribed so but he also pursued astonishingly non violence policy.

Another argument made in justifying frequent violence in Muslim world is about their deep grievances and frustrations that are ever escalated by economic, political and social factors prevailing in most part of their presence. One must not forget that entire Arabia has been a violent place and, if history is any thing to go by, unfortunately, may remain so for unknown period in future as well. It only goes to prove that best of religion, sometime, is unable to end the curse on the particular land. Violence and Arabia happens to have co existed for best part of known human history without any quick end in offing.

One view which gets formed for easier acceptance of violence by Muslims has its roots to Sunna, the example of Muhammad's pattern of behaviour, which is also taken as a important source of legislation in Islam. Its importance lies in the fact that its followers, the Sunnis account for 90 per cent of total Muslim population in the world. Sunna and Qur'an exhort Muslims to emulate Muhammad in all walks of life as the right example. But Sunna also carries encouragement to pillaging and plundering of infidels together with enslaving their children and placing their women in concubinage. The definition of infidel is somewhat porous and leaves room for stretching to suit the intentions of person explaining it or understanding it. In Chapter 9 Sura 5 is reproduced here below:

> *"But when the sacred months expire slay those who associate others with Allah in His Divinity wherever you find them; seize them, and besiege them, and lie in wait for them. But if they repent and establish the Prayer and pay Zakah, leave them alone. Surely Allah is All-Forgiving, Ever-Merciful."*
> (the reference to sacred months is for the months of Hazz and Umra when Muslims lay down their arms)

Qur'an asks Muslims to kill *'kafirs'* but such mention has to be understood in correct context of history. This chapter applied to those tribes who were continuously showing hostilities to early converts even after they have migrated to Medina to escape. It was never intended for people of other faiths as Muhammad always called Jews and Christians as "people of the book". Kafir was used to refer to idolaters opposing Muhammad and people converting to Islam in lifetime of Muhammad. But to disrepute Islam, there are numerous instances where Muslim aggressors used their power to crush opponents and took refuge to selected portions of Sunna and Qur'an to justify their actions as if they were fighting a pious war for strengthening Islam. Undoubtedly, Muhammad would never have accepted that as the right example of his life and teachings being practised by his followers.

Condition of Women in Islam

The condition of woman in pre-Islamic days was very atrocious. Different tribes were having different traditions; practices like female infanticide were very common. But to say that women condition was bad will be too simplistic. As already discussed, different tribes were having diverse customs, languages and lifestyle. North of the peninsula was arid in nature while south was blessed with soil and climate with perfect suitability for good agricultural harvest. While South was largely settled in villages and towns, the North has only few settled locations and rest of the shepherds, known as Bedouins, were continuously on the move. Ring of oases in the west had attracted permanent settlements which relied on agriculture and commerce and spoke Arabia. Mecca was situated on the spice route between Yathrib and Najran and became a caravan city having community of traders. Because violence was common, so were the fears of winner taking hostage of the females of the losers as brides or just slaves.

Many tribes used to consider girl child as a dispensable liability for the sake of poverty and fear of grace. Famines were frequent and since girls were considered less productive, it was like wasting limited resources to grow them and later send them away in marriage. On the other hand, fear of their getting captured during wars was always hovering around the head. It was obvious under these conditions that women in general were deprived of their most basic rights. It was usual to have a small dig ready near the cot of the pregnant lady where the newly born girl child was to be placed soon after birth and covered with earth. Condition of wives also was no better. Wars were common and so were the death of men. Post the death of husband; the heir apparent (could be a brother or grown up son or any other direct male relative) had full right over the wives of the dead. The heir could take them as wife or could use them as slave.

But Islam made a big difference in their plight. Actually, the advent of Islam shifted the focus of humanity from Tribe to Individuality. It made a big difference to bring a balancing concept of community and family. Islam instituted the system where everyone was, for the first time in Arabian history, equal irrespective of his or her gender, age, race, language, wealth. Also, each follower was asked to provide priority to moral and religious tradition much before his or her tribal affiliations.

This brought big relief to the female conditions and Islam certainly looked very positive for women to begin with. Some elite woman enjoyed considerable power and prestige. Women were first converts in Islam. Qur'an included many provisions for the safety and care of women. The share in property, restriction on number of wives that a man can have, forbidding killing of female children, right of divorce, right in inheritance etc. are all burning examples which surely brought cheers for women. But after departure of Muhammad, things did not remain the same for long. Most of us believe that Qur'an provides for veil system. But in reality Qur'an prescribes veil only for wives of Muhammad that was also as a mark of respect.

Sects in Islam

Islam later got divided into two groups called Sunnis and Shias. Unlike in other religions, the split here was based on politics rather any difference in doctrine. It so happened that after the death of Ali, the cousin and son-in-law of Muhammad, the Ummayads had seized the caliphate. This was not accepted by Husain ibn Ali, son of Ali and the only grandson of Muhammad. In a battle at Karbala, Ali got slaughtered by Ummayad Caliph Yazid. Although all Muslims consider this act as immoral but Shias consider Ali as a Hero and are proud that he gave the ultimate sacrifice of his life fighting for justice. They became convinced that only direct descendants of his father Ali should lead the religion. This is how they consider them separate identity

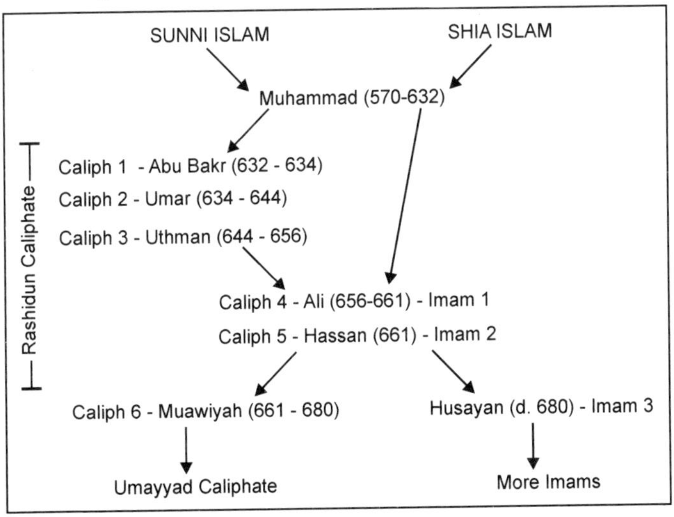

than the rest who are called Sunnis. But eventually, more people in number follow the Sunni sect which actually means "People of Traditions of Muhammad"

Sunnah, Hadith and Shariah

Undoubtedly Islam is influenced by the systems of Jews and Christian both of which grew in the same land and had developed many traditions much before Islam came on horizon. Jews have their code of conduct described in Torah. On similar pattern, Muslims also developed their own book on code of conducts based on Qur'an and the life and teachings of Muhammad. The first such guiding principle for Muslims is called '*Sunnah*' which literally means a path, a method, a way which is prescribed as normative for Muslims to follow as proper example. These religious practices got established by the Prophet among his companions and have been passed to followers by the consensus of generations. These religious practices have mostly originated from the religion of Ibrahim and the Prophet has made revisions to them or some additions where ever thought appropriate. The established Sunnah is taken at par in reliability with the Qur'an because it has been transmitted in the same way. *As such, the Qur'an and the Sunnah remain as Muslim's only primary sources of understanding Islam.* Sunnah was to be followed for fulfilling divine injunctions, religious rites and mouldings life in accordance with the will of God. To compare with Hindu systems, Sunnah can be looked as close to epic Ramayana where life and works of Lord Rama provide exemplary behaviour for other human beings to follow and get guided.

Later, based on verbal narrations attributed to the companions of the Prophet who narrated statements or stories about the Prophet, *Hadith* came in vogue. Hadith is based on verbal records, collected much after death of Muhammad, and is more of a corpus of reports of the teachings, deeds and sayings of Muhammad. The Hadith has reached Muslims through individuals or a few narrators in generations and as such is more of heresay than genuine recordings by first hand experiences. That makes Hadith not as reliable as the Qur'an and the established Sunnah. Therefore, points mentioned in Hadith needed to be verified and understood under the light of the Qur'an before drawing firm conclusions. These can be loosely compared to later *Puranas* in Hindu systems in terms of their collections. Incidentally, the time of composition of *Hadith* and *Puranas* are also roughly similar.

Lastly, we have the *Sharia Law*, which, like *Manu Smriti*, deals with topics like moral code, religious law, crime, politics, economics as well as personal codes including hygiene, diet, etiquette and fasting. Adherence to Sharia, which is also known as Islamic law, has served as one of the distinguishing characteristics of the Muslim faith historically, and through the centuries Muslims have devoted much scholarly time and effort on its elaboration. Others have left its interpretations in the hands of qaizis and Imams, which, at times, land their interpretations getting criticism.

Fast Forward

Islam has seen great successes soon after its initial spread. No one can deny the fact that it has its followers spread in more than 120 countries. As per some estimates, world's Muslims population by the year 2030 may be around 2.2 billion up from current level of 1.6 billion riding on the faster growth rate than non Muslims. As per Wikipedia, based on 2011 studies, 62% of Muslims are based in South and South East Asia with Indonesia, Pakistan, India and Bangladesh accounting for around 70% of them. The Arab world, which was home for Islam, now accounts for only 20% of the total population. Undoubtedly, Islam has seen fastest growth in number of followers in the entire history of humankind. Its impact on India and hence on Hinduism is but unavoidable. Hindus have reasons to closely watch on all developments within Islam to gear for any unfavourable development.

Faith of Islam today faces profound crisis. Its believers from main streams and adherents of radical ideologies are confronting each other like never before. Traditions of Islam were based on respect for differing religions of other people but today one can put across blatant examples where a few ideology driven Muslims are siding with violence as a justified way of forcing others to fall in line. These developments are a great cause of concerns to world at large and have far-reaching implications on the peaceful coexistence of people following other religions. Muslims themselves have a role to play to find an end to such radicalization as they themselves have been the largest target of causalities from these violent incidents.

24

Adi Shankaracharya: The Scriptor of Modern Hinduism

Adi Shankaracharya is certainly one of the most revered sages of post 9th century AD as his contributions in organizing Hinduism and taking Buddhism and Jainism head on in terms of theological debates has no parallel in Indian history. His contribution in consolidating and refining Indian philosophical thoughts under his doctrine of *Advaita Vedanta* will always be recognized as path breaking contribution for a long long time. His doctrine uniting the *Atman* and *Brahman* as one and his travel in all directions of Indian subcontinent resulted in great transformation of Vedic Hinduism to contemporary Hinduism. It was his singular efforts that pushed *Mimansa* approach of strict ritualism and its anti-monasticism into oblivion.

Within a small span of his life he started a reform movement in Hinduism proposing a better moral agenda that can successfully compete with the noble way of eightfold path advised by Buddha. At around the same time, there was also pressure of monotheist philosophies of Islam. As is often said, every Great person becomes great by responding to challenges of his times. As a reply to good working of Buddhist monasteries where many people were jointly working together and contributing for developing various studies, Shankara thought of replicating similar arrangements within Hinduism (which has always been very open and carefree religion without any central command or concerted group efforts). So, he took lead and founded four *Mathas* in four directions as pioneering centres for learning general religious studies and particularly Vedic knowledge. He left indelible impression on religious, cultural and philosophical life of India.

Shankaracharya is a commonly used title for heads of these four *Mathas* founded by Adi Shankaracharya in the ninth century CE. He is honoured as Jagadguru and certainly is the last so well known authority on Vedic knowledge and every other thing that got associated with Hinduism. Born in 788 CE, he spent all his life in promoting superiority of Hinduism over other popular religious thoughts within India. It is he who reinterpreted the *Brahma* Sutras and several Upanishads to propagate the doctrine that *Atman* and *Brahman* are not separate. He wrote a number of commentaries on various Vedanta literatures, initiated shastratha with most other thinkers of his time, and convinced many to follow his philosophy, travelled across the country to reinvigorate Vedic knowledge as the pure and Sanatan knowledge.

He was born into a high class *Brahmin* family of Kerala and is credited with many vehemently fought debates with Buddhists and constantly pursued many kings and other influential people to divert their support from Buddhism to Hinduism. Because, Shankara himself was an ascetic, there were many situations where he came in conflict even with other Vedantic for his recommended renouncing of desire and sexuality but he faced all of them with great vigour and prevailed over most thinkers of his time.

Shankara combined sharp philosophical thinking with impressive administrative and organizational skills. To defeat Buddhism and Jainism and to brand them as heterodoxies, Shankara returned to those very ancient Upanishads from which Buddhist doctrines had evolved to begin with. In well-calculated moves, he proposed an alternate superior way with new explanations for achieving salvation and knowledge. Besides incorporating and surpassing Buddhist doctrines, Shankara made use of their institutions by establishing monasteries like structures within Hinduism that got called *Mathas*.

He is credited for establishing four different *Mathas* in all four direction of the country and made each of them responsible for a specific Veda to continue the guidance to every follower and preserve the sacred powers of Hinduism. The summary of the

Mathas along with their name, location, name of Adi's disciples who was made responsible for the math, assigned Veda and Mahavakya are as under:

1. Govardhana Peetham, Jagannath Puri for Rig-Veda, under Padmapadacharya with mahavakya as 'Brahman is Knowledge'.
2. Sharada Peetham, Shringeri, Karnataka for Yajur-Veda, under Sureshvacharya with mahavakya as 'I am Brahman'
3. Dwarka Peetham, Dwarka Gujarat, for Sam-Veda, under Hastamalakacharya with mahavakya as 'Tattvam asi - That thou art'
4. Jyotirmath Peetham, Joshimath, Badrinath, for Atharva-Veda, under Totakacharya with mahavakya as 'This Atman is Brahman'

Jagadguru Adi Shankara himself finalised most of the systems for successful functioning of the *Mathas* and the fact that these have been in operation for about 1200 years already, speaks volumes of his deep knowledge of initiating systems which could withstand so much historical peaks and valleys.

All Shankaracharya are required to travel extensively in India preaching their particular sectarian beliefs. The title passes on from one person to next by personal selection by the outgoing Shankaracharya. The heir is declared well in advance and the particular disciple who is named as heir apparent must fulfill minimum qualifications of being a born *Brahmin*, completely established in Yoga, whose soul is in union with God and is divine. His knowledge of scriptures should be near perfect and he should also be well versed with other competing religious faiths of his time and most importantly, he must also be recognized as Shankaracharya by the heads of other three *Mathas*. Actually, the person identified is required to receive proper Vedic initiation by the other three Shankaracharyas according to Hindu scriptural injunctions.

As per rules laid out by Adi Shankaracharya himself, a Shankaracharya once established following all prescribed procedure detailed above, can't be removed from his position in his lifetime except if he became mentally infirm or it is proven, based on his action and judgement, that he is no more qualified to hold his title. In such eventuality a new Shankaracharya may be elected by a learned body of Pundits that include a broad based list representing all major religious head of Hindu religion. This way the *Mathas* have been maintained and handed over from Master to Disciple for over one thousand of years.

Primary purpose of these *Mathas* is to ensure deep learning of scriptures and traditions by the qualified seekers living life established in perfect Dharma.

Shankar's influence was not limited to only intellectualism. In addition to incorporating Buddhist and Jain models for faith and organizing success, he also incorporated worship of Lord Shiva particularly songs of praise. These hymns of devotion in praise of Shiva or Vishnu became foundation for the new and popular culture of Hinduism, the *Bhakti* way of worship that has endured until present day India.

Akharas and Naga Sadhus

Every subject where we have no or less knowledge, generally enhances our curiosity and desire to know more about it. This saying is so true for *Naga Sadhus* whom we come to know only around Kumbh Melas where we hear of semi naked and naked sadhus with ash smeared all across their body queuing to have dip in holy Ganga. Such curiosity gives rise to obvious questions as to who they are? Where do they live generally? What are their belief systems? How one goes to become like them? How are they organized? Where do they go back after Kumbh is over?

Actually, these sadhus arrive at material world only at Kumbh melas and rest of the time they are supposed to remain busy in pursuing their yogic and such other spiritual pursuits. These are the people who have given up the material world and started pursuing the seeking of *Moksha*. Ascetics have been part of Hinduism from the very early days and they started in parallel to Vedic system. Later, some got branched out to Jainism some to Buddhism, while remaining have remained firmly with Hinduism.

Adi Shankaracharya argued that phenomenal world of everyday experience as also the biological rounds of birth and death are unreal and the source of our bondage with this maya is to be attacked by following monastic or ascetic life of renunciation. He is supposed to have taken the idea of formal monastic order based on similar institutions operating for long within Buddhism. So he reworked those systems for Hinduism and brought out his own order for similar work to be pursued within Hinduism.

Before Adi Shankaracharya came up with a well defined and structured system of organizing and administering issues related to Hindu Ascetics, Sadhus were categorized either as followers of Shiva or Vishnu. Shiva followers were identified with carrying Trishul while Vaishnavites were carrying a single stick; Trishul vs Danda. Adi Shankaracharya founded Dashnami Sampradaya for ascetic Hindus to regulate and support monastic traditions in Hinduism specially those who have been associated with the *Advaita Vedanta* Tradition doctrine popularized by him.

Adi Shankara organized *Ekdandi* Sadhus under ten different sampradayas having its unique name out of an exclusive listing of ten names. That is how the name Dashnami Parampara came into existence. Further, each of these ten sects is attached with one specific Math for their proper governance and administration. Now, becoming Sadhu or Sannyasi is open to every Hindu irrespective of class or caste or age or gender. The distribution of ten different names and their assignments under specific Math are as under:

1. Sarasvati,
2. Puri,
3. Bharati names under Shringeri Math,
4. Tirtha,
5. Asrama names under Dwarka Math,
6. Giri,
7. Parvata,
8. Sagara names under Jyotir Math,
9. Vana, and
10. Aranya names under Govardhana Math.

In addition to above names, in North India, Ekadandi monasteries have organized themselves under *Akharas* which also were organized by Adi Shankaracharya himself in his own life time. These *Akharas* are categorises as main and sub *Akhara* where a sub *Akhara* operates under the command of its main *Akhara*. At present we have three main *Akharas* while there are some sub *Akharas* which are also part of one or the other main *Akharas* as under:

1. Juna *Akhara* with minor *akharas* of Avahan and Agni
2. Mahanirvani *Akhara* with minor *akhara* of Atal
3. Niranjani *Akhara* with minor *akhara* of Ananda

Any new aspirant to join Ekadandi system adopt one out of above ten names and has to select a particular sampradaya and initiate his joining in one of the seven *Akharas*.

It takes about twelve years to become a *naga sadhu* in which period he has to master celibacy, obtain mahapurush diksha under a guru, has to complete his own last rites to denote that he has nothing to do with his earlier name or body; a tough task where many weak people fail and get shunted out of the system. Final initiation happens only at four Kumbh Melas held at Allahabad, Haridwar, Nasik and Ujjain as per their predefined systems of time intervals.

In addition to *Ekdandi* Sadhus under Dashnami parampara, there are some other sampradayas also for people following other belief systems. These include Shaivas, Vairagis, Kalwasis and Udasins. They in turn have their own *Akharas* which are independent of the Shankaracharya directed *Mathas*. These are loosely administered by *Akhil Bhartiya Akhara* Parishad that comprises of about fourteen *Akharas* for Hindus and Sikhs. Prominent of these are *Nirmohi Akhara* (part of the Ayodhya Ram janm bhumi dispute) and *Sri Dattareya Akharas*.

25 Other Elements of Later Hinduism

Going forward in the evolution of religious traditions and customs, newer sets of faith doctrines also got evolved. This development is in line with similar processes taking place in other civilizations as well where new concepts kept emerging in response to the human nature of continuously changing the view on God and other things religious.

We should, however, remember that Hinduism has allowed unlimited variations to be tried by its followers, as it does not believe in putting any boundaries anywhere. In fact, Hinduism never had any body or agency or organization to regulate as to what can be done and what cannot be done. This aspect has been both its strength and weakness alike. But like a running river has the power of treating pollutants poured into it, Hinduism also has accepted many adverse streams and allowed them to remain for a while and than swiftly thrown such practices to its bank. So, readers are encouraged to keep the fact at their back of mind that Hinduism and authenticity don't go together. There is not much that can be said as authentic Hindu and not so Hindu. The tenets mentioned below, therefore, can be looked at with this background.

Let us look at some of these in some details.

Forms of Gods

Hinduism broadly professed only a single Supreme authority called *Para Brahma* while all other deities are considered as its forms and expansions. By the turn of millennium, Hindus have started representing Gods in innumerable forms – each of which is identified with specific aspect of divine manifestations. By this stage, the earlier Devas mentioned in Rig-Veda have gone in complete background and a new three tier arrangement emerged which continues until today.

Under this system, the *Para Brahma* is considered a faceless and formless Supreme cause of the entire Universe with many other names like Parameshwara, Ishwara, Bhagwan, *Brahman* and Paramatma. These names are just synonymous of the *Para Brahma*. On second tier we have Mahadevas namely Shiva and Vishnu. Together with *Brahma*, they form a trinity called *Trimurti*. As per modern Hindu view, this *Trimurti* symbolizes the entire Sansar where *Brahma* is designated as creator of all things and being, Vishnu takes over the role of preserver and protector while Shiva is responsible God of judgement, the destroyer.

In the last tier of this system lies the position of an Ishta Deva, which can be any one from the whole range of popular deities ranging from *Laxmi*, Sarasvati, *Durga, Ganesha, Hanuman*, etc. The choice of the *Ishta Deva* is primarily a matter of personal preference that may or may not get influenced by regional traditions, family traditions or such other factor depending solely on the choice of the devotee.

The logic for worshipping the God with some or the other form as against a faceless and formless reality is very well enumerated in *Vishnu* Samhita, a very important scripture of modern day Hinduism summarizes the concept of forms in an effective way and it says–

> *"... without a form, how can God be meditated upon? If He is without any form, where will human mind fix itself? When there is nothing for mind to attach itself, it will slip away from meditation. Therefore, the wise will meditate on some form, remembering, however, that the chosen form is a superimposition and not a reality"*

Murti Puja (Idol Worship)

It is a daily ritual by which a devotee or a seeker communion with his divine – it symbolizes the desire to offer love and devotion, thereby, surrendering one's individuality to Him. Self-surrender is considered supreme path to salvation in almost all religions. The Puja or prayers, start with a complete trust in the being to which appeal is made with a feeling of a profound need with an understanding in background that the God is indeed well disposed towards the seeker and is capable and willing to grant his blessings.

Besides seeking plentiful blessings, a properly conducted Puja is also to seek guidance and strength from God for moving on right path to live a righteous living.

Since every Hindu is expected to conduct Puja regularly, it may not be out of place to briefly touch upon right way of conducting Puja at both public and private places. Proper *Puja vidhis* is to follow the following steps:

1. *Avahana*: First of all, we should invoke the deity for whom we wish to conduct Puja. It may be our Ishata Deva for regular or may be Goddess Laxmi on Diwali or any other deity on their days.
2. *Asana*: Offer the deity proper seat to make the deity comfortable. Generally, the place is created on a higher pedestral but within reach of the person performing the Puja.
3. *Swagata*: The deity is extended unspoken welcome and requested to rest on the *asana* and be comfortable, similar to what we do to any important guest.
4. *Padya*: Cleaning of deity's feet with water similar to a real guest.
5. *Arghya*: Offering water laced with flowers, sandal or saffron. Normally, a tumblar full of water is prepared well in advance to be offered at this stage.
6. *Achamanam*: Offering of water for washing mouth and face of the deity as last activity for shedding tiredness of the long travel undertaken by the deity to arrive at worshipper's home.
7. *Madhu arpan*: Deity is offered a drink consisting of honey, sugar, milk and water as a ritual to offer food to the invited guest.
8. *Abhushanam*: Deity is presented with clothes, jewels and ornaments. Normally, threads of red colour are used as a symbol for all the apparels.
9. *Gandha*: Offering of sandalwood powder or any other substitute.

10. *Akshat*: Offering of grains of rice coloured with saffron and sindoor.
11. *Pushpa*: Offering of flowers.
12. *Dhupa*: Offerigs of lighted incense.
13. *Deepak*: Lighting of lamp for offering light.
14. *Naivedya*: As a last offering, Naivedya is to be offered which is made by cooked rice, fruits, ghee, butter, sugar and other sweets.
15. *Ashirwadam*: This is the real part of the ceremony. Here the worshipper and his family and friends, sitting quietly with closed eyes, assuming the divine presence of the deity among them, seek blessings or other desires from the invited deity.

The last part of *Puja* is *Aarti* that is supposed to establish a direct eye contact of the devotee with his Ishta deva to pass blessings of God via the flame as if the God has appeared in person to provide Darshan. The flame, kept near the God during Puja, is passed before the image of God and then brought to the devotees for them to have *Darshan* – God is supposed to see devotee's face in the flame and then transmit his power to devotee through the flame into his eyes.

Importance of Cow

Rig-Veda itself has several references to cow. In one such reference, the sacred animal is compared to mother earth. Another Rishi refers to cow as Goddess Aditi. Rig-Veda refers cow as '*Aghnya*' which literally means 'not to be killed'. Therefore, cow has always been considered as beyond killing from the ancient Indian culture time. By the time, Atharva Veda gets composed, cow's status gets upgraded to being fit for worship. There are many other scriptures as well which speak of prohibition of eating cow's meat.

"*Kamadhenu*", the so called mother of all cows is treated as a miraculous creature and is considered as a provider of plenty. Especially useful for *Brahmins*, Cow's milk and its derivatives provide them with main foods. Possession of cows has always been looked up as a symbol of wealth and hence, donating a cow to a *Brahmin* is taken as one of the largest donation providing bundle of good karma to its giver.

It is interesting that sanctity of cow protection has not only survived all through our long history, it has gathered further strength with many pro-Hindu organizations regularly calling for its protection and ban on its slaughter. Besides its revered status in our scriptures, cow has retained its great contribution in sustaining human life at the subcontinent all through. It is seen helping human at every step of its life cycle including by providing best possible leather out of its skin post death. In yet another feature of seeking harmony and balance with all living beings, Indian culture alone is to be credited for repaying the dues of this great animal with its veneration and such veneration and respect has no other parallel in any other culture.

The history of Hinduism will never be complete without a deep reference to the respect given to this simple and gentle animal for all its contribution to human life in our country in terms of providing, all through its whole life, richest possible natural nutrients, eco friendly manure supplement, agriculture power and leather.

Triads of Hinduism

Over the history, there are many triads that have evolved and made their own important place in Hinduism. It may be a good idea to have a look at main triads as follows:

- *Aims of life*: *Dharma*, *Artha* and *Kama*–Much later *Moksha* also got added to make these four. These are already discussed earlier great details at a later stage.
- *Sound of three letters of "AUM"*–Explained in very detail in Mandukya Upanishad, the word *AUM* represents primordial and powerful sound symbol of the Supreme Being. The first letter "A" is spoken with open mouth, the second letter "U" with partially open while the third letter "M" is spoken with mouth closed. This way, this single word of just three letters is revered to represents all sounds, all words, all languages, all the possible knowledge sources and all *mantras* of the entire universe. Due to its sound strength, this word is chanted at the beginning of all prayers and all other rituals. People who practise it with desired intensity can feel its serene power as an aid for all aspcts of meditations.

- *Qualities of Matter*: Called *Gunas*, we have *Sattva, Rajas* and *Tamas* representing Harmony, Activity and Ignorance and Inertia. These have been the bases of some of our main Philosophies and have been extensively dwelled upon even in *Bhagvad Gita*.
- *Doshas for Human Body:* These are *Vaat, Pitta* and *Kapha*. Heavily used for all matters relating to identification of ailments and their treatments. Indian system of Medicines, *ayurveda*, is completely woven around establishing balance in these three *doshas* in every human body.
- *Planes of Space*: These are Heaven, Earth and Hell. Used largely in all mythology based scriptures as also in exploring Hindu Darshan, the Indian Philosophy.
- *Main Gods*: The *Trimurti* consisting of Brahma, Vishnu and Mahesh. Does not find much presence outside Puranas. Most likely, it may have been Indian response to Christianity's version of God, Son and Soul because these Gods came to be regarded in their current position only in first few centuries after Christ.
- *Stages of Consciousness*: Used in Upanishads, these are Waking, Dreaming and Dreamless Sleep. Every human being on daily basis experiences all these stages. Later on the fourth stage got added named 'Turia' which is the stage where the *Atman* is supposed to be part of *Brahman* and hence, there does not remain any duality between Atma and *Brahma*. These terms are used for philosophical purposes only.
- *Main Shastras*: Three most quoted scriptures for defining Hinduism on practical basis are *Manu Smriti, Artha Shastra* and *Kama Sutra*. These will be taken up for greater explanation later.

26

Ancient India: Advancements in Sciences

Our elders have passed on several stories about highly advanced scientific progress, which has been achieved by India in its ancient times. Every time when there was some new scientific discovery coming to public domain, throughout in our growing time, like television, satellites, guided missiles, weapons of mass destruction, stories soon started making rounds about their getting linked to some or the other reference in our scriptures. We also read about *Pushpak Vimana* and floating bridge over sea in Ramayana and great weaponry system of Pandavas, live commentary given by Sanjay to blind King Dhritrastra, Arjuna punching a water stream from a single arrow so that Bhishma Pitamah could quench his thirst while on his deathbed waiting for the right moment as per his horoscope to leave his body and Sudarshan Chakra of Sri Krishna which followed its target wherever it went. But whenever we tried finding more details all was available to the loosely connected reference of such stories in epics or *Puranas*. We were also told that our ancestors have made so much of scientific progress in those days and present generation is even unable to pick up the available hints from our scriptures and related *Shastras*.

But, hold on; let us accept the fact that these are merely myths. As we have seen in the section on Mahabharata and Ramayana and all subsequent readings, there is no doubt most of these stories are just fiction at its best and there was no such advancements in technology or sciences as our elders mistakenly believed to be true.

Surely, we can salute to the narrators for taking their fictional capability to such heights that some of their hints got converted into reality over 2000 years later. But that's about all.

It is said that religion and arts, at any given point of every culture, are known to travel in the same direction. In the sense that for making advancements in both religion and arts, one must always be grounded in the perspective of history to look at the new angle of present. But in science, it is totally different as one is supposed to completely forget everything of the past to make an altogether new research which may have some continuity from the past or no. Standing today, one can say that Hindus have never been able to forget their rich past. That continued clinging with our proud ancient heritage resulted as strong shackles for our ability to make advance contributions in all fields scientific. One more strong reason of our inability to keep pace with scientific advancements is that intellectual life of Indians has all along being dominated by religious thoughts than that of any other race. As a result, for most part of our proud past heritage, a large portion of our intellectuals has given more attention to religious and spiritual accomplishments as against to basic sciences.

Let us look at some findings that one comes across from normal study of the Indian Scriptures. Though, I must admit that I have not been looking for science as specific subject of curiosity. I had been looking largely on the evolution of social systems and structures of traditions than science. In any case, my specialized education of commerce would have inhibited my ability to grasp science with all its depths; I may not have even succeeded in looking at science. So these observations are the result of secondary readings.

The earliest reference that one comes across for any scientific material is in Shulva Sutra which deals with rules of measurements. This text is dated around 800 to 700 BC. As we know that over the period of Vedic culture Vedic rituals and sacrifices had grown to fairly large proportions, it is but natural that there was a need for some well defined rules to ensure that the *Vedi* for *Yajna* and for animal sacrifices are made as per desired dimensions to ensure that the desire for divine blessing does not get hindered. It has rules for length, height, angles, etc. which is like an elementary mix of maths and geometry at best. But if you go back from that place to 1200 years early and compare it with Sindhu Sarasvati

Culture's achievements in terms of square towns and well defined water works and sewage/storm water drains, minting for metallic seals in alloys, invention of chess (very first version), the progress of Vedic people for finalizing basic measurements of *Havan Kunda* will not even qualify to be called a baby step.

Later, one comes across Vedanga Jyotisha which looks like oldest astronomical text available anywhere in our texts and one finds some progress like mention of Dhruv Star but the real breakthrough in terms of spinning of earth and it being round as against flat, will be proven by others only and only many centuries later. This was also the text that established first Indian calendar, a very insufficient attempt that finally got dumped for all practical reasons. But there was still no reference of eclipses where saros cycle of the Greeks has been much more advanced.

Only much later, it was Aryabhatta (born 476 CE) who wrote Aryabhatiya and earned a good name everywhere for his contributions in mathematics and astronomy. But let us not forget that composition of Mahabharata has started around 800 years before this development. It was Aryabhatta who argued that westward visible movement of stars gives that impression because stars are fixed and we are observing them from a spinning earth. Until that time in history, everybody had strongly and firmly believed that world is fixed and every thing visible in the space make rounds around the earth.

Aryabhatta was the first person who came up with the theory of spinning of earth. But then if you are too ahead of your compatriots, they don't believe you. Not only that, they may even ridicule you for your illogical views. This is what it happened to Aryabhatta. There was no system in practice like now-a-days where people making scientific announcements were loaded with all facts and empirical data to support their claims. Our Aryabhatta was no exception and he was ridiculed by his peers as well.

Then we come across *Brahma* Siddhanta for getting used by some Islamic Scholars for developing telescopic astronomical aids for observing the cosmos. Subsequently, we come to 12th Century and read about Bhaskara II known to have invented pi. He compiled his book named Lilawati after her dear daughter where he has used poetic riddles to discuss complicated mathematical problems. He is also credited with some great work on calculus. But his area was mainly numbers while advance mathematics is much more than mere number crunching.

Certainly, Hinduism had not been blessed by some one like Isaac Newton, the great scientist credited with "laws of gravity". Many of us may not know that Newton started from mechanics much before mathematics. He believed that a scientist should be able to draw a circle accurately before he could master geometry. Many of us may also not believe that Newton started with an attempt to explain the physical universe with God as an essential part of the system. He wanted to describe the relations between celestial and terrestrial bodies in mathematical terms so that a coherent system can be well established. His original belief was that nature was completely passive and God alone was the sole source of activity. But his findings of laws of gravity took that power away from God and rested it completely with the attractive part of matter. And that was, to begin with, original idea of Aristotle and was incompatible with Christian idea of sovereignty of God. (Armstrong, 1993)

Hinduism, on the contrary continued attracting best of its human talent to remain in awe with its glorious past. It was in these periods that Christianity allowed more of its adherents to pursue sciences with more open minds even by going against the orthodox systems that it was known for.

Another important reason for Hindus lagging behind in scientific advancements, to my mind, is our historical lack of interest in instruments and machines. We have been great in every area which involved use of mental faculties but not so good when it comes to creating and using machines. For examples, we started well with Astronomy, but further growth involved making sophisticated telescopes, which would have required presence of instrument makers and we never had that.

Another obvious weakness seems the absence of institutionalized approach. We have been an individual focused society. There are only few instances of collaborative group workings at larger scales. For example, we never had institutions like Royal Society of London, which was dedicated to collection of new knowledge in all fields, and replace that with the old knowledge. Similarly, one comes across not many instances where Hindus were having intellectual expertise in different fields getting pooled together in systematic ways to grow on each other's knowledge. Pooling of resources is supposed to be the easiest way of new discoveries. So until the time that single individuals were able to keep themselves abreast with knowledge on all fronts, we were at par with the world if not ahead of all. But no sooner, pooling became essential for assimilating wide knowledge on expanding fronts, we were found wanting. Our Kings were largely busy in pursuing their personal agendas and luxuries. Weakening the enemy was the approach rather than strengthening self.

Ayurveda can be taken as the only science stream where Ancient India did wonders. Wellness of human body has been an early area of interest of our sages. Here again, we also come across strong clues from the excavation at Sindhu Sarasvati sites that medical practices have been around at that time as well in fairly advanced stage—probably another first in the world. Medical references are found in Rig-Veda in plenty as well. It is but a different matter that in those early days evil spirits were supposed to be larger cause for human health than anything else. But that misconception got changed later. Charak-Samhita, which together with Shshruta Samhita, is acknowledged as the earliest text credited with *Ayurveda* being projected with a complete and comprehensive scientific approach to the understanding as to how a human body operates and how to make its systems respond to external intervention. Composed around 900 to 700 BC, *Charak Samhita* includes eight sections and 120 total chapters. It divided medical study into eight separate sub sections. These were:

1. Surgery with External Equipment,
2. Minor Operations performed with Superficial Pricks,
3. Medical treatment for ailments of body,
4. Ghostly treatments,
5. Medicines specific to ladies and children,
6. Treatments for poisonous bites,
7. Chemistry for healthy body balance and finally
8. Ways to improve health and virility.

Now this is something to be proud of as such an extensive classification of medical science around three thousand years earlier is no mean feat.

The language of *Charak Samhita* is Sanskrit and this *Samhita* is also written in poetry style with meter and melody. Scriptures of that time were always written in poetry form to facilitate memorizing of the contents. There are in all over 8,400 metrical verses. The focus of *Charak Samhita* is "Kayachikitsa" meaning internal medicine and the science contained is based on theory of digestive fire and treats the ailments focused on *vaata* without so much discussing *pitta* and *kapha*, the other two critical elements of Indian systems. *Sushruta Samhita* that presents the field of Ayurvedic surgery has dealt the second aspect of medicinal science of surgery. There were very frequent wars and surgery was equally critical. *Shshruta* also is said to be a redaction of oral material passed down verbally from earlier generations.

Lastly, one another area of advanced progress in the ancient history is in Metallurgy. But again, Harappa culture remains, since found, reveal that they were far ahead of every other civilization in their times. They are now known to produce metals like copper, bronze, lead and tin besides iron and gold. From Vedic time onwards. Actually, Rig-Veda uses the term Ayas which means alloy or copper or bronze. The term used for iron is *Krishn Ayas* (black metal). Recent excavations in Middle Ganges Valley conducted by archaeologist Rakesh Tewari show iron working in India may have begun as early as 1800 BC.

Going even in the past, evidence found from Sindhu Sarasvati sites in India and Pakistan show ample examples of widespread presence of copper-bronze metallurgy in the Harappa civilization. Historians are of the opinion that that civilization had developed practice of copper-smelting even before iron smelting as there is to date no proven evidence for smelted iron during Sindhu Sarasvati sites but few iron and steel items also have been unearthed where some of these are said to be dated on or before 2600 BC. These new findings force us to consider the possibility that some of these items were made of smelted iron,

In any case India has always been known for its great skills for metallurgical progress. The special alloy pillar at Qutub Minar which is there for 1600 years and even in the climate of Delhi, which sees an extreme variations from a cold night in winters to the hottest day of summer, has not yet rusted, is a great example of our ancestors reaching to great heights while dealing with metals.

27

Position of Women: From Ancient India to Present

Over last 4000 years, Indian subcontinent has been witness to a lot of shifts in the conditions of women's position in the society. To begin with, Ancient India had equal status to women in all respects like education, property rights, marriage of choice, and freedom for contributing in all religious and social functions. This status got lowered during the medieval time and worsened even further during later period of modernity.

Ancient India spans a vast period 2500 BC to 250 BC. Archaeology, ancient texts, and artifacts are but various tools to reconstruct the expected lives of women during that period. The earliest materials found by archaeological excavations suggest the worship of goddesses. The earliest recorded religious texts of around 1500 BC call on the life-giving power of goddesses to give life and to nurture and sustain it. Extensive remains at Mohenjo Daro, Harappa, and Lothal show a well organized, prosperous agriculture and commercial society that traded with other civilizations in other regions. The most famous ancient artifact is that of a young slender girl posing confidently. Numerous toys found convey a society that valued family life. While their inscribed ancient seals have not been deciphered to determine the actual meanings, extensive female images have been found that suggest goddesses played a central role. Often called fertility goddesses, very few depict pregnant women, women giving birth or women nursing children. Several of the seals suggest a goddess associated with vegetation and fertility.

Apparently this civilization succumbed to major natural disasters that changed the course of the Sarasvati River. Then came the Vedic time, which was a highly hierarchical society, led by the *Brahmin* priests, who imposed political and religious power over the rest. The *Brahmins* kept composing remaining Vedas that postulated the beliefs that continue to be revered today by the Hindus. The Rig-Veda, oldest of these texts is reported to have few women composers as well. There is a creation story, where the goddess Aditi gives birth to the earth, also personified as a goddess, Prthivi. Mother Earth's role was to be tender to the dead and Aditi was to be prayed to release from sin. Women of this time had access to learning similar to men, married at mature age and had right for selection of their life partners under the well known system of *swayamwara*.

Much of the ideal role of women can be ascertained from the images of a maiden and bride in the Rig-Veda. A daughter and maiden were praised for the characteristics of beauty, radiance, appealing adornment, sweet odours, ample hips and broad thighs. This description suggests interest in feminine sensuality, childbearing capacity of the young girl. At festival gatherings, young virgins met eligible men, with flirtatious coupling after initiating a relationship. They then turned to their parents for approval and marriage arrangements were made. To be a virgin bride was of paramount importance. Practical advice was given to the new bride like not to be angry or hostile to her husband, to be tender and to bear sons to carry forward the family lineage.

A woman's role as outlined in Hinduism at this time was to be a good wife so that the gods and goddesses would respond to the couple's requests and needs. An altar tended mainly by the father/husband, was overseen by the wife/mother when he was gone from the home. Her job was to keep the sacred flame burning 24/7. It was also the woman's responsibility to recite and sing hymns to the deities, a duty ascribed to women in most all other cultures as well. Divine couples like Indra and Indrani, and Surya and Soma acted as role models. Goddesses were generally viewed positively, although occasional glimpses of their darker side surfaced. Other early goddesses were the sisters Usha and Nisha (Morning and Night).

In the next segment of ancient texts, the Upanishads dated about 800 BC to 600 BC, writers began to reinterpret earlier Vedic literature. Now a person was able to reach the universal soul *Brahman* through self-knowledge not just through ritualistic knowledge performed by the *Brahmin* priests. In this period also, we have presence of Gargi and Maitreyi who were highly learned women and participated in theological discussions with the best in trade. Maitreyi was wife of Yajnavalkya who also had another wife named Katyayani. This second wife is projected in Brahadaranyaka Upanishad as a lady whose understanding is limited largely to look after domestic affairs. Clearly, you have only a countable few exceptions to stand against the general rule that women are objects and have limited prototype of roles at different stage of their life.

With the onslaught of urbanization and surplus produce resulting in excess of resources with average household, inheritance became an issue probably first time. Urbanization gave property rights as well as more sexual freedom to women. This freedom cautioned many fathers to give away their daughters in marriage at young age lest they do something that brings bad name to the family. Para number 6.4.7 of Brahdaranyaka Upanishad, a chapter dealing with procreation, speaks general approach of the time and it says:

> *"... if she does not grant him his desire (succumb to have sex with the husband) he should buy her a gift. If she still does not agree, he should hit her with a stick or hand and overcome her with power and glory and say "I take away your glory". Thus she will be devoid of glory."*

This paragraph is proof enough of dilution of women, say, in matters relating to her limited options as compared to men.

Women's economic contributions were important in ancient India. As India was an agricultural country, women were needed to assist the men folk in the various seasonal activities. As today, in the past also, India was made up of thousands of villages. It was the family not the individual that was the basic unit. Usually three generations of the family lived together in an essentially patriarchal structure. This patriarchal system prevailed in the religious rituals. The Indians practised a form of ancestor worship, whereby the oldest male was responsible for conducting the rites on a regular basis in the home. It was the eldest son's responsibility to incinerate his parents' funeral pyre. Women could not serve as

Brahmin priests or study the sacred Vedas. Some women could be seers, though.

After 500 BC, the economy further increased to newer heights with many cosmopolitan cities coming up like Varanasi and Kaushambhi serving the Gangetic Plains and great empires of Maurya dynasty reaching newer heights. During this period, once again, there were few examples of individual woman making her place in society on her own but again more as exception than as rule. And such women got attracted to follow alternate religions of Buddhism and Jainism as against Hinduism as they had better say outside Hinduism.

The next texts that speak about women in Ancient India are the Laws of Manu around 150 CE and *Artha Shastra*. Here we can gain insights into the legal status of women but not necessarily what was actually practised. Law codes are nearly always prescriptive not descriptive literature. Manu in particular has been rather harsh to women's plight. He seems to be against her independence at any time in her whole life. In her younger stage, she was supposed to be under the guardianship of her father, after marriage under her husband and lastly under her son. Post marriage, a woman was regarded to have her second birth with a new name and new family. However, she was to remain present in all successful religious rituals. Adultery was not punished as severely as in other ancient cultures. Divorce was possible for the woman too but only if the husband was impotent or insane. Generally, there were practices like *sati* where she was supposed to finish her life after death of her husband. In other cases, the majority of widows apparently did not remarry.

It may also be interesting to look at following eight types of marriage mentioned by *Manu Smriti*:

- *Brahma*: Where father gives away her daughter to a boy he has summoned.
- *Gods:* Father gives his daughter to the officiating priest in course of sacrifice ritual being conducted.
- *Sages:* Where father gives away his daughter to a man after receiving a gift of cows and bulls.
- *Lord of Creation:* Where he gives away her to a man of her choice saying that "may the two of you fulfill your dharma together".

- *Antigods:* Man takes a girl because he wants her and gives as much wealth to her and family as much he can.
- *Gandharva:* Both join in sexual union out of lustful desire.
- *Ogres (Rakshasas):* Man picks up the girl against her will and harms her family.
- *Pishacha:* Man has sex with her in a condition where she is sleeping, intoxicated, drunk or otherwise out of her mind.

Manu suggest that best marriage for all classes other than *Brahmins* is number four where there is a mutual liking as well as consent of the family. But he suggests only *Brahma* marriage suitable for a *Brahmin* girl. But if one is to look more closely, it will be obvious that in all the last four options there is no willingness of the girl or her family. This certainly does speak volumes of social condition of woman in India around the turn of millennium. (Doniger, 2009)

After this time, we have the time of epics of Mahabharata and Ramayana. These points we have discussed in some details under the chapter relating to epics. But suffice to say that while Ramayana tries to project a perfect picture of ideal woman in Sita, it also talks of Kaikeyi and Surpnakha. In any case one does not find any one giving birth to a girl child in both the epics. How come all the children born to Kauravas, Pandavas as well as Rama Sita are all boys? Does it speak of equality? Certainly not. Either a daughter's birth is not auspicious or it is not worth mentioning. In both situations, social preference for sons gets highlighted.

All said and done, in the epics, women are shown as having more freedom and competency than in the religious and legal literature until that time. In the Mahabharata, there is evidence of both polyandry and polygamy. Events in these stories demonstrate women's managing and problem-solving skills. In the Ramayana, the heroine, Sita, is the example of the good wife, who still shows determination to manage her life. When Sita is accused of sexual misconduct, she has to prove her sexual purity. Public opinion still negates her innocence, forcing her to go into exile, where she goes back to her mother, Earth. This ritual suicide then becomes the prototype for *sati*, the self-sacrifice of a wife on her husband's funeral pyre, which occurs later in Indian history.

But outside of the epics, one comes across tales of courtesans and prostitutes who were part of ancient Indian society. Courtesans were often literate, and skilled in music and dancing besides the usual sexual services. Regular prostitutes engaged in their trade in busy places and paid taxes. Even in *Kama Sutra,* one finds some sympathy with women but not the empathy, which remains missing. A deep look at *Kama Sutra* and one can clearly see the tone of the composer who is ultimately using women in the exploitative mould. Repentant courtesans and prostitutes sometimes went into Buddhist nunneries. Just as in the medieval west, wives and daughters in Indian traditions also could become ascetics if their present life was untenable.

But *Manu Smriti,* the so-called moral code of the day, comes out the flag bearer of Hindus oppression on women. Manu treats women as a sexual crime about to happen. Manu identifies six clear ways of easily corrupting a women which included drinking, association with people of ill repute, separation from husband for long period, wandering about aimlessly, sleeping and living in the house belonging to some other person. He is totally against her having any independence any time in her entire life.

As Hinduism developed, certain facets became dominant: the caste system, karma, dharma, and reincarnation. In certain cases a man was allowed to marry a woman of a lower caste, but a woman could not do so without disgracing her family and defiling herself. Because of the relative lower status of women in India, if you did not do your proper duty or dharma, then you did not accrue good enough karma to be reincarnated in a higher caste or life form, including being reborn as a woman, who was inferior to a man.

Padmapurana is yet another classic case of picturing women of the day. Some of the language used here comes out quite demeaning and full of shame for a culture that has been better than most others on most matters relating to morality. No wonder our sisters and mothers have suffered a lot under earlier systems and we have no right to call ourselves as *Jagad Gurus* unless we succeed in changing our complete moral fabric to provide women just and equal place with men. Nonetheless, here is a complete excerpt of *Padmapurana* about dos and don'ts for the woman of that day:

> *"In spite of any deformation, aging, infirm, offensive, immoral, drunkard, gambler, visitor to places of ill repute, having no affection for his home, living with other women, let him be blind,*

deaf or crippled, a wife should always look at him (her husband) as her God, should lavish on him all her care and attention and give him no cause of displeasure.
She must be always attentive and diligent in all her domestic duties, watchful of her temper, never covetous of the belongings of others, never quarrelsome with her neighbours, always calm in her conduct.
Should any man make proposal to her and endeavour to seduce her by offering her nice clothes or jewels of great value, she should not lend an ear to him and should hasten to flee from him.
She should laugh only when her husband is happy and feel sad when he is unhappy. She must answer only when her husband questions her. This is how she will present proof of her dispositions.
She should take heed not to remarks that other person is young, handsome or well proportioned and above all she must not speak to such person. Such modest behaviour will secure her the reputation of a faithful spouse.
Let her bath every day, rubbing saffron on her body. Let her attire be clean, her eyelid tinged with antimony and her forehead marked with red pigment. Let her hair be well combed and adorned. Thus shall she will be like the Goddess Laxmi.
Before her husband, her words shall fall but softly and sweetly; and let her completely devote herself to please him everyday more and more. Prudent in her conversation, she must be careful in conversing with the Gurus, Sanyasis, strangers, Servants and others to adopt a tone suitable to the position of each."

After going through such strict list of expectations from the wife, one only wishes that there should have been similar standards applied to the husband of that time. Let us admit that our culture has had double standards when it came to genders. One also tends to conclude that crimes generally propagated against women, including dowry, rape, sexual harassment, work place harassment, domestic violence, female infanticide etc., all have their roots in our cultural weakness of treating women as an object or piece of property. That is why we had provided them unequal status all along. Even today, many instances comes to light where their very decision making is questioned and most of the crimes against women being committed today, are deep rooted in such old practices which have badly treated them and have oppressed them continuously without bestowing them the place of respect they deserved.

Let us also discuss women's plight in mythological stories about Gods and Goddesses. Hindus came to think that various deities were manifestations or *avatars* of the *Brahman,* the world soul. Each god has had many rebirths. Goddesses of special reverence were Kali, Sarasvati, Parvati, Lakshmi, Durga, and Devi.

Sarasvati was the consort to *Brahma,* who set the world in motion, but lost importance with the emergence of the gods *Shiva* and *Vishnu*. Sarasvati was the goddess of learning, writing, knowledge, mathematics, the arts, music, magic, and eloquence. She created the first alphabet. Many consider her the mother of all life since it was her divine energy that united with the awareness of *Brahma,* who was born from the golden egg from ocean. Thus the two created all knowledge and all creatures of the world. Sarasvati was also a river goddess, and her name translates as the flowing one. She is usually shown seated on a lotus blossom throne accompanied by a white swan. She has four arms, showing that her power extends in all four directions. Two of her arms hold books and beads (showing her spiritual knowledge), with the other two arms and hands she is playing the veena, an Indian lute.

Parvati was Shiva's wife. She is often seen with him in statues and paintings. They look like the model loving couple. In some of her *avatars* or reincarnations she is also Durga, the ten armed goddess of battle, Kali, or Uma, the beautiful one who rides on a tiger. Parvati means mountain girl and she is considered the daughter of the Himalaya Mountains.

Lakshmi was the wife of Vishnu, the preserver. She is often shown seated on a lotus as she was born from an ocean of milk standing on a lotus flower. She is the goddess of good fortune, prosperity, wealth, and beauty. Representing all that is feminine, while her consort Vishnu represents all that is masculine. Many paintings show them riding on the back of Garuda, the eagle, the giant king of birds, as they fly across the land. Lakshmi chose Vishnu. They had a son, Kama, who was the god of romantic love, and in many paintings he looks similar to the cupids on valentine cards. Her attendants are white elephants. Lakshmi is also worshiped as Sita, the reincarnation of the perfect wife to Rama in the Ramayana. All Indian householders keenly invite Laxmi on Diwali for blessing them with good fortune and prosperity for the coming year. Lakshmi lives in the sky with the most beautiful jewels of all, the stars.

Durga, the warrior goddess, is one of the *avatars* of Devi. She is invincible in battle, and was created by the gods to destroy the buffalo monster that was threatening their power. Taking a weapon in each of her ten hands, she killed the beast.

The goddess Devi was the essence of being and, as Shakti, she was the one great mother goddess, and she was responsible for fire, water, earth, and air. Devi is unknowable, omnipotent, and the myth of Devi as Kali dates back to goddess worship in the early Sindhu Sarasvati culture. Kali is the most terrible aspect of Devi. Sent to earth to destroy the race of demons, Kali caused such devastation that many died. She has four arms and hands. One holds a sword and the other a severed head, both symbols of death. With the other two hands she holds a holy book and prayer beads, both symbols of life. Sometimes Kali is depicted as a black goddess, signifying the essence of all perishable things, with her dark skin reflecting the dark soil of earth. Her teeth are bloodstained fangs, and rivers of blood flow from her. In India today bloody sacrifices still are made to her at her Kalighat Temple in Kolkata, the city named for her.

Buddhism was open for all people irrespective of caste and gender but even Buddha generally discouraged women from becoming nuns. Usually it was the widows, abandoned wives, and courtesans who did become nuns, travelling to various areas, giving public talks and visiting individual homes. And nuns were always to be under the strict supervision of monks. Surviving sources from the earliest Buddhist texts suggest monks and Buddha also viewed women's sexuality as a threat to spiritual growth of men and monks, just as in later medieval Christian Europe. Buddhism also stressed that the proper relationship in India was between a married couple. Wives should be encouraged to provide the home atmosphere conducive to the maintenance of society as their main contribution.

A lot more can be said about women's plight at different stages. But they were not treated equally and gender bias appeared all around the social evolution under Hinduism. Unfortunately, on this count, Hinduism does not appear standing much away from Islam as well as Christianity.

28
Hinduism under Delhi Sultanate

Beginning 700 CE, the areas of central Asia saw a big jump in their military powers and many people from that area started eyeing riches of India with increasing confidence that these can be had. The area of today's Afghanistan was largely under the Buddhist influence experiencing non-violence and flower power rather than military power. Northwestern India (mainly Punjab) was at the next forefront and India of the day was largely fragmented into smaller kingdoms with very poor stability. Situations were rather apt for foreign aggressors.

Inspite of all this, the conquest over India has been slow and fragmented, perpetrated over many long years by many different people from Persia to Mongol. Number of advances and inroads were made into Indian territories mainly by Pashtun armies from Central Asia but footholds were not easily gained. But Indian kingdoms on the front were getting weak by every aggression and finally started caving to the increasing power of the Mongols. Ultimately it was in 998 CE that Mahmud of Ghazni conquered the area of Punjab. Again in 1019, Mahmud Ghazni attacked north India and destroyed Kannauj, the capital City of Gurjara-Pratihara Empire. Later, in 1192 Muhammad of Ghori defeated Prithvi Raj Chauhan and soon established the first Muslim Sultanate at Delhi.

Over 320 years between 1206 CE and 1526 CE, India got ruled by Delhi Sultanate which was a Turkish Muslim dominated rule under four separate Dynasties named Mamluk, Khilji, Tughlak, Sayyid and the fifth dynasty that ruled in the last was Lodhi from

Afghan. This period saw many rulers, of which Qutub-uddin-Aibak who was a slave of Muhammad Ghori was the first Sultan. But all of these rulers can be classified under a single band so far as their impacts on Hinduism are concerned.

All of these are blamed for indiscriminate destruction and desecration of ancient Indian temples after looting them of all their riches. All of these rulers were Muslims and greatly promoted Islam in all-important spheres of society, military and administration. They were almost on the move all the time and heading to either east of India, or central India or South of India (largely to Deccan) or to West of India with a single mission of looting temples, destroying temples, killing all those who were expected to rise against their rule (needless to say that most of the people killed were Hindus). The rulers of this period also encouraged converting to Islam by increasing taxes on non-Muslims, providing preferential treatment in administration positions. Another marked feature of Delhi Sultanate was recycling of sculpted stones for construction of Mosques and such other structures which got built by them (for example, the Qutub Minar complex in Delhi).

It all started in 997 CE with Mahmud Ghazni from central Asia raiding and plundering kingdoms of north western India as many as seventeen times between 997 and 1030. That process remained on in by and large similar fashion for next five hundred years. The only silver line can be called is introduction of Islamic Architecture in India which got used for most state sponsored construction of forts, monuments, palaces etc. The first female ruler, Razia Sultana who ruled from Delhi between 1236 and 1240, also belonged to this period. But her brief rule was laced with her own survival rather than any other distinct mark on history.

The background explained above is a clear proof that nothing much can grow under such conditions as the entire Hindu culture was living just for survival. On the reverse, Hindus saw many killings at the hands of these aggressors and rulers as well as large amount of forced and induced conversions to Islam that again were at the cost of Hinduism.

Again in 1398 CE, Timur, the Turkish king of Samarkand, invaded India and plundered lots of temples and treasuries, killed over 200,000 Hindus, looted most Hindu areas of Delhi for days together, carried back wealth, slaves, women and artisans with him to Samarkand. His brief aggression will always be noted as one of the most barbarian attacks on Hindu interests.

Most rulers from the Sultanate not only looted and destroyed Hindu temples; they banned repairs, reconstructions or new constructions. So much so that when some Chinese ruler sent his people to help rebuild damaged Buddhist Stupas, they were denied by imposing unreasonable amount of *Zazia* tax for such works. Temples, in that period were the symbols of religion and were used not only for worships but served as major focal points of all social gatherings and carried the best of art, sculpture, and prosperity of the kingdom which ruled over the lands where these temples were located.

The only noticeable development on Hinduism was the *Bhakti* movement that largely started and flourished under these testing times. More about it is taken up in the next section.

29
Bhakti Movement in Hinduism

The religious movement in Hinduism of medieval period that accepted inclusion of many fringe groups into main stream and promoted the belief that salvation is attainable by all. It advocated that a personal expression of devotion to God is the way to become at one with Him. But side by side there was something important also brewing underground. This was time of very active interaction among various religious movements that were also getting varying patronage from political setups. Trade and commerce was going great between North and South. South was already well connected with various trade centres in the west as well. All major kingdoms of South were going for longer times unlike those in North. This political stability was a great source of many social developments in south of India including developments on cultural, social and religious fronts.

Cholas extended their influence on some foreign lands also and were keeping their adjoining kingdoms of Cheras, Pallavas and Pandyas on a tight leash. After disintegration of Gupta dynasty in north, all artisans and cultural players have headed south making it much more vibrant than ever before. To sum it up, there was a great *sangam* of North and South traditions in all spheres.

Bhakti as a form of worship started in Tamil literary circles and soon moved to other Dravidian cousins. It was first time that some new tradition on religious front started from literate and moved on to illiterate sections. The movement of *Bhakti* soon spread all through the Indian Sub continent fertilizing by worship of Krishna at Mathura and Jagannath Puri via pilgrimages and festivals/celebrations at Temples of all Hindu sects. Along with *Bhakti*, several other Tamil characteristics of poetry and other forms of literature also came into North. Couple of hundred years back, similar thing has happened when *Brahmins* took Sanskrit with them when they went down South together with many other Northern characteristics. (Doniger, 2009)

Tamil as a language to South was occupying exactly same space as Sanskrit in North, meaning that, poetry, religious text writings and court decrees were using Sanskrit in North and Tamil in South. Tamil poems called *Cankum* (Assembly or Sangha in Pali language) were getting very popular for their content and literary concepts. Many of these poems were already singing praises for *Tirumal* (the Vishnu name popular in South), Murukan (son of Shiva) and River Goddess. The theme of these praises was called *Akam* and *Puram*. Akam means those relating to inner world of the human heart and Puram means outer visible world. Akam poetry was focused on many emotive subjects like love in union, patiently waiting for better half, anger at infidelity, anxiously waiting for lover and separation from lover, etc.

My idea of touching the subject matter of Akam poems is just to share how unique was the culture of South India vis-a-vis that of North India at that point of time in history. North was fighting for protection against Islamic influence and was high on bravery, mythology and spiritual love while South was focused on Akam and Puram. Akam poetries were mentioning love of several types; going from unrequired/unwanted love to unachievable love. One of the types of love in these poems was "love while in separation" which is known as '*Virah*' in North. This type of love got picked up by *Bhakti* poets to denote the separateness of the devotee with his Ishta. *Virah* is known to portray one-side sufferings of the lover as if the lover is unable to come due to his preoccupation in other matters. The emotional bond via these poems was very strong showing anguish of the devotee who felt separated from his God and not because God is not available but because God is busy and preoccupied.

Wandering poets and saints devoted to Shiva and Krishna Vishnu (No Rama as yet, as Rama was never a popular incarnations of Vishnu in South) were singing these poems in devotional modes and attracting popular mood. These were called '*Tevaram*' poems and, by now, developed their own unique distinct style that was different then *Cankam* poems.

Following the sectarian trends already established, *Bhakti* movement was focused on Shiva and Vishnu in South and Rama and Krishna dominated Northern movement. *Bhakti* did no harm or support to sectarian divisions as it impacted all sects equally and coexisted with all of them. On the contrary, *Bhakti* facilitated in bridging the sectarian divides and reunited the total Hindu thought. To the credit of *Bhakti,* it soon got popular among all classes and soon involved even orthodox sections including Kings and other influential power centres of the society. In fact, *Bhakti* continues to be most important mode and religious expression in modern India.

Bhakti brought a perfect level playing field among all followers as it establishes a direct contact between the seeker and the sought after – there is nothing in between the God and Bhakt. It allowed people to have less abstract and more emotive relationship with their God without any hindrance by any intermediary. Another great revolution was that *Bhakti* allowed the seeker to seek his Ishta in any form to his own liking without any restriction. *Bhakti* also allowed the devotee to have a direct physical and visual, a passionate transformative relationship with his choice of God. In other words, devotee was able to establish a direct relationship of near and dear as if in direct relationship with others within his immediate family.

This relationship could look at God as a parent as happened in case of Dhruv and Prahlad. It could be a relationship of Lord taken as a master as Hanuman denotes his relations with Rama. It could be a relationship of equals like what was there between Arjuna and Krishna. Another form was where the devotee considered lord as his/her child. The example of such relationship is the character of Yashoda. It could be where Lord is taken as husband. This is well exemplified by the characters of Sita and Rukmani. And finally, the relationship could be as between lovers and beloveds like Radha and Mira.

So depending on one's own attitude, one could look at his God as a friend, guide, lover, child, hero or any other relation. This, I think was the most remarkable introduction of *Bhakti* and a reason as to why it became so popular throughout the Hindu thought. I don't recall any other religious system parallel to this aspect of *Bhakti* in the whole world.

The first person of *Bhakti* movement in North is Sant Ramananda from Varanasi who was a disciple of Ramanujacharya. He started popularizing that simplest way to seek salvation is simply by chanting Rama's name. Nothing would have been easier for the simple population struggling in their daily life of survival. Around the same time, another sant named Vallabhachrya spread *Bhakti* for Krishna as a way of salvation. His doctrine of "salvation only with the God's grace" made *Bhakti* the easy way of seeking that grace. Chaitanya Mahaprabhu (1486-1534) is another great name for philosophizing the *Bhakti* by evolving his unique "Achintya Bheda Abheda" doctrine meaning inconceivable simultaneous oneness and separateness. It was a combo of monism and *dualism* that continues to be popular even among people from outside the Hindu religion. The same doctrine is followed by ISKCON's Hare Rama Hare Krishna movement.

There is another popular division of *Bhakti* movement popular among Vaishnavites in North India based on a matrix of *Nirguna* and *Saguna* Gods vs. Rama and Krishna. Under *Nirguna,* there are two streams; one following Knowledge and other following Love. Kabir is identified with *Nirguna* Knowledge stream. He was against idol worship or Rama Krishna divide. His God was like Vedic God. The *Nirguna* Love stream was represented by Jaysi. The *Saguna* branch also got divided into Rama and Krishna where Rama was represented by Tulsi while Krishna was represented by Surdas and Mira. We can briefly look at some of the great contributors of *Bhakti* Movement in North India which virtually empowered the entire grassroots masses spiritually cutting across class, caste, region, and language barriers of Hinduism probably for the very first time.

Emergence of Chaitanya Mahaprabhu and Tulsidas (1532-1623) are the rare bright spots about Hinduism in later Mughal period. Chaitanya was a born *Brahmin,* very learned in Sanskrit and was a great poet who specialized in the pain of separation of Radha from his beloved Krishna. This separation was way different from Sita's separation from Rama while she was under captivity. At his young age of twenty one, Chaitanya's father passed away and he got inspired to renounce the world. But public did not let him renounce. He saw people worshipping Krishna by singing and chanting. Soon he started retelling Krishna's acts particularly his love play with Gopis. Chaitanya was invited to

Puri where he got settled. He was taken as Krishna and Radha both living in one body. But this was not something very unique, as *Tantra* followers have been taking Shiva and Shakti in single body for long time.

Chaitanya worked a lot for popularizing his new form of *Virah*. His followers were called Goswamins. He is also credited for converting back Orissa's Governor and also converted many Pathans to Hinduism. It is to the credit of Chaitanya that *Bhakti* was no more extra suited to women who could be God's lover or mother, which were certainly the most intimate relationships. But with Radha and Krishna being in a single body, it allowed even men folks to experience the same intimacy with their God.

Tulsidas came out as an architect of North India Vaishnavism from a person who could never move away from his dedication to Shiva. He was known to be close to Mughal courts near Banaras and claimed that the power of Rama's name will liberate even Muslims. He wrote the famous 'Ramcharitmanas' (lake of deeds of Lord Rama) in Vernacular Awadhi as against Sanskrit which was the convention. Even orthodox *Brahmins* were up against him for such an attempt. But easy language and *Bhakti* laced characterization of Rama ended up becoming very popular among the masses throughout North India. So much so that today most people look at "Ramcharitmanas" as the Ramayana little realizing that the theology approach of the two books are quite apart from each other.

Ramcharitmanas is associated with the beginning of the tradition of Ramlila, the dramatic enactment of the text on nine days before Dushehra every year. Ramlila had blown open the story to masses like no other text in history can be compared with.

The blind saint and poet Surdas is well known for his devotional songs in praise of Lord Krishna. He is reported to have compiled over one hundred thousand songs of which only around eight thousands have survived under the famous "*Sur Sagar*". He wrote in Hindi and Brij and was greatly acclaimed in his times. Even Emperor Akbar was said to be his patron. Surdas is certainly a pioneer of fuelling *Bhakti* movement in Hindi heartland. Mira is another great name for promoting *Bhakti* like never before. Her father was from the Rathore clan of Jodhpur who died defending against Babur. She got married to the son of Rana Sanga of Chittor but never was interested in the physical spouse as she was completely devoted to her Lord Krishna. Mira is credited with over 1300 songs in Rajasthani and Brij dialects which have since been published worldwide for their contents of spiritual realization through passionate praise of Ishta which leads the devotee to a situation where one forgets all desires of the worldly attachments. Her love for Krishna overflew into ecstasy that led her to sing and dance in any setting, an approach which is so much visible with many Krishna devotees to this day.

Around the same time, we also have Guru Ravidass (1450-1520) who was born in Punjab to a Chammar family and grew to become a great socio-religious reformer, thinker, humanist, poet and a traveller par excellence. Many of his devotional compositions are also included in Guru Granth Sahib. Mira also took him as her guru. Then there was Rahim Khan, one of the nine jewels of Akbar Durbar who was a Muslim but a great devotee of Lord Krishna and composed a lot of poetry to show his dedication to Krishna. He also translated "Baburnama" in Persian for wider spread of its message. The new form of writing called "Doha" is attributed to Rahim which packed a lot of punch in sending across the message contained in the writing.

Last but not the least; we can talk about Raskhan (born in 1548) who again was a born Muslim but a great follower of Lord Krishna. He learned Hindu religion from Goswami Vitthalnath at Vrindavan which remained his city for rest of his life until his death in 1628. Son of a wealthy Jagirdar with Pathan background, he was a scholar of both Hindi and Persian and is accredited for translating *"Bhagavata Purana"* into Persian. Bulk of his poetry was around the Lilas. Besides many other contributors, he deserves the credit for popularizing 'Bal Lila', 'Chirharan Lila', 'Kunj Lila', 'Ras Lila', 'Panghat Lila'. Besides bulk of his works on Krishna, Raskhan also composed some poems for Lord Shankar and Goddess Ganga.

Thus *Bhakti* period resulted in a mass of devotional literature, music and arts which gave India a renewed spiritual impetus. Thus, the development of *Bhakti* as a major form of Hindu practice has left an indelible stamp on the faith. It is to the credit of *Bhakti* movement that spiritual quest could reach to each and every individual; the barriers built over the years of class, caste, sect, region and gender were all got broken by *Bhakti* as it traversed all social boundaries and unnecessary rituals requiring help of priests and all.

In addition to other benefits, one additional benefit coming out of popularity of *Bhakti* was that it diverted the anger of many Hindus away from Muslims. Most of the reformers of *Bhakti* period commented on religious discord among practices both with Hindus and Muslims and their teachings did contributed towards reduction of bitterness between the two religions. It also resulted in heart change for many kings of this period who started looking at their subjects in more sympathetic ways and changed their policies to help them.

The last most important benefit of *Bhakti* to Hinduism was that it almost stopped conversions from Hinduism to Islam in particular. *Bhakti* brought in Hinduism a feeling of brotherhood like never before and the idea of direct access with the godhead had everlasting impacts specially on low caste Hindus who were rapidly giving up hope of their salvation were increasing getting drawn towards Islam. In a way, later *Bhakti* teachers had taken over the role of social reformers and *Bhakti* provided them the magic wand to push back such people back to Hinduism.

30

Hinduism under Mughal Period

This period had examples on both sides of following contemporary Hindu practices with full earnest on one extreme and complete hate and disrespect for everything Hindu on the other extreme. Some of the rulers considered Hindu practices as completely blasphemous while some other had shown complete dedication for the same. Mughal is Persian form of Mongols and some people also call them Mogul that is generally used to denote a person with extravagant wealth and power. Mughals, in continuation of the other rulers coming from Central Asia and Mongolia, have been known for inflicting cruel injuries on their enemies which included blinding people by piercing rods in eyes, putting molten metal in mouth etc. for scaring the repeat by others. They are also known for killing their own family members to get the crown. And they are also known for their addictions as many remained drunk or stoned for most part of their times. But in spite of all other weaknesses, Mughals were always known for their extraordinary bravery in wars and their love for luxuries in many forms.

They ruled India for around three hundred years starting with Babur defeating Ibrahim Lodhi in the battle of Panipat. All said and done, Mughalia Sultanat made spectacular contribution to the culture of India. Trade and industry again flourished under their rule. They introduced luxury and costumiers, perfumes, jewelry, ivory carving, gunsmith, central Asian architecture, civil engineering, stone carving, etc. in India at a scale like never before. Unlike most other aggressors from Arab, Mongol and Turkey,

Mughals decided to make India their home and that allowed them to have a different focus that was long term.

Mughal Emperor Akbar was most wonderful for Hindus and respected them better than many Hindu kings while Aurangzeb was most horrid. In general most of them were a bit of both with the proportions varying from one side to another. Let us look at each one of them in some details.

Babur, the person responsible for starting the Mughal Dynasty in India, had blood of Genghis Khan from his mother side and that of Timur from his father's side. Born in Ferghana, central Asian Mountains in 1484, Babur (meaning Tiger) got educated in Turkey and adopted a deadly mix of elegance and cruelty. He is known for constructing many great gardens and knocking down many temples, killing many Hindus, constructing many Mosques on the same place where Hindu temples stood. He has written his life memoirs by the name of Baburnama that shows that he came after India having failed to win over Samarkand.

Like many others who take pride in everything in their own culture and are intolerant for contents of other's culture, he had very low opinion for most Indian things and complained that there is no charm, there is no beauty in Indian people, no grace in social interactions, no poetic talent, no etiquettes. He was not happy with India not having good horses, grapes, meat, public baths and madrassa. The only good thing he saw in India was that it was a big country with lots of gold and money. It appears that he had his complete fixation of Turkish luxury and held the view that everything else was just a waste.

Babur was not a hardcore religious fanatic as he was more dedicated to his army, more than religion. Nonetheless, he considered himself a holy warrior and, due to his Islamic background, looked at Hindus as infidel. He enjoyed wines, women, composing poetry, music, flowers, gardens and enjoyed his weakness of remaining intoxicated at odd hours on regular basis. Baburnama is full with many references of such instances. Finally, in 1530, he prayed for transfer of his karma to the credit of his son Humanyun. As the story goes, Humanyun came out healthy from his serious ailment while Babur died soon losing his great health over very few days.

Humanyun, born in 1508 in Kabul dabbled in astrology and spiritual matters, blinded his brother Hindal and took over the crown. He died young in 1556 after tripping down from his makeshift observatory in Delhi and died leaving his son, Akbar who was just 13 at that time. Akbar is famous for his tolerance for all religions that has so few parallels in history. He was a fearless and tireless rider and ruled India for a long time. His career had a bad spot when he got over 20,000 people killed while taking over Mewar's Chittor. Those killed included large number of civilians, women and children. He was apparently suffered from dyslexic as he could neither read nor write. We know his life details in much more clarity due to biogrhaphical books named 'Akbar Nama' and 'Ain-i-Akbari' by Abul Fazal who was one of the nine gems of his Darbar.

Akbar was initially very impressed with Sufi Saint, Shaikh Salim Chisti. So much so that he got Fateh Pur Sikri built to live near the place of the Saint. Akbar even named his son after the great Saint. Akbar is also known for holding regular debates on religious concepts and invited people of all faiths without any clear preference as also for wandering amongst the general public incognito for seeking first hand feedback about people's issues with the state. Akbar was more like King Ashoka and believed in religion of Humanity rather than any particular faith. Like Ashoka's own Dhamma, Akbar started his own faith called 'Din-i-Ilahi' which also failed dismally.

Akbar was first Mughal emperor born in India and was a great pluralist to the core. He was also the first foreign ruler who had Muslim enemies and Hindu friends. He married daughter of Raja Bharmal of Amer and made her Marium-uz-Zamani, the Queen Mother. This gesture, among other equal policies, brought Indians closer to the Emperor for the first time. He had *Brahmin* Birbal as one of his closest confidante and *Kshatriya* Todar Mal as his leading general. He dispensed with *Zazia* from Hindus and encouraged people to follow their religious practices without any fear. He was good to both Hindus and Hinduism and treated both with respect. Most matters of mathematics and management of state were left exclusively to Hindus by Akbar.

Akbar and Jodha's son Salim (later name changed to Jahangir) is known more as an alcoholic. He readopted Islam as the state religion but continued the policy of religious tolerance. He got several religious leaders killed including Sikh Guru Arjan Das, Shi's Qadi Nurullah Shushtari and Abul Fazal. He got his own son blinded saying that there is no father or son to a sovereign. Inspite of being a son from a Hindu mother, he saw only darkness of spirits in Hindu traditions. He got many temples destroyed during his rule that ended in 1627 on his death. Another development worth mentioning of this period was that Urdu had taken full shape and was taken as the official language of the Empire. Urdu uses Arabian script, grammatical structure of Hindi and vocabulary that is mix of Persian and north Indian.

Next Mughal, Shah Jahan was third son of Rajput Princess Manmati. He is known for his sever discrimination against non-Muslims. But he had liking for Sanskrit poetry and few other traditions of Hindu culture. He was influenced by Amir Khusro who himself was a son of Turkish father and Rajput mother. Shah Jahan was a great builder and got Fort at Agra, Fort at Delhi, Jama Maszid, Shalimar Gardens, White Marble Palace of Ajmer and finally the Taj Mahal at Agra built under his rule.

Dara Shikoh was the eldest and favourite son of Shah Jahan and was heir designated. But Dara had too much deep liking for ancient Indian Systems and was disliked by Muslims ulemmas. Being proficient in both Sanskrit and Persian, he himself translated many Indian Scriptures, (including key Upanishads) in Persian and argued that basic essential nature of Hinduism and Islam are alike. He debated with Sufis, Muslims, Christians and even Jews. Poor guy was killed, cut into pieces, paraded on Agra streets by none other than his own brother, Aurangzeb who later came to be called the Zealot.

An absolute orthodox Sunni, Aurangzeb hated the tolerant views of his predecessors and took on himself to repair them by undoing all the good things of past generations. He strongly believed that Akbar should have declared India as an Islamic country. He disrupted entire India and made best possible efforts to convert it into an Islamic State. He unleashed a twenty year long discrimination on Hindus, Sikhs, Shiites alike.

When some Muslims got reported to have joined Sikhism, he got infuriated and got Guru Tegh Bahadur killed. It was as this juncture that the 10th Guru Govind Singh converted Sikhism from a social and religious reform movement to a political and military force. Aurangzeb once again imposed *Zazia* even on *Brahmins*, rescinded all state endowments to Hindu Temples and *Brahmins* and even got all positions held by Hindus replaced with Muslim occupants to change the scale completely in favour of people from his religion. He hated every other faith and hated them hard. Hinduism, being the biggest of them all, was on the firing line so to say.

Aurangzeb got Hyderabad Temples destroyed during his attack on Deccan. The iconic temples of faith for Hindus like Vishwanath Temple at Banaras and Keshava Deo Temple at Mathura got replaced with Mosques. He ordered for immediate destruction of all schools and temples and all places of teaching anything Indian. Had he access to weapons of mass destruction, Aurangzeb would not have hesitated to destroy everything Hindu in particular and Indian in general.

He no longer allowed the Hindu community to live under their own laws but imposed Sharia Law over the whole Empire. His policies resulted in very unstable situations where large part of his subjects started opposing him and finally, he got reduced to be the last big Emperor of the Mughal Sultanate.

This period also saw mass conversion from Hinduism to Islam that sew the seeds of faster growth of Muslim population on Indian soil. Some Hindus were converted for monetary allurements and inducements, some for marriage, most to avoid punishments and discriminations and very little who actually believed in Islam. Hinduism had never seen such an attack on its roots before.

Women under Mughals

There were many women who did well under the Mughal period. They exercised great powers behind throne. Few of them had their own libraries and are known to achieve great literary accomplishments, mother of Akbar remained incharge of the administration for a good time as he was very young at the time of death of his father. Even Jodha Bai is known to lead Akbar to take much more favourable view of Hinduism and Hindu subjects. She was said to be taking active interest for advising Akbar on many issues of the state. Then we have Chand Bibi who as Regent of Bijapur is known for defending Ahmednagar against the Mughal forces of Emperor Akbar.

Another important woman was Nur Jahan who virtually ruled the kingdom since Jahangir was happy with his addiction of opium and alcohol keeping him pre-occupied. She was strong, charismatic and well-educated woman and is to be considered as one of the most influential woman of the entire century for Mughal Empire. She made significant contributions to Indian culture, charity work and commercial trade and ruled with an iron fist. She was twentieth but favourite wife of Jahangir and enjoyed complete free hand to run the administration as she deemed fit. Later she got her relative Mumtaj Mahal married to Shah Jahan.

The definition of right kind of women underwent change during Mughal raj, at least for them. This can be finely captured, on a lighter note, from the writings of Mirza who was half brother to Akbar. He wrote;

> *"Every man should have four wives; a Persian for conversations; a woman from Khurusan for household work; a Hindu woman to have children and raising them under her watchful eye; and one transoxiana who can be beaten as a warning to all others."*

Religious Fusion around this Time

The Sufism of Islam is not very far from Hindu idealism. It allowed many people to look at Hinduism and Sufism in an inextricable manner. This was ofcourse, not liked by orthodox people on both sides. But considering the fact that most Muslims of India had been converted to Islam from original Hindu background, many continued to be Hindu by culture and Muslim by religion. This "*Ganga Jamuna Tehzeeb*" continues until this day to denote peaceful and loving co-existence of Hindus and Muslims on Indian soil sharing long common traditions and customs. Mughal rulers patronized Yoga while many Hindus started worshiping Sufi Peers like their own.

Around this time, *Bhakti* movement of Hinduism and Sufi traditions of Islam got so much intertwined by each other that it is difficult to say which influenced whom to what extent. This period saw a lot of translation of scriptures from one side in the language of another. This facilitated lot of enrichment on both sides. Dara Shikoh translated Upanishads while Abul Fazl translated Mahabharata and Ramayana into Persian.

A unique mix of languages took shape called Hindustani which when written in Devnagri came to be called Hindi and written in Arabic got known as Urdu. This simple development itself speaks of what kind of fusion would have taken place between Hinduism and Indian Islam. This fusion got reflected in many things including architecture. Fatehpur Sikri, for example has a distinct stamp of Persian, Hindu and Jain forms of building architecture.

31
Social Evils Manifesting in Medieval India

The period after end of classical Indian period of 6th century is generally called early medieval period which goes until end of 12th century CE. This was not a good period for Hinduism on the Indian sub continent in many ways. We have seen how Adi Shankaracharya established his order and spearheaded a great campaign which resulted in substantial success in uprooting the home grown religions of Buddhism and Jainism. But other than this, there were not many examples of good environment for religious growth.

As discussed earlier, post-Gupta Dynasty, kingdoms from all directions including those from east, south and northwest tried attacking the Kannauj power for its attraction of *Doab*, well oiled administration and fertile lands. These brutal fights led to military actions of unforeseen proportions. Finally, after lots of bloodshed, Rajput Kingdoms of various sizes ruled large portion of north side. These rulers were very obsessed with chivalry and feudalism. Another key characteristics of this period was development of regional societies which had very fluid boundaries and their politics was defined more by languages and dialects, sectarian affiliations and temples rather than administration or welfare of subjects. Constant skirmishes on different sides took away long-term perspective from all the rulers. If today is not secured, tomorrow is always forced to wait in desperation. This was the darkest period of Hinduism as all one can hear from this period is gods, temples, inspired poets and sectarian philosophies.

Situation in South of India was comparatively better as most part was ruled by dynasties for comparatively longer periods with rulers having more energies for promoting all forms of expressions including arts, architecture, dance, music, literature and poetry. The size of the kingdoms was good enough to force all the rulers to maintain the balance without involving violent confrontations. That is the precise reason that one can trace better economic and religious advancements from South throughout the early medieval period.

But situation in North was deplorable. Most of the northeren kingdoms were constantly fighting with each other and going to extra length to weaken the enemy by going to any extremes. The conquering side was to take over what ever they could lay their hands on, including treasures and womenfolk of the losing side. The losing side was either getting killed or run away and waits for regrouping to prepare for counter attack. Everyone was constantly looking to befriend with the actual or possible enemy of their enemy. History is full of examples from this period where one side entered into treaty with some other side to stand by them when attacked.

The women who were overpowered met with great insult and humiliation. They were treated like prizes and got appropriated, exploited and ill treated, as there was no one to stand for them. In any case, the position of women in higher classes of *Brahmins* and *Kshatriyas* was much worse than their counterparts in *Vaishyas* and *Shudras*. It is because women in lower class were to contribute towards family occupation and hence it's earning. As opposed to this, higher classes were engaged only in priesthood and martial duties with practically no role for the women except to be a sexual partner to the husband, have children and help them grow. This class division of women in higher and lower classes will be very clear as soon as we relate it to the major evils involving them in later sections.

Because of this economic usefulness of women, there have been a clear gender divide in higher and lower classes. Higher class families were also supposed to accumulate large resources for marrying off their daughters as marriage functions involved large feasts and gifts for the groom's entire family. The acceptance of another family's daughter as a bride was considered some sort of benevolence that needed to be responded in material terms. As against this, lower class used to welcome addition to the family as another earning hand and has been known to provide cash and other considerations to the family of bride to part with their daughter. These practices of this time sound quite reasonable as they respond to simple economic principle of demand and supply.

The established practice of monogamy, where one male person could marry only with one female, resulted in worsening of the situation. As a natural phenomenon, the proportion of females is higher than males and India was no exception. With many males getting killed in constant wars (and wars always involved males from regenerative age group) there was double whammy on availability of suitable matches for many daughters. Many people felt that by accepting a bride, the groom and his family is taking up a onerous responsibility of supporting the bride for the rest of her life. In addition, there were inheritance issues where daughters were not entitled to share in her parent's estate post her marriage. This resulted in one-time settlements by handing over some portion of her share at the time of her marriage to her new family. Even Vedic systems provided for the best scenario of a *Brahmins* daughter's marriage where he gifts her to a suitable boy invited at her parent's place and where the bride's family was to hold a feast for groom and his family and friends. These factors covering religious, economic, demographic and traditional aspects got combined resulting in what we call dowry system.

Another important off shoot of our class based segregation, especially during early Medieval India period, was a blind desire in lower classes to adopt traditions and customs of higher classes. The superiority of higher classes projected them, at least in the eyes of lower classes, as ideals for social behaviours. Since the beginning of our society, every section sitting on lower step of the social ladder has been aspiring to move up the ladder, sometimes by aping the norms and rituals followed by higher class. As we will see slightly later in this very section, this tendency will give rise to many social evils that infected the Hinduism during this period where things relevant for one higher class (which was like an exception under specific situations) became a general norm for other lower placed castes.

There was yet another crude attack on social customs of this time after arrival of Turks beginning with first wave of invasions beginning 10th century. These invaders came with the background of tribal culture from Arabia where woman were treated as an object of possession and enjoyment. They and their soldiers were freely roaming around most of the time and used to pick up females mostly unmarried and take them away with them as part of loot. Such events had happened even before when Rajputs were fighting Rajputs but the practice was different with Muslim invaders. While Rajputs were to loot women from ruling clan only, the Muslims would do that at random without looking at class as they didn't care for class segregation. Picking up of a girl by an alien person with a different faith was to bring great disrepute on the entire family to which that abducted female belonged. As the chances of such abductions were higher with unmarried girls, presence of a young unmarried girl in the family was considered a potential invitation to disaster. By the time the Delhi Sultanate settled down in India, most people in the North of the country were found wanting marrying off their daughters at the earliest opportunity. This tendency kept reducing the bride's age and ultimately reached to the cradle. This is the background of early marriage and child marriage which are considered as great social evil of Hindu society.

By this time, another factor of sub castes also became dominant. For some unknown reasons, the similar profession based sub-class identity; the system of caste and sub-caste took over bulk of Indian social strata. To my understanding, it was leftover impact of sectarian division which always had regional colour attached to it. Somehow, similar occupation-carrying families got identified with caste/sub-castes and many of them under a single region came under influence of some sectarian saint or local deity. Occupational commonality brought them together and forced them to aspire for separate identities leading to strong cult like feeling for their caste. The typecast became stronger and stronger over the period and gave rise to many other customs including early marriages. Increase in feudalism, rivalry, personal honour, hereditary animosity and friendships encouraged parents to fix up matrimonial relations with each other family to avoid any possibility of their young ones going against their caste under juvenile passions. Since the social structure was village based, any cases of person or family going against these customs was heavily penalized. The diktats of Khap Panchyats that we come across even today coming out with their nonsensical sermons are an unfortunate continuity of the system described above.

The ruling kingdoms and fiefdoms resorted to grow each others juveniles in cross families as a safety for keeping the treaties intact in testing times. Military alliances played bigger role for these kingdoms to create, maintain or destroy balance of political and economic powers among competing kingdoms. Establishing matrimonial relations was considered even more long lasting alliances. Since these alliances were for ensuring power balance, factors like age were not given much importance. This led to many marriages without proper mutual suitability between bride and groom. Many a times, even set traditions of monogamy were kept aside to make way for these alliances. The cultural difference with Muslims chieftains gave rise to another strong reasons for erstwhile fighting Rajput kingdoms to come together against common enemy. This resulted in added urgency for yet another combinations of alliances. The fanatic zeal of foreign aggressors and their brazen and brutal ways of dealing with defeated enemies added only fuel to the fire. It was unfortunate that every such development has to end with added atrocities on women rights and resulted in their increased suppression and exploitation.

The combined effect of such social, cultural, religious, political and economic factors combined together to bring many social evils throughout Hindu society of this time. The major such problems which created severe road blocks in growth of Hinduism, coupled with foreign rules of Delhi Sultanate followed by Mughals, pushed Hinduism to one of its darkest period. For a long time at this stage of history, a bit of progress by *bhakti* period movement was the only silver line that encouraged ordinary Hindu to get attached with his cultural roots of some kind. Let us look at some of these social evils in brief details:

1. *Gender Inequality:* This was the period that reinforced position of male gender as the main earning member and one providing physical protection to his family. The enhanced gap in gender inequality converted women to third grade members of the society in general. This resulted in substantial drop in their exposure to education and forced them to observe norms like covering of head in public places. It basically pushed them inside four walls of the household and took away economic freedom.

2. *Dowry System:* Tracing of this problem will take you to classical Hinduism time of Dharma *Shastra* of Manu which

recommends how a daughter's marriage should be solemnized. A man with daughters became a cursed soul due to impending expenses involved in marrying them off. The social taboos forced parents to spend on daughter's marriage beyond their own financial capacity. Customs forced them to take loans and sell their land holdings to ensure meeting marriage expenses. The original system of voluntary gifts to grooms family got to the state of negotiated demands. Alas, the custom is still prevalent in many parts of the country. The unfortunate part was that tribals and lower caste people who were known to pay for getting bride, also adopted the dowry system leading it to get infected all strata of society.

3. *Caste Discrimination:* Vedic society was based on four classes that were based on professions of the people. In due course it became hereditary in nature where class got decided by birth and not by profession. With increased number of professions, even in Classical Period of Hinduism, the class got expanded into castes to accommodate new professions. By the medieval time, the exponential increase in caste resulted in unthinkable rigidity forcing number of social interaction within very close range of own casts. This system soon percolated down to village level with even stronger biases. This was the time when eighty per cent of Indian population was still living in villages. Villages were as it is suffering from lack of education and covered with ignorance were facing lots of superstitions. Rigid caste discriminations brought in deep divides among various castes and sub-castes resulting in greater social barriers in terms of access to places of worship, celebration on festivals, say in administration, employability of weaker section, untouchability and such other social interactions got impacted.

4. *Female Infanticide:* Female birth got compared to curse from God. This prompted parents to take extreme steps of killing their new born girl child to avoid social stigma and potential hardship to the finances and honour of the family. The main problem behind this evil is burden of dowry. First of all the problem got reported among Jats in Punjab region but later it was well acknowledged in other areas spanning from Gujarat to Uttar Pradesh. This soon resulted in unbalanced proportion of male and females. The basic problem which converted to evil was the fact that originating with higher classes, it got spread to lower classes as well and most

unfortunately, even after the social misbalance reported, the problem could not get eradicated. So, what started as an economic problem got transformed into a social evil. And as is the case always, the worst effected of this were the backward classes that suffered the most.

5. *Sati:* Self immolation by wife of a deceased person on his pyre got social acceptance and was looked as an ideal step by the widow to protect the husband's family's honour. This was preferred by *Kshatriya* women to save themselves from worse than death treatment if they were captured and taken alive by the conquerors. In other classes, the real reasons were largely economic. Prejudices of sanctified virginity of a bride prevented any chance of remarriage. A widow, specially a young widow, was feared to fall for her sensuous passions and was treated as a burden for the family carrying potential risk of bringing bad repute.

Her very presence, after her husband's death, was taken as a dead weight around the neck of the family. Her sight, her voice, her touch and her very name were considered a bad omen. She was to keep away from every good event of the family including festivals or marriages. It is not hard to believe that most cases of immolation of the wife, along with the deceased dead body of her husband, were inspired, encouraged or tacitly executed by the family members by playing on the weak emotions and sensitivity of the unfortunate woman.

While one could have justified some stray cases involving some Rajput families going for group suicide by ladies to avoid capturing by enemies, as in case of Rani Padmini of Chittor in Rajasthan, in most other cases *Sati* was encouraged to get rid of the unwanted wife. It was yet another example of double standards favouring males, as being widow did not make males underprivileged lot. The females were treated like cheap commodity, which can be easily dispensed with. The people in-charge of religion matters encouraged such practices as false pride.

6. *Polygamy:* The evil of Polygamy crept into Hindu society in due course forced on the social practice where it was mandatory for every girl to get married but many males were adopting the life of ascetic that forced them out of counting. Many others were also known for taking celibacy as a preferred way of life. Originally, this practice was to correct the gender imbalance but later influential persons used it to secure more than one wife just for

pleasures. But finally, it was in 1952 that the legal provisions were introduced to ban this wrong practice.

Inspite of relative different circumstances of South India, the impact of social evils had infested that region as well albeit in varying proportions. The position of women in South was marginally better than North and the imparting of education to female also was far better. But untouchability and sectarian divides were far stronger in South. Caste based inequalities were equal in all regions. South had yet another custom of having Devdasis attached with Temples who were like married to the deity and lived on Temple resources. They learned classical dance forms and performed before temple deity with full social sanctions.

Some of them also had marriage with already married patrons from outside temples. Society respected them well and their children were extended due acceptability. The number of Devdasis attached with a temple was in proportions to the financial capacity of the temple and its patrons Kings included. As per one record, the temple of Tanjavur patronized by Cholas was having four hundred Devdasis on its roll. Dance and music was a necessary part of daily Puja of Deities at Temples. The tradition was based on old scriptures as Kalidasa's Meghdhoot is quoted to have references to dancing girls present at functions in the temple at that time. But destructions and plundering of temples under West Asian attacks depleted financial resources of the temples. Even capacity of patron states went down to continue support. This scenario brought most of Devdasis on street forcing many of them to join the world's oldest profession. The understanding of Britishers for these girls was, like in most other cases, very wrong, as they compared them and treated with petty dancing girls on the street and dealt their plight with their well-known casual and high handed approach. Here again, the ultimate sufferer of the social customs was the woman once again.

32

Hinduism Under British Raj

East India Company was one of the many companies from Europe, particularly Dutch and Portuguese which came to Indian subcontinent looking for a pie of trade and commerce in Asian countries. All these companies were keeping their private armies and were constantly competing with each other for larger size of the trade. British East India Company (EIC) got major boost to their efforts in 1612 after they secured exclusive business facilitation approval from Jahangir to freely stay and carry out their business any where in his empire. By diplomacy and deceit, the company also got control for revenue collection in the province of Bengal. This provided the company a great opportunity to exercise indirect control over the Provincial administration and a peep into the working of governments in this part.

EIC also remained focused on expanding from one region to another. They traded in spices, cotton, tea, and opium and later kept adding items to their list. In this process, they also expanded their operations to Afghanistan, South East Asia and China. The fact that at one point in history, this company accounted for half of the entire world trade, spoke volumes about their success in business. Expanded business also allowed them to expand their army which was having best of European weaponry of its time and employed only British rank and file while all the sepoys were hired locally.

Between 1750 and 1755, one third of Bengal population died of famines. This catastrophe saw a big surge in worship of Goddess Kali in her aspect of Annapurna. This was in continuation where the features of the rising deity were matching in the need of the hour.

Then in 1757, EIC had first major success to keep firm foothold in taking over territories on the subcontinent. In the battle of Plassey, EIC defeated independent Nawab of Bengal, Siraj Ud Daulah who was affiliated to the Mughal King but EIC was ready to take on their original friends who had since weakened drastically. EIC had already established a number of treaties with many smaller kingdoms to extend their military support in exchange of exclusive trade rights. They also developed local understanding and took advantage of weakening of Marathas and snatched the area of *Doab* to have their control on Oudh to Agra and later many other territories in Gujarat and Maharashtra as well. They had spread right upto Mysore where they defeated Hyder Ali and Tipu Sultan in 1799, who alone offered them some resistance. The Marathas, the Sikhs and rulers of Mysore could never unite to confront the foreign adversary and ultimately succumbed to their dirty designs and intrigue one by one.

By this time EIC had full control on all economic matters in most part of the subcontinent. They forced farmers to switch over to cash crops and replace the food crops and got most industries closed down so that the entire subcontinent was only to offer crops for trade at their terms. Our farmers were reduced to work like supplier of raw materials of cash crops of British choice. Materials so procured were exported to England to feed the factories and finished products were brought back for sale in India making double profits. Large-scale diversions of cultivable land from food crops to cash crops resulted in substantial reduction in food buffers.

Coincided with bad rain cycles, food non-availability resulted in enormous famines. As per British records, between 1800 to 1900 CE, India saw regular deaths of over 25 million people exclusively because of wide spread famines. But what the records fail to tell is the fact that British people had forced change of India's indigenous crop pattern to divert large track of food growing area to produce jute, cotton, tea and oil seeds so that EIC can meet its targets for supplying these items as raw materials to feed the factories back home. By this time, industrial revolution had turned Britain into world's workshop and India proved their largest raw material source and its 300 million populations was treated as a backyard market for readymade goods. There was no one to think that loss of food crops meant catastrophe in times of shortage of rains.

These developments had very bad impact on Indian economic conditions. Earlier invaders looted only wealth from temples and treasuries but the new rulers were looting it by snatching away work from hands of labourers and by forcing them to die of hunger. Muslim invaders had concentrated their loot only on temples and monasteries based in main urban centres but British were making life difficult for almost everyone including people living in villages as they collected taxes in form of crops leaving little share with the farmers to survive on.

Even at this point, a large portion of the subcontinent continued to be independently governed by large and small kingdoms that numbered around 560 and had treaties with Raj for mutual cooperation. Both the EIC and Maharajas proved good ally to each other and both made increasingly higher profits at the cost of poor subjects. Raj officials played cozy with the rulers and exposed them to European luxuries and encouraged them to close eyes to the problems of the common man. There are so many stories and books already available on the luxurious life lived by most heads of kingdoms and fiefdoms.

These were very bad times for social harmony on the sub continent. Muslims were fighting with each other in many areas for seeking dominance post Mughal empire's got disintegrated, many Rajput kings were fighting with their Rajput neighbours, there were Muslim fighting with Rajput kingdoms in west area, Britishers were fighting with both Muslims and Rajputs in different parts. In some pockets, both Muslim and Rajputs had joined hand and were fighting with Britishers. Soldiers, both Hindu and Muslims were fighting for money and were known to switch side with whosoever was winning. Allegiance to any specific king or territory was not in vogue as soldiers wanted only salary and share in loot. Starvation and taxation policies of the Raj were killing farmers and labourers alike. The subcontinent was never more unfortunate. Muslims had made India their home. So whatever they looted was not going out of the sub continent. But plundering by Britishers has turned India from a 'Golden Bird' to 'Lame Duck' and a pauper for everything small and big.

True that they have invested in creating railroads, road network, telegraph, dams, bridges, irrigation canals, sanitation, public health, schools and colleges. But the entire investment was focused on facilitating their trade and commerce and nothing else.

Their methods and ways of dealing with the people of subcontinent sparked instant hatred for them and they could never succeed in creating any place in the hearts of public at large.

Social Significance of Britishers Arriving in India at Different Periods

Let us briefly analyse the characteristics of Britishers arriving in India at different times with their changing agenda on the social and religious fronts. Britishers' arrival in India had three distinct periods. To begin with we had people connected with trade and commerce who came to India in the first phase when they were focused on trade and less on governing. They came with limited purpose and looked at things Indian with some curiosity. They mostly came without families and intermingled with locals with many having local marriages and children. As first batch of Orientalists, they were genuinely trying to learn India with open minds and were open for new learning and maintained social sensitivities by staying clear of India's socio-religious sphere. They stayed clear of all religious matters altogether.

They could relate to Indian class divide with the similar system in Europe and only encouraged the gaps among classes. Their own brand of diplomatic deceit was intended to pursue the policy of divide and rule. They were happy that Hindus don't take Muslims kindly and brought in much segregation which only fuelled the mutual distrust and resulted in much confrontation among Muslims and Hindus to begin with. For Hindus, who have been used to see different aggressors over last 1000 years or so, they were yet another rulers in the series. Britishers of this time intermingled socially with *rajas* as they took themselves also as *Kshatriyas*.

In their effort of sowing the seeds of segregation, to *Brahmins*, they encouraged to consider themselves as elite and focus more on their food and cleanliness. This was dubbed as their efforts of Sanskritisation and aimed at continuing with class-based divide that allowed larger role for new rulers to weaken both sides and enhance their own importance. Towards end of 18th century, however, many Englishmen started bringing their families to live in India and that created a lot of divide as the interaction of wives and children with locals became different. It was like a relation of masters and slaves with barricades and no-entry zones. Such behaviour was new to most locals and saw the seeds of 'us vs they'. Each memsaab had 20-25 workers at her disposal and ruled them like animals. Slowly, religion also started coming in between as new English arrivals started finding many local practices as unbearable and soon it was the religion that made Britishers treat Hindus as devils.

Then in 1813, under pressure from English religious groups, new charter of the Company allowed Christian Missions to operate in India. The arrival of Evangelicals socn resulted in conversions of many Dalits and lower class Hindus to Christianity. Slowly slowly, the Raj officials also started their interference in Hindu's religious matters like non acceptance to remarriage of widows, cancellation of inheritance rights of converting out to other religions, all castes to share same rail coaches, teaching children at missionary schools and making them realise that the religion of their parents is something to be ashamed of, etc. The changes made by Raj in these matters slowly lead to a big divide in the relationship between Britishers and Hindus.

Muslims were still found better by English people as both Britishers and Muslims had basic books of their religions and shared manners in social governance. But soon the increased number of missionaries and their activities, coupled with racist attitude of British officials, threatened traditional Indian life creating new fear in the minds of most Hindus. It may be added that the problem was with Protestant Christians who came fresh from England with the belief that their ruling power was result of their religious superiority over Hindus and treated Indian as devils, downtrodden and duffers with no respect and regard to their religion and social customs. Their behaviours antagonised many Hindus on personal basis but the brutal power of Raj officials crushed all such incidences with increasing punishments.

Christians Missionaries used to look at Indian religion also in light of their own systems and took the Vedas as equivalent to the Bible. They classified all popular manifestations as superstitions. Translations and explanations of Vedic scriptures also followed heavily on the model of Christianity and the role played by the Bible. They were looking to rule Hindus also by a Book (as the case in Islam and Christianity). But they realized that most Indians were illiterate and did not understand scriptures and rather followed oral and visual traditions. Their own effort of segregating real Hinduism and popular Hinduism did no good for their actual understanding of the depth of the whole gamut of religion in practice. They were confused to find so many commonality and variations over regions that taking out a single stream, as a single representation of entire Hinduism became impossible. Back then, most of Western scholars could never had the humility to try and understand/appreciate the basic tenets of Hinduism. Up until 1800, most European found Hinduism quite disgusting and ridiculous, as they could not handle the prevailing multiplicities of the religious practices. It was to take them another hundred years to change that attitude to tolerance.

In the early decades of 19th century, British Raj took many legislative steps to curb and ban many Hindu practices that they considered as barbaric and impinging on women rights. The laws so made included banning infanticide, human sacrifice, and practice of *Sati*. These, by themselves, were welcome steps and should have created a positive impact but Britishers had lost their respect in the eyes of Hindus who had reasons to believe that all these are unwanted interference in their social life. As a result, and as a token of the first sign of disobedience, the number of *Sati* cases drastically increased in the first year after the ban by Raj as compared to a year earlier. This was first sign of defiance by Hindus. It gave them a reason to respond to British rule collectively.

It was by pure accident that Britishers, in their own ignorance, forced a sense of unity and community that Hindus have never ever felt before. English Raj officials, made the arrogant mistake of considering all Hindus as a single combined community. For their goodness, they were awarded with large-scale protests from Hindus from one corner of the country to another. But in the process of their unintended arrogance, they ended up doing a great service to Hinduism by unknowingly forcing all Hindus to gather under a common umbrella. These legislative changes for social reforms together with missionaries, injected a sense of unity among all Hindus who got propelled to come together in self-defense leaving behind their sectarian identities leading to first time "unification".

The Great Indian Rebellion of 1857

The year 1857 proved to be the tipping point and saw one after the other instances of rebel from Hindus. In some cases, Muslims, to oppose Britishers, also joined Hindus, in another first in the history of the subcontinent. To begin with it was rebellion by Mangal Pandey, and then there was mutiny of sepoys at Meerut where 85 sepoys got arrested. Little later there was massacre at Cawnpore (Kanpur). But the last nail in the coffin was the controversy of new cartridges having animal fat, which required to be kept in mouth before being used. The rumours spread that it contained both beef and pig fats (these were a big no to both Hindus and Muslims respectively) and that it has been done by the Britishers intentionally to corrupt the religion of Indian sepoys from both religions. The distrust exiting between Britishers and Indians raised the issue beyond proportions where the rebellion took unmanageable proportions leaving the Company Officials found wanted in their situation management.

Events of 1857 culminated in British Government taking over India from East India Company and introduced new harsh administrative changes. The third round of Britishers' arrival at this time was branded as Utilitarian and Anglicizes. They were genuinely misplaced to think that Western education and religion was extremely superior to the traditions of East and gave them right to rule over Indians with an iron hand. Lots of counter measures were introduced to bring normalcy and for cooling religious fervours to normalize the situation. But the landscape had changed forever. From now on, Britain was forced to use most of their energy in managing administrative matters over India leaving lesser energy to enlarge their business further. The situation was also contributed by some bizarre situations like disparity of salaries between an Indian and an Englishman at the same post where there salaries were 1:20 times apart. Indians had well realized that they are being treated as second-class citizens irrespective of their social, educational or economic status. Top posts in ICS (Indian Civil Services) were not given to Indians, Indian origin judges had no jurisdiction to provide judgement if the person involved was a Britisher.

By this time, many Indian had come out of English based education systems with some of them also getting higher education at British universities. They had seen through the double standards being applied to Indian rule. Later 1800 time saw some Indians asking for greater role in their own governing as the loss of trust with Britishers had given rise to feeling of unrest in many quarters. Modernization and Westernization coupled with physical connectivity of regions like never before sparked the feeling of national identity and self-rule. This was first time that both Hindus and Muslims got united as they found common enemy in British rule.

Social Reform Movements of 19th Century

The entire 19th century can be said to be a reforms driven century for Hinduism. With the banes and blessings of British Raj, Indians in general and Hindus in particular got a unified sense. New education and exposures to cultures and systems of Europe and other parts of the world helped them understand the evils infesting their culture. These feelings resulted in emergence of some very dedicated sons of Hinduism who got connected with its rich past and started galvanizing Hindus to fight for eradication of the social evils.

This was the first time in history where Hindus accepted the word Hindu as their own representation. To many readers, this may be unbelievable but this is the reality. Hindus never considered themselves identified with this word before this time. Earlier, it will be recalled that many outsiders were calling people on Indian subcontinent by this name but it was mostly with derogatory connotation. Looking, back to the history of the Hindu as a word, one has to go back to Persians who used the word to refer to all residents living on other side of River Sindhu (the word S is pronounced as H in Persian language).

By the time Britishers got settled, the word got accepted by the local residents to identify as a name for geographical identity rather than cultural. But thanks to colonial exploitation and intolerable attitude to subcontinent's culture, all the people having their links with Sanatan Dharma, living across in all regions of the subcontinent, forgot their internal differences and accepted to be collectively called Hindus. It was under this acceptance that they took Britishers as common enemy. The word Hindu got accepted to encompass whole of native culture as opposed to Muslims first and followed by Christians. The seeds that got sown at the time of arrivals of Muslims got germinated into solid shapes with English Raj.

Coming into contact with European systems caused cultural and religious matters to gain political value like never before. This further provoked a strong sense of unity among all Indians (with

Hindus and Muslims alike). The main reasons contributing to this sense of unity can be summarised as under:

1. Cultural gap between those dominated and those dominating were much greater than among various groupings of those dominated.
2. Spread of English language in India, which exposed some Indians to an outsider's view about preconceptions inherently present within Indian society. This made it easier to spot the social evils that were weakening the social systems.
3. Change in the direction of Colonial rule which changed colours from non-interference on religious matters to the one dictating changes without any prompting or consultations undertaken.
4. Deep distrust between rulers and subjects bringing in deep divides on restrictive measures being taken as unwanted and undesired interference.
5. Insensitivities of Britishers with many Hindu practices and persistent denial of expressed feelings that resulted in Mutiny of 1857.
6. Acceptance of Hinduism, by Hindus as a common umbrella covering all of them consolidated their unity and providing them a force never felt before – the feeling of oneness realized for the very first time.
7. Existence of infrastructure of transport and communication resulting in knitting the previously independent regions of subcontinent. This was single largest unifying force to germinate Indian independence struggle under one banner.
8. Emergence of very class of Indians who benefited from British education system and were exposed with concepts of fair play, justice and functioning of parliament in Westminster style, the democratic systems of decisions. They saw with naked eyes, all these concepts being ignored under rule in India.

Britishers are generally blamed for successfully applying the principle of "Divide and Rule" which they used to acquire territories by pitching one local ruler against the other. History does not forget anything. It was time to pay Britishers in their own coins. There are benefits that come out from otherwise bad situations and this is what happened precisely when all Indians started coming together to "unite and gain independence".

This situation gave rise to many individuals to initiate unification efforts and start reforms on social evils in bits and pieces. Soon like-minded people started coming together and many groups started to get formed championing common causes. Interestingly, these initiatives started the ball rolling in almost all regions of the subcontinent around the same time. As is expected, the individuals were fired by different forces and had varying point of views about possible solutions. Social movements of 19th century had religion and its resurrection by eradicating infested evils at the core unlike later period when all such efforts got a political tone aimed at independence from the colonial rule. To understand the wide range of reformation initiatives, one can group the views under specific brackets as attempted below:

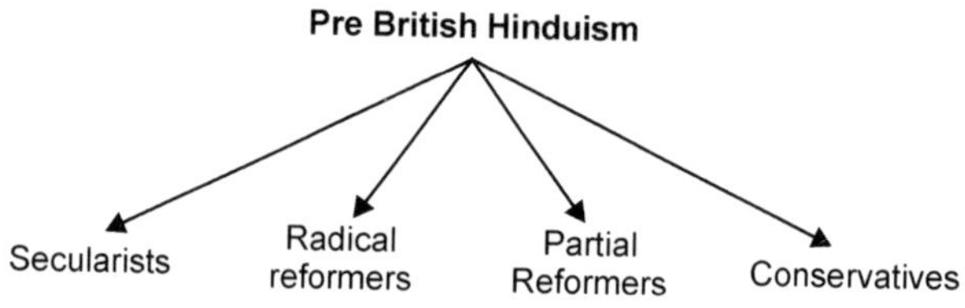

Adi Shankaracharya had in 9th Century emerged as a great intellectual, organizational and physical power that uprooted Buddhism and Jainism from the subcontinent and established Hinduism as a stronger force to stand. He convinced people across the regions that if the world around us is just an illusion, as were the view of these competing thoughts of that time, then there is no encouragement or incentive for any human being to try to understand its working or to derive any empirical knowledge from it. Some thing similar happened again to Hinduism. In otherwise pathetic situation of the period, Hinduism got united again with many people working for its resurrection and to provide it strength to stand against Islam and Christianity.

Most of the groups/organisations of this time had strong belief in Hinduism values and ancient traditions to take its rightful space as the world religion. It will be seen that all such organisations had focused around one or more of social evils of the Hindu societiy while spreading the basic values of Sanatan Dharma, as envisaged in its purer form pre Puranik times. They also got in contact with each other and explored, for the first time, a grand common ground to resurrect Hinduism.

1. *Secularists:* This group include those rationalists who typified by individuals who publically discarded sacred thread, *Janeu,* as a mark of finishing class based divide which allowed the *janeu* to be worn only by upper three classes to the entire exclusion of *Shudras, Dalits, Adivasis* and all other lower class. These people also refused to swear by water of holy Ganga, they established modern libraries providing access to ancient scriptures to all sections as well as advocated modern knowledge on wider subjects. Many of these people donated their resources and land for promoting education for women and also refused to marry child brides. The focus was to stand against obvious social taboos by providing personal examples and create awareness in the Hindu society to embrace knowledge in place of undesirable traditions. To end the class divide was their main agenda. But most of these were individual examples rather than groups.
2. *Radical Reformists:* This group consisted of people who have come up based on English education including higher education on foreign soils and who desired to radically reform Hindu society in light of Western morals and rationalists ideals. The largest group under this classification was Brahmo Samaj, Prarthana Samaj and other individuals such as Dr. B.R. Ambedkar.
3. *Partial Reformers*: Under this group can be included all those organisations and individuals who were engaged in defending old traditions and ideals of Hinduism. This group will include organisations like *Arya Samaj,* Rashtriya Swayamsevak Sangh, and Vishwa Hindu Parishad, etc. Some of these have strong ideals and wish to make Hindu social polity. There looks to be stiffness in their approach as they suffer from the bias of neither tolerating nor acknowledging the existence of other forms of Hindu thoughts and practices. But not all of these need be associated with hardcore mentality.

4. *Conservatives*: Defenders of conservatism included those people who considered Hinduism superior to all other faiths. The followers of this approach find no fault with any Hindu tradition and are intelligent enough to find shortcomings with other faiths. These were people for whom a mere mention of *Pushpak Vimana* in Hindu scriptures was sure shot guarantee of Hindus having achieved great advancements in scientific fields ahead of others. They don't need to listen to argue that to make a Vimana one required to assemble parts, equipments, navigation systems and what not, things for which scriptures do not provide any reference anywhere. The organizations such as Sanatan Dharmarakshini Sabha and Ramkrishna Mission find grouping under this category. Vivekananda, the genius disciple of Ramakrishna Paramhansa, married universalistic idea of Swami Rama Krishna Paramhansa (his Guru) to strange idea of social service, is one of the most befitting examples of classification under this school. Followers of this category had a sort of pride and arrogance towards outsiders as they had Hinduism in awe as a most superior thought of the entire human history. Some followers of this thought can be found even today, largely at school and college levels, who strongly believe that ancient Hinduism were so advanced in natural sciences as modern West and credit Hinduism for most sophisticated firearms, television, airplanes and bridge technology. Slightly misplaced with hard facts but this spirit also contributed towards Hinduism finding its pride and lost relevance. (Farquhar, 1914)

Main Social and Religious Organisation during Raj

Among many exploitative features of Raj in India, there are silver linings that helped Hinduism to encourage many thinkers of that time to shred away isolation and come out against many social evils prevalent in contemporary Hindu society. Beginning of 19th century was pivotal that saw creative excitement of new hopes, new culture, dream of a new nation, revival of deep cultural values inspired by own luminous past. Many illustrious individuals emerged out of this exciting cultural spark. It is interesting to see that many of these individuals and movements have their connection with Bengal. It was precisely due to the fact that Bengal had significant influence that helped produced new English educated group with varying degree of European exposure.

Let us briefly look at some of the major organizations contributing to resurrection of Hinduism as an umbrella holding many different thoughts under its wide wing. The sequence taken below is guided by the period in which these got founded and not by any means by the comparative significance these hold in the resurrection process:

Brahmo Samaj

Raja Ram Mohan Roy initially founded it in 1828 after he returned to India after spending good amount of time in Europe. As a young boy he got mastery over Sanskrit and Hindu Philosophies at Banaras and learned Persian, Arabic and Qur'an at Patna. After settling down at Calcutta (now Kolkata) in 1814, he dedicated his remaining life to light the candle of social and religious reforms. He advocated Hindus for studying maths, philosophy, anatomy and other life sciences to obtain modern day education and develop wide view about its society. Himself a staunch Vedic follower, he was against Puranicl Hinduism focusing more on issues like puja, temples and pilgrimages. The social evils he worked for included *Sati*, Child Marriage, Polygamy, female infanticide and caste-based discrimination

The Samaj was based on doctrines of Upanishads and worked on propagating new tenets incorporating new developments. But after death of the founder, the membership got dwindled fast. Again, in 1839, Debendarnath Tagore, father of Rabindranath Tagore resurrected the doctrines under the new name of '*Tattwabodhi Sabha*'. The Sabha got Katha Upanishad translated into Bengali language helping it to become popular in that time. It was like modern day Vedanta adoptable to middle class Hindus. The Sabha also attracted Iswar Chandra Vidyasagar as its active member. Eventually, they came up with a new version of Vedantik Hinduism named 'Adi Dharma' which continued for many decades and eventually faded into obscurity in early 1900 when all energies of the entire nation got channelized towards Independence Movement.

Prarthana Samaj

Later in 1867, Atmaram Pandurangan formed the Prarthana Samaj in Bombay (now Mumbai). Their doctrine was also to encourage people to believe in one God and worship only one God. Here again, the members of the Samaj were intellectuals who advocated their preferred philosophy as the basis for reforms in social systems of Hindu society of that time of Maharashtra. The members met regularly and followed teachings of saints like Vitthal, Namdev and Tukaram. The Samaj later started working for cultural change and social reforms in entire western part of the subcontinent.

In their doctrines, Vedas were not to be taken as infallible. They called for abandoning class segregation and abolish child marriage. They also raised voice for encouraging female education and remarriage of widows and banning of *Sati*.

Arya Samaj

Arya Samaj was founded by Swami Dayanand, as a religious and spiritual organisation to promote a unique model of Hinduism incorporating some of the original core values of Vedic Dharma. These included belief in One Supreme Almighty, Vedas as infallible scriptures, rejection of idol worship, holding of havans as important rituals, and equality of all followers of the religion. In addition to the religion, the Samaj worked a lot for many issues of social reforms including empowerment of women, protection of cow from slaughter, etc. Swami Dayanand is known to denounce much of contemporary Hinduism, which, in his opinion, has got corrupted, and directionless due to polytheism, idolatry and many superstitions and narrow beliefs together with stranglehold of *Brahmin* class on sacred lore of religious practices. His religion was in form of pure Vedas and all his efforts were aimed at reinstating the Dharma of Vedas in its purity.

Since beginning, the Samaj has stood for cultivating strong ethical and moral values as well as advocacy of peaceful coexistence of all human beings. The Samaj has unwavering devotion to universal truth and promoted love, justice, righteousness towards all irrespective of race, caste, and creed and follows the principles as espoused in the Vedas. Swami Dayanand was a profound Sanskrit scholar and firm believer in Vedic ideologies. He was also the first person to talk about "Swarajya" a motto, which was later promoted by Lokmanya Tilak on political level. Called as one of the makers of modern India, Swami Dayanand established many Vedic schools even before founding *Arya Samaj* in 1875.

He also communicated closely with Brahmo Samaj and found many similarities but his firm belief in Vedas supremacy was so uncompromising that he could not be a part of Brahmo Samaj. Later, the Samaj activated a lot of people to contribute towards reforms through education. Even today, one can find so many educational institutions under the "Dayanand Anglo Vedic (DAV) Society".

Rama Krishna Mission

The mission was part of Vedanta movement and was founded in 1897 as philanthropic voluntary organization by yet another great son of India, Vivekananda. The Mission had focused on providing health care, help in disaster relief, rural management, tribal welfare, elementary education and higher education besides Vedic Hinduism. The people contributing their might in running such a huge organization included hundreds of ordered monks and thousands of householders dedicated to the path of Karma Yoga of Swami Vivekananda. Born in 1863, Vivekananda became a key figure in introducing Indian Philosophy of Vedanta and Yoga School to western World. His world famous speech of 1893 at Parliament of World Religions, Chicago has been credited as a milestone in bringing ancient Indian Philosophies and religious theories to the attention of whole world. His works have certainly contributed a great deal in showing the world about Hinduism. His works also inspired lot many youth of the time to wholeheartedly stand for nationalism under Colonial rule.

Rashtriya Swayamsevak Sangh (RSS)

Founded by Keshav Baliram Hegdewar in 1925 with Headquarter at Nagpur, the organization took up its goal to reunite all Hindus by rising above caste differences with an objective of making India a Hindu Rashtra. RSS has character building of the youth at the core of its ideology to make them dedicate their life for the cause of making India a strong nation with proud national identity. It is generally branded as right-wing, charitable and educational and volunteer organisation. Based on its strong principles, many important people of their generation as Veer Sawarkar and Bhim Rao Ambedkar got influenced by RSS. Later this ideology got identified with political ambitions, which came to be known as Hindutva.

Besides above mentioned few, there are many more individuals and groups who worked for social reformation in late 19th and early 20th centuries riding on ancient Hindu philosophies. Sri Aurobindo (1872-1950) a nationalist, philosopher, poet, and spiritual thinker developed 'Internal Yoga', a special method of spiritual practice. Ramana Mahershi (1879-1950) who got his enlightenment at the young age of sixteen years practised and preached that silence was the purest form of reality. He turned out as an outstanding Hindu preacher with a wide following. Swami Sivananda (1887-1963) was another Hindu spiritual guru who worked on Yoga and Vedanta schools of philosophies after studying Medicine and working as a Physical for many years under Britishers. Later he took to monasticism and founded Sivananda Ashram at Rishikesh. Under this *Ashram*, the society named Divine Life Society spread his philosophy through its many centres spread all over the globe.

Other Great Indian Teachers

Swami Ram Tirtha (1873-1906) was one of the first Hindu teachers who started lecturing about Vedanta through a series of lectures in different parts of America. He popularised these teachings under 'Practical Vedas'. He also worked to get many scholarships in America so that students from India could come to America for studies in many fields. After his academic achievements, he opted life of a sanynasi under direct influence of Vivekananda. In India he worked on the theme of education for women and children of poor families.

Paramhansh Yogananda (1893-1952) was another great Indian teacher who is credited for popularising Indian ancient thoughts in America. Yogananda became a close disciple of Swami Muktananda Giri in Calcutta and learned his Sadhana under his close watch while pursuing formal college education. He was inspired by his Guru to move to America for spreading the Sanatan Dharma teachings under what he called 'Kriya Yoga' techniques. Before going to America and establishing 'Self Realization

Fellowship', he established a boys school in India at Dihika, West Bengal where he combined modern education with Yoga training and spiritual ideals in a residential environment.

Yogananda spent his later life in America from 1920 onwards where he established many centres for popularising Kriya Yoga to help achieve understanding of universe being a cosmic motion picture by God where human beings are just actors to perform as destined in the divine play. Combining some Buddhist values with Vedic ideas, he preached that human sufferings were rooted in wrong identification by the actor with the role assigned. Over the years, Yogananda achieved phenomenal success and his centres are still active spreading 'Kriya Yoga' teachings and techniques through on site and on line courses.

Another great name in the series of Indian thinkers and promoters in academic world of 20th century is of Dr. Sarvpalli Radhakrishnan (1888-1975). In addition to be a great scholar of Vedanta, he developed detailed understanding of Western Philosophy and thereby created a bridge between East and West in very acceptable manner. He is accredited with translating all major Upanishads in modern English with his commentary where he defined and defended the ancient spiritual strength of Hinduism. His detailed commentary about Gita is another great service to Vedanta philosophies. He had a very lengthy writing career helping Hinduism create its respected place on world map of religions. He belonged to *Advaita* (Non-*dualism*) school of Vedanta philosophy of Adi Shankaracharya.

Radhakrishnan hierarchy of religions is well-known and his "Hinduism" accepts all religious notions as facts and arranges them in the order of their more or less intrinsic significance. The worshippers of the Absolute are the highest in rank; second to them are the worshippers of the personal God; then come the worshippers of the incarnations like Rama, Krishna, Buddha; below them are those who worship ancestors, deities and sages, and the lowest of all are the worshippers of the petty forces and spirits. Later he got known for championing the cause of education and nationalism and went on to become first Vice President of free India.

33 Hinduism and Independent India

During first half of 20th century, people from across India got involved in the struggle for Independence from Colonial Rule of Great Britain. All types of energies got diverted to mobilize protests and demonstration to create civil disobedience so that the foreign rulers are forced to go back. Under the leadership of Congress and inspirations of Mahatma Gandhi, all castes and creed, religion and sectarian variations got galvanized to keep their differences aside and contribute their might to support for freeing the nation. People from all walks of life including social thinkers, religious leaders, educationists, professionals, even farmers and workers and all sorts of self employed people from all age groups contributed towards a single objective of freeing India. This did not leave much room for growth on any religious front. Hinduism was no exception and practically there was no worthwhile progress to write about.

To start with, Indian Muslims were also equal partner in this endeavour. For first two decades of the century, Muhammad Ali Jinnah, who was active member in Congress had also acquired prominent position in Muslim League, argued in favour of unity among Hindus and Muslims. But by 1940, his political ambitions forced him to change his stand and he also started to push his weight behind "two nations" theory. Leaving the political discussions away, suffice to say that 1947 saw independence for India and Pakistan came to existence which involved migrations of about 10 million people from one place to another, largest ever in human history, and more than half a million got killed in Hindu and Sikh vs Muslim violence on both sides of demarcated borders. The distrust between these communities had never reached to such heights before.

Most Hindus were obviously on Indian side and the political leadership decided to build a modern nation where people from all castes and religions were to live harmoniously with mutual respect, trust and with tolerance for each other's religious faiths. But it was not to be. Tragedies and violence between 1946 and 1948 destroyed many illusions of the Independent India's leadership under Pandit Jawaharlal Nehru. Mahatma Gandhi's death in 1948 proved to be a watershed moment in this respect. Sardar Patel had made all of 560 princely states, having special status under the partition, to be a part of India that put lid on any problem from their side. He also managed the situation with strong-arm tactics to quell opposition from people making linguistic and/or ethnic based claims for formation of states. Some people thought that good days are not far and new found freedom, democracy, new constitution and peace will enable progress on all fronts including religion. But it was not to be. The distrust between Hindus and Muslims never got eliminated. The demons that divided these two in pre independence period raised their ugly head again and India saw riots one after another, from one part of the country to another, killing a large number of people on both sides.

India, a subcontinent in size is a giant country but it had extremely diverse cultures where people have cohabited for millenniums in narrow proximity but have never merged. What is more interesting is that those original inhabitants have believed in having differing faiths without really getting worried. This diversity was never a roadblock in its unity. Even when Buddhism and Jainism emerged from within, people accepted them easily because Upanishad-based common philosophy and feeling of a well-accomplished civilization contributed towards national bonding and developed a revered tolerance as far as religious faiths were concerned. There was an undisputed sense of accommodating each other's desire and free will to pursue all sorts of religious dispensations.

But things had changed by now. The Hindu pyramid had *Brahmins* and *Kshatriyas* sitting on top but the largest proportion of the population consisted of the lower caste that, after independence, got divided into different connotations like "Backward Class" and "Other Backward Classes". The lowest of lower that were socially treated as untouchables due to their identification with unclean but necessary professions got segregated as "Scheduled Castes" while the *Adivasis*, the aboriginal people got clubbed under yet another list called "Scheduled Tribes". As if thousands of castes and sub castes (*jati*) which originated on the basis of blood purity, colour of skin and tradition of occupations was not enough, this further division of Hindu Samaj ended up in deep divides in the society and gave basis for demanding additional pie of government sponsored benefits like reservation in jobs and education.

Let no one think that the divides were there only among Hindus of India. The position of Christians and Muslims was not much better either. Muslims of India may appear monolithic to someone looking from far above but reality is far from this impression. To begin with, Islam came to India on coasts of Malabar and Coromandel where Muslims sailors settled soon after Islam came into existence in Arabia. These were well accepted and got absorbed in local population without many problems. Many others in South got converted to Islam from lower castes who were tired of their poor treatment by higher caste Hindus. But in North, Muslims are taken as invaders and identified with Turks and Mughals who have had strong association with tyranny and oppressions. But in reality, most Northern Muslims remaining in India after partition are also converts from lower castes who could not or did not want to part with their motherland even after Pakistan came into existence. There is but only a thin crust of Muslim population who can easily trace back their roots to foreign origin. Now, the caste-based segregation has persisted in converts even after conversion and their plight in terms of class-based segregation is as bad as Hindus.

Looking from another angle and leaving aside classification based on sects, schools of philosophy and practices followed, most Muslims in India are Sunnis with the exception of few from princely families of Shi'as (twelvers) and few Ismaeli Shi'as settled in West India. In yet another way of looking at Muslims, it is safe to accept their segregation between orthodox and heterodox being followers of Mosques and shrines respectively. Heterodox Muslims are extremely tolerant themselves and they and Hindus alike visit their shrines and saints. There worship tradition of Quawalli also is just like another way of Hindu Kirtan. But the orthodox people believe in one Prophet, one God and one Scripture to the exclusion of everything else. And this intolerance for multiplicity pitches them sometimes in conflict on religious level with Hindu practitioners. In addition, there are so many other reasons, such as, desecration of religious sites, indiscreet loud noise from places of worship, overlapping of festivals, cow slaughter, etc. which give rise to infrequent riots involving these two communities. The trust deficit refuses to die away even after so many decades after independence.

In addition to Hindus and Muslims, India has a lot of other religious minorities on the margin of Hindu world. To begin with we have Parsis (Zoroastrians) who were forced to flee at the downfall of Sassanid Empire at the hands of Islamic Arab conquerors. Than we have Christians who arrived here in first century after Christ with St. Thomas who were largely Evangelical, followed by new arrivals of Syrian Christians in 15th and 16th Century CE who are largely based in Kerala. These are largely Catholics and own their allegiance with Oriental Churches. Finally, we had third round of Christians arriving in India under English Raj who belong to 18th century Protestants. These are the people who resorted to mass scale conversions under patronage of the state and created direct animosity with oppressed Hindus of the time. Besides, we have a host of other smaller minorities that have culturally merged well with the original Indians and live in social harmony.

The crux of inter faith tensions prevailing in India of 20th century lie in a basic difference in approach of the practitioners of different faiths. Ancient India has been a land where changing the manner of worship does not change anything. Indian thought has accepted God to be capable of calling by different names by different people. The soil of India is said to have ingrained love and respect for all faiths and religious beliefs. But Islam and Christianity are based on One Prophet, One Scripture and One God. They proclaim loudly that other than the one suggested by their Prophet, there is no other path of salvation of the human soul.

These basic differences would have been overcome by now but the electoral politics at the root of democratic India encourages politicians to promote their vote banks. Divided society that India is, fuelling of religion, sect and caste based passions of poor electorate has been taken as the easiest route to secure a win by many political outfits ignoring the adverse impact on the unity of the people of this great civilisation. Lack of strong political wills on the part of statesmen governing Indian polity and petty election gains is the biggest bane of free India in terms of continued deep divide among various communities of the society.

This unfortunate situation results in serious disadvantage to Hinduism, the faith of most Indians. Coming out of one thousand years of foreign rules where the faith of majority got oppressed and infested with many evils, it was expected that the political leadership of the country will pay urgent and immediate attention to take concrete steps to promote the good parts of religion and will push out not so good practices and systems. Alas, Hinduism continues to suffer apathy and ignoring attitude by the state. Under the disguise of secularism, Hinduism stand completely ignored. Whatever little get done is based only on the initiative of hand full of individuals. It is unfortunate that even after over sixty years of independence there are no large-scale efforts to spread the basic knowledge of this great religious heritage. Our political leaders have done great injustice by not promoting pure and universal traditions of Hinduism. On the contrary, what they have allowed is to force Hinduism to stand in line of comparison with prophetic faiths of Islam and Christianity. It is like comparing large size continent with islands; comparing ocean with ponds; comparing most inclusive religion with most exclusive ones; comparison of most tolerant with absolute intolerant; comparison of most peaceful with astute violent; comparison of a library with a book; comparison of a beautiful and big garden with a single plant.

This apathy by Indian governments is not doing any good with the national aspirations of achieving its deserving position of leadership in the world in terms of financial powers, spiritual wisdom, political representation, social inclusiveness, advancements in cultural accomplishments, maintaining equilibrium with tradition and modernity, development and sustaining environment. Indian cultural richness can show way to the world in most challenges of the humanity at present or in future. The need is to enrich our real Sanatan Dharma concepts with its pure philosophy and harmonious inclusiveness. We should separate the ways of worship from human religion. Because any thing that divides can never be a religion.

India has lost couple of generations post its independence. But there is still time for making course corrections. If it can leave behind Puranic Hinduism of Temples and Deities, Mosques and Churches and create national awareness for the core of Sanatan Dharma, the eternal Human code of life, all Indian citizens will soon get united and prosper jointly. The feeling of "Vasudhaiva Kutumbkam" where the whole world is to be treated as a single family has great power and relevance today than ever. But to inculcate that, Indians have to forget their immediate affiliations in terms of cast, sect, creed and way of worship and connect to the Sanatan values for peaceful coexistence in harmony with nature and focusing on internal peace and prosperity and channelise all their energies for fighting with ignorance, lack of wisdom and aligning with the cosmic powers through spirituality.

Can it be done? Or it is just a pipe dream? The answer to this will depend on how the Indians decide to respond individually and collectively in future. But outside India one can see many positive developments for concepts of Sanatan Dharma where many people with clear thinking and open-minded approach are increasingly accepting and appreciating the values that Hinduism has been so proud of. And this is precisely the subject matter of our next section dealing with global spread of Hinduism.

34

Global Spread of Hinduism

Many a times, past is known to hold indications for future. Until as late as 1700 CE, Hinduism had remained strong in areas far and wide from India. It was a major force in Indonesia, Cambodia and Vietnam in the East and up to Iran on the West. So, global relevance and dimensions are nothing new to Hinduism. It was only later when it came under total siege of foreign powers that it started contracting from many areas of its influence.

Since beginning of 20th century, one can identify traces of Hinduism starting its positive influence on the spiritual psyche of many people in Europe and especially in America. It is easy to see that so called industrial and financial development pushes humanity towards materialism and that is seen creating erosion of traditional values of these developed societies. Materialism leads people to rely on external inducements and the doses required for stimulation keep increasing to experience same kind of excitement. This leads to emptiness on inner planes forcing people to see through that the external stimulation are not the real answers. It is at that stage that they feel natural inclination to move towards alternate solutions, therapies and such other options. It is somewhat similar to the historical trend where people have been inventing new Gods when the earlier Gods stop meeting newer expectation of newer followers challenged by newer space of their existence. To my mind, this is how elements of Hinduism, albeit in bits and pieces, started attracting attention of Western World around middle of 20th Century.

Yoga can be identified as the first such element connecting with America followed by meditation. Vedantic Philosophy kept touching American bases through many teachers that started arriving in America in increasing numbers since 1965 themselves. During last 50 odd years, Yoga and Meditation have spread to all cities and towns of America at such a fast pace and a good portion of American population is connected with it in one or the other way. The penetration of these systems is best explained by Dr. David Frawley's speech (delivered in Hyderabad in 2010) excerpts about his town in South Western Desert area and I quote *"with population of about 100,000 they have 65 Yoga teachers, 20 odd Meditation Centers and the number of devotees arriving to listen Ma Anandmayi at her annual congregation crosses the count of 5000"*. Any one travelling to towns of America can say with confidence that these numbers are no exaggeration as similar trends are visible in most parts in entire America.

In fact, spreading of Yoga and its popularity in America has outpaced the same in India by several notches. To borrow the terms from Car Industry, today America has vintage versions, Indian-American versions, Pan American versions, cross-over versions, hybridized versions, specialized versions, and localized versions. The variety of Yoga available in America includes Pure Yoga, *Raja Yoga,* Hath Yoga, Bikram's Hot Yoga, Ashtanga Yoga, Iyenger Yoga, Anusara Yoga, Restorative Yoga, Jivamukti Yoga, Prenatal Yoga, Ananda Yoga, Integral Yoga, Kundalini Yoga, Power Yoga, and Shivananda Yoga. And, as the names suggest, some of these are no more addressing to physical health issues as was the case couple of decades earlier.

Increasingly, one comes across spiritual aspect of ancient Yoga getting increasingly assimilated in the Yoga practices in America. Most of these centres all across are manned largely by local instructors or trainers and some of whom are thoroughly well versed with all ancient aspects of Yoga practices and its Philosophy. As per one estimate, the number of people in America practising Yoga in one or the other form exceeded 20 million in 2010. (Dr. Christoper Chapple's article dated 29 June 2010).

The basic reason of Yoga gaining popularity is its being soulful alternative to the otherwise mechanical life style of people in general. It is proven fact that capitalistic life had devoid them from the tranquil balance among body, mind and life. Yoga helps them connect with themselves and offers consolation hideout or retreat. As more people in other countries go down that very lane of materialistic development, they will also get automatically attracted to Yoga.

Initially, Yoga came to America without any direct reference to its embedded roots in Hinduism and many practitioners didn't even know its connection with India or Hinduism. But increasing presence of Indian diaspora, trends of globalisation, India's own place at international scene, arrival of many teachers from India, training of many instructors at Indian institutions, have all contributed to a situation where Yoga's proud connectivity with ancient Hinduism promotes both India and Hinduism. Baba Ramdev is one of the contemporary popular instructors. Yoga certainly is a worldwide phenomenon already and stands out as the single most visible globally accepted feature of Hinduism as on date. So what if global Yoga has obscured its roots to Hinduism directly. Slowly and steadily, practitioners are bound to see through its origin source and shall get attracted to other equally important parts of Sanatan Dharma.

Sizable migration of Indian origin families, post relaxation of migration in 1965, from as far as Fiji, South Asia, South Africa, Trinidad, Kenya, UK, Uganda has taken their population in America to over 20 lacs which is close to one per cent of total population. They are well spread and have arranged construction of over 200 temples already and some of these temples will easily find place among some of the largest Hindu temples any where in the world. These temple complexes contribute a lot for spreading Hindu practices of worship besides working as centres for all types of cultural activities including classical music and dance, festival celebration, marriage and other rites and such other aspects of devotional and symbolic Hinduism. Hindus are one of the best educated and financially well off religious minority of America behind only the Jews. Average earnings of Hindus in America are pegged at two times of average earnings of Christians. Further, education standards of American Hindus continue to outpace others even in new generations. These all are factors towards positive environment for faster growth of Hinduism in America.

Besides the religion followers, important aspect is that an increasingly larger population of America is getting inclined towards some of the major tenets of Hinduism. For example, about one fourth of all Americans do believe in concept of reincarnation. The concept of Karma is yet another great example which is very easily accepted by Americans. One comes across many times where people may not relate these concepts directly to Hinduism. But if one has to put two critical facts together, one can clearly visualise the future of Hinduism in America. Firstly, about 25 per cent of Americans do not follow the religion of their birth. Secondly, they are getting connected with the concepts of Yoga for health and spirituality, meditation as an internal peace and salvation, karma to get inspired to do good to others and reincarnation as an universal truth. Thirdly, Hinduism is the religion getting the largest number of voluntary converts from other religions in America. And lastly, one hardly finds a Hindu leaving his religion and adopting some other religion, exceptions apart.

Couple of decades back some aspects relating to Hinduism were also attracting some adventurous natured Americans. This was the time when many in West knew Hindu religion as a plethora of faiths riddled with polytheistic, magical, fertile, erotic and violent aspects more than its positive sides. These included aspects like Goddess Kali. She was invoked and adopted by countless modern Pagans in America, sometimes with little to no knowledge of the religion or culture she sprung from. Than we had *Tantra* infatuating some people in early 20th century who wanted to develop their own cults for sexual freedoms aimed at ecstasy based on Tantrik practices and doctrines from India. *Kama Sutra* is yet another tool used by few to popularize its sexual positions as if that is what *Kama Sutra* was all about. These aspects were surely used by people in non-religious exploitations but they did harm to Hinduism. Those were the days when the Hippies were experimenting with their unusual ways and wanted to experience satisfaction by going down every possible lane, good or bad. But with increasing spreading of true Hindu concepts through teachers and preachers and after the Act of 1965 opening door for large scale immigration of Hindus to the land of opportunities, these concepts showing Hinduism in a negative or exotic manner, got pushed back from the major part of American systems. Today, there is very appreciative environment for Hinduism and Hindus, which augur well for further expansion of Hinduism in America.

So it is clear that key Hindu concept of Yoga has already acquired pan global status and that increasingly Americans are becoming Hindus at least ideologically as the basic concepts of karma, dharma, reincarnation, originating exclusively from Hinduism, are percolating indelibly into the American psyche. Much of their present day thinking revolves around finding a perfect balance among life, body and mind. This yearning for a balance is bound to draw them to Hinduism as the way forward as Hinduism alone is the reply for such a balance, that is, if it exists. While Christian proselytism is known to prey on the poor and the ignorant all around the world to covert for allurements and inducements, Hinduism is seeing conversion purely on voluntary basis and most new converts are well educated, urban, affluent and spiritually inclined Westerners.

The academic circle in America also is engaged in pious work of spreading good aspects of Hinduism and is credited for generating lots of good publicity and interest among newer generation from far across. As per Dr. Christopher Chapple's article dated 29 June 2010 placed at patheo.com, there are more than four hundred Professors trained as specialists in India who are currently teaching at various Universities in America. These scholars are generally trained in Sanskrit and other modern Indian languages and have extensive field experience in India. Scholars of Hinduism may be experts in the worship of Krishna or Shiva or Goddess or Yoga or in Vedanta or any other school of Indian Philosophies or even in ritual practices. All these Professors roughly teach Hinduism including other aspects of History, Geography, Philosophies and religious practices. By any standard of comparison, this kind of promotion of Hinduism in America is far better organised and practised than any where within India.

Pluralistic society with no established religion, Australia is another example seeing fastest growth of Hinduism in comparison to all other religions. As per their census of 2011, Hindus recorded a growth of 97 per cent in five years since 2006 with total population of Hindus in 2011 standing at 280,000. While, Australia is also experiencing migration of Indian origin people, there are new converts who are taking to Hinduism by choice. As per last census figures, as many as 17 per cent Hindus are born in Australia itself.

The spread of Hinduism in Ghana, a western African country is yet another example of great success in spite of no one pushing for Hinduism expansion. With about 70 per cent of population being Christian, Muslim is the second dominant faith there followed by Indigenous Africans. But as per census of 2010, Ghana had over 20,000 Hindus including about 2000 Indian migrants. The growth of Hinduism there is by locals adopting to it by choice. Indigenous people there find many of Hindu traditions reflecting their own basic traditions. Recent presence of many Hindu movements like Divine Life Society, ISKCON, Brahma Kumaris and Sri Satya Sai Baba has also helped people getting exposure of Hinduism. As per Kwesi Anamoah, National president of the African Hindu Temple of Ghana;

> *"Today there are 2000 to 3000 families worshiping in our temples which is a big increase from 24 people who participated in the first ever training camp in 1976 to become disciples. We have not achieved it by winning the souls as other religion do, but we have attracted people into practice of Hinduism simply by the lives we lead. Our lives shine in the community to attract people"*

One person who studied Vedanta at Sivananda Ashram, Rishikesh and became an African Swamy and started Hindu Monastery of Africa (HMA), now has seven centres running in Ghana and one each at neighbouring countries of Togo and Ivory Coast. Such small candles are going to slowly light more and more candles to help the darkness disappear and replace universal love and peace.

35

Sanatan Dharma: The Real Hinduism

Real Hinduism is synonymous to Sanatan Dharma. But because of its intrinsic nature Sanatan Dharma cannot be straight jacketed into any specific definition. To understand real essence of Sanatan Dharma, let us look at the literal meaning of these two words. Sanatan means eternal, universal, abiding, ever present, unceasing, natural and enduring the fundamental principles behind this marvelous universe like the Law of Karma and Karma Sansara. Similarly, Dharma, as we have already seen, means harmony, righteousness, compassion, natural law, divine conformity, cosmic norm, wisdom, purest insight or law of being or moral duty. Putting these together, Sanatan Dharma denotes a dharma applicable to all people, at all times, inherent in and inclusive of all, loving to all and excluding none, both immanent and transcendent, the whole and the parts all together. And this is the real Hinduism, a fact that needs to be understood by many Hindus themselves.

In its normal nomenclature, Sanatan Dharma can be taken as a synonym for the universal teachings of Hinduism which remain relevant at all times and transcendent all historical changes, which seek to unite humanity as one large family, which overlooks all petty differences like class, caste, sects, genders, regions and includes all pure virtues for peaceful existence of all living beings and entire environment.

While Hinduism has been Sanatan Dharma's main experience, it does not mean that it is limited to only Hinduism or India. We must not forget that Sanatan Dharma has many of its reflections in many other religious thoughts of cultures in the past. A deep reading of cultures such as Egyptian, Babylonian, Greek, Celts, Persian and Chinese will clearly display that many aspects of the universality and inclusiveness identified with Sanatan Dharma have been in existence out there as well. But it is to the credit of India that Sanatan Dharma took deeper roots and continued to remain in practice all through. It is not out of place to say that before the emergence of prophetic religions on the radar of humanity, all cultures did embrace eternal Dharma in varying proportions but it got trampled and gave way to other thoughts. But Hinduism has survived itself as it never remained far away from its deep roots embedded in Sanatan Dharma.

One can come up with a question as to why Sanatan Dharma in India allowed diverse forms to get created as vitiated versions of universality? We must understand that Sanatan Dharma, by its very nature, is against uniformity as uniformity results in some sort of artificiality. It always promoted diverse localisation by the people that it served. We can appreciate even in today's context that any thing to become universal will have to allow adaptation suitable for local digestion. Again to the credit of India that in spite of emergence of variety of forms over the years, the soul of entire Hinduism has firmly remained Sanatan. And this very quality necessitates that India and its people recognize their responsibility to take up the role of global gurus for guiding the world to seek spirituality by firmly remaining grounded to Sanatan Dharma.

Every time we talk of Hinduism, we must keep the Sanatan Dharma perspective in mind so that we perceive the right angle. Hinduism is like a great landscape of rivers, forests, snow-clad mountains and many more things in between. But how can such vast scenery be captured in a single camera image? Best of photographer will never be able to capture such a vast view in the best of best camera that he may have known to exist. So, best of best single image will show just a glimpse of the entire reality. To capture the entire scene, he must look at each of the part from close range and then only he would appreciate the switching over from one aspect to another in any meaningful manner. Unfortunately, many people do that injustice to Hinduism as they wish to put it in comparison with such other Prophetic religions, which do not offer such large view and are capable of getting fully captured in a single shot.

Having been through the entire historical journey of this great tradition, let us now try to look at its core by ignoring unwanted and unrequited issues on its periphery. Hinduism has been recently dragged into controversies by only discussing about some limited aspects either deliberately or under some gross ignorance. So, let us look at it in its purest form once again. When we say Hinduism, it is not to be looked at in same manner that we look at Islam or Christianity. The word Hindu may get used as religion alone. But Hinduism, the subject matter of our study in this book, is far wider in scope and far more comprehensive in terms of human existence on this earth.

> *The word Hinduism, every time we read it, refers to the eternal code of human conduct; that which has no beginning and no end; that which is firmly rooted in nature and honours all aspects of natural world including mountains, river, rocks, trees, flowers, birds and consider them all as sacred and holy; which has completely pluralistic approach and accepts and appreciates all methods of worshiping the God in all its aspects or human imaginations without the exclusion of any one; which does not believe only in one book but considers every word and every letter as a guide for proper human behaviour; which does not require any one to be a middleman between a human and his God but encourages every man to contemplate his own inner self and connect with the God of his choice and imagination; which prompts human to seek his own experience of divinity rather than just blindly follow experience of some other human being; one which accepts multiplicity of beliefs being true and which does neither persuade or dissuade anyone to change his belief under any fear or favour; and one which considers every human as a separate soul by itself with no difference between long or short, thin or fat, black or white, Eastern or Western, male or female.*

Besides multiple forms of worship, Hinduism includes Ancient Culture, Philosophies, Literature, and Principles of Eternal Dharma. Looking at Hinduism from the narrow meaning of only way of worship is the greatest injustice one can do to this longest practised live human way of life. Methods of worship are temporary as they change every few hundreds of years. Hinduism is not only about how we seek our God. As we have many Gods, we also have as many ways of seeking to that. Actually, Hinduism also accepts as a good Hindu to any one who does not have any God. How many of us are confident that we know a little bit of our great Dharma in all its spectacular expanse in terms of its long traditions, its teachings and teachers, its never rejecting attitude of all aspects of human religious aspirations, its philosophy of coexisting in harmony with everything alive or dead on this earth, its commitments to non-violence, its spiritual traditions, use of all types of imagery as aspects of God, its beliefs in all sorts of rituals as means of maintaining disciplined life at different stages of life, its techniques and approaches to meditation to connect with the core of humanity well within our own hearts and its practices of *Ayurveda* and Yoga to ensure a perfect healthy balance between mind, body and soul.

I have no hesitation in assuming that, unfortunately, most Hindus themselves may not have looked at Hinduism with so much of clarity. Most of its own followers have not been able to secure required exposure to understand it with all its vastness. Our schools and colleges have refrained from touching any subject under the disguise of secularity; our parents have been rather sucked up in normal life challenges for securing comforts of life for us ahead of teaching us about our great ancient traditions; and until two generations before, the entire energy of all our countrymen was in any case dedicated for securing independence from foreign rulers. Yes, we have gone through these challenges but the time has come for each one of us to do our bit of reconnecting with the best of principles enumerated by our learned sages.

Let us not follow any thing blindly neither keep our eyes closed. I think we owe it to our coming generations to let them look at this grand mosaic with all its colours and reflections. Surely, this understanding will only widen their outlook to everything around; will encourage them to gain advancements in all fields requiring human intelligence; will ward them of all pitfalls that transient attractions of material world are only false shadows and are not to be pursued for long; that we as human have a moral duty to find our spirituality in our own way; that a person bestowed with the wealth of wisdom is the real super rich guy.

Undoubtedly, if we fail to expose them with this treasure, outsiders will take over this also and that day Hindus of India will be the real losers.

Hinduism offers many tools and components that need to be understood and practised for adopting and adhering to this way of life in its true sense. These include *mantras, asanas,* rituals, pilgrimages, meditations, symbols, mind and body balance, astrology, astronomy, spiritual science, and the most scientific language Sanskrit. It is the way that is ever inclined for absorbing and reinventing new innovations all the time. This attitude of reinvention and smooth adaptation with changing landscape of its surroundings has helped it to survive for over 5000 years of history and kept it relevant at every step. In its long journey, Hinduism has witnessed many other religious and cultural systems that failed to invent and adopt and faced wiping out all together. Being an open-ended theology, any new finding at any stage and in any stream is never at risk of crossing its path. Compare it to some other prophetic monotheism faiths that are time and again confronted with new discoveries challenging their basic assumptions or new social trends standing in their way with mouth wide open.

Speaking spiritually, as per Hinduism, the whole human life is supposed to be a unique journey where the individual soul remains in search to reach the goal of Self-realisation. And Self-realisation is what leads to realisation of God or, to say in other words, union with the divinity. Hinduism alone offers multiple choices of the tools or aids or inspirations that may be required by the soul which is aspiring for that union with the divine. Hinduism provides that the karmas one accumulates with each of its thoughts and actions determine the time taken or lives required for such Self-realisation. The array of choices on offer for the spiritual journey is observed to be the most attractive proposition influencing most new converts from the western world, who take up Hinduism on their own accord. Unlike the religions of book, there is no one in Hinduism who is there to encourage or cajole or initiate any one for adapting to it. On the contrary, many Hindus still suffer from trust deficit with non-Hindus and during their interactions with outsiders, Hindus most observant reaction is a very defensive approach, as they generally fear attack from Non-Hindus.

Sanatan Dharma encompasses a rich treasure of literature created over centuries, which is larger than written material available for any other scientific stream until today. This speaks volumes of contributions made by learned Rishis, Munis, Yogis, Philosophers, Scholars, Thinkers, and Teachers. The concepts contained all through its great literary heritage have been refined with utmost collective wisdom of these great souls. Against this, other religions came up with collection of single Saint of their beliefs with the writings responding to prevailing conditions of that very specific time and place of history. Certainly, the legacies of Hindu scriptures do not deserve to be downgraded to get compared with others. While Sanatan Dharma constantly talks of inclusivity and acceptance for all, other religions focus on rejections. Such rejections are also not based on logics or philosophies but simply because their Book said so. Hinduism encourages each person to constantly remain in search of Truth by knowledge or actions or devotion or Yoga but other religions simply tell the individual to follow what is told.

Similarly, Sanatan Dharma recognises that besides many active organs, the human body is blessed with five distinct sense cognitive organs and a rational mind. Besides mind, it recognizes presence of a higher intuitive power called, *Buddhi* which needs to be accessed and applied along with mind, to search the Truth. This accessing of *Buddhi* using mind and body as tools is advised to be undertaken only in deep silence of meditation. Any person with sustained practice of meditation can access that and once accessed, this experience will provide a direct perception of ultimate Truth. Also that, every person has to find his own Truth, as truth found by some one else is not capable of helping you to reach your truth. Obviously, reaching to such truth depends on seeker's own capacity, capability, determination, and perseverance.

So the onus of leading his journey on the road to pursue his truth is centered in driver's own hand and while there are milestones and directions available for travelling all through the road, the reaching to destination will firmly remain with the endeavours of the seeker himself. Contrary to this, other popular religions make the whole process very simple and provide that any one can follow the truth by simply accepting teachings of the Prophet or seeking pardon for the sins committed. People having mind of their own can draw their conclusions about which systems looks more logical and likely to meet their aspirations i.e. by exploring your own or simply by following others.

Sanatan Dharma fundamentally believes in unity among all religious thoughts. People knowing about peaceful co-existence among Buddhism, Jainism and Hinduism in BC centuries can well appreciate this aspect. These home grown systems, which were always in competition to each other, have remained in active communication and continuously borrowed from each other and lend to each other with out any problem whatsoever. These are known to respect each other. It was common in those days for members in a single family to get influenced by one of these thoughts and individual members were practising these alternate systems under the same roof without any problem. Can one imagine that kind of inclusiveness in other major religions of today? Can one imagine the fate of marital bliss of an average family, just for general understanding, if a middle-aged husband is practitioner of Islam and his wife wishes to converts to Christianity and his adolescent son comes home and declares at the dining table that he is influenced by Hinduism and wishes to go to temple for puja? But among Hinduism, Buddhism and Jainism, this is precisely the way it was happening.

36 Challenges Being Faced by Hinduism

Global afflux of Hinduism is, however, only one side of the story. Journey of Hinduism is certainly not a bed of roses with only beauty and grace embracing it on its off take. There are many challenges and roadblocks standing tall to get resolved with urgency. Some of these are rather serious questions and are likely to shape its future course. The beauty of the situation, however, is that most of these challenges relate to the land of its own origin.

Apathy in Education

To begin with, entire academic spectrum in India is not paying due importance to exposure and growth of Hinduism through deep studies and researches in the realm of formal education. Leave aside special Universities focused exclusively on this great heritage, we don't even have general exposure on entire spectrum of Hinduism any time in his entire academic career of a student. Any level of our education system does not include the discipline of religious studies the way many Universities in West are known to have. A University course is just not a course by itself, it include Professors, evolving syllabus, research for study material, tracking of articles and books written, discussions, further writings and so on. It is a process, which certainly has a snowball effect.

As a result, most people engaged in entire religious spectrum including the priests of temples, are not well trained in a scientific manner. Whatever training they get, takes place only outside the University settings and which at best is equivalent to residential seminaries. Use of scientific methods for promoting religious studies will help our society in more than one ways. I am not at all suggesting such system for Hinduism alone. Let it be followed for all the religions under practice by Indian citizens. If proper academic system helps to promote all other streams of sciences why not expect the similar results for Religious Studies. Because if you don't study some thing, you lose the chance of helping it to flourish, exuberate, prosper and grow.

Lack of Public Debates about its Character

Hindus in particular have this pious responsibility to strongly work for enlarging the sphere of Hinduism. Will the future of Hinduism get limited to its ritualistic practices being followed in homes and temples? The reply to this question lies in hands of Hindu practitioners. Today, there is a greater need for Hindus to work on public character of Hinduism. No, it should not get left to appear only addressing to symbolism alone.

Hindus must make choices for initiating debates on all aspects of their religion/way of life. Ignoring or closing eyes from the stark realities will not help but harm the core of Hinduism. There is need to debate as to what our public values are and how do we rely on our traditional teachings and wisdom to shape our value system. Pushing the issues under carpet or leaving it for some one else will not help. Yes, Hindus have suffered immensely from gender bias, from castes divides, from social divides but so what? Shall we continue allowing past demons to remain ever stronger? Hindus will need to leave aside their individual focus and need to learn how to make use of their shared past to evolve public values and public behaviour.

Resurrection of Intellectual Discussions

Hindus have to share the blame that in recent past, they have been shying away from intellectual debates and discussions to reinvent Vedanta for the present day environment. Remaining limited to idols and temples and conducting pujas at home with half knowledge is not our total religious practice. We have to go back to our doctrinal contents to redefine and reinvest the new forms of our proven doctrines of past. Leaving Hinduism to only Temples and Pujas will surely result in losing relevance as a modern-day religion capable of providing credible alternatives to many people who look for rational, logical and philosophical religion to help them guide their day-to-day life and address to that natural spiritual hunger better than other religions around the block.

Focus on Whole rather at its Parts

Another problem arising is that most of the teachers of our time who are in any way engaged in proliferation or dissemination of Hinduism, end up taking some particular aspect of it as a personal branding and stop mid-way from connecting with it directly or completely. For example, all the teachers who got big ticket popular in India and abroad can be seen focusing on their own brand and not so much with Hinduism in totality.

They are all doing a great work for their own selected aspects but how much they could promote Hinduism in totality? This has resulted in a situation where in America you come across people appreciating a teacher but not knowing that what he practices is just another small module of Hinduism. As such Hinduism is looked down in many quarters while its individual parts get appreciated. Teachers and Preachers have to recognise that it is their obligation to also promote the big picture; after all, any part cannot be bigger than the whole.

Swamy Narain temples may be seen as somewhat exception to this rule as they show all sects of Hindus with their promoters and founders to help the visitor know about the total Hinduism spectrum in addition to the deities founded in the temple. All involved must desire more such efforts. Our learned teachers must be proud of universality of Hinduism concepts and traditions. Now, there should be no fear or mishmash as there is nothing to hide or be ashamed of.

Need for Combining Hinduism with Ayurveda, Vedanta and Astrology

Actually, the crux of all its challenges can be summarized in a single point as to how do we resurrect the great sense of Sanatan Dharma with its complete package involving the well-being of body and mind by *Ayurveda,* complicated but effective science involving astrological predictions under Jyotish, worship of Ishta Deva at house or temple to secure mental peace and guidance for refraining from bad karmas, widely examined multiple philosophies, alternate concepts of Karma Yoga/Gyan Yoga/*Bhakti* Yoga as promoted by Gita, exotic concepts of *Tantra, Mantra, Kundalini* and Chakras and what not. The fact that Hinduism alone offers unmatched inclusivity for all forms of worship, room for all sort of sects, all possible options to choose what suits one particular individual's own orientation for Self-realisation, in itself is a great portal for it to deserve whole hearted promotion so that more people benefit from this great tradition.

Forcing Support from Governments

Interestingly, Hinduism faces more challenges at its home than on foreign soil because all past governments in free India have remained completely apathetic rather than indifferent or nostalgic towards it. Under the disguise of being secular, most Indian politicians have done great injustice to not let its citizens know the great powers, which can be unleashed by proper propagation of this great tradition.

The argument is that they have many other priority areas seeking their attention and resources. Actually, the prevalent social tension and ignorance of the main strata of Indian population serves their political interests because change in status quo might make them less powerful and can make it more difficult for them to win elections. Just imagine if just *Ayurveda* is given a total boost for a decade or two. What impact it can have on rural health, on economy of all Himalayan states, on tourists arrival for alternate healing, on generating employment for teachers, practitioners, processors, laboratories, research centres. This is just one such example. Point is that promoting our own great tradition will only bring greater advantages than blindly following traditions of others. This kind of promotion is beyond individual's efforts. These kinds of changes require political will and commitment of national resources.

Promote Unity among all its Practitioners

Another well-accepted challenge before Hinduism is the lack of unity among its practitioners. The sectarian divisions, the caste based biases, the difference in methods of worship are some of the issues we have to accept as they are. But these have always been there and these have not come in the way of our unity. Again, going back to the basics of Sanatan Dharma as the way forward will remove all differences.

Concepts of the eternal Dharma are accepted and appreciated by all Hindus. They have to forget the sectarian variations and consider them as private matter away from public domain and come together to galvanize under Sanatan Dharma in its purest form where it has no disunity even with outside religions. Existence of some points appealing to some and not appealing to others is but an important feature of Dharma. This variation is to be celebrated and not confronted. Sanatan Dharma is the trunk of all subsequent branches which developed their own colours and shapes for their leaves and flowers. But our trunk is absolutely common and nourishes us all. Let us come down a bit from our leaves and flowers and assimilate upon this trunk.

Not to Shy Away from its Superiority

We also have to call spade a spade and deal with the situation accordingly. It is fine to say that all religions are same and they all teach good things. But wait a minute, all religions are not alike. Are all flowers are same? Are all foods same? Are all individuals same? If we have to compare on some very basic level, these all may be accepted as it is. But they have their own unique features, which make them special or ordinary. At deeper levels, we have to ask, what the purpose of religions is. Is it not to help seek individual's association with his divinity, with his God? But if one is told to follow the path of some great person from past and follow him blindly without even asking any question, is it not a case where freedom of individual's own experience is taken away? And if other religions prescribe that while there is one that does encourage the individual to experiment and choose the right suitable option, from very many, to seek the divinity, are they similar or not so similar? Hinduism is unique and must be accepted as such.

Promote its Unity on Collective Basis

Yet another major challenge for Hinduism is the missing sense of "Hindu Unity". Vedic path of spiritual progress offering great individuality and freedom to choose is the logic quoted behind Hindu's individualistic approach. But it has to change if Hinduism wishes to survive in future. Hindus have to learn from Muslims and Christians who have developed strong community feelings and are together when it comes to making political selection, opposing anyone writing against their faith, custom or any individual. Hindus have to learn to react in groups. Closing eyes from group working will create serious problems for sustaining its longevity. Pressure groups have a role to play. If a single Hindu cannot take part in a group, he or she can extend their support to some group.

To begin with, new generation people active on social media at least can start showing their resentment every time some media reports something against Vedic path or some politician comes in favour of some unreasonable point favouring others. It is sad that organisations like RSS and VHP are being disliked and written against by majority of Hindus forgetting how much important role they play for reducing the pressures that many other Muslim groups wish to exert. The lame duck attitude that Sanatan Dharma is ever lasting and will remain valid forever is like not learning anything from last 1200 hundred years of history. Should Hindus forget that their not being united allowed Turks, Mughals and English rogues to rule over all Hindus in their own land for such long period and should they forget that all the plundering of India done by those foreign looters. Lack of Unity can create similar situation again. Like all Muslims and Christians, Hindus must throw their political weight behind those politicians who have atleast strong Nationalistic attitude if not clearly Hindu religion.

Need for Shunning Caste and Creed differentiations

Hindus are unable to through their castes or immediate group for their identification. Even today, caste based divisions have not been thrown out of window. On all-important occasions like seeking marital alliance or seeking reservations, even young age Hindus are seen clinging to their immediate groupings. While it is true that every group must gain identity and must stand on its own but changed social conditions must be given a chance. World of today is different than earlier. In the past, local identities were important to secure benefits by working as pressure groups but today are the times of meritocracy. In a highly networked environment where most people are exposed to work and spend life in places far away from their places of birth, the clinging to groupings will not help in any way. Hindus must think as a Hindu first and then bring in their other identities for their public interactions.

Extend Protection to Weak and Suppressed

Hindus have a lesson to learn from others in terms of organising and extending protection to its poor or suppressed members. Donation and charities are considered very highly for bringing instant karmic dividends but options available today for such philanthropy are limited to temple "Dan Patras". But Hindu temples are not known for running socially useful programmes at all. And temples have never been considered favourably inclined towards the Dalits, backwards, untouchables, the *Adivasis* and those poor Hindus who deserve to be helped. This is the same part of Hindus that is prone to conversions in distress.

Other religions like Christianity come forward and offer inducements and allurements and get them converted out of Hinduism. Now Hindus are open for charity, do not lack resources but there are no proper organised instruments to connect the intention with delivery. Hindus philanthropy needs proper direction and some credible organisation with pan India spread need to take the lead to come up socially beneficial schemes to address Hindu poor. Looking for such help to only governments is never a solution for a democratic federal structure in India where average politician is not encouraged to have a longer than five year's horizon for implementing their schemes. Handfull of well oiled organisation operating in any area can bring a seechange in the positivity for Hindu religion and can have a far reaching impact.

Under such situation, it is but natural for an individual to look aside with the feeling that what can I do alone. But sea is made from collection of drops. Let each one of us contemplate as to what little can we do to secure, promote and preserve our great traditions for our next generations and some options will emerge. This is the least that we owe to our faith. Turning a blind eye will leave it orphaned. Most of us privately agree for individual and moral responsibilities of its practitioners but we are very weak when it comes to take some concrete steps. We must always remember that waiting for people like Adi Shankara or Vivekananda carry its own risk and is not a good option.

37

Future of Hinduism

These are great times for flourishing of traditions of Sanatan Dharma. Churches in America and Europe are going empty like never before. As per one estimate, around one fourth population of American Christians is disillusioned from the religion of their birth. Out of various Christian sects, the hardest hit are Catholics and Protestants. Evangelicals alone are seeing some growth in their following. But Christianity is clearly on decline throughout the world. Evangelicals are seeing additions of very poor and less educated segments of people from developing nations as it promises them with quick fix solution of salvation by simply seeking pardon from God. Such easy religion will prevent or promote evils or bad deeds, is any body's guess. Even in America, where they have one of their largest populations living, Evangelicals are seen as representing bad parts of American culture.

Islam has got its own identification with some unwanted elements and looking to what is happening in the heartland of Arabia, the place where Islam originated, it is not being looked as a system to provide answers for the challenges being faced by humanity in times to come. Then what is the solution? Where does one find hope and aspiration?

Before we jump to conclusions, let us look at what kind of requirements need to be addressed by the future global religion. It is because the requirements of today are much different than those of the past. Scientific progress achieved by humanity has raised curtains from many unknown and unresolved surroundings. The basic attitude of present day person to entire religious scenery is far open and subtle as well as meticulous. The terrifying mysteries of wonders attached with unseen and unknown God is a thing of past. But human beings are essentially spiritually oriented and still aspire to find meaning and value from human life.

Gallup, which is a world-renowned company engaged in conducting surveys, has been conducting regular survey in America asking for people's belief in God. The percentage of Americans having this faith in God was 96 per cent in 1944, and went up to 98 per cent in three surveys carried out from 1954 to 1967. But the percentage has come down to 92 per cent in 2011. As per the summary of the 2011 survey prepared by Frank Newport in his article dated 3 June 2011, there is yet another important trend noticed which relates to significant drop of the respondents in their identification with a particular religion and it says "*Other indicators of religiosity in America have shown more dramatic changes in recent decades, most significantly Americans' self-identification with a religion. At some points in the 1950s, almost all Americans identified themselves with a particular religion. In recent years, more than 1 in 10 Americans tell survey interviewers they have no formal religious identity.*"

The points to note, based on the reputed survey findings of last 60 odd years, are (a) more than 9 out of 10 still believe in God but only 9 out of 10 such people identify themselves with any particular religion. In other words, around 10 per cent of population has come out from their original religion. This trend clearly points out to the void, which is there to be absorbed by a better option.

Let us try to list out what expectations normal person of today has from his religious faith. Let us keep the age until adolescence away as parental influences operate more until formative years as against logics and own thinking. As a young man, he or she is engaged in running his family where his issues are selection of mate for life together, births and deaths in the family, child rearing, schooling, holidays, health, sports and work and life balance. He is looking for a system that guides him to bring sanctity to his thoughts and actions, help him achieve his spiritual aspirations by offering right kind of solutions as per his individualistic orientation, help them for living a stress-free life, help them develop accommodating approach with mutual respect, help them stand as ideals for their next generation, help them avoid conflict in marital blessings, makes them stronger for avoiding all types of violence, help them collaborate with all others, and finally help them in perceiving God's divine and overarching presence in their life.

The concept of flattening of world and working in boundary-less environment also require the future religion to promote world peace, reduction of all sorts of conflicts and violence, harmony between progress and environment. And all this is required to be met without losing individual identities. All these approaches must be universal in character and global in reach.

If above assessment of individual and social needs is accurate then Hinduism is poised for secure future because it is the only religion, which has depth and dimensions to address all those future requirements. Sanatan Dharma in terms of its ideas, principles, teachings, knowledge, values, practices and wisdom is the only right choice for a safe and secure future for human to remain on this planet for long time. The philosophies of Hinduism are treasures of humanity and are fully capable to meet aspiration of people from all regions, races, languages and orientations.

Let us drive ourselves to real Hinduism as quickly as possible. It is not enough that one was born as a Hindu. It will be meaningful only when the born Hindu adopts real Hinduism with full knowledge and conviction and start living those ideals in everyday life. Other religions have grown by resorting to mass conversions as the basis. But Hinduism has to rely first on real converts out of its own followers and it is not going to be easy as conversion to real Hinduism will require lots of efforts and understanding. But if we strongly believe in its intrinsic strengths and if we are committed to uphold the values preached by Sanatan Dharma, we have to be ready to go that extra mile and inculcate all these values in our own lives and educate our next generations about the same.

Our generation is better off than earlier ones as most of us have taken birth in an independent India and our normal life achievements have secured better futures for us as compared to our predecessors. Therefore, it is our responsibility to pass on this rich heritage to next generation with better value addition, with better understanding, with better conviction and with better confidence that ours is the right culture and traditions for future.

Surely, our pluralist traditions offer lots of choices to be made but better knowledge always leads to better choices. But better choices need not be simpler choices. Plural choices offered by our traditions enhance our obligation to make informed choices. Let pluralism not result in poor choices and let it not suggest us to do nothing. Let us work for our self and our next generations to understand and build on the rich past. Let us teach our next generations to practise Sanatan values to help them develop capacity to stand against negatives in life. Let us teach them ability to see through difficulties in their life using the prism of virtuous path shown by Sanatan Dharma, the real Hinduism. That will surely lead us towards more fulfilling human life and make us strong to face questions of Why are we here? What shall we do? and Where do we go from here?

Because what we do today will impact the future of Hinduism tomorrow.

Bibliography

A Brief History of Hindu Temples. (2000). From sanathanadharma.com.
Agarwal, M. (n.d.). *The India Renaissance*. Retrieved 2014 from historydiscussions.net.
Armstrong, Karen, *A History of God*, Ballantine Books, New York, 1993.
Armstrong, Karen, *Buddha*, Phoenix, 2000.
Armstrong, Karen, *The Great Transformation: The Beginning of Our Religious Traditions*, Anchor Books, A Division of Random House INC, New York, 2006.
Burton, S. R. (1883). *sacred-texts.com*.
Chapter, I. S. (2012). *Mystery of Saraswati River*. Retrieved May 2014, from Institute of Scientific Research on Veda web site: www.serveveda.org.
Chopra, Deepak, *Buddha a Story of Enlightenment*, HarperCollins, 2007.
Compilation of *The Complete Works of Swami Vivekananda Volumes 1 to 9*, 11th Edition, 1989.
Doniger, Wendy, *The Hindus: An Alternate History*, The Penguin Press, New York, 2009.
Dubois, Abbe J.A., *Hindu Manners, Customs and Ceremonies*, Rupa & Co., 2006.
Easwaran, Eknath (introduced and translated by), *The Bhagawad Gita*, Nilgiri Press, 2007.
Easwaran, Eknath (introduced and translated by), *The Dhammapada*, Nilgiri Press, 2007.
Easwaran, Eknath (introduced and translated by), *The Upanishads*, Nilgiri Press, 2007.
Frawley, D. (n.d.). *The Aryan-Dravidian Controversy*. Retrieved from Dharma Universe LLC websites: www.hindunet.org.
Gadkari, J. (1996). *Society and Religion: From Rigveda to Puranas*. Mumbai: Popular Prakashan Pvt Ltd.
Gandhi, V. R. *The Systems of Indian Philosophy*. In D.K. Dixit (Ed.). Sri Mahavira Jaina Vidyalaya, Bombay.

Keller, Warner, *The Bible As History*, William Morrow And Company, INC, 1981.

Luce, Edward, *In Spite of The Gods: The Strange Rise of Modern India*, Little, Brown, 2006.

MacDonell, A. A. (1900). *A History of Sanskrit Literature*. D. Appleton & Company, New York.

Marchand, Peter, b. o. (n.d.). *Sanatan Society*.

From www.sanatansociety. org.

Radhakrishnan, S., *The Hindu View of Life*, HarperCollins, 2009.

Radhakrishnan, S., *The Principal Upanishads*, HarperCollins, 2011.

Rao, S. (n.d.). *Tantra-Agama*. (S. Rao, Producer) Retrieved from sreenivasaraos.com: www.sreenivasaraos.com.

Rodwell, J.M. (Translator from the Arabic), *The Koran*, Phoenix, 1994.

Sen, Amartya, *The Argumentative Indian*, Penguin Books, 2006.

Society, A. (n.d.). *Jati: Caste System in India*. From www.asiasociety.org.

Sonawani, S. (n.d.). *Ramayana: A Story Behind Story!* From sanjay-sonawani.hubpages.com.

V.J. (n.d.). *Ahimsa in Indian Religious Traditions*.

From www.hinduwebsite.com.

V.J. (n.d.). *Know All About Shaivism*. From www.saivism.net.

Vedant Tirth, Acharya, *Rigveda* (in Hindi), Manoj Publications, 2008.

Vedant Tirth, Acharya, *Yajurveda* (in Hindi), Manoj Publications, 2008.

Vedas, I.O. (2012). *Mystery of Saraswati river*. sarveveda.org.

Wikipedia. (n.d.). *Shaivism*. From www.en.wikipedia.org/wiki/Shaivism.

Yogananda, Paramhansa, *Autobiography of a Yogi*, Yogoda Satsanga Society of India, 2010.

The Supreme Court judgement quoted in the Preface came on July 2, 1995 in the matter of the Ramakrishna Mission's petition to be declared a non-Hindu, minority religion, under the constitution. The words quoted are part of para number 29 of the judgement delivered by a three Judge bench of Civil Appellate Jurisdiction, Civil Appeal No 4937/85, 5676-78/85 which was a case of Bramchari Sidheswar & Others etc versus State of West Bengal etc.The entire judgement is available on www.hinduismtoday.com and www.judis.nic.in

Index